SMUGGLERS AND STATES

COLUMBIA STUDIES IN MIDDLE EAST POLITICS

COLUMBIA STUDIES IN MIDDLE EAST POLITICS

Marc Lynch, Series Editor

Columbia Studies in Middle East Politics presents academically rigorous, well-written, relevant, and accessible books on the rapidly transforming politics of the Middle East for an interested academic and policy audience.

The Suspended Disaster: Governing by Crisis in Bouteflika's Algeria, Thomas Serres

Syria Divided: Syria Divided: Patterns of Violence in a Complex Civil War, Ora Szekely

Shouting in a Cage: Political Life After Authoritarian Cooptation in North Africa, Sofia Fenner

Classless Politics: Islamist Movements, the Left, and Authoritarian Legacies in Egypt, Hesham Sallam

Lumbering State, Restless Society: Egypt in the Modern Era, Nathan J. Brown, Shimaa Hatab, and Amr Adly

Friend or Foe: Militia Intelligence and Ethnic Violence in the Lebanese Civil War, Nils Hägerdal

Jordan and the Arab Uprisings: Regime Survival and Politics Beyond the State, Curtis Ryan

Local Politics in Jordan and Morocco: Strategies of Centralization and Decentralization, Janine A. Clark

Religious Statecraft: The Politics of Islam in Iran, Mohammad Ayatollahi Tabaar

Protection Amid Chaos: The Creation of Property Rights in Palestinian Refugee Camps, Nadya Hajj

From Resilience to Revolution: How Foreign Interventions Destabilize the Middle East, Sean L. Yom

Sectarian Politics in the Gulf: From the Iraq War to the Arab Uprisings, Frederic M. Wehrey

The Arab Uprisings Explained: New Contentious Politics in the Middle East, edited by Marc Lynch

Smugglers and States

NEGOTIATING THE MAGHREB AT ITS MARGINS

Max Gallien

Columbia University Press
New York

Columbia University Press
Publishers Since 1893
New York   Chichester, West Sussex
cup.columbia.edu
Copyright © 2024 Columbia University Press
All rights reserved

Library of Congress Cataloging-in-Publication Data
Names: Gallien, Max, author.
Title: Smugglers and states : negotiating the Maghreb at its margins / Max Gallien.
Description: New York : Columbia University Press, [2024] | Series: Columbia studies in Middle East politics | Includes bibliographical references and index.
Identifiers: LCCN 2023032166 (print) | LCCN 2023032167 (ebook) | ISBN 9780231212885 (hardback) | ISBN 9780231212892 (trade paperback) | ISBN 9780231559614 (ebook)
Subjects: LCSH: Smuggling—Africa, North—History.
Classification: LCC HJ7094.5.A6 G36 2024 (print) | LCC HJ7094.5.A6 (ebook) | DDC 364.1/3360961—dc23/eng/20231020
LC record available at https://lccn.loc.gov/2023032166
LC ebook record available at https://lccn.loc.gov/2023032167

Printed and bound by CPI Group (UK) Ltd, Croydon, CR0 4YY

Cover design: Chang Jae Lee
Cover image: © Ana Nance, Female Moroccan porters stopped by civil guard police before entering the passageway of crossing the border into Melilla, Spain from Morocco

CONTENTS

ACKNOWLEDGMENTS vii

NOTE ON TRANSLITERATION xi

LIST OF ABBREVIATIONS xiii

Chapter One
On the Radar 1

Chapter Two
Smuggling in North Africa: Stakes and Structures 20

Chapter Three
Regulating Smuggling at the Border 59

Chapter Four
Regulating Smuggling in the Borderlands 85

Chapter Five
Smuggling Rents and Social Peace 112

Chapter Six
Tunisia: Smugglers and Revolution   145

Chapter Seven
Morocco: Smugglers and Reform   174

Chapter Eight
The Valley and the Mountain: Lived Political Settlements   199

Conclusion: Remaking the Maghreb   226

APPENDIX 1. STUDYING SMUGGLING IN NORTH AFRICA   243

APPENDIX 2. INTERVIEW LISTS   259

NOTES   269

BIBLIOGRAPHY   317

INDEX   343

ACKNOWLEDGMENTS

I wrote this book. Its flaws and limitations are mine. Its strengths are a result of the kindness and insight of the people and communities that helped me research and write it. Many, without whom this project would have been impossible, I am not able to name here. Some appear as anonymized sources in the following chapters, some do not. I will be forever in awe of people in the border communities of Tunisia and Morocco who gave me their time, their trust, their hospitality, and their stories, and I hope that I have been able to do them justice. There are, however, some people I can name.

First and foremost, I am indebted to Kate Meagher, who has been everything you wish for in a mentor and without whose guidance I would not have made sense of much of this. Similarly at the London School of Economics and Political Science (LSE) I am grateful for the support and insight of John Sidel, Steffen Hertog, Portia Roelofs, Nicolai Schulz, Valentina Zagaria, Catherine Boone, Moritz Schmoll, Susan Hoult, Rose Harris, and Nina Craven. Florian Weigand and all the contributors to the *Routledge Handbook of Smuggling* have been a source of advice and inspiration. At Oxford University's Middle East Centre, I am indebted to Adeel Malik and Michael Willis for their encouragement and insight, as well as Noa Schonmann, Maria Bruckmann, Jennifer Ruth Shutek, Anna Jacobs, and Megan O'Donell. Grace Fussell created the maps used in chapter 2. Peter Andreas,

ACKNOWLEDGMENTS

George Joffé, Thomas Hüsken, Matt Herbert, Chloe Skinner, Sofya Shahab, Diana Kim, and Ferdinand Eibl provided valuable advice, insight, and feedback. I would also like to thank my colleagues at the Institute of Development Studies and the team at the International Centre for Tax and Development, who allowed me to finish this book and who make it a joy to be in this profession.

In Tunisia, I am most indebted to Mohamed in Ben Guerdane, for his fantastic translation, his patience and trust, his driving and part-time bodyguarding skills, and his insight and perspective. I am also grateful for the support and advice of two legends of the Centre d'Etudes Maghrébines à Tunis (CEMAT), Larry Michalak and Laryssa Chomiak, as well as Monica Marks, Hamza Meddeb, Rafaa Tabib, Kamel Laroussi, Mohamed Dhia Hammami, and Safa Belghith. In Morocco, I am particularly indebted to Jaouad and Mawya, not merely for their translation, but also for the engagement, heart, and care that they brought to the project. I am also grateful to everyone in Oujda who took me in and offered me their perspective: Isabelle, the Znasni boys, Soumia, Larbi, and Ute. In Nador, my particular thanks go to Fouad and his team, who shared their insights and included me in their travels, and in Melilla to Laia Soto.

I was fortunate during this project to have spent some time as a visiting scholar at the Hilary Clinton Centre for Women's Empowerment at Al-Akhawayn University Ifrane (AUI) in Morocco, and at the German Institute for International and Security Affairs (SWP) in Berlin. I am very grateful to both institutions for their support. At AUI, I would particularly like to thank Doris Gray, and Katja Žvan Elliott; at the SWP, I would like to thank Isabelle Werenfels, Stephan Roll, Luca Miehe, Wolfram Lacher, Jürgen Rogalski, Barbara Heckl, and the entire wonderful team of the FG06.

I acknowledge and am grateful for the financial support of the Economic and Social Research Council, who funded my studentship, fieldwork, language training, and overseas institutional visits. I am also grateful to the British Society for Middle Eastern Studies, who awarded me the Abdullah Al Mubarak Al Sabah Foundation prize, which further supported my fieldwork.

At Columbia University Press, I am grateful to Marc Lynch, Caelyn Cobb, and Monique Laban for taking this on, and for their guidance along the way, as well as Anita O'Brien, Marisa Lastres, and Reshma Sumitra.

ACKNOWLEDGMENTS

Parts of chapter 3 have been published in the context of my article "Informal Institutions and the Regulation of Smuggling in North Africa" in *Perspectives on Politics*.

Aside from curiosity and anxiety, caffeine is the main input into the academic production function. Most of this book was written at The Elgin in Maida Vale and the Backwood Café in Brighton, which unfortunately did not survive the pandemic. Whittard's marvelous Milk Oolong and Bird & Blend's Butter Brew worked secret wonders.

These have been long and not always easy years. I am deeply indebted to all of you who stuck with me, put up with me, and had my back. Andy, Varshini, Safa, Sandhya, Charlotte, Phil and Ciara, Hayley, my brother Oskar, and my parents Andrea and Martin, to whom this book is dedicated. You know what you did. Thank you.

NOTE ON TRANSLITERATION

Transliteration of Arabic in this book is based on the transliteration guidelines of the *International Journal of Middle Eastern Studies,* unless different but frequently used local transliteration variants were available.

ABBREVIATIONS

BAT	Brigade Antiterrorisme (Tunisia)
DfID	Department for International Development (UK)
CESE	Economic, Social and Environmental Council (Morocco)
FATF	Financial Action Task Force
FCO	Foreign and Commonwealth Office (UK)
GBP	British pound sterling
ICBT	informal cross-border trade
IFI	international financial institutions
INDH	Initiative Nationale pour le Développement Humain (Morocco)
IPSIE	Impuesto sobre la Producción, los Servicios y la Importación (Melilla)
IS / ISIS	Islamic State / Islamic State in Iraq and Syria
LSE	London School of Economics and Political Science
MAD	Moroccan dirham
NGO	nongovernmental organization
NIE	New Institutional Economics
ODECO	Office du Développement de Coopération (Morocco)
ONE	Office National de l'Électricité (Morocco)
OTLB	Organisation of Tunisian Libyan Brotherhood (Tunisia)

ABBREVIATIONS

PAM	Parti Authenticité et Modernité (Morocco)
SME	small and medium enterprise
TND	Tunisian dinar
UNCTAD	United Nations Conference on Trade and Development
USIP	United States Institute of Peace

Chapter One

ON THE RADAR

We are the children of this republic, we believe in the state, and we will reinforce the state. And the informal economy is a phenomenon that risks striking the state at the heart of its existence. And we will fight it with the same spirit as we fight terrorism. Actually, in Arabic the words are similar.

—MEHDI JOMAA, FORMER PRIME MINISTER OF TUNISIA, 2014

In the summer of 2014, I was sitting on the visitor's platform of the Tunisian Constituent Assembly in Tunis, watching as delegates voted to increase punishments for smuggling goods across Tunisia's land borders. Just three years after Tunisia's revolution, the debate was framed as a newly democratic state fighting against the forces that sought to subvert it. Many of the statements in the discussion mirrored the quote from Mehdi Jomaa: the "fight" against smuggling had become a common talking point in postrevolutionary Tunisia, connected to concerns about increasingly porous borders, and a conception of smuggling as a fundamental attack on the stability and sovereignty of the state. In a conversation afterward, a representative from Tunisia's borderlands with Algeria described such practices as "economic terrorism."[1]

Naturally, this perspective is not unique to Tunisia. It sits firmly within a broader contemporary policy discourse that frames smuggling and wider forms of informal and illegal economic activity as ascending and alarming. In this narrative, smuggling is both riding the coattails of globalization to establish nefarious networks along the "underbelly" of global trade and itself a fundamental threat to the global order of nation-states. It is presented as undermining states' control over borders, a discourse that has become increasingly nervous in both Europe and the United States in recent years, hollowing out state apparatuses through corruption and extortion, or engaging in "dirty entanglements" with terrorists, armed groups, or other subversive actors.[2] In these accounts, smugglers and states are framed as principal antagonists in the struggle for order in the twenty-first century. Recent years have seen states use this notion of a fundamental attack on their very existence to justify huge expenses and infrastructure investments to "control their borders"—from the U.S.-Mexico border wall to various foreign and domestically financed new fences, moats, and walls across North Africa's borders.

But as scholars—or residents—of many borderlands would point out, this is hardly the whole story. To illustrate the point in Tunisia, one only needs to head a few hundred kilometers further south. Just a couple of weeks after the parliamentary debate, I was sitting in the town hall of Ben Guerdane, a city in Tunisia's southern borderlands and the country's most well-known smuggling hub. Proudly, the municipality's secretary-general described a new agreement on stall fees that the municipality had reached with the vendors of the local market. And yet all the vendors in the market were informal cross-border traders, every single item sold in the market having been smuggled into the country from neighboring Libya. The harsh punishments mandated in Tunis seemed far away now—the market even has a small built-in police station, protecting and serving the traders there, rather than investigating them.

And markets were not the only place where Ben Guerdane's smugglers encountered a constructive, normalized, and well-structured interaction with state officials. As they made their way across the border into Tunisia, in complete violation of any formal customs agreements, they would make payments to customs agents and security forces. However, such bribes were typically not paid randomly, but in accordance with an informal agreement with state officials, specifying the quantity and types of goods that could be smuggled, and their costs. The agreement was negotiated between local smugglers, civil society actors, and representatives of the Tunisian state. On the ground, the regulation, governance, and negotiation of the smuggling economy with the participation of police, customs, municipal officers, and the national guard stood in sharp contrast both to the reputation of the city as a lawless "wild west town" and of smugglers and states as fierce antagonists.[3]

One might suspect the Tunisian experience to be somewhat extraordinary here, this observation being located on the border between one state that was just reconstituting itself after a revolution and Libya, which was entering another phase in its civil war. And yet, a bit further west, the border between Morocco and the Spanish enclave of Melilla provided an even more striking example of a similar dynamic. Every day, thousands of informal traders pushed through the small iron turnstiles of the Barrio Chino border crossing, carrying heavy bundles of goods across the border without paying formal tariffs, and having earned the crossing the reputation as a "zone of lawlessness."[4] But here, too, a closer examination revealed structures of regulation, and the involvement of state agents. The extensive system of rules and arrangements that structured smuggling across this border included queues of carriers organized by the police, systems of numbers and symbols on the bundles of goods, and even small written tickets that indicated the ownership of smuggled goods and let customs officials know that the necessary bribes had been paid. Perhaps the best indications of the institutionalization of the trade at this border crossing were the signs that hung over some of the lanes through the turnstiles. Showing the silhouettes of a man and a woman carrying a heavy bundle of goods, their message was clear: "Smugglers go here" (fig. 1.1).

As this book will highlight, neither of these examples is unusual. Its inquiry begins with the observation that smuggling in North Africa is an economic activity that is regulated, and, moreover, that its regulation, governance, and negotiation are much more closely connected to the state than both common perceptions and the political rhetoric cited earlier frequently suggest. This observation is also not unique to North Africa—references to informal arrangements and practical norms can be found in some contemporary work in borderland studies from Sub-Saharan Africa to Southeast Asia. Nor is it intended here as a pedantic or sensationalizing corrective to common accounts, to highlight hypocrisy, corruption, or contradictions in the discourse of the governments in question. Instead, the observation that smuggling is not per definition or even commonly unregulated by states provides an entry point into its politics through a striking puzzle: Why do states engage in the toleration, organization, and regulation of smuggling? As noted, neither arrangement mentioned is entirely untypical. Furthermore, neither arrangement is purely small and local—they cover thousands of traders and operate with the explicit involvement or awareness of multiple different organs of the state, including higher officials. And while bribes are frequently paid, there are examples of regulated

FIGURE 1.1 Sign at the Barrio Chino border crossing. Photo courtesy of Cope Melilla.

smuggling across both case studies in which no bribes are required, or in which state actors participate without any financial gain. Simple explanations of "bad apples" among low-level officers, principal-agent dynamics, or petty corruption are hence insufficient to explain these dynamics.

Asking why this happens, then, leads directly to asking about its wider meaning and consequences. How can these dynamics be squared with the idea—frequently propagated by state officials themselves—that smuggling undermines states? Clearly, a more empirical reevaluation of the relationship between smuggling and states is needed here. This, then, is our starting point: as this book aims to demonstrate, an analysis of the real regulation of smuggling provides a productive entry into examining its politics. Recognizing that smuggling is in fact regulated points the focus toward its structures and away from common explanatory models around individual instances of corruption and "bad governance." It helps structure discussions of the powers and pressures of the actors involved, and of historical continuities and recent changes. It provides an opportunity to reexamine, in the concrete and the specific, this suggested struggle between smugglers and states for order in a globalizing world and examine what its consequences are, not merely for the modern states of North Africa, but also for the smugglers themselves, and for the borderland communities that get caught in the middle.

This book argues that the phenomenon of states regulating smuggling, which appears puzzling from a "law and order" perspective, can be resolved by providing a political contextualization of the "law" and the "order" at play. Based on an examination of smuggling in North Africa in the past two decades and a structured political economy framework, it demonstrates that states have tolerated and regulated smuggling because they continue to rely on it to maintain order—that the rents generated through regulated smuggling have long been and remain a necessary part of North Africa's political settlements. The order that has emerged is not subversively encroaching on the state in the periphery but is the result of a specific model of state-building that purposefully placed the region's borderlands in economic dependence on tolerated illegal activity in a context of formal state neglect. The primary threat that smuggling contains for North Africa's states does therefore not lie in its sheer existence, but in their dependence on it, and in the vulnerabilities that decades of smuggling-based development have created in the region's borderlands.

There are important lessons in these dynamics beyond the context of smuggling, or North Africa. They illustrate that spaces that are commonly assumed as unregulated or anarchic can be a space of complex regulation. They provide a reminder that even within spaces of illegality, spaces that are more commonly associated with nonstate governance, self-governance, or private ordering, we can still at times find the long arms of states, providing regulation, protection, or favor. Studying smuggling in this way therefore illuminates and encourages us to explore "real governance"—to trace overlooked dimensions of regulation and the complex array of tools that states employ to provide order and distribute power, access, and resources in the twenty-first century.

INFORMAL AUTHORITARIAN BARGAINS

The focus of this book lies on the smuggling economies of Tunisia and Morocco, and in particular their borders with, respectively, Libya, Algeria, and Spain. Rather than relying on contexts of conflict or areas of limited statehood, where we might more easily imagine fragile regimes having to make deals with illegal traders, the emphasis here is purposefully on two states that have seen stable political structures in much of their postindependence era. Beyond expanding across the Sahara discussions on borderlands that have too often been confined to Sub-Saharan Africa, exploring these dynamics in North Africa is especially important on two levels.[5]

On one level, North Africa is particularly well positioned to contribute to our understanding of smuggling. It has long been home to a large and diverse smuggling economy. Since the 1980s the oil wealth of Algeria and Libya and resulting price differences have given rise to extensive fuel-smuggling economies. Estimations suggest that in 2014, 17 percent of Tunisia's entire domestic fuel consumption was covered by contraband gasoline from Libya.[6] Variation in tariff and subsidy regimes has fueled the informal trade of a vast array of consumer goods, ranging from tea to makeup to textiles.[7] Other networks trade in illicit goods—both as a production hub of cannabis and as a transit space for cocaine, the region has become increasingly central to the global drug trade, while the wars in Libya and Mali have provided both demand and supply for the smuggling of arms and military equipment.[8] In recent years, accelerated through conflicts and the politics of migration, North Africa's border economies have stood at the center of regional and global anxieties about stability and border porosity, often without a detailed analysis of their actual working. This has coincided with external challenges to preexisting smuggling arrangements: the civil war in Libya and an increasing crackdown on contraband in Algeria. The resulting renegotiations provide an ideal opportunity to observe the mechanics of the politics of smuggling and the behavior of the actors involved.

On another level, studying smuggling provides an important perspective to understand the modern politics of North Africa far beyond the borderlands. Specifically, it can contribute a missing piece to our understanding of how citizen-state relationships are constructed, perceived, and renegotiated underneath revolutions and reforms, democratization, and authoritarian reconstruction. Again, Morocco and Tunisia provide fitting and complementary case studies.

Having shared relatively stable authoritarian politics in the 1990s and early 2000s, both countries have in recent years seen their politics characterized by a questioning and renegotiation of domestic political settlements with a focus on issues of economic opportunity, inclusion, and entrenched regional inequality. In this they have mirrored the region more widely, as the protest movements of 2011, commonly referred to as the "Arab Spring," highlighted deep regional and structural inequalities within North African countries.[9] Protesters across the Middle East and North Africa have pointed to the insecurities and vulnerabilities that resulted from the increasing erosion of the populist social contracts of the postindependence era, as increasing unemployment and informal employment fell short of many expectations of a dignified life. Today this narrative is most commonly retold with reference to Tunisia, and Mohamed Bouazizi, the informal vendor who set himself on fire after an altercation with a municipal officer, quickly became a symbol for both the increasing indignities experienced by those seeking to earn a livelihood and the failures of the state. In Morocco, however, the February 20th movement similarly highlighted regional and economic inequality alongside poor public services and demands for democratization.

From here on, the national politics of the two countries starkly diverge. In Tunisia, a revolution in 2011 set off a restructuring of the country's politics, which saw multiple rounds of free and fair elections, the exclusion of former president Ben Ali's networks from the country's political settlement, and the inclusion of previously banned actors such as the Ennahda movement. At the same time, the country's economic structures saw less transformation, as successive postrevolutionary governments failed to see through larger reform programs. The country's poor economic performance in the postrevolutionary era both kept issues of economic inequality and unfulfilled expectations on the political agenda and fed an increasing disillusionment in Tunisia's democratic institutions. They contributed to the election in 2019 of Kais Saied, a relative outsider to Tunisia's political elite to the presidency, and his successive dismantling of the country's nascent democracy.

While issues of economic inequality and access remained on the agenda in Morocco after 2011, the kingdom did not see a revolution. Compared to Tunisia, the country's political settlement remained comparatively stable, centralized, and authoritarian. Instead, changes were characterized by a series of top-down reforms since the ascent of King Mohamed VI to the throne a decade earlier. These have included constitutional reforms, an economic program closely tied to new trade agreements, and programs aimed at addressing regional and economic inequality, such as the National Initiative for Human Development (INDH). While the particular effects and effectiveness of these programs is a matter of ongoing discussion, calls for more economic equality and in particular frustrations about regional inequality and the indignities experienced by informal workers have remained. If Mohamed Bouazizi became both symbol and rallying point in Tunisia, the death of Mohsen Fikri played a similar role in Morocco. The informal fish vendor died in October 2016 in the northern city of Al-Hoceima, crushed to death in the back of a garbage truck when he tried to rescue his goods that had been confiscated by the police. The subsequent series of protests across the country picked up on issues of regional inequality and historical injustice as well as on a perception that making a living in Morocco for many involved navigating illegality and indignity.

Scholarship across North Africa and much of the Middle East has noted the ongoing renegotiation of a social contract underneath these dynamics. This has often been framed as the renegotiation of a postindependence "authoritarian bargain"—where citizens received formal benefits such as state employment and subsidies in exchange for their acquiescence to authoritarian rule. The focus, not unjustifiably, of these analyses has often been on how economic and demographic change have eroded the formal aspects of this relationship, from subsidy reforms and increasing youth unemployment to demands for procedural democracy. At the same time, many have noted that economic liberalization in the region has come with an informalization of livelihoods and income-earning opportunities, with people "helping themselves" in the face of insufficient state support.[10] While these trends have explicitly affected formal politics, as new income streams have given rise to new political groupings, strategies, and frustrations, they are most easily and commonly framed as sitting outside of the old authoritarian bargain, as the "encroachment" of the state by nonstate actors, logics, and orders.[11]

This book suggests a slightly different perspective. Rather than just the erosion of the authoritarian bargain, it implies that the past decades have seen the increasing transition of more and more people from one type of bargain to another—one that had always been part of the picture. I argue that alongside the more formal exchange of services and acquiescence of the suggested postindependence social contract has always existed a second, informal authoritarian bargain, in which political acquiescence is exchanged for the explicit toleration of informal and illegal income-generating strategies, from street vending to cannabis cultivation to smuggling. These activities do not happen under the radar of the state, but while it purposefully and visibly turns a blind eye, they remain part of an arrangement with the state, not outside of it.

This distinction has important consequences, both in how we understand what characterized citizen-state relationships in the second half of the twentieth century and in terms of what is being renegotiated now. The existence of informal authoritarian bargains explains why, when livelihoods that are funded through technically illegal activities are threatened, be it through the police or through economic change, this can still trigger demands on the state—the demand to hold up its end of the bargain, to provide a different bargain, or to face the withdrawal of political acquiescence. This relates directly to the symbolism of both Mohamed Bouazizi and Mohsen Fikri. And it explains why, when Libyan authorities closed a border crossing in 2016, Tunisian smugglers aimed their protests not at Libyan authorities but at the Tunisian state, demanding a political intervention to secure their (illegal) income streams.

This book, then, uses smuggling as a case study to illustrate this aspect of citizen-state relationships. It presents an activity that has quintessentially embodied this informal authoritarian bargain for decades but is now also facing its renegotiation: toward a more formal bargain, or something new altogether. In this, it seeks to add a crucial additional layer to our understanding of the modern politics of North Africa that is relevant far beyond the borderlands. Smuggling can provide a perspective on the "real governance" of the regions' states that is almost entirely absent in an increasingly crowded literature.[12] Smuggling is not merely in itself a sizable part of this informality in North Africa, contributing to livelihoods for hundreds of thousands across the region, but provides a study of the informal politics, the "deals and dealings" that states in the region have drawn on to survive, that they have shaped and reshaped in recent years, and that have consequently fundamentally structured the relationship between many citizens of the region and their states.

As expectations between citizens and states about informal activities, tolerated illegality, acquiescence, and development are renegotiated in North Africa, and the politics of the region is, so to say, being remade at its margins, it is important to highlight that these margins are not primarily geographic, but economic and political. Borderlands provide a space where these negotiations are heightened, where they are particularly visible—but they are just as relevant in the capital cities. Examining the role of borderlands and smuggling economies offers insights into wider themes in the modern political economy of North Africa that are not confined to them: dynamics of inequality and inclusion, the effects of economic globalization, and the relationship among economic exclusion, radicalization, instability, and violence.

Youth unemployment and informal employment, both of which have been at the center of recent discussions about the region's crumbling social contracts, are commonly higher in the region's borderlands than in the political center.[13] When Tunisia's postrevolutionary transitional justice process became the first such process that allowed entire regions to file as victims of the previous authoritarian regime, Kasserine, a border region in the country's Northwest, became one of the first to do so.[14] The protests after the death of Mohsen Fikri had a particular political significance because Al-Hoceima is at the heart of the Rif, a region that has experienced substantial political and economic marginalization throughout Morocco's modern history. Consequently, recent years have brought back into question the territorial politics of North Africa's countries and how peripheral communities are really included in the region's politics and changing social contracts.

Border communities also stand at the heart of the interaction between economic vulnerability and securitization that North Africa has experienced in recent decades. A series of events in the past decade has increasingly brought smuggling to the forefront of public debates within and outside the region. The global war on terror and the wider effects of the conflicts in Libya, Mali, Syria, and Iraq alongside increasing international concerns around migration all have pushed "porous borders" in North Africa onto the agenda of politicians and policymakers. Connected to this has been the fact that borderland populations have been overrepresented among the people leaving North Africa both for the battlefields of Syria and Iraq and the boats to Europe. Many of the young men who joined the Islamic State came from North Africa's borderlands, particularly southern Tunisia.[15] At the same time, many of the Tunisians who made up the surge in irregular migration in 2017 were from the country's southern border regions, while legal and irregular migration has been a central part of economic livelihoods in Morocco's northeastern borderlands for decades.[16] Consequently, as discussions about security and development in North Africa increasingly engage with the interconnectedness of crumbling social contracts, economic marginalization, radicalization, and insecurity, borderlands are increasingly noted as spaces where these connections are heightened, and of additional urgency. It is interesting to observe how, building on strong assumptions around the role of border control in sustaining state sovereignty, communities that were previously framed as politically peripheral are now being positioned in a much more central role, as capable of striking the state at its very heart, of undermining its institutions by subverting its boundaries.

As the second half of this book chronicles, examining the negotiations of informal authoritarian bargains from the perspective of the borderlands of Tunisia and Morocco can provide correctives to the larger narratives about their changing politics. While Tunisia's formal political development has been characterized by a flurry of change and domestic transition in recent years, an examination of its borderlands finds evidence of continuity: of a continuous reliance of the state on informal rent streams, of a continuous vulnerability to external factors. While Morocco's political settlement has been characterized by comparative continuity, a look at its borderlands allows us to trace changes under the surface and examine how new trade agreements and ascendant political elites have changed patterns of economic incorporation, leading to an increasing formalization of the incorporation of its borderlands—with winners and losers. In both countries, a closer look at the dynamics that are often described as challenges to the political and economic center provides further insight into the politics of political and economic centralization.

One further commonality between the two case studies gives rise to the final and perhaps the most urgent reason that a new analysis of smuggling in North Africa is needed today: its structures are currently under immense pressure, at once crumbling and rapidly transforming. Following anxieties about porous borders, states in the region and in particular the international donor community have invested heavily in new border infrastructure. Alongside the conflicts in Libya and the Sahel, new trade agreements, and the Covid-19 pandemic, this has created new pressures for smuggling networks. By the time of writing, much of the small-scale smuggling along the Morocco-Melilla border had all but collapsed. Many smugglers at the border between Tunisia and Libya, in particular those operating in gasoline, have experienced some of their hardest years in decades. Reactions to this have been varied—as subsequent chapters will discuss, shaped by the different resources and capacities of different networks. Some borderland actors have expanded their connections with state actors, diversifying their activities into formal businesses or even politics. Others have shifted to more highly capitalized illicit activities such as narcotics trafficking, while still others have left the region altogether. For decades, smuggling has played a huge role in the border economies of North Africa, supporting livelihoods of hundreds of thousands of residents. As this book argues, it has played an important role in their politics as well. Understanding that role is critical to understanding what is currently under pressure, and what the consequences will be.

STUDYING SMUGGLING

Researching smuggling naturally comes with a particular set of challenges. This is often framed as the task of making visible something that doesn't want to be seen, recording something that is frequently beyond the realm of typical bureaucratic methods of documentation. Scholars have employed a wide battery of methodologies to do this, ranging from deeply embedded participant observation to satellite imagery and complex econometric modeling.[17]

This challenge of making visible what is hidden is somewhat mitigated in this project, which finds that there are structures of regulation that are applicable to many smugglers and widely communicated in borderland communities. While they can be studied through observing them and interacting with those involved, they require particular attention to where the somewhat visible ends, what is still obscured, and where the limitations of this approach lie. In addition, for this project, another, larger methodological challenge presents itself. Seeking to both trace in detail the regulatory structures and institutions that organize smuggling and connect them to the larger structures of changing political settlements, to revolutions, reforms, and trade agreements, requires both a micro- and a macroperspective, both carefully contextualized detail and comparative insight.

This book seeks to tackle this challenge by combining deeply localized political ethnographies with a structured comparative setup. It draws on extensive ethnographic fieldwork, using both participant observation and in-depth interviews in two different field sites in order to describe the practicalities of smuggling, the regulatory institutions, norms, and perceptions they are embedded in, and the changes these have undergone in recent years. At the same time, its analysis not only draws on observations from both sites but also structures these insights through a doubled paired comparison. On the one hand, it compares the changing politics of smuggling in two different locations, the borderlands of southern Tunisia and northern Morocco. On the other hand, it also compares smuggling networks in these two locations, examining in particular the difference between textile smugglers and gasoline smugglers (chapter 8). The following chapter will expand further on the logic behind this case selection. As noted, this analysis has also benefited from various political upheavals and disruptions to the structures of smuggling in both case sites that have functioned as shocks, prompting the observable renegotiation of the organization of smuggling that chapters 6–8 examine.

Most of the data for this project was collected during eleven months of fieldwork in Tunisia and Morocco in 2016 and 2017. It also built on three months of fieldwork in Tunisia conducted in 2014, as well as additional interviews and research collaborations and documents collected between 2018 and 2021. During these periods, I conducted over two hundred interviews, many of them with members of different smuggling networks, including those involved in textiles, gasoline, white electronics, kitchen equipment, drugs, pharmaceuticals, leather, foodstuffs, and people smuggling. Other interview subjects included local bureaucrats, civil society leaders, politicians, journalists, academics, and formal sector actors. I also conducted a small number of focus group discussions, primarily among informal traders, alongside one group of unemployed university graduates and local civil society activists engaged in formalization projects. A complete list of interviews can be found in appendix 2, alongside the codes that are used to cite them throughout.

The data collected through interviews has been complemented by extensive participant observation, which included observing informal markets, roadside vendors, border crossings, local administrations, public discussions, and festivities. Needless to say, doing participant observation and in particular interviews with smugglers comes with additional methodological challenges around negotiating access, positionalities, ethics, and security. It required building relationships and trust, finding the right intermediaries, tone, and vocabulary to develop more open conversations, and negotiating my presence in an area of at times heightened security concerns. I do not want to test most readers' patience before moving on to the book's main arguments and findings, but I suspect that these methodological questions and how this project has approached them might be of interest to other researchers working on smuggling and illegal activities. Consequently, I have added a substantive discussion of these issues in appendix 1.

I will limit my discussion here to three issues that I imagine to be of particular relevance to readers, namely, anonymity, triangulation, and gender. Given the sensitive content of the conversations, almost all interviews for this project were conducted under the condition of anonymity and are cited here merely by occupation, date, and location. Naturally, recording interviews electronically was almost never an option, but I could often scribble into a small notebook during these conversations. While this has allowed for the verbatim quotes in this book, it is also the reason their length tends to be limited to two or three sentences.

While anonymity eliminates some incentives for smugglers to misrepresent information, many others remain. Building on these interviews has therefore required extensive and careful triangulation facilitated by the large number of interviews I was able to conduct, alongside a collection of documents, secondary literature, and experience gained through participant observation. This has become particularly important in a context of necessary anonymity, as there is a worrying tendency in some writing on smuggling to make arguments based on one single unnamed source, frequently with no discussion of its positionality or credibility. In the remainder of this book, there are very few instances where I rely on a single anonymous source, and none of them is fundamental to the argument I am presenting. When I include single sources, I do so to present an interesting detail, to give a distinct voice to a more frequently shared perspective, or to provide a personal observation, and I have included them only where I believe them to be credible, to have detailed knowledge of the processes they are describing, and to have no incentive to misrepresent them. Again, I expand on these issues in appendix 1.

Finally, the vast majority of the interviews conducted and the voices cited here are men. This is partially a consequence of the fact that both smuggling networks and the political structures around them in North Africa are predominantly male. Interviewing women in this context also brought additional challenges, given women's packed schedules in the face of the double burden of professional work and housework and the conservative social structures in both field sites. While the thirty interviews conducted with women were the result of a concerted effort to include some of these perspectives, this remains a real limitation—there is much to be said about women and smuggling that I have missed here. There is a whole other book in need of writing, though it would benefit from an author with a different positionality than mine.[18]

REGULATION AND INCORPORATION

This book is made up of nine chapters. Following this introduction, chapter 2 reviews the theoretical stakes at hand and introduces a political economy framework for the analysis of the relationship between smuggling and state-building. It then moves on to the empirical context of smuggling in North Africa, mapping out the main flows of goods and their macro-structure, reviewing central themes in the historical development of smuggling economies in the region and situating the project's case sites within these structures and histories. After this, the remaining chapters can be grouped into two sets.

The first set of chapters explores the regulation of smuggling in North Africa, the actors involved in it, and the rents that are generated through smuggling economies and their regulation. Their empirical focus is on more microlevel dynamics at one point in time, and their theoretical focus is on institutions. Each chapter draws on material from both Tunisia and Morocco as they explore similar dynamics but highlight differences between networks within case sites.

Chapter 3 provides a detailed mapping of the regulation of smuggling activities at different borders in the Maghreb. It highlights that these activities are largely regulated through informal institutions that have been negotiated between state and nonstate actors. Examining these institutions, the chapter notes their divergence from common caricatures of informal institutions: many of them generate impersonal rather than personalist access structures, and they commonly contain third-party enforcement that is provided through state agents. While contemporary policy discourses frequently stress the "porosity" of North Africa's borders, this chapter highlights the degree to which this porosity is regulated, as informal institutions segment the routes of different goods and determine the volume of smuggled goods that pass through the borders, as well as their costs.

Continuing this analysis of regulation, chapter 4 focuses on two additional aspects: First, it examines how the distribution of smuggled goods in the borderlands is regulated, tracing hybrid institutions that have allowed municipalities to tax the sale of smuggled goods. Second, it examines the ways in which moral and religious conceptions have shaped how borderland populations engage with smuggling, pointing out how different elements of smuggling alongside evaluations of the state have affected local moral perceptions.

Chapter 5 begins to connect regulation to actors by tracing the rent streams that emerge from the institutions discussed in the previous two chapters. It discusses the rents that benefit state agents and structures, elite networks, and the borderland population more widely. It highlights the importance of smuggling rents for the social stability of the borderlands and builds on the analysis of the preceding chapters to situate smuggling in the political settlements of Tunisia and Morocco. It argues that smuggling has not undermined state-building but has been an essential feature of political settlements in both countries, incorporating borderlands through an "informal authoritarian bargain."

With these building blocks established, the second set of chapters then examines changes in the incorporation of smuggling in the political settlements of Tunisia and Morocco in recent years, in order to explore power dynamics among the actors involved and to trace their heterogeneous ability to navigate the terms of their incorporation into political settlements. Compared to the previous set, these chapters have a more macrolevel focus and look at change over time.

Chapter 6 examines the changes that Tunisia underwent in the years after the 2011 revolution from the perspective of its southern borderlands. These years have seen important developments for the local smuggling economy: a complete collapse of state enforcement in 2011 and its gradual return, new security infrastructure, the emergence of legal civil society organizations representing smugglers, an ISIS attack on the smuggling hub

Ben Guerdane, and the civil war in Libya. Tracing the renegotiation of the role of the smuggling economy throughout these events, the chapter argues that these developments have played out on the surface of a larger continuity, as the post-2011 Tunisian political settlement still relied on the smuggling economy to incorporate its southern borderlands.

The changes that Morocco has undergone are discussed in chapter 7, from the perspective of the country's northern borderlands. Rather than a revolution, a set of reforms, including new formalized markets and trade agreements, have affected the country's smuggling economy in recent years. Tracing the negotiations and effects of these changes, the chapter argues that while the past decade has looked quieter than southern Tunisia, it has seen a fundamental restructuring of many rent streams, with heterogeneous effects for different actors. As a result, when border fortifications installed by Algeria caused the collapse of large sections of the local smuggling economy, these reforms crucially conditioned the ability of groups to adjust to the changes.

Chapter 8 draws on the two preceding chapters to delve into effects of the informal incorporation of borderlands into political settlements on stability, formalization processes, and borderland communities themselves. Focusing on the comparison between textile and gasoline smugglers, it examines the attempts by different groups to navigate and improve the terms of their informal incorporation and points to reasons for their heterogeneous experiences. Based on these considerations, it reexamines the effects of the increasing border fortifications in recent years and looks at what these past years can tell us about the likely developments in the years to come. Finally, chapter 9 concludes by drawing out the central arguments alongside their implications for the region, smuggling more widely, as well as state-building and political economy scholarship. It also notes central policy implications and articulates perspectives on this field of research looking forward.

ILLEGAL TRADE AND EVASIVE TERMINOLOGIES

Before proceeding, two brief notes are in order. The first is on the limitations of this project. Seeking to connect granular detail on the regulation of smuggling in two different case studies and across networks and time, and then connect them to the wider macropolitics of Tunisia and Morocco, this book covers a huge amount of material. As a consequence, it has to be, at times, selective in its focus and analysis. In Tunisia the book's story begins broadly in 2010 and in Morocco a few years earlier, while the first interviews for this book were conducted in 2014. As chapter 2 notes, these dynamics have a longer history that lies within the interests of this book, but less within its empirical focus.[19]

Because it provides the vast majority of employment and stands at the center of most informal regulation, this book primarily focuses on the smuggling of licit goods. While chapter 8 mainly considers textiles and gasoline, the previous chapters take into account a broader set of goods. This largely comes at the expense of less frequently traded but more often discussed goods such as firearms or psychotropics, which I will cover, to a smaller extent, in the final chapters. Naturally, these limitations are also affected by methodology—both the Libyan and the Algerian sides of the border are less discussed here, as they remained inaccessible to me throughout my fieldwork. A further discussion of these limitations in relation to fieldwork on smuggling can be found in appendix 1.

Second, a note on terminology. In the words of the people interviewed for this study, its main subject has many names: some call it *tijāra muāziyya*, "parallel trade," or *tijāra bainiyya*, "intraborder trade." *Tijāra ghayr rasmiyya* and *tijāra ghayr muhaykil* are commonly used, and both translate approximately as "informal trade."[20] Sometimes Arabic is dropped altogether, and people switch to the language of the old colonial powers, using the French *contra* or the Spanish *trabando*. It is a sensitive subject, and people pick their words carefully, either aiming or avoiding to confer legitimacy to what they are describing. The man selling gasoline out of jerrycans in northern Morocco may call it *tijāra ʿaīshiyya*, "survival trade," while politicians and World Bank officials in Tunis are most likely to use the terms most familiar to us: *tahrīb*, or "smuggling."

There is a similar tendency in academic writing on the subject. While economics and security literatures are quite comfortable with the term "smuggling," other scholars are cautious of its negative associations, and it typically gives way in geography and borderland studies to "informal trade" or "informal cross-border trade" (ICBT). I use both terms: smuggling to describe all forms of cross-border trade that violate the formal law applicable at the respective border, and informal cross-border trade to describe the smuggling of licit goods, meaning all goods for which a legal trade corridor exists that is not subject to additional security clearance, in contrast to the smuggling of illicit goods, such as narcotics, expired medicine, firearms, endangered animals, or historical artifacts.[21]

I trust the reader not to consider common connotations of these terms, in particular, the word "smuggling" to be an indication of any normative position that I or the people interviewed for this book hold with respect to these activities. Instead, chapter 4 contains a detailed discussion of the legitimacy of smuggling from the perspective of those who are engaged in it, while this book as a whole should be sufficiently indicative of mine.

Chapter Two

SMUGGLING IN NORTH AFRICA

Stakes and Structures

Recent years have seen a new surge in interest in the borders of North Africa, and particularly their subversion, spurred by the civil war in Libya, the creation of new border fortifications, and the increase in migration across the Mediterranean.[1] This stands in contrast with a so far relatively sparse literature on smuggling in the region, especially when compared to Sub-Saharan Africa. Yet North Africa provides a fascinating environment for the study of smuggling and state-building: the region is home to large and diverse smuggling economies, the political role of which has been framed in various ways throughout the region's history—from peripheral to unruly, marginal to subversive. As this book seeks to demonstrate, a reexamination of the role of North Africa's borderlands in the region today can speak to two wider discussions. On the one hand, it contributes to our understanding of critical themes in the study of the Maghreb's modern politics, from the future of its security infrastructure to the erosion of its social contracts. On the other hand, it can also make a critical intervention into wider global discussions, both of smuggling itself and of the political economy frameworks in which it is located, from institutional theory to state-building.

The purpose of this chapter, then, is twofold. First, it seeks to establish the stakes of this book, both theoretical and empirical. It begins by reviewing how previous scholarship has understood the relationship between smuggling and state-building. It argues that this has too frequently been siloed from the ways in which structural political economy has conceptualized regulation and state-building and outlines the key concepts of the political economy model that subsequent chapters develop.

In its second half, the chapter provides an introduction to the landscapes of smuggling in North Africa today—a mapping, in the geographical, economic, and political sense. It traces both the historical making of the region's borderlands and the modern macrostructure of illegal trade, and it introduces the two localities in which this book will spend most of its time: Tunisia's Medenine and Morocco's Oriental.

FROM DIRTY ENTANGLEMENTS TO NEGOTIATED STATES

One of the primary challenges in scholarship on smuggling and state-building today is that there is not one singular space within which these conversations happen. Instead, parallel discussions exist in different disciplines and fields, often siloed from each other, often not reading or responding to each other, and drawing on different methodologies, traditions, and conceptions.[2] Critically, as Peter Andreas has noted, mainstream political science and political economy scholarship has been conspicuously unengaged in these discussions, despite their direct relevance for theories of state-building.[3] Notwithstanding the diversity of approaches to the topic, reviewing their development in recent years highlights an increasing focus away from examining smugglers and states as natural opposites, and an increasing interest in the results of their interactions as cocreators of order and profit.

A further challenge follows from the study of two social phenomena that are fundamentally unequal and yet closely entwined. States are typically represented as large, highly normative, and abstractly theorized structures, while smuggling is typically conceptualized as highly localized, often comparatively small, and negatively defined as illegal trade. States are often studied from their centers; smuggling, from their peripheries—both geographically and often theoretically.[4] Yet both are inherently linked in their conceptions. States are omnipresent in the definition of smuggling itself, as they set both the geographical and legal boundaries of what turns trade into illegal cross-border trade and hence smuggling.[5] At the same time, smugglers challenge what are often considered essential feature of the modern territorial state: the rule of law and the control of borders.

The latter point features prominently in scholarship that frames the two as fundamentally antagonistic. Academic writing on state fragility and "failed states" has often joined policy papers in assuming that smuggling, by definition, undermines state-building, by subverting a central feature of state control, corrupting executive institutions, and undermining revenue collection. R. I. Rotberg's list of indicators of a failed state, for example, explicitly lists "smuggling" alongside "civil wars" and the "cessation of functioning legislatures."[6] Smuggling features as one of the main "risk areas" to states in Ulrich Schneckener's work on the issue.[7] Commonly, this is folded into a wider literature on "weak," "fragile," "failing," "failed," and "collapsed" states, particularly in an African context, in what Christoph Heuser has described as a "crime-fragility rationale."[8]

Smuggling as an inherent threat for states is often framed through an economic lens. One fairly obvious point is the fact that smuggling undermines state budgets through evading taxes and tariffs.[9] Notably, however, there has also been long-standing scholarship and policy advocacy that has framed smuggling as a positive economic force. On a localized level, smuggling has been noted to provide food and other items necessary for the survival of peripheral communities, as described by Judith Scheele in the case of southern Algeria and northern Mali.[10] On a more macrolevel, smugglers have been framed as free trade entrepreneurs, as a constituency that could push for trade liberalization, as representing a new "indigenous bourgeoisie," or a potential trade hub connecting regions.[11] As companies have colluded with smugglers to bring their products into new markets or avoid tariffs, states might tolerate smuggling or even get involved in it themselves if it brings in cheap or otherwise unavailable products.[12]

Irrespective of the economic effects of smuggling on states, a frequent concern is that the existence of smuggling economies may hollow out the state administratively by creating interactions between state agents and criminal groups and by incentivizing and normalizing corruption. These issues have become associated with concerns about a "criminalization of the state," as well as worries that spaces created by one form of illegal actor—smugglers—might then be exploited by other, more nefarious groups.[13] "Terrorist groups," one report warns, "can use the same techniques and routes as smugglers of tomatoes do."[14] Particularly in recent years, some scholarship has thus sought to expand the connection between illegal trade and corruption into wider "dirty entanglements" among smugglers, criminals, and terrorists threatening the global state system.[15] While these accounts can point to a range of interactions between smugglers and terrorist organizations, a key point of criticism has been that, given the rather broad remit of these terms, some points of connection do not make a wider strategic alliance or explain the reluctance of smugglers to engage with terrorists in many localities.[16]

Another common factor connecting smuggling to state fragility is its relationship to the outbreak or sustenance of violent conflict more broadly.[17] While smugglers almost always feature as important actors in "war economies" and hence might be easily perceived as guilty by association, more recent work has often highlighted a more diverse and contextually dependent role of smugglers in conflict. They appear as profiteers, but also at times as patriots shoring up support for states; as creators or economic shortages, but also as providers in need.[18] The empirical picture on the relationship among smuggling, wars, and conflict remains contested.[19] Recent scholarship, however, seeking to unpack the role of smuggling in violent conflict, has also increasingly focused on the nature of the relationship between smugglers and local providers of order, be they state- or nonstate actors.[20]

Albeit that a substantial part of his work focuses on drug production rather than smuggling, Jonathan Goodhand's writing on Afghanistan is instructive here.[21] It describes how the opportunities created through the drug trade gave wartime military entrepreneurs a stake in a peacetime economy, providing a perspective on how illegal economies can contribute to the stability of some form of central governance in fragile contexts. Notably, whether they actually emerge as stabilizing forces depends on a variety of contextual factors: the level of centralization, the role of outside actors, and the relationships and agreements between rulers and private actors.[22] Goodhand's work here draws closely on Richard Snyder's analysis of the political economy of extraction and lootable wealth, which argues that if resources are subject to regimes of joint extraction, where both state and local actors require the assistance and cooperation of the other, the relationship tends to be less violent and may contribute some stability.[23] In the Afghan case, opium production presents an example of this—it is difficult for private actors to monopolize the trade without state collaboration, and it is hard for the state to entirely run the opium trade. What is particularly instructive about this account is that the effects of smuggling on state-building are not foregone conclusions but are rooted in their negotiation over income streams. In Goodhand's terms: "War economies and shadow economies may, therefore, be seen as part of the long and brutal politics of sovereignty. Illegality and the state have been constant companions, and revenue from illicit flows, and their control, may actually strengthen the state."[24]

Within what is typically broadly conceptualized as "borderland studies," the historical relationship between those "constant companions" has provided two archetypal ways of framing the relationship between smugglers and states. In their positioning of smugglers and states as strategic antagonists, many of the perspectives discussed earlier mirror—in this and often little else—James Scott's seminal study of borderlands in Southeast Asia, "The Art of Not Being Governed." Scott most prominently makes the case that borderlands are, by definition, aiming to resist inclusion into the state. For him, they are the "last enclosure," and he argues that "virtually everything about these people's livelihoods . . . can be read as strategic positioning designed to keep the state at arm's length."[25] While he does not claim that borderlands are always successful in their endeavor, smuggling and cross-border trade are inherently presented as conscious acts of rebellion, resistance, and subversion against the state. More recently, Thomas Hüsken and Georg Klute have similarly argued that governance processes in borderlands may have become so removed from the logic of the political center that state-centered analyses are not useful in order to assess them.[26] It is worth noting that these accounts build their description of the distance between smugglers and states on detailed empirical observations. They still contrast with accounts that assume illegal activities and economies to be a priori unconnected or anachronistic to state structures, and framed as inherently as "underground," "shadow," "hidden," or "under the radar of the state."[27]

The seminal contrast to this casting of smugglers and states as polar opposites can be found in a field-defining study of the Ghana-Togo frontier, where Paul Nugent traces the role that smugglers and wider borderland populations played in the construction and maintenance of the border as an institution. He concludes that, in their use of the border for their livelihoods and in their interaction with border guards and customs, smugglers contributed to the border's entrenchment and hence "helped to render the border more legitimate and not less so." Smugglers, here, are not subverting the state but benefiting from one of its institutions—the border—and engaged in its maintenance. While Scott frames borderlands as the last refuge from the state, Nugent emphasizes "that even the most marginal border communities have been closely intertwined with the state."[28] His conclusion is echoed by scholars such as Johny Egg and Javier Herrera or Judith Vorrath, who argues that "informal borderland activities do not necessarily advance the process of state failure, and they even reproduce and sustain the state in its current condition."[29] Analyzing the role of smuggling "tycoons" in Uganda, Kristof Titeca concludes: "Although the regulatory authority of the cross-border contraband trade is different from the state, it therefore still contributes to state power: support to government officials is essential and the tycoons help the state in various other ways."[30]

Following this perspective, a range of recent scholarship has sought to unpack the hybrid governance arrangements created by these regulatory interactions, particularly in African borderlands.[31] These studies have often emphasized the positive regulatory implications of these trade networks as local and legitimate alternatives to weak state institutions in a difficult context. They suggest that these hybrid arrangements may not simply undermine the state but diversify its regulatory influence, allowing it to transform its authority from one based on force to one based on recognition and obedience by interacting with local legitimizing structures.[32]. Hüsken, for example, argues that local tribal structures between Libya and Egypt have contributed to an embedding and regulation of smuggling in the borderlands, where the Awlad 'Ali tribes function as "the de facto producers of trans-local order," demonstrating the "stabilizing effects of transgressive borderland economies."[33] Kristof Titeca and Tom de Herdt make a similar point in their analysis of practical norms in the borderlands of Uganda—rather than seeing these norms as undermining the state, they are "essential to the functioning of state institutions" and part of a continuing negotiation of the status quo, rooted in "fundamentally different perceptions of licitness."[34]

As Meagher has noted, however, the empirical evidence—constant waves of conflict in East Africa, the region of focus of many of these authors—raises questions about some of the more optimistic interpretations of hybrid governance in borderlands.[35] Similarly, the works of authors such as Béatrice Hibou and William Reno have emphasized the risks of these forms of hybrid orders to the integrity of state institutions themselves, in particular focusing on the "criminalization of the state."[36] Within observations of hybrid governance, perspectives on what this hybridity means for the state itself remain highly contested.

A central question emerging from the existence of these hybrid regulatory structures in the borderlands is whether they represent a shift of the locus of power away from the center and toward the periphery. Timothy Raeymaekers describes the state as being "engulfed" and fundamentally *reshaped* at its border: "Through the gradual colonialization of bureaucratic practice, this highly regulated cross-border market exchange even seems capable of imposing its normative order on state agencies and institutions."[37] Similarly, Titeca and de Herdt, in their study of informal cross-border trade in northwestern Uganda, find that the trade is structured by "practical norms" that are "mediated through the power wielded by the cross-border traders, who effectively dictate terms to government officials."[38] If we want to learn about the changing nature of the state, it is argued, the front line of its negotiation is at the border. In contrast, others have noted that the creation of new regulatory structures in the periphery is also shaped by the center itself and does not necessarily imply a shift of the locus of power away from the center. In addition, many large-scale smuggling operators have their apex markets in major cities and the capital, rather than in the periphery. "Far from creating new sites of power," Meagher argues, "these networks have played a key role in consolidating state power, using symbiotic relations between political and clandestine commercial elites to oil patron-client networks and mobilize electoral support for those in power."[39]

The question of how its interaction with smuggling shapes the state is similarly central in Peter Andreas's work on the role of smuggling in state-building processes in the United States and Bosnia.[40] Here, smugglers again appear as a group of actors that can both subvert and at times collude with or shore up the state. Critically, however, they influence the development of the state apparatus itself beyond its manifestation in the immediate borderlands. Smugglers have appeared as combatants in independence struggles and have contributed to the expansion of states' bureaucratic and coercive power by motivating the creation of new enforcement agencies.[41] Notably, as for example in the case of the U.S. Drug Enforcement Agency, smuggling has even played a role in justifying the expansion of executive agencies' jurisdiction beyond their state's borders.[42] These points notably echo previous historical scholarship on banditry, for example, in Egypt or the Ottoman Empire, where the real or imagined threat of bandits has similarly accompanied the expansion and centralization of the coercive apparatus.[43]

At the heart of the variation in the perspectives reviewed here on how and if smuggling subverts or reshapes the state lie not only empirical differences, but also deeper conceptual positions. Even though they are rarely discussed explicitly in the literature, the authors' perspective on central themes in political science and modern political economy, such as the conception of the state, state fragility, the role of informal institutions of development, or perspectives of what "good governance'" looks like, drives analyses and answers to these questions. Scott's perspective on the Zomia highlands is explicitly shaped by his interest in anarchism—as expressed in the subtitle of the book itself.[44] Similarly, much of the work that connects smuggling with state fragility tend to rely on conceptions of governance that emphasize the normative priority of formal institutions, such as neo-Weberian or new institutional economics perspectives.[45] From this starting point, perceiving a weakening of the application of formal laws as a weakening of the state itself follows almost by definition. While dominant in much policy literature on this topic, however, these perspectives are often limited in their ability to trace variation, helping us understand the heterogeneous effects different relationships between smugglers and states and, more broadly, unpack microlevel dynamics. It is therefore unsurprising that many of the approaches that are grounded in empirical examinations of borderlands have opted for more microlevel and bottom-up perspectives of state-building and governance, often rooted in anthropology, from "states at work" to hybrid governance and practical norms.[46]

Hybrid governance and legal pluralist perspectives are by their very nature more agnostic about the normative primacy of the state in governance[47]. Consequently, they typically don't view the existence of smuggling, its regulation through the state, or its emergence as a regulatory actor itself as inherently subversive—it's just a different form of order. This has allowed this literature to pose questions about the heterogeneity of these arrangements and ask what features of such regulatory arrangements drive their effects on states and communities. Kristof Titeca and Rachel Flynn, for example, distinguish between forms of illegal trade that are tolerated because they are rooted in local norms and distributional ideals while others, perhaps more maliciously, continue without any local legitimacy due to "strategic groups" of local businessmen and bureaucrats who defend their interests.[48] Similarly, Titeca and de Herdt write that "the concrete manifestation of norms will depend on the specific configuration of power that sustains the modus vivendi of different social actors in a specific domain."[49]

How do these different local configurations of power then drive how smuggling affects states? Here, the agnosticism about the normative primacy of state- and nonstate governance and the lack of a clearly delineated conception of the state in legal pluralist and hybrid governance approaches appear to function as a limitation. Consequently, there is often relatively little structural connection between local configurations of power and wider theories of the state. Similarly, calls for an analysis of practical norms and hybrid governance structures in borderlands that put questions of power front and center have become increasingly present within the literature and among many of the authors cited here. Raeymaekers, for example, calls for an analysis of the political geography of cross-border relations that can "highlight the more subtle dimensions of power and authority at the border, which are seen to operate through particularly gendered constructions and political hierarchies."[50]

What is at stake here is not merely the effect of smuggling on the state but also the question of how relationships between states and smugglers shape the nature of the state for the people involved. Do they primarily provide opportunities for otherwise powerless communities to assert themselves or for the powerful to further game the system? Is smuggling a "weapon of the weak" or a "weapon of the strong"? Titeca, discussing this question in the context of Northwest Uganda, argues that smuggling often straddles the two: smugglers frequently need to maintain relationships with state officials, on the one hand, but also with local populations, on the other. Their activities are characterized by an "economic and political ambiguity," a constant negotiation between different constraints and loci of power that can empower and disempower.[51] This is echoed in recent work on the role of brokers in borderlands.[52] Here, too, the effects of these interactions are traced not to the definition of the state or the types of goods smuggled, but to the nature of these negotiations that take place between smugglers and states, what determines who has access to them, and what kinds of order they produce in the end.

As this brief review has highlighted, scholarship on why states engage with smugglers and what its effects are for state-building has produced substantially divergent perspectives, driven by varying empirical focuses but also different conceptual perceptions of the state itself. What has been visible throughout much of these discussions is an increasing move away from the seemingly confrontational struggle for order between smugglers and states, or a priori concern about their "dirty entanglements," toward a desire to untangle them. This has been motivated by the assertion that rather than a peripheral issue, the "view from the margins" can provide insights into the heart of the state and its mode of governance itself, and that it might be here where states are remade—or where they reveal themselves.[53] With this have come difficulties in how to connect localized bargaining and brokerage processes with larger macroquestions about power, state-building, and development. In this context, it appears surprising that, as noted earlier, mainstream political economy and political science scholarship has been comparatively invisible in many of these discussions. As the next section highlights, this book seeks to close this gap by building toward a political economy framework to unpack the relationship between smuggling and states.

INFORMALITY AND STATE-BUILDING: A POLITICAL ECONOMY APPROACH

The previous chapter started by observing the existence, empirically, of structured interactions between smugglers and states. If we do not categorize this a priori as subversive but want to dig deeper, then the central conceptual challenge in examining the effect of smuggling on state-building is to determine its wider political function. As already reviewed, a whole range of political and economic, symbolic and material incentives of different actors intersect here. Which of these dominate and which are side-effects—which matter most for states? This connects to another challenge highlighted in the section above—that of connecting the granular and detailed accounts of the realities of smuggling, which have stood at the heart of rich ethnographic literatures, with the larger structural processes of state-building and economic development trajectories.[54]

This book argues that there are ongoing conceptual developments in modern political economy that can advance these questions by providing a structure and framework to connect granular observations of smuggling to their wider political functions. This does not imply that previous accounts are not political or do not cover politics—they emphatically do—but that they are often missing a framework that systematically and comparatively structures their connection to wider discussions about state-building. Notably, making this connection is productive in both directions: a political economy approach can contribute to our understanding of smuggling, just as bringing illegal trade into conversation with key political economy concepts enriches and challenges contemporary discussions in political science and development politics. It is in these connections that this book seeks to make a contribution to both literatures—to offer an account of the political economy of smuggling but also use the empirical realities of smuggling to make wider observations on the nature of governance and inclusion. Through this account, as the subsequent section will highlight, it seeks to provide an important addition and corrective to our understanding of the modern politics of the Middle East and North Africa, to reexamine the center through a view from the margins.

As noted, the empirical and conceptual starting point is the practical regulation of smuggling. The book's analysis of state-building, then, does not primarily refer to historical processes of state formation but to the continuous ways in which modern states engage with borderland populations and smuggling networks. It therefore requires a conception of the politics of regulation. Here, it relies on two bodies of scholarship that have both emerged as criticisms of New Institutional Economics but have thus far remained largely unconnected: critical institutionalism and political settlement approaches. The remainder of this section provides a brief sense of how they structure the upcoming analysis, but it will not discuss them in full—instead, I will come back to them in turns in subsequent chapters.

Institutions, "humanly devised constraints that shape human interaction," provide a common starting point for a discussion of regulation.[55] While most analysis of regulation begins with formal institutions, codified in laws and decrees, discussions about the effects of nonstate and hybrid governance have frequently clustered around the features and role of informal institutions. In his canonical work on institutional theory, Douglas North draws a firm distinction between the two, and throughout mainstream institutionalist scholarship, informal institutions are typically conceptualized as personalistic, lacking third-party enforcement, as unwritten and small-scale, and as self-enforcing institutions that are difficult to maintain at large scale or high levels of complexity.[56] Consequently, economic activities regulated through informal institutions are similarly perceived as made up of small units, personalized relationships, insecure property rights, and clientelistic relationships with state agents.[57]

With informal institutions framed as a less effective form of economic and political regulation, from the perspective of mainstream institutionalist approaches such as New Institutional Economics (NIE), good state-building was therefore in essence formalization—the replacement of informal institutions with formal ones.[58] From this angle, informal and hybrid institutions around smuggling either are antithetical to state-building or could be seen as second-best solutions and temporary fixes. In its primacy of formality, New Institutionalism is essentially Neo-Weberian and has, as a consequence, given rise to various empirical and normative critiques. Perhaps the most prominent alternative to Weberian approaches to state-building can be found in the work of Charles Tilly, who has pointed out that some informal institutions—such as trust networks—can be central factors in democratization, creating a structure where they intertwine with state authority, building trust between citizens and the state.[59] Tilly's analysis is echoed in more contemporary work on informal networks within formal politics and development, such as Tom Goodfellow's analysis of "political informality" and recent discussions around the role of "deals" in development.[60]

New work on the role of informal institutions in recent years has also highlighted the diversity of informal and hybrid institutional arrangements that exist in practice. Critical institutional scholarship has in particular sought to step back from the broad a priori assumptions about the developmental or democratic inferiority of informal institutions that are still inherent in NIE.[61] Instead of focusing on formalization or codifying what the "right" institutions are, scholars have increasingly concentrated on examining how they interact in practice, how people navigate and negotiate them.[62] In the face of this institutional diversity, and having moved away from a focus on formalization, many scholars have sought to restructure the results of relationships between formal and informal institutions as an empirical question.[63] A seminal contribution has come from Gretchen

Helmke and Stephen Levitsky, who suggested that whether informal institutions are "complementary," "substitutive," "competing," or "accommodating" to formal state institutions depends on the formal institutions themselves—or, more precisely, their effectiveness and goals.[64]

These approaches to institutional regulation provide a first framework to unpack the regulation of smuggling: this book does not consider the existence of informal and hybrid governance arrangements around smuggling to be a priori detrimental to state-building but is instead interested in how its regulation is negotiated in practice, and how this affects the actors and forces involved. Helmke and Levitsky's framework, however, already points to a further difficulty. If the role of these institutions depends on the goals of the state, how do we determine the goals of the state in the context of smuggling? What really is the "state" in a context where state agents are themselves involved in smuggling, or where illegal traders are involved in shoring up support for the state?

What is required is a conceptual approach toward the state that can conceive of a state that operates beyond formal institutions alone and does not draw a priori inferences from the mere existence of informal arrangements to a subverted state. Here, this book relies on the concept of political settlements as popularized by Mushtaq Khan, Hazel Gray, and Lindsay Whitfield et al.[65] Having emerged as a critique of New Institutional Economics, political settlement analysis similarly examines the institutional arrangements that determine the distribution of resources in a given political system. A political settlement is here defined as "a combination of power and institutions that is mutually compatible and also sustainable in terms of economic and political viability."[66] Contrary to NIE, political settlement theory approaches state-building and development not merely as a process of getting the "institutions right" but considers the distributional consequences on institutional arrangements as critical for the stability of the whole. State-building is not dependent on the establishment of the right type of formal institutions, but on the establishments of institutions that distribute resources in a way that is compatible with the balance of power. In Khan's terms, "Institutions and the distribution of power have to be compatible because if powerful groups are not getting an acceptable distribution of benefits from an institutional structure they will strive to change it."[67]

Consequently, scholarship on political settlements diverges from NIE in its evaluation of rents. While NIE primarily frames rent-seeking as antithetical to political and economic development, a political settlement approach argues that rent-seeking can be developmental if it contributes to the stability of the settlement. It is here, then, where political settlement also differs from NIE and more classical neo-Weberian approaches on the role of informal institutions in development and state-building. Rather than framing them as inherently antithetical to state structures, in political settlement scholarship they can play a role in reallocating rents and resources in a way that brings the overall distribution of resources in line with the balance of holding power and hence maintain the stability of the system as a whole, thereby supporting the performance of both formal and informal institutions. Consequently, a political settlement approach suggests the possibility of a nonsubversive role for informal institutions and consequently smuggling economies in state-building processes, if the rents generated through them help to bring the distribution of resources in line with the wider distribution of power. Political settlement scholarship therefore provides a different interpretation of the function of informal institutions.

Traditionally, applications of political settlement scholarship have centered on industrial policy, although more recent applications have expanded to a wider variety of contexts from postconflict settings to urban politics.[68] Its application to illegal economies is still rare and so far primarily found in Goodhand's analysis of drug economies in Afghanistan.[69] As discussed in the previous section, his work highlights the utility of the framework in placing local illegal economies within national political dynamics. It also illustrates the ways in which their previous thematic focus has limited political settlement analyses, and how it can be expanded by an application to illegal economies and smuggling in particular. As Goodhand and Patrick Meehan have pointed out, the framework traditionally struggles in its analysis of space and territory.[70] Similarly, scholarship on political settlements has been skewed toward questions of stability and growth rather than issues of justice or equity. Its analytical focus tends to be top-down, examining the role of different groups and actors within the settlement, rather than their experience of navigating it. Chapter 8 will present a sketch of what a more bottom-up approach to political settlements—"lived political settlements"—can look like. Political settlement approaches have also largely mirrored NIE in their description of informal institutions, even if they give them a different role in state-building processes. They are still primarily conceptualized as personalistic, small-scale, and unwritten. Here, both an empirical application with a focus on informal institutions and a combination with more critical institutional approaches can expand key tenants of this approach, as chapter 3 and 4 will highlight.

Critical institutional scholarship and political settlement approaches do not imply a priori judgments on whether the sheer existence of informal and hybrid regulation of smuggling already subverts states. Instead, they structure empirical questions about when and why smuggling might subvert or support state-building. From these frameworks emerge the central building blocks and related questions of this book's analysis of the politics of smuggling.

First, there are the (formal and informal) institutional arrangements that regulate smuggling. Empirically, these institutions provide a compelling starting point as they promise granular insight into the actual practices of smuggling and a natural focal point for interactions between state structures and smuggling networks. The analysis begins by asking what kind of institutions these are, how they are negotiated and sustained, and how they relate to formal state institutions. It asks what role state agents play in their maintenance, and whether they are sustained through active enforcement or because they are embedded in local beliefs and moral economies. A critical institutionalist angle further asks how what is often described as small-scale personalistic arrangements can structure large-scale smuggling economies.

The second set of questions relates to the rents generated both through smuggling itself and through its institutional regulation. It asks how these rents are distributed, and who has access to them. This provides a first look at the motivations of different actors and the economic effects of these smuggling economies. Most important, however, it connects these institutions to wider questions of state-building along the criteria that a political settlement approach suggests. It asks which groups and structures benefit from smuggling rents and whether this helps bring the distribution of resources in line with the distribution of power. Are smuggling rents used to pacify groups that could destabilize the state, or are they emboldening groups that seek to upset the wider settlement?

Together, these questions seek to build toward a structured answer as to why and how states engage in regulating smuggling, and whether this subverts or supports state-building processes. Consequently, much of the focus is on how what happens in the borderlands affects the state. This is not where this analysis ends, however. Instead, it seeks to explore not merely what smuggling means for the wider political settlement, but also what these arrangements in turn means for the smugglers and borderland communities involved in it. Are they "reshaping the state from the margins" or being trapped in vulnerable livelihoods and increasingly alienated from state institutions? And, critically, how are these dynamics changing as states are themselves changing in the wake of revolutions and reforms, free-trade agreements, and increasing global concerns about porous borders in the context of migration and terrorism?

MAKING NORTH AFRICA'S BORDERLANDS

To begin unpacking these questions in the context of North Africa, the remainder of this chapter provides an introduction to smuggling in the region. Before getting to its modern structures, however, it is important to briefly put them into a historical context. Notably, as in most of the world, trade in North Africa predates the borders that now make it "cross-border" trade. Scholars of informal trade in Algeria, Tunisia, Libya, or Morocco have highlighted long histories of trade stretching back to the caravans that have for millennia connected and supplied a vast territory from the Sahara to the Mediterranean and from Fez to Cairo.[71] Mobility of goods related closely to the mobility of people, as patterns of trade and nomadic patterns of movement overlapped and connected.[72] As Scheele, Matthew Ellis, and others have noted, while trade in the region predates the economic regulatory systems of the modern nation-states, it has been structured by—and contributed to the formation of—centers of tribal and religious power.[73] Historical accounts of this relationship provide a corrective to a narrative of only dominance and subversion, noting shifting and at times shared forms of governance in the periphery.

As early state structures developed in the region, their relationship with centers of power in their territorial periphery was characterized not solely by competition over control or legitimacy but also by coexistence and indirect rule. The most famous sociological history of the region, Ibn Khaldûn's "Muqaddimah," is centered on the relationship between the tribes of the *makhzan*, the proto-state, and *siba*, the nomadic periphery.[74] It describes a circular, dialectic vision of rule, in which dynasties rise, until the relationships that maintain them weaken, and they are conquered by tribes from the periphery, who form a new dynasty to rise and eventually fall. While Khaldûn's description of the relationship between centers and peripheries is at first glance antagonistic, the two still remain closely intertwined in shifting alliances, raids, and connectivities, the periphery both a refuge and a center in waiting. More modern historical accounts primarily highlight a coexistence between political centers and centers of power in the periphery alongside forms of selective and indirect rule. Ellis notes the Egyptian state's reliance on tribal communities in Siwa as indirect providers of order and regulation.[75] Lisa Anderson's account of state-building in Tunisia and Libya points out relatively limited interactions of tribal communities in southern Tunisia with the central state, which rarely interfered in tribal matters and limited itself to the collection of taxes through regular military campaigns, the so-called *mahalla*.[76]

Any account of the history of smuggling in North Africa, however, needs to begin without a notion of borders and of territorially defined centralized polities with a claim on regulating trade. The emergence of both in North Africa, and hence of smuggling in the region, is intimately related to the history of colonial rule. The modern borders in North Africa, as in most parts of the continent, were largely established as borders between colonial territories. While the infamous Sykes-Picot agreement of 1916 has become a popular shorthand used by scholars and activists to decry the artificiality of colonial borders in the Middle East and North Africa, the region's borders were largely defined in a set of separate agreements with Spain, France, the Ottoman Empire, Italy, and the United Kingdom, and only slowly enforced on the territory.[77]

Alongside the demarcation and control of geographically fixed borders, colonialism also contributed to a shift in the conceptualization of statehood in the region from population to territory. The Ottoman Empire had claimed sovereignty over all Sunni Muslims; the Kingdom of Morocco, over all those who said their prayers in the name of the Caliph of the West.[78] Ibn Khaldûn conceptualizes state power not as territorially delineated but emanating outward from a political center over populations.[79] As I. William Zartman notes, when the two conceptions—the territorial state and its traditional predecessor—met, the new demarcation was still first limited to areas of higher population density. While French colonial control of Algeria led to the official drawing of a line limiting the northern part of

Morocco in 1845, the line stopped south of the small desert oasis of Figuig, as a border further south was considered "superfluous" because there were no people there.[80]

The colonial period also contributed to the organization of borderlands as distinct spaces. When borders split long-standing tribal territories, colonial regimes employed policies aimed at sedentarizing nomadic tribes within these territories, while structuring and accessing trade routes, heralding "the end of the political autonomy of the hinterland."[81] Colonial administrations became directly involved in setting up trading posts, markets, and entire urban centers in borderlands, occasionally bringing in populations from other regions to populate settlements.[82] Frequent use of military zones along newly established borders also saw borderland communities commonly experiencing a more militarized form of governance under colonial rule than their counterparts in the political and economic centers.[83] Unsurprisingly, the colonial period saw a range of anticolonial uprisings in the region's newly created borderlands.[84] The Werghemma tribal federation on the border between Libya and Tunisia, for example, which had seen its territory divided, became a primary site for resistance against colonial occupation, taking advantage of the newly divided jurisdiction by providing resistance fighters refuge across the border, and by continuing to move goods and arms—what had now become smuggling.[85]

Despite their colonial origins, North Africa's borders, borderlands, and state system have survived the end of colonial rule and the establishment of independent states. A brief period of enthusiasm around pan-Arabism and plans for the creation of a federal union that could have diminished the importance of the region's borders quickly devolved into competition, rivalry, and border disputes. The region's colonial borders were formally accepted at the Organisation of African Unity summit in Cairo in 1964. Since then, even though some actors have challenged the legitimacy of these borders and some disagreements remain, they have been remarkably stable and have become a resilient element of the modern political structure of the region.[86]

While independence reshaped the region's politics, state-building projects across North Africa maintained many of the centralized political institutions inherited from the departed colonial powers, as Michael Willis notes, "not just out of necessity but in full consciousness of the fact that the colonial structures had been designed with the specific objective of establishing full and exclusive political control of the country."[87] Even though actors from peripheral regions were involved in the independence struggles, postindependence politics, especially in Morocco and Tunisia, was primarily located in the political centers, with elites from peripheral regions frequently marginalized at the expense of increasingly personalistic regimes.[88] Uprisings in the region's peripheries, such as revolts in Morocco's Rif Mountains, and Tunisia's interior regions, were defeated militarily and did not significantly counteract the centralizing tendencies of postindependence states.[89]

Partially tied to nationalist, personalistic, or Pan-Arabist programs, many states in the region set about to pursue national ideologies that were largely antagonistic to the idea of peripheral communities as alternative markers of identity and political spaces. In Tunisia in particular, the postindependence regime of Habib Bourguiba abolished tribal lands, decried tribal structures as "archaic," and systematically undermined local identities at the expense of a direct allegiance to the nation-state.[90] In contrast, the consolidation of the monarchy in Morocco involved an incorporation of tribes into the national narrative, alongside their political co-optation by the palace, relying on them as a counterweight to urban elites. However, this too coexisted with an increasing centralization and domination of national politics by the palace, particularly at the expense of tribes in peripheral regions, as colonial provisions granting autonomy to Amazigh regions were rescinded.[91]

While the postindependence years across North Africa shared centralizing state-building processes, their underlying political projects were marked by institutional and ideological divergences, alongside rivalries, distrust, and shifting regional and international alliances. A rivalry between monarchic, economically conservative Morocco and socialist, Third-Worldist Algeria, fueled by diverging ideological positions, international alliances, and disputes over the status of the Western Sahara, has dominated regional relations in the postindependence period.[92] Further east, a failed attempt at uniting the two countries deepened distrust between the Tunisian and Libyan administrations.[93]

Crucially for the topic at hand, divergent political trajectories also spawned divergent economic projects and contributed to a failure to create institutional structures for economic cooperation and coordination across the Maghreb.[94] Essentially, a failure of regional integration had direct impacts on the mode of integration of borderlands into domestic economic systems. Formal trade between North Africa's states remained limited, trade relationships were primarily with Europe, and projects to build regional trade infrastructure stalled.[95] This not only left the region as one of the least economically integrated regions in the world but also limited formal employment opportunities in the borderlands. At the same time, divergent price, tariff, and particularly subsidy regimes, driven in particular by the hydrocarbon wealth of Libya and Algeria, created opportunities for arbitrage trade. Increasingly, borderland populations began exploiting arbitrage opportunities and their ability to move across the region's borders, bringing across gasoline, couscous, and other consumer goods. As these activities expanded, informal cross-border trade—smuggling—began to rival formal trade volumes at various borders in the region, providing employment and income to borderland communities.[96] It was at this moment of political and especially economic divergence, in the 1970s and 1980s, when smuggling in North Africa developed the broad macrostructure that can be observed today. A subsequent section of this chapter will provide a systematic mapping of this structure, alongside its key trade corridors, goods, and drivers.

What are the politics of this expansion of informal cross-border trade? Anthropological accounts of borderlands in the region have noted that despite nationalizing discourses from the political center, tribal markers of identity have not entirely disappeared.[97] This has led some to argue that today's smuggling routes may reflect the resilience of traditional nonstate structures of authority.[98] As related work in the African borderlands literature has pointed out, however, the continued observation of the transgression of borders does not necessarily imply continuity in the motivation, structure, and organizational form of the trade[99]. At the same time, the expansion of smuggling has also seen interventions by elites from the political center in structuring and influencing informal trade in the borderlands for their own financial benefit, such as the clan around President Ben Ali in prerevolutionary Tunisia[100]. As a result, the role of smuggling in postindependence politics, and whether the organization of the trade represents the continuity or reemergence of nonstate organizational forms or is more closely connected to state structures, political elites, or simply corruption, has remained an open question.

As noted earlier, a range of developments in the first two decades of the twenty-first century have brought renewed attention to borderlands and their role in regional politics. Three in particular stand out.

The first has been the expansion or rising prominence of jihadi movements in the region. Notably, these have both ideologically decried the illegitimacy of the region's national borders as colonial and oppressive constructs and repeatedly used the region's borderlands to move people and arms, establish temporary footholds, as well as stage attacks against neighboring jurisdictions.[101] An analysis of the origins of North African IS members noted a particularly high number of recruits stemming from Tunisian border regions.[102] Consequently, fears of an "unholy alliance" between smugglers and jihadi groups became increasingly prevalent in policy and media narratives.[103]

The second and directly related development has been the increasing regional and international concern with border security in North Africa. Key factors here have been the post-2001 "War on Terror" agenda, the conflicts in Libya and Mali in the 2010s, as well as increasing European concerns with the regulation of mobility in the region following the increase of irregular migration across the Mediterranean in the mid-2010s.[104] These interlocking developments led both to an increasing attention to borderlands in the region and to increasing investments in physical security infrastructure along the region's borders. This has brought the creation of new walls and fencing alongside sections of the border between Morocco and Algeria, a trench along sections of Tunisia's border with Libya developed in 2016, substantive expansions of the fencing around the two largest Spanish enclaves in Northern Morocco, Ceuta, and Melilla, alongside substantial international investment in electronic border infrastructure.[105] With this have come some visible effects on smuggling networks, and protests in border regions—sparking a new conversation about the form of their economic integration and potential alternatives.[106]

The third and perhaps most important development in the region in the past decade has been a set of popular uprisings in 2011 that led to the downfall of regimes in Tunisia, Egypt, and Libya and provided a shock to the region's politics. With the self-immolation of an informal vendor in Tunisia as one of the early symbols of the "Arab Spring," youth unemployment, economic informality, and socioeconomic marginalization emerged as prominent themes in the protests.[107]

Consequently, the post-2011 years across the region have seen renewed discussions on the fragility of the region's social contracts, their effects on youth and labor markets, and the need for more "inclusive" development.[108]

Across the region, the somewhat stylized picture of postindependence social contracts had been one of "authoritarian bargains"—the exchange of political acquiescence to authoritarian rule for a set of primarily formal benefits including expansive subsidies, opportunities for public-sector employment, high public spending, and expansive state intervention.[109] Toward the end of the twentieth century, however, changing demographics alongside growing pressure to decrease public spending in the context of structural adjustment programs in the region had increasingly constrained states' ability to hold up their end of the bargain. At the same time, the old distributional regime had fostered insider-outsider divisions within the private sector, hampered its ability to create private employment for a new generation, and increasingly segmented the labor market.[110] As the portion of public-sector jobs decreased, much of the region's youth moved on to finding more precarious employment in the informal sector, seeing a decrease in their future prospects and increasingly dissatisfied with their role in the dominant social contract.[111]

Borderlands have played a particular role in these dynamics. Levels of informal employment were already disproportionally high, and arbitrage trade made smuggling economies indirectly dependent on subsidy regimes.[112] Most important, however, the years after 2011 increasingly saw borderlands framed as a space where these different dynamics—crumbling social contracts, a dissatisfied youth, popular mobilization, radicalization, migration, and insecurity—interacted with and reinforced one another, and hence where new discussions of political and economic inclusion were of particular urgency.[113] Tracing these dynamics in these spaces, however, requires an analysis of their political economy and how it has been affected by these developments. Studying North Africa's border economies post-2011, therefore, can both contribute to understanding the role of smuggling in the region's politics and provide wider insights into some of the central discussions on the politics of the region today.

MAPPING SMUGGLING IN NORTH AFRICA TODAY

While smuggling is at times conceptualized as a product of individual-level incentives and hidden networks, borderland scholarship has long highlighted the existence of persistent and researchable macrostructures of smuggling, shaped by territorial arrangements, political institutions, economic structures, and global trade routes.[114] This section outlines the contours of a macrostructure of smuggling in North Africa. As discussed earlier, many of the modern smuggling routes broadly developed their current directions starting from the 1970s, in the context of political divergence and poor formal economic integration in the region. While the past decades have seen a variety of changes in flows and drivers and the collapse of an increasing number of networks, this section will focus on the larger structure that existed throughout most of the first two decades of the twenty-first century, with later chapters focusing on the more recent disruptions and their consequences.

Identifying a macrostructure of smuggling in North Africa is complicated by the immense diversity of goods traded that follow different routes, drivers, and structures. Varying tax and especially subsidy regimes have created price differences and significant incentives for arbitrage trade, especially on the borders of the hydrocarbon-rich Algeria and Libya. At the same time, high tariffs and nontariff barriers, a widespread feature in the region, have created incentives for trading outside of formal channels, both within the region and in connection with global trade links.[115] While trade in illicit goods similarly both reacts to demands within the region and connects it to wider global corridors of the drug and arms trade, drivers here are less structured around price differences and more around the unavailability of formal trade channels for certain goods and actors. This section provides a brief overview of the main trade routes for the most commonly traded goods before drawing out the crucial nodes that make up the geography of informal trade in North Africa.

Gasoline

Although it has not received the same media attention as drug smuggling or human trafficking, there can be little disagreement that in terms of its dollar value, quantity, and employment effects, gasoline has been the most central informally traded good in the region in the past few decades. Price differences created through subsidies have acted as the key driver. The region can be easily divided into two production countries—Algeria and Libya—which supply their neighbors, Morocco, Tunisia, Mali, Chad, Niger, Sudan, and Egypt. This dynamic is illustrated in figure 2.1. Smuggled quantities here have frequently been large enough to plausibly have a significant effect on expenditure on gasoline in destination countries—in 2013, for example, estimates suggested that around one-quarter of the gasoline consumed in Tunisia had been smuggled in from Libya or Algeria.[116] There has always been a huge diversity in the quantities of gasoline traded—while some is transported in 20-liter canisters across borders on donkeys and motorcycles, especially Libya has in recent years also seen large-volume quantities smuggled toward Italy and international markets via oil tankers.[117] By building primarily on price differences driven by subsidies, which make up a significant section of state expenditures in Libya and Algeria, the rent streams created through gasoline smuggling thereby are directly connected to state budgets and mechanisms of redistribution. This is particularly noteworthy in Libya, which is a large exporter of crude oil but still largely imports its refined gasoline from abroad.[118] As later chapters will discuss, the past decade has seen increasing pressure on gasoline smuggling networks, as a result of novel border fortifications in Algeria and Tunisia, alongside the deteriorating security and economic situation in Libya.

Main Corridors for the Smuggling of Gasoline

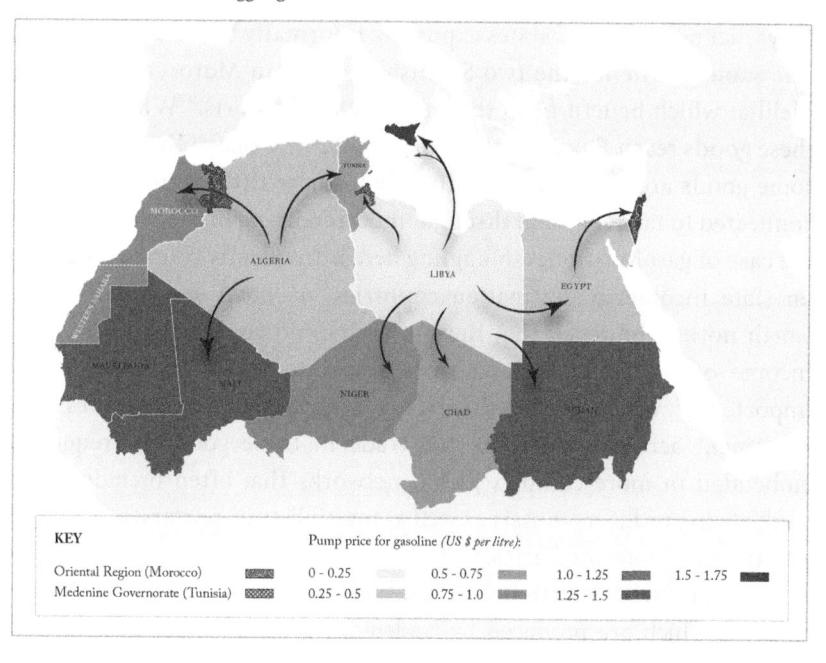

FIGURE 2.1 Key corridors for gasoline smuggling in North Africa, price differences (for 2018), and case studies. Map drawn by Grace Fussell based on author's data.

Nonhydrocarbon Licit Consumer Goods

Nonhydrocarbon consumer goods not produced in North Africa represent a wide set of commonly informally traded goods in the region. Their origin is typically China, Japan, or South Korea, as well as Turkey, the special economic zones of the Arab Peninsula, and to a lesser degree the European Union. Key drivers are usually heterogeneous tariff regimes, tariff evasion, and to a lesser extent the unavailability of specific goods in local markets due to sanctions or poorly developed formal trade channels.[119] The most commonly traded goods in this category include a variety of fabrics such as clothes, carpets, and bedsheets, white electronics like microwaves, fridges, air-conditioners, and phones, household items and kitchenware, stationery, cosmetic products, and toys.[120]

As figure 2.2 shows, this trade connects the region to wider global supply links that ship to selected countries in the region, from which goods are distributed across the region through smuggling networks. Countries with lower import tariffs than their neighbors, Algeria and Libya, act as "entrepôt" states exporting informally to their neighbors.[121] The same is true for the two Spanish enclaves in Morocco, Ceuta and Melilla, which benefit from their status as "free ports." While many of these goods reach Egypt, Tunisia, or Morocco via one of these entrepôts, some goods are also imported directly to these three countries but are connected to tariff evasion through underreporting in the ports.[122] As in the case of gasoline trade, smuggling here is frequently framed as a drain on state income in destination countries via tariff shortfalls.[123] It is worth noting, however, that these networks do contribute to the tariff income of the countries and free ports into which they are legally imported.[124] While the gasoline trade described usually involves only movement across one border, the trade in these goods is frequently embedded in more complex global networks that often include direct contacts to producers in Asia as well as multiple transporters, merchants, and financial intermediaries.

Informally traded cigarettes are also a common feature across the region, many of which are produced by trademark owners based in Free Trade Zones in the UAE and either consumed in the region or smuggled onward.

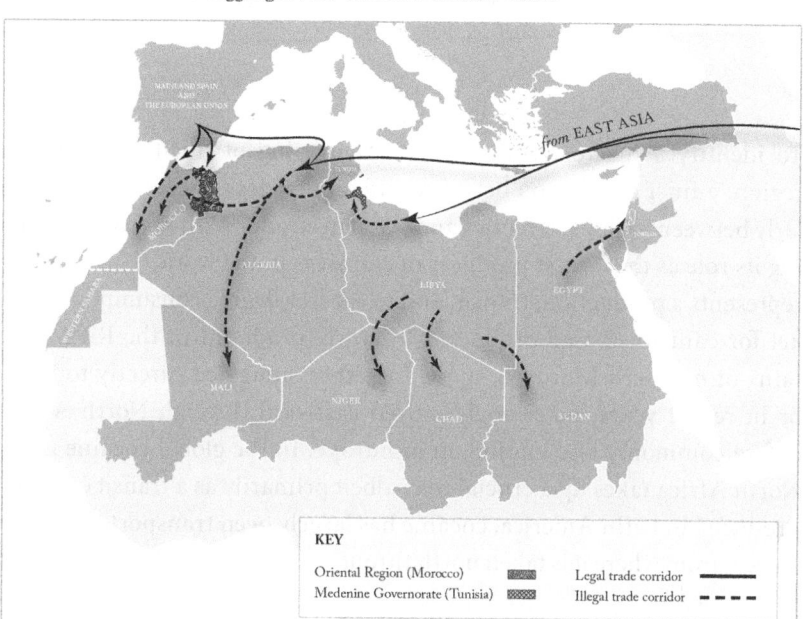

Main Corridors for the Smuggling of Non-Gasoline Consumer Goods

FIGURE 2.2 Key corridors for the smuggling of nonhydrocarbon consumer goods in North Africa, and case sites. Map drawn by Grace Fussell based on author's data.

Food

The informal trade of foodstuffs in the region is as widespread at it is diverse. Both packaged staple product like couscous, spaghetti, or olive oil and fresh products like fruits, vegetables, or livestock are commonly traded informally due to price differences or domestic availability.[125] Food shortages, particularly in times of conflict, have repeatedly given this trade additional importance. Scheele argues that the food supply in northern Mali would be impossible to sustain without informal trade networks from southern Algeria and that their absence would likely lead to a severe humanitarian crisis.[126] A similar argument likely applies to informal trade networks between Egypt and the Gaza strip, as well as at times during the civil war in Libya.[127] However, with the diversity of different foods traded across the region's borderlands and frequently shifting patterns, no clear macrostructure for this trade emerges in the region.

Illicit Goods

To identify a macrostructure of the smuggling of illicit goods in the region, a finer distinction between different trades is necessary, particularly between various narcotics and the arms trade. With Morocco retaining its role as the largest producer of cannabis in the world, North Africa represents a production, transit, and to a lesser degree consumption market for cannabis-based products.[128] Largely produced in the Rif Mountains of northern Morocco, these are either smuggled directly to Spain or in recent years increasingly moved eastward through North Africa, before commonly also ending up in Europe. In the global cocaine trade, North Africa takes up a crucial role, albeit primarily as a transit corridor. Produced in Latin America, cocaine has largely been transported to West Africa, from where it is taken north through Morocco or Libya, and finally to Europe.[129]

As figure 2.3 highlights, North Africa primarily functions as a country of origin and transit for drug smuggling, with destination markets primarily being located further east or in Europe. In recent years, however, it has become an increasingly important consumption market for a variety of synthetic drugs and amphetamines, including ecstasy, Tramadol (an opioid-based painkiller), and a variety of psychotropic prescription drugs, many of which are produced outside of the region and imported through its ports.[130]

The 2011 uprising in Libya and the protracted civil war that started in 2014 have transformed the regional macrostructure of weapons smuggling. Libya has emerged as a crucial consumption market of both weapons and ammunition, and likely increasingly a transit country as well. This trade has seen the engagement of a wide variety of actors, including international backers of factions in the Libyan conflict, the Touareg and Tebu groups in southern Libya, some members of borderland populations, as well as international criminal networks.[131] As research by Small Arms Survey indicates, an increasing amount of the organization of this trade is now conducted online and increasingly ties the region to manufacturing centers in Europe, China, and Russia, as well as conflict zones in the Sahel.[132]

SMUGGLING IN NORTH AFRICA

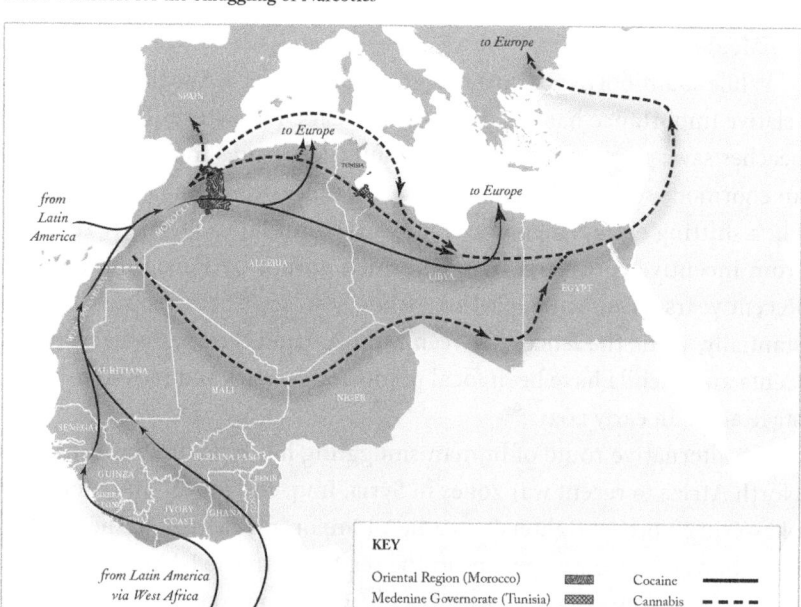

Main Corridors for the Smuggling of Narcotics

FIGURE 2.3 Key corridors for the smuggling of cannabis and cocaine in North Africa, and case sites. Map drawn by Grace Fussell based on author's data.

Migration and Human Trafficking

This book's focus is on the smuggling of goods—it does not endeavor to cover in the same terms or logic the dynamics of human trafficking, migration, and the various forms that human mobility has taken in the region. These have been at the center of some excellent scholarship in recent years but have also, through their central role in policy discussions, increasingly shaped how political actors have approached the region's borderlands more widely.[133]

While migration and human trafficking from North Africa have been long-standing issues that have fundamentally structured the relationship between North African states and the European Union, their political prominence has expanded in particular since 2011, as the weakening of the security infrastructure in Tunisia and Libya opened up new routes for migrant smuggling, and the civil war in Syria, alongside a protracted economic crisis in the region, increased the number of those looking to cross the Mediterranean.[134]

While south-north human smuggling routes exist across the region, their relative importance has varied in recent years. Departures from Tunisia's beaches saw spikes in 2011 and 2017, while departures from Libya reached an enormous scale in the years after 2011 before decreasing in 2017 following a shifting enforcement environment within Libya, partially resulting from incentives provided to local armed groups by European actors.[135] Recent years have seen departures from Morocco's beaches increase substantially, while the fences between Morocco and the Spanish enclaves of Ceuta and Melilla have been focal points for decades and moved to center stage again in early 2021.[136]

An alternative route of human smuggling has linked the countries of North Africa to recent war zones in Syria, Iraq, and Libya. The smuggling of aspiring "foreign fighters" became an important element of the military operations of extremist groups in the region, with the Islamic State gaining particular prominence after 2014.[137] Common routes here connected Morocco, Algeria, and Tunisia with Libya, from which fighters either joined the Libyan segments of IS or flew to Turkey, crossing from there into Syria. Given the vast geographic reach of these networks, they have included a wide variety of local and regional actors, reaching from recruiters in Sub-Saharan Africa to criminal networks in central and southern Europe.[138] With the collapse of ISIS territory in Syria and Iraq from 2017 onward, the movement of fighters back to North Africa has caused increasing concern in the region.[139] In Tunisia in particular, concern about these movements has often been closely interwoven with how cross-border movements more widely have been framed.

Geographies of Informal Cross-Border Trade

As this brief mapping of some of the main smuggling routes in North Africa has demonstrated, there is not one generalizable macropattern of informal cross-border trade in the region but a variety of different structured patterns for different commodities. While the commercial logics of these streams appear relatively separate, this is not to imply that they are in no way interdependent. At least two points of connection between different trades are worth pointing to. One involves financial services: while poor currency convertibility is not a driver behind smuggling activities in the region in the same way that it has been in areas with uneven landscapes of currency convertibility, a variety of different networks are relying on parallel foreign exchange markets.[140] In some cases, such as southern Tunisia, informal financiers not only buy and sell currency but also provide a variety of financial services such as credit and loans for large-scale wholesale trade.[141] In addition, they organize international transfers, typically through *hawala* networks. Hawala banking involves a system of brokers in a variety of countries, who conduct transactions with each other primarily through a system of debt, trust, and promise that does not typically necessitate the transfer of any actual currency.[142]

A second factor that connects different informal trade routes in North Africa is the emergence of nodes of informal trade across the region, as particular border towns with a position close to a formal border crossing and large informal retail markets and infrastructure have become places where different trade routes converge and intersect and have come to dominate local economies. The formal centers of commerce in North Africa—Cairo, Alexandria, Tripoli, Tunis, Algiers, or Casablanca—are familiar to the casual observer of the region and have served to embed the region in the global economy primarily through ports and North-South linkages. If we observe the central nodes of smuggling routes in the region, however, another geography of regional trade emerges. At its heart are places like Nador, Tamanrasset, Zuwara, or Ben Guerdane—medium-sized cities in the geographic and economic periphery of their respective nation-states and logistical centers of commercial networks that include strong East-West links across the region, alongside connections to Europe and the wider global economy. They are the centers of transport and wholesale for the region's informal economy, and their networks employ a significant section of the region's labor force. This, of course, does not imply or postulate that these nodes are also where all the "action" is, that the region's formal political and financial centers don't hold any power over informal trade, or that influential traders in these networks are not still located in the capital cities, but it makes these nodes well-suited sites to begin studying smuggling and its governance in the region.

Figure 2.4 gives an overview of some of these key nodes. It is not meant to be exhaustive but highlights larger cities where a variety of different trade

SMUGGLING IN NORTH AFRICA

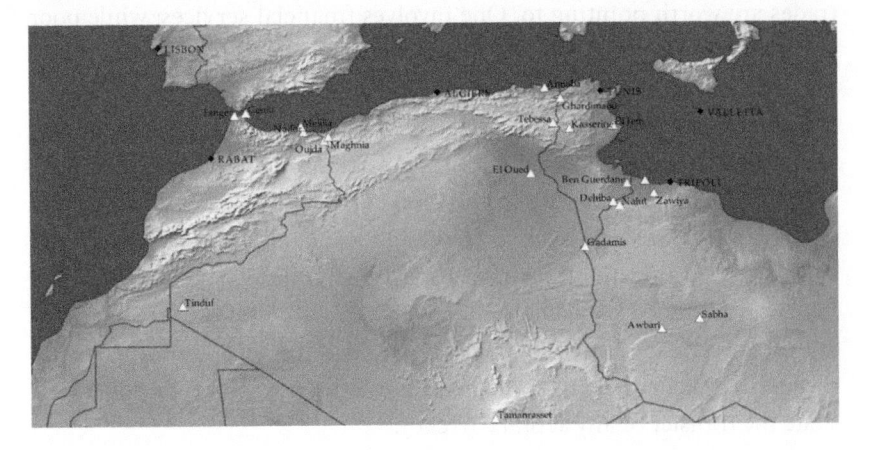

FIGURE 2.4 Key nodes of informal cross-border trade in the Maghreb. Map by author.

corridors intersect. Together with the trade corridors outlined earlier, it presents a first mapping of the geography of informal trade in North Africa, which provides a starting point to introduce and situate the cities in which much of this book is based.

CASE STUDIES

The majority of the following chapters will focus on two borderlands in North Africa: the Oriental region in Morocco, which includes the cities of Oujda and Nador, and the Medenine region in Tunisia, which includes the cities of Ben Guerdane and Medenine (see figure 2.5). As the other figures in this chapter have highlighted, both regions are central nodes in the trade of licit and illicit goods.

These regions also share a range of structural characteristics that make them good representations of the wider borderlands in the region. Both lie in the political, geographic, and economic periphery of their respective countries. In both regions, informal cross-border trade accounts for a significant part of the local economic activity and employment. While Morocco and Tunisia have developed different political systems (Tunisia abolished its monarchy in 1957, while Morocco's remains intact), both have sustained relatively effective and centralized administrative institutions. For most of their postindependence history, they have shared broadly

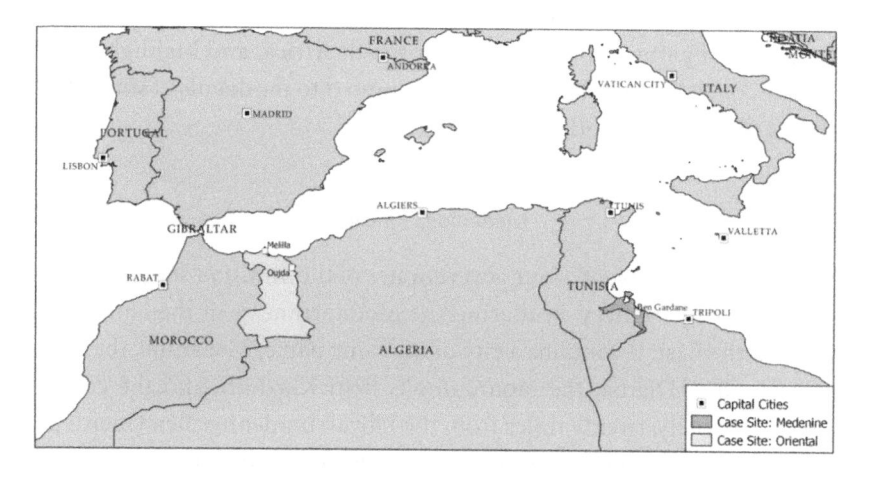

FIGURE 2.5 The two case sites within North Africa. Map by author.

authoritarian regimes alongside clientelist political settlements which included the co-optation and enrichment of politically connected elites and repression against oppositional groups. Both settlements visibly benefited elites from the political center and sustained uneven economic geographies, which in the periphery have been accompanied by lower formal state investment alongside histories of resistance and narratives of exclusion.[143]

Alongside these similarities, the two case sites diverge in aspects that allow us to explore some of the key questions of this book. While both countries have seen renegotiations of their national political settlements in recent years, which have included new constitutions, gestures toward more horizontally inclusive political settlements, and renewed public discussions on the role of smuggling and the wider inclusion of the periphery, this has happened under fundamentally different contexts. In Tunisia, these changes were triggered by a revolution and saw a shift toward more democratic political structures alongside a temporarily decreased state presence and enforcement capacity in the borderlands. In Morocco, the changes were guided through a top-down reform agenda and were not accompanied by a decrease in state capacity or the establishment of genuinely democratic political structures. The two regions also offer geographic variation, containing three structurally different borderlands: one urban, two rural, one closed border, two open ones. The remainder of this chapter will provide a brief introduction to the two case sites, situating them in the historical and geographical patterns of smuggling in North Africa, and highlight some of their context before the next chapters jump into the details of smuggling and its regulation in both sites.

Medenine, Tunisia

Medenine, one of twenty-four governorates of the Tunisian state, lies in its southeastern periphery, bordering the Mediterranean in the North and Libya in the East. It contains a city of the same name, Medenine, the touristic island of Djerba, the mountainous Beni Khedech, and the coastal Zarzis. Crucially, twenty miles from the Libyan border lies Ben Guerdane, a town of seventy thousand inhabitants and the central hub of informal cross-border trade in Tunisia.

Medenine's history closely reflects major themes in the history of borderlands in North Africa discussed earlier. Large parts of its territory form part of the Jefara, a tribal territory that spans around 10,000 square kilometers across the modern border and into western Libya and has been a space of nomadic movements dating back to before the colonial occupation.[144] While Tunisia and Tripolitania were different political entities under the Ottoman Empire, the border was never clearly defined until the early twentieth century, creating a zone of ambiguity and refuge for dissidents.[145] This ended when the convention of Tripoli finally demarcated a border between the French protectorate of Tunisia and the Ottoman rulers of Libya in 1910. This caused a short-lived uprising by the Tunisian Werghemma tribal federation, which had so far experienced limited interactions with the central state, limited primarily to the collection of taxes through military campaigns.[146]

Ironically, the city of Ben Guerdane, now a smuggling hub accused of subverting Tunisia's borders, originally developed out of French colonial strategies aimed at sedentarizing local tribes and controlling commercial routes. In 1895 the Service des Affaires Indigènes outlined a territory of 174 hectares for the construction of a market and fields and began with the construction of what today is the city center. As the dominant local tribe, the Twazine, refused to participate, the city center was populated by neighboring tribes, groups from Djerba and even Malta, alongside Jewish merchants.[147] Only slowly, Twazine began to construct houses in the periphery of the city, giving it its modern shape: a small, narrow city center surrounded by vast suburbs of expansive family homes, usually made up of two or three houses on a small piece of land surrounded by a wall, sprawling out into the desert. Today, many of the original residents of the old city center have left, and most of the city identifies as Twazine, while the second-largest group, the Rabai'a, makes up about 10 percent of the city's population.

After Tunisia's independence, a split between its leaders Habib Bourguiba and Salah Ben Youssef over the terms of independence escalated into clashes, in which Ben Youssef found strong support in the southern regions, including in Medenine. As Bourguiba's victory became clearer, Ben Youssef hid near Ben Guerdane, before fleeing across the border into Libya. Repressions followed for Ben Youssef's supporters across the country.[148] As Bourguiba emerged as Tunisia's first president, the country maintained a populist authoritarian political structure and a political settlement embedded in a clear economic geography, with the new regime largely made up of an elite from Tunis and the northern coastal cities around Sousse and Monastir, Bourguiba's birthplace.[149] The political settlement throughout the tenure of Bourguiba and his successor Ben Ali remained broadly clientelist: alongside redistribution through formal institutional structures, such as high levels of public employment, subsidies, and some of the highest levels of social spending in the region existed informal side-payments to politically connected groups vis-à-vis crony capitalism and patronage as well as targeted repression against excluded groups, such as the country's Islamic Tendency Movement.[150]

Formal state investment remained unevenly distributed: between 1973 and 1985, Medenine received less than 1.5 percent of formal state investment, despite accounting for 4 percent of the country's population.[151] While many people in Medenine frame their economic marginalization as a "punishment" for their support of the Youssefist uprising, it is worth highlighting that the state's approach toward Medenine largely maps onto the wider development of an economic geography in Tunisia that continued to benefit the northern coastal regions and, as Anderson has argued, already finds its roots in the country's precolonial and colonial economic institutions.[152]

While largely marginalized in terms of formal income streams, Medenine began to occupy a central role in the development of the post-1970s structure of informal cross-border trade in the region described earlier. With Libya functioning as an entrepôt state for the informal trade of both gasoline and foreign-made consumer goods such as textiles and white electronics, informal trade in southern Tunisia is largely focused on import. Textiles, white electronics, and similar consumer goods are shipped to the port of Tripoli, loaded on fleets of smaller cars, and brought into Tunisia, where they are sold on markets throughout the country. Arms and narcotics trade are small but high-value operations. Informal export from Tunisia to Libya consists largely of food staples and agricultural goods but generally remains on a relatively small scale. Under the Ben Ali regime, these activities appear to have been largely tolerated, alongside the selective integration of figures closely connected to the regime into lucrative positions within the trade.[153]

Medenine provides a fitting setting, not merely because it represents typical features of the region's borderlands, such as the disruption of peripheral politics through border-making, postindependence economic marginalization, and the development of employment-intensive smuggling economies. More crucially, the past decade has seen the role of smuggling in the country's politics contested, challenged, and negotiated, providing a unique opportunity for observation.

In 2010 a closure of the main border crossing prompted large-scale protests in Ben Guerdane, which only briefly abated before the 2011 revolution dramatically changed Tunisia's political landscape. As security forces and customs had left their positions, 2011 became a boom year for Tunisia's smugglers, who moved huge amounts of goods, licit and illicit, in a relatively short time, creating enormous opportunities for accumulation. As security forces returned and the Tunisian state began to reconstitute itself, the role of smuggling in Tunisia moved again to the forefront of political discussions, alongside local negotiations between smugglers and state representatives, repeated protests, and strikes. At the same time, the civil war in Libya and increasing pressure for new border fortifications have provided new challenges for smuggling networks, especially in the late 2010s and early 2020s. This renegotiation of the role of smuggling in the context of post-2011 Tunisia and its interaction with the development of the postrevolutionary state provide an ideal context to observe the interaction of smuggling and state-building in action.

Oriental, Morocco

The Oriental, one of the twelve regions of the modern Moroccan state, lies in its northeastern periphery, bordering the Mediterranean and the Spanish enclave Melilla in the North and Algeria in the South and East. Its two main cities are Oujda, near the Algerian border, and Nador, bordering Melilla. Like Medenine, the Oriental shares in the wider themes of the history of borderlands in the region: the disruption of economic networks through border-making, resistance, postindependence economic marginalization, and the emergence of large smuggling economies.

While largely regarded as a provincial city today, Oujda was an important commercial center throughout much of Morocco's precolonial history, owing to its strategic place on the intersection of important trade routes between Fes, Tlemcen, Sidjilmassa, and the Mediterranean.[154] The Lalla Maghnia Treaty of 1845 formally established a border between Morocco and the then French territory of Algeria but originally had little practical relevance for the local population, as trade continued and Algerian traders, settlers, and refugees continued to play a large role in Oujda's social fabric.[155] State penetration of the area remained limited for most of Morocco's precolonial history, and, similar to southern Tunisia, interactions with the central state were largely structured through a system of limited and indirect rule through tribal structures.[156] This changed when the protectorate period split the region between the North, administered by Spain, and the South, administered by France. In both regions, colonial construction of economic infrastructure was limited and primarily geared toward extraction of natural resources, mainly iron, sedentarization of tribes, and control of regional trade routes.[157] With the establishment of local borders running across traditional trade routes, a flourishing contraband trade began to develop, both between the two protectorates and outside of them.[158]

As in Tunisia, the end of French colonialism in Morocco was comparatively swift, but it set the scene for new conflicts rooted in disagreements over the legitimacy of the colonial borders. As a trading center on the border, these conflicts shaped the destiny of Oujda in particular, leaving it in a "quasi-permanent state of exception."[159] The "War of the Sands," a conflict between Morocco and Algeria over their respective borders, caused the border to be temporarily closed in 1963, while the two countries' disagreement over the status of the Western Sahara saw the border closed between

1975 and 1988. After Morocco accused Algeria of complicity in the Marrakesh bombing of 1994 and reinstated visa requirements for Algerians, Algeria promptly closed its land borders with Morocco. Officially, they remain closed today, with smaller disagreements about their location still occasionally returning.[160]

The evolution of Morocco's national postindependence political settlement was shaped by conflicts between the monarchy and nationalist movements, particularly of the Istiqlal Party, with the palace increasingly solidifying its position at the center of the country's centralized political structures.[161] Alongside the repression of oppositional groups, the strategic co-optation of political elites has frequently been described as a modus operandi of Morocco's regime.[162] Consequently, the broad structures of the political settlement developed clientelistically, including informal opportunities for accumulation for political groups and business elites close to the palace alongside kinship ties and more formal distributive institutions.[163]

As in the Tunisian case, Morocco's postindependence political settlement included an uneven geographic distribution of formal rent streams, focusing on the coastal commercial centers, cementing preexisting segmentations between rural and urban, coastal and interior, and economic centers and the "Maroc inutile."[164] Economically, the second half of the twentieth century in the Oriental saw the complete absence of any development strategy to overcome the region's social and spatial marginalization.[165] In another similarity to Tunisia, this marginalization is commonly portrayed in northern Morocco as a "punishment" for their resistance against the postindependence strongman. After personally heading his father's campaign to put down uprisings in the Rif Mountains in 1959, King Hassan II's dislike for the country's northern regions was well-known—remarks referring to its people as savages and thieves are still commonly cited in the region today. Still, as in Tunisia, the economic interests of the dominant postindependence elites, the centralization of the Moroccan state apparatus, and the legacy of colonial extraction and economic neglect likely played as large a role in the economic marginalization of the Northeast as any particular personal dislike.

As in Medenine, the Oriental's economic survival drew on its international connections. Emigration—first legal, then irregular—became a preferred strategy that was the state tacitly encouraged. By the 1990s an estimated two million Moroccans had emigrated illegally to Europe, with the Oriental consistently making up a large proportion of emigrants.[166]

At the same time, smuggling networks began to expand. As mapped out in the previous section, northern Morocco primarily functions as an importer within regional informal trade structures, driven largely by subsidies in Algeria and tariff avoidance on the border with the Spanish enclave of Melilla. From Algeria, gasoline smuggling in particular began to be a hallmark of the region's economy, alongside a wide range of consumer goods that were cheaper in Algeria, such as textiles, processed foods, electrical appliances, pharmaceuticals, car parts, and beauty products.[167] Moroccan goods smuggled in the other direction included fresh fruits and vegetables, dried fruit, fish, some appliances, and, most important, cannabis. Morocco remains the largest producer of cannabis in the world, most of which is grown in the Rif Mountains and smuggled both directly to Europe and eastward toward Algeria.[168]

Alongside Algeria, informal cross-border trade between the Oriental and the Spanish enclave of Melilla expanded significantly. While the port of Melilla had mainly been used for the export of iron during the protectorate period, the city later reinvented itself as a free port, bringing in goods from the European Union and East Asia at extremely low tariffs.[169] Many of those goods were then smuggled wholesale into Morocco.[170] Mohamed Berriane and Andreas Kagermeier estimate that by the 1980s, this trade already involved one-fifth of households in Nador, the city bordering Melilla.[171] Economists in Melilla estimated that by the early 2000s about half of the goods that entered the city were then smuggled into Morocco, mainly through the official border crossings via extensive networks of carriers, the so-called portadores.[172] Common goods traded on this route are textiles, beauty products, processed foods by European brands, and alcohol.

Like southern Tunisia, the Oriental region in Morocco suggests itself as a fitting case study not only by sharing many of the common structural features of borderlands in the region, but also as a result of a range of changes and transformations in recent years, which beg new questions and observations.

The ascendancy of King Mohamed VI in 1999 set off a process of adjustment within the economic and political strategies of the Moroccan state. His father had not set foot there for decades, but the young king made a triumphant return to the Oriental. In a historic speech in Oujda, he set up a development fund to signify the end of the region's economic marginalization. This process accelerated once again in 2011, aiming to contain the kind of uprisings that had swept away the Ben Ali regime in Tunisia. At the same time, recent years have seen an increasing securitization of the Algerian border by the Algerian government, directly threatening informal trade networks and leading some networks to collapse and others to restructure. In an effort to soften the resulting economic crisis in its borderlands, the Moroccan state intensified its economic engagement in the border region, reaching out to communities it had had very little relationship with in the past.

Taken together, these events present another series of shocks to the routinized informal trade system in northern Morocco, mimicking in some aspects the shocks in southern Tunisia and diverging from them in others. They precipitated a renegotiation of the relationship between informal traders and the state, and a shift in the institutional environment and the political settlement more widely, while maintaining the Moroccan central state as a significantly more dominant actor than the postrevolutionary Tunisian state. This makes the Oriental a particularly fitting counterpart to southern Tunisia for an analysis of the relationship between informal trade and state-building.

Chapter Three

REGULATING SMUGGLING AT THE BORDER

The informal economy here is like geography, it is a sedimentation, layer after layer, and it created its law, and its reality.

—MEMBER OF PARLIAMENT, OUJDA, 2017

"Our border problem," a United States Institute of Peace (USIP) report quotes an Algerian border official as saying, "can be summarized quite simply as a problem of tomatoes and terrorists. Terrorist groups can use the same techniques and routes as smugglers of tomatoes do."[1] The quote reflects a common narrative in contemporary writing on smuggling: the invocation of a general, unregulated porosity, of "ungoverned spaces" in global borderlands through which small-scale, informal traders of food or textiles move alongside drug smugglers, terrorists, and other "global outlaws."[2] "A culture of low-level corruption engendered by generations of smugglers makes it easy for terrorist groups to move people and supplies throughout the region," the same report concludes.[3] All this is imagined as "under the radar" of the state, a radar that is presented as weakened by low state enforcement capacity, administrative corruption, economic crisis, or conflict. As a result, policy recommendations commonly call for either an improvement in the state's "radar," as illustrated by the German and U.S.-funded installation of surveillance equipment along Tunisia's southern border, or a stringent limitation of the border's porosity, as illustrated by the dramatic increase in border fortifications in the region since the early 2000s.

This chapter begins the analysis of the regulation of smuggling in North Africa by presenting a detailed account of the institutions that have regulated smuggling at the point where goods cross the border. Consequently, it directly challenges the idea of an unregulated, general porosity in North Africa's borders. It demonstrates that smuggling in the region has typically been a highly regulated activity, structured through a variety of formal, informal, and hybrid institutions that do not always working in accordance with the law. These institutions can not only regulate porosity—for example, by only allowing the smuggling of a limited set of goods through selected nodes along the border—but also affect the quantity of goods that can pass through a certain area, the costs of smuggling, its labor intensity, and who can participate. While these forms of regulation can be found at different points and times across the region's varying borderlands, systematic differences in regulation can be highlighted between goods and different sections of the informal value-chain. Most notably, this regulation is not located under the radar of states but negotiated and maintained with the heavy involvement of the region's states.

Beyond this observation, this chapter also seeks to make a wider theoretical contribution. It employs the analysis of the regulation of smuggling in North Africa to examine some of the dominant assumptions about informal institutions and the regulation of illegal economies. As discussed in chapter 1, mainstream political economy typically conceptualizes the regulation of informal and illicit economies as the domain of informal institutions, which are commonly characterized as personalistic and lacking third-party enforcement. This chapter questions these assumptions empirically by pointing to informal institutions that operate impersonally and involve third-party enforcement. It argues for renewed attention to the roles of states in constructing and enforcing informal institutions.

The remainder of the chapter is made up of five sections. The first three provide a detailed analysis of the institutional environment that has regulated smuggling at key nodes along three different types of land borders in North Africa: an open rural border (Tunisia-Libya), an open urban border (Melilla-Morocco), and a closed rural border (Morocco-Algeria). They highlight that much of the smuggling activity in North Africa has long been subject to regulation through informal institutions, which determine the process and costs of smuggling, alongside the goods permitted at key nodes along its borderlands. Characterized by impersonal structures and third-party enforcement, these institutions provide an interesting challenge to common assessments of informal institutions. The fourth section discusses trade that occurs outside of border crossings. The final section examines how these accounts of the regulation of smuggling in North Africa can advance our understanding of informal institutions and the regulation of informal and illicit economies in political economy scholarship.

As previously mentioned, the institutions that regulate of smuggling have often been in flux—sometimes in their details, sometimes more fundamentally—and their change and renegotiation will be the focus of later chapters. The rules, procedures, and practices presented here are therefore snapshots of these institutions at moments in time. For many of them, this will be at a point where I was able to trace them in most detail, in 2017. As later chapters will note, the events covered here have led some of these networks to collapse—some, like gasoline in Morocco, as early as 2014, others more recently. For these cases, this chapter reviews their regulation before their collapse which allows a discussion of the nature of these networks and the features of the institutions that structured them. Subsequent chapters will tackle their rise and fall in recent years.

TUNISIA-LIBYA: REGULATION AT AN OPEN, RURAL BORDER

The Ras Jedir border crossing lies at the northern tip of the border between Tunisia and Libya, twenty miles from the Tunisian town of Ben Guerdane. The vast majority of informal cross-border trade operates through the Ras Jedir crossing and has done so for the past three decades. A wide variety of internationally produced consumer goods are shipped to the ports of western Libya, packed on smaller cars, and brought into Tunisia through the border crossing. At the crossing, the goods are either completely undeclared, misdeclared, or underdeclared, with the avoidance of the full legal import tariff making up a significant section of the profit margins of local traders. The trade is highly routinized and can be observed in broad daylight. Hundreds of young men from Ben Guerdane earn their livings as drivers carrying smuggled goods between western Libya and southern Tunisia. As this usually occurs alongside a payment to the customs agents at the border, media reporting on the border crossing typically connects the procedure to issue of corruption and frames Ben Guerdane as a "lawless, Wild-West-like town."[4]

Upon closer examination, however, fundamental regularities appear in the procedures at Ras Jedir. For decades, informal trade at the border crossing has been regulated through an informal agreement among local traders, customs officers, and the Tunisian and Libyan state apparatus. This agreement regulates the types of goods that may pass informally through the crossing, their quantity, the means of transport, and the cost of this trade—meaning both the practice of underreporting and the side payments made to border agents. This agreement has not stayed fixed: many of its terms have varied over recent years, based on a set of negotiations that will be discussed in later chapters. However, its claim over the regulation of these features of the trade, has, with the exception of a few months after the revolution in 2011, remained constant. A similar version of this agreement has in fact made it through all the turmoil at the heart of subsequent chapters and was still in practice in the summer of 2021.

To be precise, and for the purpose of illustration, this is the agreement as it existed in April 2017:

- Traders who were transporting goods with a value of less than 2,000 Libyan dinar (LYD) (GBP 1,097) plus 150 liters of Libyan gasoline were not required to pay anything at the border crossing—neither the official tariff nor any standardized bribe or other informal fee.[5]
- Traders who were transporting goods with a value of over 2,000 LYD (GBP 1,097) would pay 1,500 LYD (GBP 822) to an intermediary on the Libyan side, while 300 Tunisian dinar (TND) (GBP 76) would be paid to the Tunisian customs officials.[6]
- While the money on the Libyan side would be divided between multiple groups that exercised some claims over the border crossing, including the nearby Libyan municipality of Zuwara, the money on the Tunisian side would partly go toward the tariff income of the state, while some would go directly to the private income of the customs agents.
- Weapons and narcotics were excluded from the deal and not allowed to be imported through the border crossing. Medicine is only allowed to be imported informally if paperwork by a doctor can be provided. All goods that were brought in had to pass through a scanner at the border crossing to ensure that they are in accordance with this rule.[7]

The procedures and payments outlined in this agreement are—as all actors involved generally readily admit—entirely in contradiction with Tunisia's laws on customs and tariffs.[8] Formally, the trade conducted here is illegal. Tunisia's tariff system does not mirror the "minimum threshold" included in the agreement; it specifies different tariff rates for different goods, employs tariffs as percentages of the good's value, not a lump sum as in the agreement here, and naturally does not contain a split of the tariff incomes between state accounts and the personal income of customs agents.[9]

It is also worth noting that the agreement outlined here represented one of the more "deregulated" versions of this institution. Its immediate predecessor, for example, in effect from January until April 2017, had set an upper limit per car of goods with the total value of 4,000 LYD (GBP 2,187) plus 150 liters of gasoline, and a later iteration again introduced a maximum limit of 5,000 LYD (GBP 2,733).[10] While this agreement prohibited only the informal import of illicit products alongside medicine, agreements that had been in place before 2011 placed additional restrictions on the types of goods that could be brought through the crossing without paying the formal tariffs, mainly to protect goods that politically connected business elites in Tunis had an interest in protecting from competition through informal trade. This included, among others, almonds, pistachios, high-value electronics, and bananas, which famously had been a part of the enterprises of Chafiq Jerraya, a controversial businessman who was arrested on corruption charges in 2017 and had frequently been connected to smuggling networks.[11] He was sentenced to ten years in jail for forgery of contracts in 2021.

Earlier agreements, including between 2012 and 2016, had also included specific restrictions as to the type of cars that could be used for informal trade through the border crossing. As local traders pointed out, this boiled down to a prohibition against the use of large transport vehicles, as the use of smaller cars combined with the traffic jams at the border crossings that would commonly surpass four or five hours made the trade substantially more labor intensive. Negotiators for the agreement with whom I spoke highlighted that this had been negotiated in the knowledge that it would both help to employ young men from the region and make the practice less accessible for traders based in Tunis.[12] In addition, smaller cars were easier to search, facilitating the enforcement on the ban of smuggling weapons through the border crossing.

The agreement described was unwritten, but knowledge of it and its details was widespread among traders in the area. A wide variety of traders in different locations and networks were able to recite its precise details to me. However, an earlier version was even written down—against the expectation of common characterizations of informal institutions as inherently unwritten, as I will discuss in more detail shortly.[13] Between January and April 2017 a written text existed, a "Memorandum of Understanding" that had been produced by an earlier round of negotiations between local actors around the status of the border crossing.[14]

Apart from listing the goods and quantities that are allowed to be brought through the border crossing informally, and at what cost, the agreement included sections that justify its purpose, affirming "the spirit of cooperation and brotherhood between the Libyan and Tunisian peoples" and "foster[ing] cooperation through it, without proceeding to hurt the national sovereignty of both countries."[15] It also contained a list of demands toward both the Tunisian and the Libyan governments, reflecting common frustrations of the traders, such as long lines at the border crossing, the absence of a special passageway for humanitarian emergencies and families, and even increased security cooperation between the two governments.[16]

The agreement states that it was signed in the Libyan city of Zawya and includes the signatures of multiple actors on the Libyan side of the border, alongside two Tunisian signatures (figure 3.1): Ahmed Lamaari, a Tunisian member of parliament for the Medenine region and a member of the Ennahda Party, and Adel Ben Belqassem Neji, a civil society activist and informal trader from Ben Guerdane. The agreement also lists as "present" a variety of other actors, including multiple military officers from armed groups in western Libya, ranging from the "Situation Room of the Western Military Region" to the "Brigade of the Martyr Jamal Gha'eb," an armed group that was founded in 2011 and had since made repeated claims to playing a role in the operation and securitization of the border crossing.[17] It is likely that the large number of actors involved and conflicts and mistrust between some on the Libyan side necessitated a written form for the agreement, although this practice was soon disbanded and the agreement returned to being unwritten by April 2017. It is also worth noting that the member of parliament is listed in the agreement merely as the "President of the Tunisian Delegation," not as a member of parliament or of a party that was, at that point, in government.

Even the most formalized version of this agreement remained at its essence in clear contradiction to both Tunisian law and state practice, as

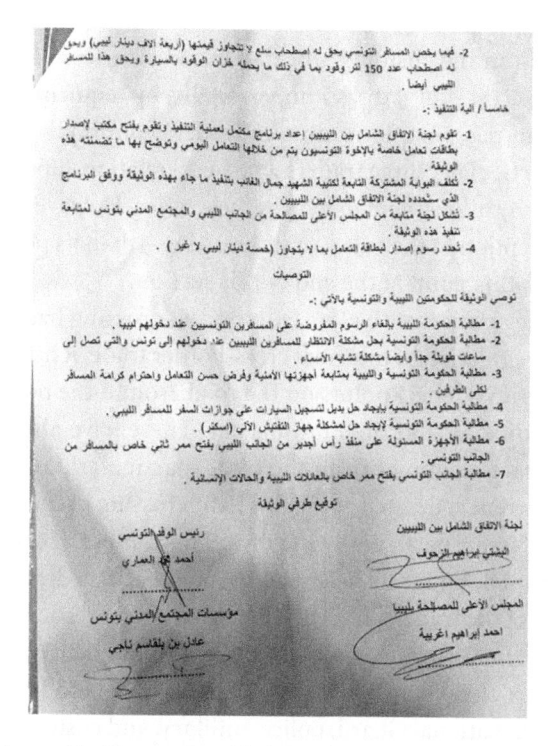

FIGURE 3.1 Final page of the Memorandum of Understanding, with signatures. Photo by author.

it circumvented not just tariffs but also the usual process on who could negotiate agreements with foreign actors. In my interviews with them, the negotiators of the Memorandum of Understanding emphasized that this is "not an official accord," that it is "not legal," and that while both the prime minister and the minister of interior had explicitly allowed their negotiation of the agreement, it has not been signed formally by a member of government.[18] The agreement hence remained informal, yet it is worth noting that its negotiation, enforcement, and maintenance involved a wide variety of state actors, including regional governors, a member of parliament, and police and customs officers, some but not all of whom stand to financially benefit from the agreement.

It is worth noting that while the agreement was informal, it was also impersonal. While large parts of the political economy literature on informal institutions assume that they are personalized and small-scale, being able to trade under this agreement did not depend on particular contacts, having a cousin in the customs office, or even being from Ben Guerdane. It did restrict access, but it did so impersonally, by requiring all traders to have a Tunisian passport, for example. Traders commonly told stories of some of the particularly large traders who build relationships with customs officials that may allow them to bypass these rules. However, this suggests more of an exception to the rule—or its breaking—than its personalization. I will return to this point at the end of this section.

While the regulation at the Ras Jedir border crossing had been the primary form of regulation of informal cross-border trade, it has usually coexisted with a series of checkpoints on the road around the border crossing, on both the Tunisian and the Libyan sides. These have allowed different groups to extract resources from the trade, particularly if they were not included in the rent generated at the Ras Jedir crossing itself, which became a controversial issue, particularly in Libya. The number of checkpoints has waxed and waned, but at its heights presents a serious drain on the time and resources of the traders. In February 2017 a trader recounted to me that in order to informally bring couscous to Libya and return with carpets, he would pass four checkpoints between Ben Guerdane and Ras Jedir, set up by the Tunisian National Guard, police, military, and customs officers, and another five checkpoints between Ras Jedir and Zelten in Libya, set up by a variety of local authorities and armed groups.[19]

Both the creation of checkpoints and the level of bribes demanded are usually less predictable for traders than the institutionalized agreements at the border crossing. Bribes range from nothing to their whole profit margins. Stories of violent abuse at checkpoints, especially in Libya, are available in abundance among traders and have been a significant source of conflict in recent years. In this context, traders also presented the different agreements for the procedure at Ras Jedir as a simpler, more predictable, and more desirable form of organization. Especially after 2011, both the agreement at Ras Jedir and the existence of checkpoints not only represented coordination between traders and elements of the Tunisian state around the regulation of informal trade but also became a space of negotiation around rent extraction from the border crossing between different groups vying for influence in Western Libya. This will be discussed at more length in the second half of this book.

MELILLA-MOROCCO: REGULATION AT AN OPEN, URBAN BORDER

Although commonly portrayed and imagined as such, smuggling in North Africa is not limited to the rural periphery. In the institutionalization and regulation of informal cross-border trade, the procedures around the small Spanish enclave of Melilla have long rivaled those of the Ras Jedir crossing. Covering less than 5 square miles of territory, Melilla borders the Mediterranean in the North and Morocco in the South. Largely due to concerns about migration, its 6.8-mile border has been heavily securitized in recent years, including two parallel fences topped with barbed wire, watch posts, and a buffer zone. As others have noted, Melilla's border fortifications are characteristic of a recent fortification trend that seeks to be porous to the free movement of goods but demonstrate a capacity to regulate the movement of people.[20] What is particularly noteworthy about the case of Melilla is that this significant expansion of its border infrastructure has for many years left it porous not just for the legal trade of goods, but also for a large wholesale smuggling trade. Based on an estimation published in 2014, at least half of the goods that arrived in the port of Melilla were brought into Morocco illegally, with the trade being driven (and made illegal) through its bypassing of any official trade or tariff regulations on the Moroccan side.[21] The most common goods traded this way have been textiles and foodstuffs, alongside a variety of European consumer goods. Many of the dynamics described here were mirrored in Ceuta, the second largest Spanish enclave in northern Morocco, before new interventions in 2020 began to increasingly disrupt this trade.

On both sides of the border, there are significant economic interests in maintaining illegal trade—wholesale merchants on the Spanish side and informal trade and distribution networks on the Moroccan side are both significant drivers of the local economy. In another parallel to the Tunisia-Libya border, informal trade out of Melilla has for decades occurred primarily through the city's official border crossings. I focus here on the two most prominent crossings, at Beni Ensar and Barrio Chino. Bustling with traders and transporters carrying goods through the narrow border crossings in defiance of any customs regulation, the crossings have been described as "a space of lawlessness."[22] As in the case of Tunisia's Ras Jedir crossing, however, upon closer observation and following conversations with local smugglers, clear rules and regulations emerge.

Let's begin by taking a stroll through the Beni Ensar crossing on a cloudy day in 2017. Named after the Moroccan suburb that borders it, the crossing has three main lanes going into Morocco: one for cars, one for normal walking traffic, and one reserved for informal cross-border trade on foot. Especially since the construction at the Farrakanh crossing, it had for many years been the main avenue for car-based informal cross-border trade between Melilla and Morocco. Late at night, Moroccan drivers can be seen lining up in a long queue of cars in the Moroccan town of Beni Ensar, to be let into Melilla early in the morning and drive to one of the countless warehouses just on the other side of the border. They fill their cars with clothes, tires, foodstuffs, or other imported products, before making their way slowly back to Morocco, where the goods are sold on markets in Nador or transported across the country. Most of the cars are ancient—waiting in line at the border crossing most of the day does not require much horsepower.

The lines of cars on both sides of the borders have been regulated so as not to interfere with local traffic. As the cars pass back into Morocco, their imports are let through unregistered and untaxed in exchange for a bribe to the Moroccan customs officers. While the bribes are relatively standardized, they are dependent on the value of the goods and typically range between 50 and 200 Moroccan dirham (MAD). Importantly, the cars are inspected by Moroccan customs officers. This allows not only some estimation of the value of the goods (and hence the level of the bribe) but also the enforcement of some restrictions on goods that are not allowed to be traded this way—for example, alcohol, medicine, or drugs.[23] While there is no official restriction on how many cars can engage in this trade. They are limited through standardized and strictly enforced times during which the trade is allowed to occur—usually between 6 a.m. and 1 p.m. Moroccan time, after which the trade shuts down and the traders offload their goods and get in line for the next day.

Car-based trading is only one of the two streams of informal cross-border trade through the Beni Ensar border crossing—trading on foot is even more common. At six in the morning, screams and chatter fill Beni Ensar, as traders push against the small gate until it is opened and they are let into Melilla to buy their products. Although the group of waiting traders has been separated by gender (women are let through first), the scramble still presents a serious health hazard for the traders. Spanish riot police who were manning the checkpoint have shown me videos on their phones of traders stepping on other traders who had tripped and fallen. Once they have bought their goods, traders make their way back to Morocco through the border crossing. Two lanes are open for foot traffic. One is open for tourists, visitors, and other travelers without a car. It can also be used by small-time traders with only a few goods, usually one bag that can be carried in one hand. For all the other traders, there is a special lane. A member of the Spanish *guarda civil* directs people into the correct lane. The specialized lane for traders usually is significantly busier, and around half a dozen members of the Spanish police are typically involved in getting traders to line up at a large open space near the border crossing and then walk through the narrow, fenced-off path, through an iron turnstile, and then past the Moroccan customs officers and into Morocco.

The Spanish police, mainly riot police brought in from mainland Spain on two-week rotations, have for years played a crucial role in organizing the procession of traders. They have come to understand their role as ensuring that the onslaught of traders trying to get through the small turnstile doesn't result in injuries and at times mediating when conflicts break out.[24] However, they have not been directly involved in the central transaction of the trade: the payments made to avoid the application of Morocco's customs law are given to Moroccan customs officers, on the Moroccan side of the border. These payments can be differentiated into three categories. The first group are independent traders with very small amounts of goods, often older women from the Oriental region who are selling their products to local stores. While they used to pay small bribes to Moroccan customs officials in order to pass, custom officials stopped systematically demanding bribes from them in 2010 and 2011 and have not done so since. There are still occasions in which bribes are demanded or goods are confiscated, but traders reported that the systematic taking of bribes from very small-scale traders seems to have stopped, simultaneous with a similar development along the border between Morocco and Algeria that I will also discuss.

The second group are traders who also work independently but are carrying larger amounts of goods. They typically pay a bribe to the Moroccan customs officers, which, similar to the car traders, is roughly proportional to the quantity and value of their goods and usually ranges between 50 and 100 MAD.

The third group are traders who work for a wholesaler. While many of the traders working in Beni Ensar work independently, there are also a significant number who are employed by a wholesaler, picking up their goods either at nearby warehouses or directly near the border crossing. Alongside their goods, they are usually supplied with a ticket, which carries their name, the name of their boss, and the goods they are transporting. As they pass the Moroccan customs officers, they use the ticket to identify themselves as employees of a particular wholesaler. They hence do not have to pay a bribe, as the bribe to the customs officers would be part of a larger, regular arrangement between the wholesaler and the officials. The traders then deliver their goods to a transporter working for the same boss on the other side of the border, with their ticket again identifying them as employees of a certain wholesaler and specifying the goods that they have to deliver, as well as the payment they are entitled to receiving.[25]

As in the case of Tunisia, as well as the car-based trade through Beni Ensar, these procedures have not been open to all types of goods. Medicine and alcohol, for example, even little sanitary wipes that contain alcohol, have not been traded through these mechanisms.[26]

Interestingly, after Morocco imposed restrictions on the use of plastic bags in convenience stores for environmental reasons, traders reported that these bags could also no longer be brought through the border crossing,

FIGURE 3.2 Cars waiting at the Moroccan side of the Beni Ensar crossing. Photo by author.

FIGURE 3.3 Traders lining up at the Spanish side of the Beni Ensar crossing. Photo by author.

demonstrating the existence of a dynamic and purposeful selection of goods that can be traded this way.[27] Some features of these procedures have also limited the quantity coming through—as with the car-based trade, there have been strict temporal restrictions on informal cross-border trade by foot, typically between 6 a.m. and 1 p.m. Moroccan time.

Beni Ensar is not the only crossing where such regulation could be observed. Let's go on another walk then, in 2017 once more, to the Barrio Chino crossing. As the crossing does not cater to other travelers and is used almost exclusively for smuggling, we cannot walk through but have to approach it first from Melilla and then from Morocco, trying to linger and observe until we arouse the suspicion of the security forces on either side.

Located in the southwestern part of the city, this crossing has been used almost exclusively by large-scale, informal cross-border traders and their transporters. The routinization of the process observed here is even more striking than in Beni Ensar, especially as recent years had seen the construction of additional infrastructure on the Spanish side to organize the trade. Barrio Chino has three lanes that lead into Morocco, all of them for foot traffic. In 2017 nothing signified their purpose for informal cross-border trade more clearly than the three signs over the entrances to the border crossing. On top of the Spanish and Arabic words for "Entrance," there are two silhouettes depicting *portadores*: one man and one woman, carrying a large bundle of goods (figure 3.4).

FIGURE 3.4 Border crossing at Barrio Chino. Photo courtesy of Cope Melilla.

If we walked to the crossing early, between 7 a.m. and 11 a.m. Moroccan time, we would find three lanes incredibly busy.[28] At this point, Barrio Chino is the epicenter of the large-scale wholesale, informal trade operations between Melilla and Morocco. Transporters, so-called portadores or hamala, wait in lines under sheet-metal shelters on a large space near the crossing. Trucks can be observed as they bring goods from the nearby warehouses, prepacked in bundles wrapped in plastic sheets and marked with numbers and symbols that indicate they are the property of a particular owner. Organized by the Spanish police, transporters then pick up the bundles and carry, push, and roll them up the small passageway to the border crossing.

Here, three metal turnstiles present the key bottleneck of the border: the police let traders approach them in small groups, and local intermediaries, employed by the larger traders, stand at the turnstiles to facilitate a smooth flow of carriers through them.[29] Similar to the Beni Ensar crossing, there

REGULATING SMUGGLING AT THE BORDER

are payments to the Moroccan customs officials, but they depend on the type of transporter. The large group of traders who work for one of the bigger wholesalers do not pay a bribe, as this is organized centrally by the wholesaler. While there are at this point essentially no independent small-scale traders in Barrio Chino, groups of transporters organize transport for smaller wholesalers, usually exploiting personal relationships with customs officials in order to negotiate low bribes.

On the Moroccan side, traders are quickly ushered to larger vans, in which the numbered bundles are stacked and then transported across Morocco. Contrary to Beni Ensar, there seems to be a lot less scrutiny of the content of the bundles at the moment they cross the border. This most likely relates to the absence of small, independent traders—the traders operating here, as well as their goods, are well known to Moroccan customs and security services. Still, it appears that some goods that cannot be brought through Beni Ensar, such as alcohol, are being traded in Barrio Chino.

Even though the border between Melilla and Morocco is located in an urban setting and contains a significantly higher level of infrastructure and surveillance capacity on both sides of the border than the border

FIGURE 3.5 Shelter for traders, police surveillance tower, and border fence at the Barrio Chino crossing. Photo by author.

FIGURE 3.6 Marked truck at the Barrio Chino crossing. Photo by author.

between Tunisia and Libya, the way in which smuggling has long been regulated at both borders shares important similarities. As in Tunisia, the procedures observed at the border between Morocco and Melilla were entirely illegal and yet highly routinized and organized, regulated primarily by state officials. While no written version of these procedures existed in the Melilla case, they were widely known to everyone involved and included some form of written documentation, such as the tickets at the Beni Ensar crossing.

As in the Tunisian case, these institutions regulated the types of goods that can cross the border informally and, through the combination of the temporal restrictions and the pace and size of the turnstiles, created a strict limitation on the number of goods that could pass through. As in Tunisia, large elements of this regulation were impersonal: anyone with a Nador residency card (which allows free movement to Melilla without a passport) could work as a transporter, and no particular connections to customs officers were required. Even for people not from Nador, a residency card is easily acquired—transporters from outside the area told me they were able to purchase residency cards for villages near Nador for around 2,500 MAD.[30] Still, personal connections, as well as capital, have guaranteed larger traders advantageous positions within this system—a theme that later chapters will return to.

MOROCCO-ALGERIA: REGULATION AT A CLOSED, RURAL BORDER

As the previous sections have outlined, formal border crossings have long played a crucial role in the organization and regulation of smuggling at the Tunisia-Libya and Melilla-Morocco borders. They provide crucial nodes at which the trade can be easily coordinated and surveyed, and where payments can be extracted. The border between Morocco and Algeria provides an interesting case study to examine the regulation of smuggling in the absence of formal border crossings, as the land border between the two countries has been formally closed since 1994.[31] As this section highlights, the regulation of smuggling at this border still exhibited significant similarities with the procedures at the border crossings of Melilla or Ras Jedir, as smugglers and security forces quickly established informal crossing points along the border. While regulation along these points was not always uniform, they provided points of coordination and predictability.

The trade in gasoline, which for many years dominated the informal cross-border trade before collapsing in the face of new border infrastructure, is instructive here. Algerian gasoline, cheaper than Moroccan gasoline due to the Algerian subsidy regime, would be collected at Algerian gas stations by filling up tanks and then refilled into jerry-cans in large storage facilities on rural farms near the border. They would then be brought by Algerian traders to prearranged meeting points along the border. As former traders have recounted, there would usually be a set of about ten potential meeting points, with the one that would be used by the Moroccan and Algerian networks prearranged on a day-to-day basis.[32] At these points, the gasoline would be sold wholesale to Moroccan "first buyers," who would transfer it to depots in rural Morocco, where it would typically be resold to "second buyers," who would transport it across the country. These exchanges were exclusively conducted at night. However, Moroccan and Algerian traders would not be the only ones in attendance at these meetings: soldiers from both countries were involved in the organization of these exchanges, with the Algerian soldiers usually playing the dominant role. The soldiers would not only observe the procedure but also act as mediators in the case of conflict between the traders, or as enforcers of a quiet and orderly exchange if anyone was making too much noise. Both Moroccan and Algerian soldiers would receive a payment from the traders—commonly the Algerian traders would pay the Algerian soldiers, and the Moroccan traders would pay the Moroccan soldiers. The level of these payments would typically be fixed; for example, Moroccan soldiers would receive 5 MAD (GBP 0.4) for every 30-liter canister that a trader was buying that night. The rates for the Algerian soldiers would occasionally change when a new captain was assigned to the local force.[33]

Further crucial fix-points within the trade were "gates" in the border fence on the Moroccan side that the Moroccan military would operate in order to organize and regulate informal trade. A variety of these points existed around the border near Oujda, along with specific times during which they were open. One gate was opened every night between 7 p.m. and 2 a.m., another one between 8 p.m. and midnight.[34] During this time, Moroccan soldiers would let traders pass across the border, as well as back into Morocco. These crossings did not appear to be operated in coordination with the Algerian soldiers and continued to function even when Algeria started to crack down on the trade and increase its own border security. Traders reported that Moroccan soldiers would screen and inspect traded goods as traders entered back into the country—at least in the case of new traders.[35] It appears that illicit goods were not traded through these gates; dominant goods here were gasoline, cigarettes, fabrics, and household items. Prior to 2010–2011, soldiers would collect bribes from traders of all goods. In 2010–2011, in parallel with similar changes at the Melilla border crossings, this procedure appears to have changed: small scale-traders, especially of gasoline, were not asked to pay bribes anymore by the Moroccan soldiers and could pass through the gates for free. Bribes for larger quantities and higher profit margins remained. While some traders report that this change came after demonstrations by traders against the high costs of bribes, others say they did not know what prompted the change. Similar to the traders between Nador and Melilla, however, they all agree that this change implied an effort by the Moroccan government to decrease the burden on poorer informal cross-border traders. In the words of one former gasoline trader:

> This was to make it easier for people. The order came from the very top, from the King. . . . Oujda is not a touristic city, we don't have any other projects, we have nothing else, so people would starve. So, if the government stopped this, trust me, there would have been the biggest demonstration in the world. This came all the way from the top, from the king, to not take bribes, and to

let them pass easily. But if someone brought cigarettes, for example, he'd make a lot of money, so he would have to bribe a little bit. If there were four soldiers, for example, he would have to give them each 200 [MAD].[36]

Another gate that requires special mention is that near Beni Drar, a town approximately fifteen miles north of Oujda and one of the key distribution centers for informally traded goods, and particularly gasoline, in the region. The informal border crossing near Beni Drar appears to be the only one in the region that operated both during the day and at night. Additionally, while many other border crossings saw people brining goods through by hand or on the back of donkeys, there are many reports of entire trucks, or even entire buses, passing through the gate and directly on to Beni Drar, where they were unloaded and distributed among local vendors.[37]

While these informally arranged points along the border were not formal points of entry like the border crossings at Ras Jedir or Melilla, they share important features for the regulation of smuggling. They facilitated the structure and regulation of the trade and made it easier to monitor through the security services. They were connected to institutions that restricted the types of goods that could pass through these channels and made the process of paying to security services standardized, predictable, and affordable even for small-scale traders. The existence of these regulatory structures at the Morocco-Algeria border during the heyday of the gasoline trade suggests that the regulatory structures found at the official points of entry on the other two borders were also not merely a side-effect of the existence of official points of entry but were wider features of the politics and regulation of smuggling.

OUTSIDE THE NODES:
EVASION, VIOLENCE, AND BORDER GAMES

While the previous sections have highlighted key institutions regulating three borders in North Africa, it would be misleading to suggest that these institutions control all smuggling activities across these borders. To quote a Moroccan official in a local development agency: "The doors, they were made for control. But there were other things going on."[38] While the institutions described here have regulated the smuggling of the majority of goods, they do not account for most illicit goods, which, as discussed earlier, cannot be traded through these institutionalized procedures. This applies in particular to drugs—cannabis, cocaine, and synthetic psychotropics—for which there are large smuggling routes running through North Africa, but also to arms or ammunition. In addition, some well-connected traders may seek to trade licit goods outside of the impersonal systems described if they believe they can generate opportunities to trade on better terms by doing so. On the Tunisia-Libya border, these goods are typically transported on 4x4s across the border south of the Ras Jedir crossing, through rugged terrain that requires experienced drivers, locally dubbed the "contra route." Similarly, on the border between Algeria and Morocco, smugglers try their luck outside the informally arranged border crossings, many of them moving cannabis-based products grown in Morocco.

As the focus of this book is on licit goods, the vast majority of which are exclusively regulated through the institutions listed, they are also the focus of this chapter. However, by providing one regulatory environment for one set of goods, these institutions still affect the opportunities, geographies, and risk profiles for trade outside of their jurisdiction, while not directly regulating them. For example, by offering structures that incentivize traders in particular goods and quantities—small amounts of licit goods, for example—to trade through points of entry, they shape the expectations that soldiers outside of points of entry have of the traders they encounter there. Microwaves, carpets, or children's clothes would not usually be traded illegally outside of the more normalized nodes, which would offer a vastly superior cost-risk trade-off, especially for small-scale smugglers. Nodes and spaces outside of nodes also together form part of a wider regulatory geography of smuggling across these borders. The availability of nodes of regulation has shaped routes, and the choices of smugglers to trade outside of border crossings have waxed and waned with the changes in the conditions for smugglers at the crossings themselves. As later chapters will highlight, these geographies structured the options of smugglers when their trade was thrown into crisis.

At this point, however, some observations can be made that give good reason to question whether even the trade outside of these more institutionalized channels is conducted in a fashion that is entirely unregulated, or under the radar of the state. Two dimensions of this are worth highlighting here. First, traders, security forces, and politicians across the two large border case studies (Tunisia-Libya and Morocco-Algeria) report the existence of "security arrangements" in which smugglers, even as they are trying to evade security forces as they are crossing the border, will still report suspicious activities along the border and the presence of unknown individuals back to the security forces.[39] While some of these agreements seem to have developed out of clientelist relationships with security forces, others appear to have grown historically out of similar agreements with pastoral communities in the borderlands.[40] Farmers watching livestock out in the borderlands had maintained arrangements with security forces, informing them of unknown individuals operating on the border. It is worth noting that there is an incentive for smugglers to engage in these activities: increased perception by security forces that the part of the border that they operate in is unmonitored and used by dangerous individuals might lead to higher security force presence there, increasing the cost of smuggling.

Second, even though there did not seem to be clearly institutionalized rules on smuggling across the contra routes, there do appear to be at times certain regularities and predictabilities in the interactions between smugglers and security forces in these areas. These perhaps more resemble "border games" or "cat-and-mouse' games," which through their own rules institute a certain regularity and an observable and predictable outcome.[41]

An example may serve to illustrate. In March 2017 I was sitting in a roadside café in southern Tunisia—the only café in a small village near the border, south of Ben Guerdane. I was talking to the only other customers: a friend of mine who was working nearby and a local smuggling boss who had around ten young men working for him. On most nights, they drove across the desert to Libya and returned with a variety of goods, some licit, such as tea and cigarettes, and some illicit. Recently, with the closures at Ras Jedir, more people had started working in this territory. The installation of a ditch and surveillance equipment to improve border security in recent years had not yet done much yet to change this trade: drivers either put boards over the ditch and drove across it or simply threw the goods across. Most of the traders did not own their own cars—they leased expensive and fast SUVs, for one principal purpose: to outrun the local customs agents. "Our cars are much faster than theirs," the man bragged. It was easy for us to verify this from the little café: while many of the smugglers' cars were parked next to the café, the customs agents' cars were parked next to their small headquarters on the other side of the street. While smugglers and customs agents played cat and mouse at night, they were sitting right across the street from each other during the day. They know each other. "It's like a game." If they get caught, they negotiate a bribe. They don't resent the customs officers for their role in this; it's "normal," he told me.[42] If they made it through uncaught, they were home free. Once they were home, as the sun rose, their goods were no longer up for scrutiny. The likelihood and price of getting caught were part of the smugglers' calculations. Their expected income was subject to a game that is well established, repeatedly played, and understood by every player. When one of the customs agents refused to take bribes, the smuggler recounted, they knew his superior and could easily arrange for him to be transferred somewhere else. And the game continued.

As this example suggests, the absence of regulation through rules does not imply that even illicit smuggling is entirely unregulated, or that it is regulated in the absence of the state, or entirely through personal relationships. Even arrests of smugglers, in this context, do not necessarily need to be proof of an attempt by state security forces to eliminate smuggling. I was speaking to a human trafficker in Morocco about the time he was arrested, which led to him spending a significant amount of time in jail. Still, he didn't perceive his arrest as part of any kind of police strategy to stop human trafficking, which he felt they "tolerated." Once in a while, however, they would have to arrest someone to show that they were doing their job, he explained, and that time it hit him.[43]

One final caveat is in order here. When highlighting that, even outside the more institutionalized "nodes," smuggling is not necessarily without predictable structures, it is still worth noting that these activities have also not been without violence. Its most extreme expression has come with the deaths of young traders, usually from the borderlands, who have died crossing the border, shot by security services or as the result of car crashes after nightly chases through difficult and dangerous terrain. Along the Morocco-Algeria border, traders have reported that this phenomenon has decreased since the 1980s, especially under the regime of Bouteflika (1999–2019), but did not entirely stop.[44] The past few years have also seen multiple deaths along the Tunisia-Libya frontier. Deaths have also not been limited to the rural borderlands—as discussed earlier, the vast numbers of traders seeking to move through the small spaces of the Melilla border crossings have caused altercations, stampedes, and injuries and have resulted in multiple deaths in recent years. Much of this violence, like the cat-and-mouse game described, appears both unpredictable and random on a microlevel and broadly expected on a macrolevel. But it remains real, deadly, and a source of grief and trauma in the borderlands. The next chapter will return to this point.

INFORMAL INSTITUTIONS AND THE REGULATION OF SMUGGLING IN NORTH AFRICA

This chapter began by describing a common notion of a general "porosity" along North Africa's borders, where smugglers of licit goods, smugglers of drugs and arms, or terrorists all slipped through the same spaces, under the radar of the state. As the chapter has demonstrated, this is not an accurate description of how most smuggling activity has typically looked in the region. Instead, what has emerged from this mapping is that smuggling in North Africa is a densely regulated activity. Informal institutions at border crossings, meeting points along the border, police checkpoints, and markets serve to structure, normalize, and control the trade. They are able to affect the number of goods that come into the country illegally through physical bottlenecks like turnstiles, regulations on the size of the vessels in which goods may be transported, and time limits on when goods can be traded. Most smugglers observed trading through Ras Jedir and Melilla were not spending their days evading their police—they were spending their days standing in line.

Crucially, the regulatory structures described here can and do differentiate between types of goods. Across the three diverse borderlands studied here, different regulatory nodes covered different goods. A pattern emerges that separates most licit goods from illicit goods: contrary to the quote that opened the chapter, the path that contraband tomatoes—or textiles or TV sets—would take across the region's borders is not available to terrorists aiming to smuggle weapons, or to networks smuggling narcotics. Returning foreign fighters or those on travel blacklists would have serious difficulties passing through these nodes and even face difficulties outside of them. This is not to say that the smuggling of illicit goods does not occur in the region—it certainly does. But its origins do not lie in a general, unregulated porosity of the region's borderlands, which smugglers of gasoline and guns alike can use. Instead, the porosity of North Africa's borders, even where illegal trade occurs, is regulated and, in its regulation, segmented.

As this chapter has highlighted, the regulation of smuggling at these nodes is not just structured through petty corruption, but through institutions, the systematization of which—organizing an interaction based on commonly understood and coordinated rules of the game—differentiates them from individualized instances of corruption. Despite their normalization and visibility, the institutions regulating illegal cross-border trade must be classified as informal, as they remain in direct contradiction to the formal law, communicated through the "officially sanctioned channels."[45] And while state actors play a crucial role in their maintenance, they do not do so in an official capacity, differentiating them from the hybrid institutions that will feature more prominently in the following chapter.[46] And yet these institutions reveal some features that are in contrast with common characterizations of informal institutions in modern mainstream institutional scholarship, as described in chapter 1. Two points in particular stand out, both allowing us to zoom out from the borderlands of North Africa to wider questions about the features of institutions and their role in development and state-building.

First, the regulatory structures described in this chapter provide an example of informal institutions that are capable of providing impersonal regulation. One of the traditional theoretical distinctions between formal and informal institutions in mainstream political economy rests on the assumption that informal institutions are inherently personalistic. "By definition," Khan writes, "while most or all formal institutions are impersonal, informal institutions are never impersonal."[47] The classic characterizations of informal institutions as small-scale, inefficient, and unwritten ultimately follow from this primary assumption. If informal institutions cannot be impersonal, it is easy to see why they are so frequently framed as incompatible with and antithetical to the development of states, of "good governance," or of functioning markets, all of which we typically associate with impersonality. The analysis presented here, however, does not support this assumption. The informal regulation of smuggling at the Ras Jedir border crossing, at the Melilla border crossings, and at the gates alongside the Algerian border with Morocco are all largely impersonal. They require certain characteristics of the people involved in them, such as Tunisian passports or a residency card for Nador, but this is not untypical for impersonal institutions. They are not tied to personal identities—surely, family connections help in the smuggling business, but in the same way, they also do in the formal sector: beyond regulatory institutions, not as a feature of them.

Second, the regulation discussed provides examples that informal institutions can contain third-party enforcement. Some of the logic behind the assumption that informal institutions are incapable of operating impersonally often lies in the expectation that they lack third-party enforcement, that they are self-enforcing, and that those adhering to them are required to avoid persecution when they stand in opposition to the formal law, requiring them to operate on a basis of trust or mutually rational equilibrium behavior.[48] Once more, in the context of the institutions observed here, these expectations do not hold: police, customs agents, and soldiers, albeit unofficially and illegally, systematically act as enforcement agents for these institutions and tolerate illegal activities within the realm of these institutions. While in some cases they appear as corrupt patrons of individual smugglers, in others we observe them enforcing informal rules, either collecting no bribe at all or collecting a fixed bribe level that has been agreed as part of the institution itself. Crucially, they create interactions that are predictable and necessitate neither trust nor evasion.

The observations that informal institutions can operate impersonally and with third-party enforcement can be extended to noting that informal institutions do not necessarily need to be "stateless" in order to be informal. Even when they are in direct contradiction to the rules communicated through the officially sanctioned channels, they can still be supported and enforced, informally, by these same channels. Here, state officials involved in the maintenance of these institutions are acting systematically and in accordance with a negotiated role rather than through individualized corruption. While this will not surprise most observers of the politics of regulation, this has been critically underappreciated as a systematic starting point in modern institutionalism, and in its use as a foundational principle of modern political economy from New Institutional Economics to Political Settlement Theory. This observation extends the argument of the literature on "forbearance," which describes the purposeful nonenforcement of formal institutional regulation, to the purposeful enforcement of informal institutional regulation.[49] This chapter therefore supports the case, more well-established in anthropology and economic sociology by critical institutional scholars and legal pluralism, that assumptions about any inherent, a priori distinctions between formal and informal institutions should be questioned.⁵⁰ It suggests instead that the features of institutions are best analyzed in their political context—that rather than viewing informal institutions as inherently personalistic, political economy scholarship needs to ask what it is about these institutions that makes them personalistic in some settings and impersonal in others. This shifts the focus back to the actors involved, to their interests, and fundamentally to the function of these institutions. It thus offers the structure for a new comparative politics of informal institutions.

Applying these observations once again to the institutions in this chapter, and in particular the role of state actors in their functioning, provides a starting point for the analysis of the politics of smuggling. It directly points to central questions of future chapters: Why do states engage in such regulation, and why in a way that maintains impersonal structures (chapter 5)? How are these institutions negotiated, and how do they change (chapters 6–8)? First, however, the following chapter will complete this mapping of the regulation of smuggling by looking at the regulations that engage with the trade once smuggled goods have crossed the border.

Chapter Four

REGULATING SMUGGLING IN THE BORDERLANDS

While crossing a border is a crucial and prominent moment in the organization and regulation of smuggling, it is not the only point at which smuggling networks encounter regulation. From production to transport within a country, accompanying financial flows, storage, and sale, different forms of regulation influence smuggling activities. While providing a complete account of all of them would fill a library, this chapter aims to highlight two additional dimensions of regulation. One is the regulation of the distribution of smuggled goods and particularly their point of sale, and the other is their regulation through local conceptions of morality, religion, and legitimacy. While they are not the only place in which smuggled goods are being sold, regulated, or thought about, I have located both discussions in the borderlands.

The previous chapter highlighted that the regulatory institutions at the borders of Tunisia and Morocco have long differentiated between different types of goods and rely on the toleration and involvement of state agents. This chapter extends this finding to the regulation of the distribution of smuggled goods. It notes that the institutional structures regulating the distribution of smuggled goods in city markets involve a hybridization of informal institutions and, in contrast to the border itself, officially recognized state involvement that has largely developed out of a desire to tax these goods. At the same time, the distribution of smuggled gasoline in roadside stations has been selectively tolerated and subject to resource extraction by security forces but has not undergone a similar hybridization process.

A small literature on religious and moral evaluations of smuggling in North Africa has emphasized the importance of nonstate references such as religion and tribal identities in legitimizing informal trade in the eyes of the local population.[1] Expanding on these perceptions, albeit briefly, is important for two reasons. One is that popular discussions of smuggling in the region are ripe with assumptions about how borderland populations perceive it that are at best anecdotal. The other is that strong local norms could provide a potential rival explanation to the more structural and political account of the regulation of smuggling in the following chapters. If there are strong norms around smuggling as a traditional and legitimate local practice that is preferable to other income streams, this might in itself provide a reason for other actors to tolerate it. If there are commonly held norms about how it should be regulated, this might drive regulatory structures from the bottom up. This chapter does not advance a singular, definite place of smuggling networks in the moral perceptions of the region's borderlands; it finds little evidence for strongly and communally held normative perceptions as a key driver of regulation. Instead, it highlights the diversity of moral evaluations of smuggling in the region that are shaped by varying perceptions of the moral status of different goods, the permissibility of breaking the law, and the ability to sustain livelihoods. Overall, it finds that smuggling has an uneasier relationship with local normative perceptions than is commonly suggested.

Combined, two discussions in this chapter advance a point of caution with respect to hybrid governance in the regulation of North Africa's borderlands. A range of the regulatory structures considered in this chapter represent hybrids, drawing on formal and informal institutional structures. However, as the chapter's discussion on local normative perceptions demonstrates, these informal institutions are not necessarily locally accepted and legitimized in the sense that some of the more optimistic hybrid governance literature has at times suggested. What we find is a functional hybridity—formal institutions combined with local practice, not necessarily local norms.

The remainder of this chapter is divided into three sections. The first section discusses the regulation of the sale of (licit) smuggled goods in the borderlands of Tunisia and Morocco. It reviews the "Libyan Markets" in

Tunisia's Medenine region and the city markets in Morocco's Oriental, and draws conclusions from their comparison and contrasts the markets with the regulation of the sale of contraband gasoline. The second section explores how smuggling is conceptualized in local accounts of morality, religion, and legitimacy, seeking to understand both how regulatory institutions are perceived locally and if this in itself exerts a regulatory influence on smuggling networks. A final section briefly suggests conclusions.

CITY MARKETS AND ROADSIDE GAS: REGULATING SMUGGLING AT THE POINT OF SALE

The dynamics of the regulation of smuggling at the point of sale are substantially different from the regulatory dynamics at border crossings. As previously discussed, the objective of border regulation is the management of its porosity and the control of the type and quantity of goods that are brought into the country through certain channels. In contrast, the objective of the regulation at distribution points inside the country is the maintenance of a distribution system that can be monitored and taxed, while at the same time remaining segmented from the distribution system of formally imported goods.

As this section demonstrates, this change in objective also affects the type of institutional governance. While the regulation of smuggling at the border in the previous chapter relied on the routinized and systematized involvement of state actors, this was never officially communicated, acknowledged, or connected to their formal institutional roles. In contrast, the institutions governing the distribution of some informally imported goods include institutional elements that are officially supported by the state while still maintaining elements that are illegal. As this section argues, this is once again limited to selected types of goods and has largely resulted from efforts by local municipalities to generate tax revenues from informal markets.

To illustrate this argument, I will discuss the main distribution channels for informally imported licit goods in Tunisia, known as the "Libyan Markets," followed by the city markets in northern Morocco. These can then be contrasted with one stream of goods that largely falls outside the remit of these markets: the sale of contraband gasoline, which is regulated through a combination of enforcement strategies that tolerate the point of sale but make the transport of goods between points of sale costly.

Tunisia: The Libyan Markets

As the informal cross-border trade of consumer goods expanded in Tunisia in the 1980s, it required a distribution system that was reputable, predictable, and safe enough to attract local—especially female—customers. The rotating weekly markets, a century-old institution in rural Tunisia, which in their organization largely mirrors periodic market structures that are common across Africa, provided an ideal platform.[2] They required little infrastructure investment and could easily be expanded or imitated in other public spaces.[3] Most important, they were only very loosely regulated. While market fees were collected by either municipal agents or tax farmers to whom the right to tax the market had been sold, vendors in the markets were generally not required to hold a permit, as other Tunisian vendors usually do.[4] For many of the vendors who bought from local farmers and sold products on the markets, there was not even a legal category in which they could apply for a permit or an entry in the commercial registry.[5]

Vendors of smuggled goods, especially fabrics, carpets, and kitchenware, quickly flooded the local weekly markets. The growth in demand strained the infrastructure of the markets and produced problems for municipalities—vendors expanded into roads, clogging traffic, and began to overstay the usual market times. Seeking to both organize the markets and find ways to extract money from them beyond the market fees, municipalities began to "formalize" sections of these informal markets that were largely selling smuggled consumer goods. This typically included the provision of additional market space specifically for the vendors of smuggled goods, the walling of new markets, or the provision of additional infrastructure. The "Souk Libya" was born. Tunisia's smugglers hence followed a common global trajectory of informal traders from roadside vendors to state-built markets and in a way mirror the sedentarization of the southern tribes a century earlier. Today, Libyan Markets exist across Tunisia, from Medenine's Souk Libya all the way up to the Souk Moncef Bey in Tunis. Needless to say, there is heterogeneity in the organization and regulation of these markets; I focus here on two of the most prominent markets of the Medenine region.

One of the largest markets lies, unsurprisingly, in Ben Guerdane. A bit outside of the town center, on the road to Zarzis, it consists of a wall, more than four hundred concrete shops, parking spaces, and a field that is filled up by even more vendors on the weekend. Especially on Saturdays, the market is buzzing, as both locals and customers from surrounding towns navigate among the colorful piles of blankets, carpets, clothes, and kitchenware to haggle for bargains. The market includes sanitary facilities and used to have an ATM, which was burned in the 2011 revolution.[6] And while all the goods sold have been brought into the country illegally, no policeman would attempt to disrupt the goings-on in the market.[7] On the contrary, the market has a small police station, tasked with protecting the market and ensuring its functioning. While most markets of this kind in Tunisia are just colloquially referred to as "Souk Libya," a brief enthusiasm around the idea of the Maghrebi union in the 1990s gave this one its current name: Souk Maghrebi. The history of its creation is shaped by the efforts of the municipality of Ben Guerdane to create a controllable and taxable distribution structure for informally imported goods through creative institutional innovation.

Having decided to build a market structure for the group of vendors who were selling smuggled goods to an ever-growing number of customers in the late 1980s, the municipality faced two obstacles. First, they did not have the funds to construct the market themselves, and second, they did not own the land. As with all territories in Tunisia that contained significant amounts of salt, the land was officially the property of the Ministry of Defense.[8] Since this made it impossible for the municipality to either claim or transfer full ownership rights, they opted for an unconventional approach: they built an enclosure and rudimentary market infrastructure in 1991 and gave out permits to local traders, instructing them to build stalls themselves, and allowing them to operate out of them in exchange for a yearly fee.[9]

The fact that the land did not belong to the municipality was not communicated to the traders, and both the construction of the stalls and the extraction of a yearly fee were therefore not entirely legal.[10] On this basis, a hybrid regulatory system developed around the Souk Maghrebi market, made up of an informal trade distribution network governed by an improvised but officialized regulatory structure through the local municipality, which continued until the 2011 revolution.[11] This regulation of the use of the land was done officially and with a high degree of bureaucratization, despite the fact that the municipality was not acting strictly legally.[12] One high municipal official in Ben Guerdane described the arrangement to me with a phrase that fittingly summarized authorities' strategies toward this trade more broadly: "informal but controlled."[13]

During this time, the municipality not just tolerated but actively encouraged, supported, and regulated the activities of the market. It provided sanitary facilities and organized the cleaning and security of the market. It never made an issue of the origins of the products that were sold there—quite the opposite. As buses brought more and more customers from around Tunisia to Ben Guerdane, they would often have problems with customs officers who stopped them on the road north, asking about the origins of their goods and demanding a bribe. So the municipality set up a booth in the market where it issued receipts that could be shown to police or customs agents in order to prove the legality of the goods. Of course, and as local administrator confirmed to me, this practice was not legal.[14] It was, however, at that point an official practice by a state institution. And, of course, the municipality collected a fee for this activity. Alongside the fee that it collected from the vendors, ranging from 120 TND (GBP 30) before 2005 to 300 TND (GBP 77) in 2009, the income from the market began to make up a significant portion of the municipal budget.[15]

Apart from the collection of fees, this organization of the market also allowed the municipality to exert some control over the allocation of spaces and to use this as a basis for clientelist influence.[16] It also allowed it to monitor the ownership and usage of the market. I was able to receive from the municipality a complete list of the operators of all the stores in the market, along with their phone number and payment history. The market regulation also included the prohibition of certain goods from sale there: large-scale items such as cars could not be sold in the Souk Maghrebi. More important, flammable liquids were not allowed, which left the gasoline traders to develop a separate distribution mechanism outside of the Libyan Markets.

Alongside the regulation produced by the municipality, there lies a small degree of regulation that is entirely informal and maintained among the vendors, including a designated day every week on which the market is closed (Monday), and a minimum wage of 300 TND paid to the employees in the market's stalls.[17] Vendors also organized among themselves to provide additional security for the market, as what the police provided was insufficient, and cooperated in the construction of roofing for the small passageways through the site.

REGULATING SMUGGLING IN THE BORDERLANDS

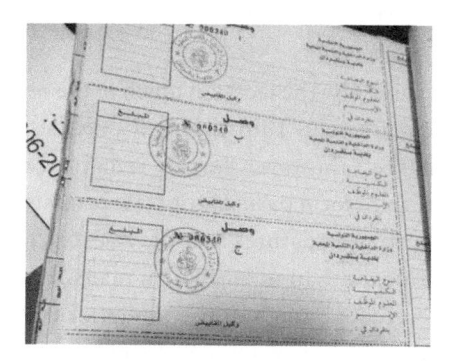

FIGURE 4.1 Receipts for the payment of the yearly fees to the municipality by the vendors of the Souk Maghrebi. Photo by author.

While the complications of the landownership shaped the institutional setup of the Souk Maghrebi, other Libyan Markets provide a variety of other institutional hybrids. The Souk Libya in the city of Medenine was constructed by the municipality in 2002, after a preexisting market had burned down under disputed circumstances. The municipality directly rents the stores to 123 vendors and has written contracts with them, which stipulate some restrictions on the types of goods that are allowed to be sold in the markets, excluding, for example, flammable liquids. The contracts, however, make no mention of the goods' origins. Bureaucrats in the municipality of Medenine expressed the opinion that it was their responsibility to enforce local rules and regulations, and only those.[18]

The vendors in Medenine's Souk Libya typically do not have a permit, so they do not pay income taxes, but they pay rent (around 40 TND per month) to the municipality and pay a market tax to a private revenue collector who purchases the right to tax the market on a yearly basis. In 2014 the city began planning the construction of another market on the same model to deal with the high demand for commercial space.[19] At the same time, it still operates another market, the Wadi Market, which consists of more shabby stalls built by the vendors themselves, who pay a relatively minor fee of 90 TND a year to the municipality. And on the weekend, and especially early on Sunday morning, a huge market fills Medenine's dry riverbed. Alongside agricultural products and animals, many of the goods sold are smuggled. Here, the early institutional setup of the weekly market dominates the regulation of the trade, with no formal registration, little control over the type of goods, and a set fee paid to the municipality or a tax farmer.

This is partly explained by the fact that much of the organizational structure of the periodic markets in Tunisia largely predates the modern Tunisian state.[20] The markets, however, largely remained regulated by these embedded practices, with local parts of the state primarily attaching themselves to these preexisting structures in order to extract some revenue and integrate them into local urban management plans. The resulting institutional bricolage has created much of the modern institutional structure through which the distribution of smuggled goods interacts with the Tunisian state.[21]

However, the sale of informally imported goods in southern Tunisia is not limited to these market structures. As the Libyan Markets grew, so did a vast distribution network of traders who would buy goods in Ben Guerdane or Medenine and transport them across Tunisia.[22] With this came the demand for more wholesale trade in smuggled commodities. While large-scale traders originally began selling at a large space behind the Souk Maghrebi, the ground there was of poor quality, and traders started building warehouses along the road between Ben Guerdane and the Ras Jedir border crossing. Here, larger quantities of goods were sold directly to other traders.

Here, too, the municipality of Ben Guerdane managed to engineer institutions that allowed it to tax these activities. While they could not extract rent from traders, who owned the land they had built stores on, or charge market fees, as the traders were selling outside of a market, the municipality instead picked up on the practice of traders storing goods in front of their stores and using the space on the side of the road to load and unload vehicles. Hence they charged the vendors a yearly fee for the "temporary use of public space." In 2010, for example, this fee was set at 150 TND (GBP 38) per year.[23]

Morocco: The City Markets

In their historical development, structure, and institutional hybridity, the regulation of the distribution networks of licit smuggled goods in Morocco shares significant parallels to the Tunisian case. Recent years in Oujda have seen intense activity in the creation of new market structures that have

FIGURE 4.2 Wholesaling of smuggled tires on the Ras Jedir Road. Photo by author.

established new regulatory institutions and have further solidified the ability of local municipal authorities to extract revenue from these markets.[24]

As in the Tunisian case, distribution networks for informally imported consumer goods in Morocco began to build on local traditional market structures as they expanded, taking advantage of their regulatory informality and flexibility. Oujda's most prominent market for the sale of smuggled goods from Algeria, like its counterpart on the other side of the border, still betrays that heritage in its name: Souk Fellah, "farmer's market." While in the 1970s it functioned primarily as a market for fruits and vegetables, they are now nowhere to be found in the narrow alleys between self-constructed stalls that sell a wide variety of consumer items associated with the informal trade to Algeria: electronic goods, construction materials, cleaning products, and beauty products.

The land on which the Souk Fellah was built is privately owned by a single landlord. Vendors sell out of a mix of temporary stalls built in the 1990s and self-built concrete structures, mirroring the case of the Souk Maghrebi.[25]

Just a few hundred yards down the road, the municipality has built a new market for the vendors currently selling in the Souk Fellah. Many of them, however, are skittish about moving to the new location—they are worried whether their customers will follow them, and whether they will be able to maintain the Souk Fellah "brand" as a market for cheap (and smuggled) goods.[26] If the vendors decide to move, the new Souk Fellah will be the completion of a decade-long strategy by the municipality of Oujda to formalize its informal markets. As in Ben Guerdane and Medenine in Tunisia, these attempts have produced a variety of hybrid arrangements, all of which allow the municipality to officially regulate, organize, and tax the sale of smuggled goods.

One of the largest markets in Oujda is located just across the road from the Souk Fellah. The Souk Melilla is named after the origin of most of its goods—for decades, it has specialized in informally imported goods from the Spanish enclave, especially in clothes, fabrics, and shoes. While traders who were importing smuggled goods from Melilla had originally sold on the roadsides in the city center, the municipality began directing them onto an empty piece of land in the 1960s—the location that now houses the market. The original stalls were self-built and rather rudimentary. Even in this early form, however, the market was already taxed by the municipality.

Before the creation of formalized market structures in the 2010s, the municipality had developed two mechanisms through which they could tax informal vendors, and especially vendors selling informally imported goods, the city's primary commercial activity. First, law 30/89 stipulated a fee that the municipality could charge roadside vendors.[27] However, due to the fact that the operation of these vendors was technically illegal, this fee was taken out of the law in 2008. The change left both the municipality of Oujda and the roadside vendors in a "delicate" situation, as a senior municipal official noted.[28] The municipality had depended on the income, while the vendors had relied on the receipts from the fee as a legitimizing mechanism in their interaction with local law enforcement officers—a strategy that scholars of informality, legitimacy and taxation have repeatedly noted.[29] But the municipality learned to adapt. Another section in the same law allowed the municipality to charge fees for the "temporary use of public space for commercial purpose."[30] As the first fee disappeared in 2008, the municipality began to "migrate" vendors to the other fee, which swiftly was applied to most informal vendors in the city and by 2011 covered most of the vendors in what now is the Souk Melilla.[31]

Vendors did not have licenses, and their goods were smuggled, but they now held "temporary permits" for their commercial operation. Similar to the receipt slips under the previous arrangement, this gave them not just an important piece of leverage against harassment by the police but also a formal, official, and predictable relationship with the municipality.[32] When I talked about the early phases of the market with Oujda's mayor, Omar Hajiira, he fittingly summed up that relationship: "They were not really informal. Well, informal, but they were on our territory."[33] The similarity to the "informal but controlled" approach in Tunisia is notable here.

In 2011 this relationship was transformed by tragedy. On the night of August 26, a fire broke out in the Souk Melilla, destroying a wide swath of its stalls and infrastructure. Its reconstruction took over eighteen months and was conducted with heavy financial input not just from the local vendors but also from the state through the regional administration, the Agence Oriental, and the National Initiative for Human Development (INDH). While the state built most of the market infrastructure, significant investment and labor in the furnishing and construction of the individual shops—again, similar to the situation at the Souk Maghrebi in Ben Guerdane or the Souk Fellah across the road—came from the vendors.[34]

The result was a large roofed market structure with electricity access for the vendors, a sanitary infrastructure, and even a small mosque. Over its entrance, the market carries the name that signals the origin of its goods—Souk Melilla—as well as the INDH logo and a picture of the king. Still, vendors do not own their own stores in the market. Instead, they made an initial payment for the "key," the right to operate out of a particular store, and then rent the stores from the municipality, typically for around 150 MAD (GBP 12) per month.[35] They pay a separate fee for the electricity, and some of the vendors pay an additional fee for their membership in the market association, which can provide them with some medical benefits. Many of the vendors don't have business permits, are not listed in the commercial registry, and hence pay no commercial taxes. But even for the ones that do pay, the taxes are "declarative"—they are dependent on the revenue that vendors report, and according to a senior official in Oujda's tax service, controls in the market are barely existent and generally negotiable.[36]

Oujda's different markets display a wide variety of regulatory arrangements. In the Souk Tanger, just across the street from the Souk Melilla, opened by the king in 2013, people own their stores but pay an "urban tax" of 504 MAD per year to the municipality.[37] In the large number of smaller markets that the INDH has been building in Oujda's urban periphery, stalls are rented, though typically at negligible fees.[38] Despite this diversity, however, there are important commonalities that characterize the regulatory arrangements of these markets, and by extension of the distribution of smuggled consumer goods in Oujda.

First, an increasing number of the city's vendors are operating in an infrastructure that is to some degree constructed and owned by the municipality but commonly also included some labor and financial investment by the vendors. Second, with the exception of some of the vendors in the Souk Fellah, the municipality has created institutions that allow it to extract some revenue from the sale of informally imported goods, primarily through permits for the temporary use of public space for commercial activities, market fees, and stall rents. At the heart of this stands the substitution of stall and market fees for commercial taxes, the toleration of vendors operating without formal business permits and entries in the commercial registry, and the flexible handling of the declarative nature of taxation. This still leaves most vendors with a lower tax burden than if they were fully formal, while at the same time ensuring a stable and official relationship with local state authorities.

This connects directly to a third point: the relationship between the markets and state institutions, primarily the municipality and the region, is managed and negotiated through market associations, all of which are legally recognized, and represented in the Chamber of Commerce. Fourth, while there are some limits to the types of goods that can be sold in each market, there are no mechanisms that in any way account for, trace, or penalize the smuggled origin of the goods sold. The main mechanism for this appears to be a siloization of the responsibilities of different state institutions. Authorities on a municipal level, of course, are fully aware of the origin of the goods in the Souk Melilla. However, they do not see this as their concern. To quote a senior official in Oujda's Chamber of Commerce: "If you have a locality, a fixed locality, and you are in the commercial registry, it really doesn't matter where the products come from."[39] Or, in the words of the head of one of the market associations: "The government doesn't care about whether the products are legal, it's whether the market looks legal."[40]

The objective behind the construction of these markets was never, as a leading administrator of the Agence Oriental confirmed, to limit or restrict the distribution of informally imported goods: "We wanted to formalize the contraband, and make it visible."[41] If any reference to goods' origins comes up, local authorities have referred me either to the standards inspectors, who in turn claim not to be able to inspect informal markets, or to customs agents, who claim that they are both legally unable to operate within the city perimeter and would likely cause riots if they were to try to do so. "We are not allowed to enter the Souk Melilla," a high official in the regional customs office told me, "but also, it is just impossible. Just imagine—there would be riots."[42] The customs agents therefore focus their efforts on controlling goods—or extracting money from their owners—when they are moving, both across the border and across the country. I will return to this point below.

Informal Markets and Hybrid Institutions in Tunisia and Morocco

As this section has demonstrated, the regulation of the sale of informally imported consumer goods in Morocco and Tunisia through city markets is remarkably similar. Generally, the institutionalization of these markets and their embedding with official state institutions appear to be a little bit more advanced in Morocco, although it is worth noting that a similar development in Tunisia might have been delayed by the 2011 revolution—the municipality of Medenine, for example, has had the plans for another market finalized for years but has not been able to begin construction due to the political turmoil.[43]

In both cases, the regulatory structures around the markets reflect the interaction of the largely informal institutions of the traditional periodic markets with the novel institutions utilized by local municipalities in order to sufficiently formalize the markets so that they could extract resources from them. The result of this particular form of "institutional bricolage" is a set of hybrid institutions that combine formal and informal elements. Strictly speaking, various elements of the markets' activities and regulations—from the lack of business permits to the faked letters of origin—are still illegal. However, contrary to the institutions at the border crossings discussed in the previous chapter, the regulation of the markets sees not merely a de facto involvement of state structures but an official involvement, communicated through officially sanctioned channels. Local state authorities are openly transparent about their role in the market regulation in a way that they are not about the regulation at the border, to the degree that markets are branded with the logos of state institutions and presented as model development projects.[44]

Going one step further, the institutional development around the city markets in Tunisia and Morocco in the past decade resembles a process not just of hybridization, but of officializing—of creating documents and institutional structures that provide claims to formality for both the municipality and the vendors, without formalizing the markets entirely. This strategic use of official documentation to create selective areas of "officialdom" that are deeply embedded in informal systems has been a frequently noted feature within processes of hybrid governance.[45] This employment of officialdom relates not just to the vendors but also to the goods themselves, which, by passing through these regulated distribution networks, are transformed from smuggled goods to goods that can comfortably be bought by consumers and are thereby introduced into the mainstream consumer economies of Tunisia and Morocco.

Across the case studies described here, municipal authorities have drawn on these institutions in order to tax city markets. As has been frequently noted in the literature on taxation, informal vendors are often willing to engage in taxing institutions to the degree that they also provide them with claims to legality.[46] Taxation has structured the relationships between municipalities and vendors while transforming organizational structures in the markets. In both countries, this has been accompanied by the creation of market organizations and associations. Some of the literature on informality and taxation has suggested the possibility that this may lead to more accountability of state institutions to informal actors.[47] Chapters 6–8, which trace the renegotiation of the markets' regulation, will pick up on these issues.

Toleration of Roadside Gasoline

While a wide variety of illegally imported goods are sold in the markets described so far in this chapter—from cosmetics to foodstuffs, carpets to kitchenware—there are goods that are prevented from being sold on their premises. Similar to the structures at the border crossings, the regulatory structures of the markets do not permit illicit goods, such as narcotics or weapons. In addition to that, gasoline, one of the most widely traded smuggled goods in the region, is typically not sold in these markets.

In both Tunisia and Morocco, the sale of contraband gasoline is primarily conducted through informal roadside gas stations.[48] Some vendors, especially in the vicinity of the border in Tunisia, directly supply themselves from the smugglers who have brought the gasoline across the border. Most of the other informal vendors are supplied through transporters, who buy from large-scale wholesale vendors and then act as distributors across the country.[49] During the heyday of contraband gasoline in both case studies, these structures functioned as the dominant supplier of fuel in both southern Tunisia and northern Morocco.[50]

Amid widespread concern about vendors selling adulterated gasoline, establishing trust with their clients and transporters is a central concern for roadside vendors. Apart from establishing a sense of brand identity—a characteristic red light made of a plastic jerry-can, or a hand-painted "Total" sign (figure 4.3), the ideal strategy for vendors is hence predictable repeat interaction with their customers. Most of the roadside stations in the region are relatively stationary, even though the permanence of their

FIGURE 4.3 Informal gasoline station near Medenine, Tunisia. Photo by author.

infrastructure differs vastly, from a single jerry-can placed beside the road to wooden, iron, or even garage-like stalls built out of cement.

Despite their stationary and visible character, informal gasoline stations do not exhibit similar regulatory structures as the city markets and do not fall into the remit of hybrid institutions. Though illegal, they have for many years been tolerated by the police in both southern Tunisia and northern Morocco. While some traders mention having to pay occasional bribes, most of the vendors I spoke to claimed that they did not have to do so. However, the blanket toleration of informal gas stations by the police and the absence of hybrid regulatory institutions do not mean that there is no regulatory superstructure that manages the selective integration of these goods into the Tunisian and Moroccan markets. In the context of illegally imported gasoline, in both countries, the regulation of distribution is best described as a form of geographic zoning of the phenomenon, limiting it primarily through border regions. This is achieved through a toleration of points of sale of contraband gasoline that exists alongside the prosecution or limitation of its transport within the country.

In Morocco, while there is no general crackdown against informal roadside gas stations, cars transporting gasoline across the country, and especially from the northeastern borderlands further south and inland, are commonly stopped on the road by police and customs agents. If caught, they usually face high fines, the confiscation of their cargo, and even the confiscation or destruction of their cars.[51]

This has shaped the activities of different actors within the gasoline networks. While the so-called first buyers at the border, embedded in informal institutions that regulate their trade, and the vendors on the roadside, generally tolerated, are not particularly concerned with avoiding detection or fleeing from law enforcement, the "second buyers," the transporters between the border crossing and informal gas stations across the country, face a markedly different situation. With their cargo being unprotected by any institutionalized arrangement, they must constantly fear arrest. And so their cars can be heard on the streets of Morocco's Northeast, driving at full speed, often at night, without lights and without stopping, as if the devil were behind them. Locals call them *muqatila* (fighters), for their strength, their powerful engines, and their recklessness.[52] It is a dangerous business—apart from the risk of arrest and confiscation, accidents are common and, with a car full of gasoline, particularly perilous.

REGULATING SMUGGLING IN THE BORDERLANDS

Crucially, this has created a distinct spatial pattern. Every mile that a *muqatila* has to transport gasoline inland from the border increases the risk of detection. This makes contraband less available and more expensive as the distance from the border increases. In effect, this mix of toleration and prosecution creates a tolerated integration of contraband gasoline into a geographically limited space—primarily the border regions.

The situation in Tunisia is similar. Here, too, roadside gas stations are generally put up with and can be observed throughout the southern borderlands. And while transport across the country is not dangerous, it is equally costly. Here, the cost is not imposed through the risk of arrest or confiscation—this may occur but appears to be rather rare. Instead, the cost of transporting contraband gasoline inland is induced by the police checkpoints that are ever-present across Tunisia's interior regions. Gasoline transporters are expected to pay a bribe at each roadblock. As gasoline traders report, the level of these bribes is usually relatively stable at one checkpoint over time but increases the farther away from the border a checkpoint is positioned.[53] It is unclear whether this is due to a conscious strategy or the result of a changing position of power of law enforcement vis-à-vis local traders as the distance from the borderlands increases.

In effect, the checkpoints appear to account almost completely for the price differences in contraband gasoline in southern Tunisia, as the price rises with distance from the border, but primarily with the number and size of checkpoints between the point of sale and the border. Contraband gasoline on the island of Djerba, for example, is significantly more expensive than in Medenine, even though Djerba is closer to the border geographically. In early 2017 I noticed that 20 liters of Libyan gasoline were on sale for around 10 TND at a wholesaler in Ben Guerdane, 13 TND in Medenine, and a hefty 17 TND in Djerba.[54] According to transporters of contraband gasoline, the police at the large checkpoint at the entrance to the touristic island of Djerba usually take a bribe of 4 TND per canister from transporters, hence driving up the price.[55]

As in Morocco, this combination of tolerating the sale of contraband gasoline while making its transport costly has led to the integration of contraband gasoline into the Tunisian economy in a geographically segmented fashion, with availability and price going up with distance from the border. In the Tunisian case, it is interesting to note that this geographic distribution has waxed and waned over the past years. While the tolerated sale of contraband gasoline was limited to the immediate border regions before 2011, informal roadside stations could be observed across the countries in the years after the revolution, before receding again, reaching about as far as Gabes, where a crackdown against roadside vendors in 2017 led to the confiscation of 24,000 liters of contraband gasoline.[56] In this context, it is worth noting that enforcement operations against informal gas stations seemed to occur as the geographic remit of the phenomenon changed, especially as it contracted again after 2014, as a measure of controlling the territorial spread of the phenomenon, but not as a measure to reduce its prevalence within the territory where it was still tolerated.

In both cases, when revenue is extracted from the contraband gasoline trade, this occurs through security services—contrary to the city markets described earlier, there are no institutions that allow local municipalities to tax the sale of contraband gasoline. As a result, distributors and vendors of contraband gasoline do not benefit from the officializing processes described in the case of the city markets. When asked why they haven't attempted to tax the gasoline trade, municipal officials have at times described these activities as "more illegal" than some of the activities from which they have managed to extract revenue. A high official in the Oujda tax office, having just explained the mechanisms through which they tax illegal street vendors, when asked about gasoline merely exclaimed: "We can't tax what is illegal."[57]

The heterogeneous and less officialized treatment of the sale of gasoline at first appears surprising, as its economic dynamics are rooted in the subsidies of neighboring countries, leading it to technically represent less of a challenge to the state resources of Tunisia and Morocco than smuggling that is more heavily driven by tariff evasion. There are a range of potential dynamics that this difference in the perception and treatment of these goods could point to. One is a feature of gasoline itself. As a flammable good, the sale of gasoline is not allowed everywhere: many rent contracts of vendors in city markets specifically prohibit flammable goods, and there are specific requirements that formal gasoline stations need to fulfill. It is worth noting, however, that gasoline is not the only product that is subject to additional restrictions. The sale of food products, for example, is connected to additional regulatory requirements but can still be found in city markets.

Chapter 8 will pick up this puzzle again, by comparing the institutional histories and the relative power of gasoline and textile smuggling networks.

The remainder of this chapter, however, addresses another form of local informal regulation: moral perceptions. If hybrid institutions are conceptualized as the interlinkage of formal and locally embedded informal institutions, local norms appear as another potential explanation for the heterogeneity in regulation.

INFORMALITY, ISLAM, AND LEGITIMACY

How do borderland populations evaluate the dominance of smuggling in their local economies, and particularly its regulation? Aside from being a relevant part of the picture empirically, there are at least three reasons why this is also relevant to our questions on the nature and meaning functioning of this regulation itself. First, local belief systems and normative perceptions about criminality and justice, particularly if they are hegemonic, can present another form of informal regulation, normalizing certain behaviors and making others more costly.[58] Second, writing on hybrid governance has frequently assumed that informal regulatory arrangements are embedded in local belief systems, thereby enjoying local legitimacy even if they are formally illegal and lending additional durability and efficiency to hybrid institutional structures.[59] As Meagher and others have noted, however, this does not necessarily have to be the case and should be treated as an empirical question rather than an assumption.[60] Third, analyses and discussions around smuggling in the region have hypothesized a central role for systems of norms that present alternatives or challenges to the nation-state, on the basis of either tribe or Islamist imaginaries.[61]

The remainder of this chapter examines local normative perceptions of smuggling by looking at local conceptions of licit and illicit goods, lawbreaking, and the right to a livelihood. It does not aim to advance a singular and exhaustive place of smuggling in the moral perceptions of the region's borderlands—in my conversations with smugglers and borderland residents, local perceptions and evaluations of smuggling and its regulation were diverse, differentiated, and conflicted. Two observations, however, stand out. First, while local perceptions of smuggling also differentiate between different smuggled goods and types of activities, they do not necessarily reflect one unified position on their respective appropriateness. Second, it becomes noticeable that across the borderlands discussed here, smuggling and its regulation rest uneasily against local moral and religious evaluations and are more commonly put in relation to a need to survive and a lack of alternatives than a right embedded in traditional practices or religious opposition. This provides an indication that the hybrid institutional arrangements described here are mainly functional hybrids—they have primarily developed out of states adapting to local practices, not necessarily local norms. I discuss Morocco and Tunisia together, as perceptions in both case sites were remarkably similar and will highlight differences whenever relevant.

Political and policy analyses of smuggling typically differentiate between licit and illicit goods. In her seminal piece on smuggling in southern Algeria, Scheele notes that local communities similarly separate their moral evaluation of smuggling based on the types of goods that are being transported, drawing on the Islamic concepts of *halal* (permitted) and *haram* (forbidden).[62] Similarly, this distinction is common in both northern Morocco and southern Tunisia. While this partly maps on the distinction between licit and illicit goods, there are occasional differences, and the categorization of goods as halal and haram is not universally agreed on. Alcohol, for example, not typically considered an illicit good in the wider literature on informal cross-border trade, is, by religious definition, haram. Class A narcotics are both illicit and generally agreed to be haram, with particularly synthetic psychotropics also increasingly standing at the heart of local moral anxiety around immorality and drug consumption by the local youth. At the same time, however, opinions diverge over the status of cannabis, the consumption of which has a rich and culturally embedded history in the region, particularly in Morocco. While cigarettes are usually considered halal, opinions appear to diverge over the status of firearms. Notably, though somewhat unsurprisingly, none of the conversations I've had framed gasoline as haram, or as a good that was morally different from nonhydrocarbon licit consumer goods such as textiles or kitchenware.

Apart from the classification of goods as halal or haram, much of the diversity of moral evaluations of smuggling that I observed are driven by differing opinions on the issue of breaking the law, and particularly bribery. This is reflective of diverse positions on the respective primacy of formal state laws, informal local practices and agreements, and religious rules and laws. Again, this argument is often framed in religious terms. The most common explanation given by those arguing that all smuggling is immoral was that bribery is haram, as all illegal actions are. "What is halal and haram is really clear," one avid opponent of smuggling liked to tell me. "People just make it complicated because it helps them."[63]

Yet many people did highlight some more complications to this approach. Some drew a moral distinction depending on how directly people were themselves involved in bribery. I met deeply religious men who objected to much contemporary music and poetry on religious grounds and considered the payment of bribes as forbidden but were operating a wholesale gasoline business, arguing that it was not they themselves who were paying their bribes, but the transporters who supplied them.[64] More commonly, however, disagreements around the permissibility of bribery revolved around the legitimacy of both the formal law and the state that issued it. If the state is not legitimate, if the law is not legitimate, this argument goes, then transgressing it is permitted. In the words of trader of smuggled shoes in Morocco:

> Smuggling has nothing to do with religion. It's commerce, I am getting something, selling something, making profit out of it. It's trade, the prophet encouraged us to work in trade.... In the time of the prophet, they brought fabrics and spices from India, from other countries. All that is happening now is the same thing. In the prophet's time, the money, the tax, it was also not going to the government, it was zakat, that went to the poor people. Now it goes to the government, not the poor people. The government forces you to pay the tax but doesn't do anything good with the money. I will tell you—I am against the government.[65]

The same argument is often extended to the police who either try to enforce the law or ask for bribes. Some traders argue that, religiously, the police should not be classified as a legitimate enforcement institution of just laws, but as *qaata'a tariq*, as highwaymen, bandits. As a consequence, bribery would then be religiously permitted. "Even the prophet was robbed by bandits they say, the police are not legal, and hence it is not haram to give money to bandits."[66] This language of banditry, of an illegitimate, predatory state, is common. It is often tied not merely to religious critiques of the Tunisian state and its security services, but also to an economic and political history of structural exploitation of the Moroccan North or the Tunisian South. "The police take their goods, so they have the right to attack them.... They sometimes make new laws, because they hate Ben Guerdane, they just take the goods," argues one of the city's residents who is not himself a smuggler but currently working on a construction site.[67] "The Sahelians are doing robbery, they are not considering Ben Guerdane as part of Tunisia," says a local textile smuggler referencing the Sahel, Tunisia's coastal regions from which much of the country's political elite has hailed.[68]

Local perceptions of the permissiveness of lawbreaking as a central part of smuggling appear to be complex and contested, but not random. Instead, they are closely connected to different views on who has the legitimate right to tax, to control, to ask for money. As demonstrated earlier, this in turn intersects not merely with religious convictions but also with evaluations of state security services, accountability, and the history of center-periphery relationships and the local economy.[69] It is worth noting, however, that critiques of the state or doubts of its legitimacy are not generally framed through reference to alternative normative orders such as tribal laws, traditions, or a failure to adhere to certain Islamist ideas of what states should look like. Instead, more common references are to state performance, accountability, and, crucially, the provision of livelihoods.

In fact, the livelihood dimension gives rise to the most dominant theme in these conversations around moral evaluations of smuggling. The notion of a right to work, a need to earn a living, and an absence of legal employment opportunities was ever-present across both case sites. It comes up again and again: "Of course, people have a right to do this kind of commerce, because they have a right to live, and this is a universal right, and in order to live, you need to work. They are working, not robbing banks," one Ben Guerdane resident told me.[70] "We don't want to work as informal traders with Libya, but there is no other option. I mean, I literally brought goods over under fire. I need to do anything to bring food on the table for my family," argued a wholesale smuggler selling off the Route Ras Jedir.[71] "I have a right to smuggle, because if I don't, I will die of hunger. And I have a family, I have a daughter," added a transporter working for a wholesale smuggler.[72] Some traders explicitly mention the absence of factories as a synonym for high unemployment, such as a textile smuggler in Oujda: "There are no factories here. If they close the door, honestly, people will kill each other. There is no other place to work. The only way to work here is this way."[73]

In the words of one Medenine resident: "We do illegal things here, because there is nothing else. Because the government lets us. Actually, because the government forces us."[74] The question of alternatives, too, relates more directly to a wider discussion in Islamic thought over criminality in the context of economic adversity and hunger.[75] One Ben Guerdane resident recalls the story of Umar ibn Al-Khattab, the second caliph, and the thief: "Someone had captured a thief and beaten him. The caliph said to him, don't beat him, give him the money that he took, and give him a job, and food. If he still robs you then, cut off his hand. But now, he is in need of food and it is haram to punish him. Now, here, it is the same for the people. They should pay bribes—what else can they do? Especially when they have a family. It is only a real bribe if you have a choice."[76]

This argument, of course, does not apply to all smugglers—not everyone who is smuggling is devoid of other options; not everyone is just making enough to get by. Staying with the theme of the need to make a living, local moral evaluations of smuggling commonly differentiate between the "little guys," the "portadores" and "ants," and the "big guys," the "barons" and "bosses," which are unlikely to fit the role of the thief in the story.

It is worth noting that the permissibility of smuggling is not just assumed to have consequences for the fate of smugglers in the afterlife. Many local residents, even among those who argue that smuggling might be permissible, argue that the profit made from it has a different status from that made from honest work. There is a sense in some conversations that nothing good, nothing productive, will come from this money, and that the consumption patterns of many of the young smugglers, being viewed as immoral by much of the borderland community, are a direct result of the way this money has been earned. "People here will make good money, very good money. And then, when the border closes, in two days, it is all gone. They earn the money in a haram way, and they spend it in a haram way—on girls, or on alcohol," one resident of Ben Guerdane, who himself quit smuggling some years ago, argues.[77] "This is not honest work, so God will not make *baraka* with that," a vendor in Oujda's Souk Melilla says, referencing a concept (blessing) commonly employed in this context. "I may make money, but it may affect someone I marry, or it might affect my son, it might give him an illness, or a drug addiction, I may be rich but I will lack inner peace."[78] It is not clear, however, that these beliefs have strong regulatory effects on smuggling networks so far—there are no indications that even smugglers involved in the drug trade are socially ostracized, or that they find themselves in a tricky position on the marriage market. They are likely to affect personal choices in activities—but, as emphasized earlier, the available choices are often perceived as limited.

An illustrative case study for the normative framing of smuggling can be found in the memorandum of understanding that outlined the agreement on the border procedure at the Ras Jedir border crossing in early 2017. As mentioned in the previous chapter, the document that was negotiated between local political, military, and civil society actors on both sides of the border represents one of the few written versions of an otherwise largely unwritten agreement. It is interesting to note that the text of the agreement itself is very cautious about its legitimacy, stating that it "puts forward exceptional solutions to some of the problems that are faced by travellers and trade movements on all sides, without entrance of the official side of any party in the commitments or measures contrary to the law or international agreements . . . without proceeding to hurt the national sovereignty of both countries."[79] Its authors are careful to point out that the process by which this has been agreed upon, without the official sanction of the Tunisian state, is not ideal, but they situate it in what approximates a "state of exception," noting the particular political circumstances in both countries.[80] While one of its authors argues that the fact that they are the ones who negotiated the agreement with municipalities in Libya, a feat that the formal diplomatic channels were unable to achieve, does give them certain rights to determine the procedures.[81] Another argues that "for the accord to gain legitimacy, we need the state."[82] There is, then, even among the authors of the agreement, no unanimity on the legitimizing role that only the state can or should play in this context.[83] While the agreement references the historical relationship between the two countries in its preamble, which is described as "eternal" and "inherited from our ancestors," as well as the nations' shared "religion, race, and language," it does not draw on this as a source of legitimacy or specific normative order that explicitly outweighs or challenges that of the state.[84]

Naturally, the perspective of the authors of the agreement is not necessarily the same as that of most of the traders operating under it. When talking to local smugglers about the agreement, its evaluation was rarely connected to its relationship with the state or the formal legal system. Instead, many noted that the agreement was preferable to the situation before, but still only positive in the context of a lack of alternatives. "Obligée," one large-scale wholesale smuggler told me—"we are obliged to work with this, what else is there?"[85] "It's okay... but it's a galley" said another.[86] "It's only good because there is no alternative," said a third, before voicing a common complaint about the agreement: "Is it good to pay money, and to get nothing in exchange? No."[87]

As in the discussions of informal regulation more widely, references to livelihoods and social justice also frequently came up in evaluations of the agreement, referencing the lack of alternatives for many traders. Some traders expressed concern about the fact that the Ras Jedir agreement specifies a unit price rather than a percentage price, hence benefiting those who import larger quantities. Similarly, there is an acute awareness that some of the very large players may have options to trade outside of the agreement: "There is always an option for the big ones, and an option for the small ones, and for the small ones it is always bad. The poor ones always suffer," a gasoline trader from Ben Guerdane commented.[88] As discussed earlier, there are some general disagreements on the legitimacy of security forces extracting resources from the trade at all.

Once more, discussions of livelihoods also closely connected with the issue of indignity and notions of decent work. Every smuggler in Tunisia has a story of mistreatment by Libyan customs officials or militias manning checkpoints along the way, stories of verbal and physical abuse and humiliation. "They do things beyond the laws of humanity," one Tunisian trader complained about a militia manning checkpoints in Libya.[89] This theme echoes across the different cases studied here. Despite the regularity of much of the trade, there is still a significant element of violence and indiscriminate harassment experienced by traders, introducing an element of physical and financial insecurity fundamentally at odds with how people locally imagine decent work, or more widely, *karama*, or dignity.

This section has noted a diversity in the moral evaluations of smuggling in the borderlands, structured around evaluations of goods, of the permissibility of breaking the law, and the lack of alternatives or right to livelihoods. At least based on the conversations that this project draws on, moral evaluations of smuggling in the borderlands appear to fall not only on a "religious" versus "less religious" scale, but on a multidimensional spectrum as people navigate the complex terrains between formal state laws, informal arrangements, religious laws, and moral perceptions.

Neither the uneasy position of much of the smuggling economy in local moral perceptions nor the terms on which they are typically justified support the idea that smuggling or the institutions that regulate it are deeply embedded in local norms or necessarily seen as legitimate, even by those participating in them. Local traditions of trade, tribal identities, and pan-Islamic or jihadi identities are rarely evoked in these discussions, which more commonly frame smuggling as a way of making do in the absence of alternatives. Here, religion is primarily pointed to as a moral system that permits or doesn't permit certain acts or types of smuggling, but not as one that demands it, perhaps to avoid or subvert an insufficiently religious state.

In these conversations, smuggling is generally not framed as an act of rebellion, resistance, or political subversion against the state. There is an awareness of confrontation with the state as a feature of smuggling, for example, in the descriptions of the gasoline transporters in Morocco as *muqatila* (fighter), and some of the frustrations with the role of state security services as bandits. As discussed earlier, however, this confrontation is directly connected to narratives of being forced to smuggle due to a lack of alternatives, and hence to state neglect rather than subversion.

Consequentially, this suggests that where hybrid institutions exist around the regulation of smuggling—as discussed in the first half of this chapter—they should be conceptualized primarily as functional hybrids. While they contain combinations of formal and informal institutions, this section strongly suggests that the informal institutions that these hybrids connect to (as well as the informal institutions that regulate smuggling at the border) are not primarily a feature or construction of local norms.[90] Local normative systems are grappling and engaging with smuggling, influencing choices and perceptions, but they do not present themselves, at least discursively, as its primary driver. The regulation of smuggling, therefore, cannot be conceptualized as states engaging in institutional compromises with bottom-up local traditions of smuggling in a more traditional image of "hybrid governance." Instead, the concepts that anchor local perceptions of smuggling point less toward local norms and more toward a reaction and coping with the uneven economic geographies and political power structures created by the region's states themselves.

WHAT DRIVES REGULATION?

This chapter has reviewed the institutionalized structures that regulate the sale of licit smuggled goods in Morocco and Tunisia, as well as some of the central themes in the relationship between smuggling and local moral and religious beliefs. Together with the previous chapter, it has once again emphasized that smuggling in North Africa is neither unregulated nor typically occurring under the radar of the state. Instead, it is closely embedded in a range of informal and hybrid institutions, which segment the trade depending on different categories of goods, influence its costs and access, and allow various actors to extract revenue. Not only does this frequently rely on the official or unofficial toleration or even active participation by state agents, but it also has created points of contact and negotiation between state organs and traders.

In tracing these institutions, these chapters have provided the first step toward a political economy analysis of smuggling and state-building in North Africa. They have highlighted that the existing regulatory structures around smuggling suggest a less simplistically adversarial relationship between state structures and smuggling networks than is frequently assumed. Instead, they have pointed toward some of the central mechanisms through which smuggling is controlled and through which rents are generated and distributed, and toward some of the actors involved. As a result, novel questions have emerged.

If the informal institutions in these structures are not driven by local norms or traditions, what are they driven by? Why do state institutions tolerate and engage in these institutions, at times even without taking any bribes? Why do borderland populations accept them, given their rather contested position in local religious and moral understandings? What drives the way in which these institutions segment between different goods? How are these institutions maintained and negotiated, and which actors can influence and benefit from this process? And finally, how should they be understood in the context of state-building? The next chapter will begin to address these points by focusing on the rents generated through smuggling and its regulation.

Chapter Five

SMUGGLING RENTS AND SOCIAL PEACE

Sometimes, it is the law that secures the social peace. But here, we have a special situation. Here, it has never been just the law that secured this.

—SENIOR MUNICIPAL BUREAUCRAT, BEN GUERDANE, 2017

While the previous two chapters have mapped and analyzed the regulation of smuggling in North Africa, this chapter seeks to understand its function. In other words, it seeks to answer the question why regulated smuggling exists, and why the various actors involved continue to engage in it. To do this, the chapter traces the rent streams that are generated through North Africa's regulated smuggling economies, alongside the groups among which they are allocated. This allows a discussion of the questions raised in the previous chapters and an opportunity to advance this book's main argument on the relationship between smuggling and state-building.

The previous two chapters have noted the central role of state agents in the regulation of smuggling. At the same time, the systematic nature of their involvement has complicated simplistic images of individual corrupt members of security services as primary causes of the region's smuggling economies. Notably, these chapters have even pointed to interactions between smuggling and state agents in which illegal activities were tolerated but no bribes were paid at all, such as in the case of roadside gasoline stations or small-scale smugglers operating on the Algerian border. This begs the question of why state agents are participating—systematically—in the regulation of smuggling. The same can be asked of borderland populations, as the previous chapter has argued that local popular norms are unlikely to have been key drivers behind the regulatory structures that surround the region's smuggling economies. Both point to a deeper question of what or who drives and structures smuggling in North Africa.

This chapter answers these questions in three sections. First, it discusses the different rent streams that are directed toward different state actors, differentiating between security services, and municipalities. It highlights that while both sets of actors have extracted substantial rent streams from the smuggling economy, this is not their only or even primary reason for engaging with it, as they cautiously balance extraction with maintaining rents to borderland populations. The second section discusses the rent streams that have been directed toward nonstate actors, differentiating between elite networks and the broader borderland population. It argues that maintaining accessible survivalist rent streams for broad sections of the borderland population is the primary political function of the smuggling economy and explains both its toleration and much about the precise nature of its regulation.

The chapter's final section connects these observations to the book's wider theoretical questions. Sketching the role of smuggling in North Africa's political settlements, it argues that smuggling does not undermine the region's states. Instead, through the provision of income to borderland populations bereft of meaningful formal development, smuggling economies have been essential to maintaining the congruence between the balance of power and the distribution of resources between the political center and the periphery, thereby acting as a stabilizing element not just for the ruling regimes, but also for the formal institutional structure and the distribution of formal rent streams. It notes that the common characterization of postindependence citizen-state relationships in the region as an authoritarian bargain is incomplete unless it is accompanied by a description of another arrangement in the periphery: an informal authoritarian bargain.

As mentioned before, rent streams and political settlements shift and transform. I sketch a temporal context for the rent streams I am describing, using more recent data wherever possible. This chapter discusses both case studies together, drawing on variation whenever relevant and illustrative.

RENTS TO STATE ACTORS

Are state actors primarily engaging in the regulation of smuggling because they are getting access to its rent streams? Speaking of rent streams to state actors involves multiple conceptual difficulties. First, the state does not always present itself as a unitary actor. Different organs—the police force, municipalities, ministries—might play occasionally contradictory roles, which this section aims to address by discussing them separately. Second, there is a notable difference between state actors as individuals and as members of a state body. In the case of "classical" corruption, rent streams are directed to the private accounts of individuals, linked to their position within a state structure. Here, the rent is not collected by the state agency, but by the agent. If corruption is systemic, however, this becomes more difficult to separate. If interior ministries are able to pay very low salaries to police because there is an expectation that they will be able to top up these salaries through bribes, the agency is involved more directly.[1]

This section argues that while some rent income is or has been directed toward individuals working for the state and mirrors more individual corruption, rent income from the illegal trade of licit goods is generally highly systematic and needs to be conceptualized by examining structures and organs of the state, rather than individual agents. It notes that varying interests and jurisdictions of different state organs with respect to smuggling have allowed a segmentation of responsibilities that has facilitated the creation of spaces of toleration and hybridity. Crucially, this section argues that while state agents have benefited financially from the trade, they can be observed to balance rent extraction with other considerations, particularly the maintenance of stability and social peace in the borderlands. Rent therefore does not seem to be the primary reason that state actors have engaged in the regulation of this trade and continue to do so.

Security Services

Defying the caricatured conceptions of Tunisia's and Morocco's borderlands as lawless spaces, members of state security services—police, military, national guard, and customs—are highly visible and present in both. For some, being assigned to the border areas can be a highly lucrative position. There are stories of officers throwing a party once they found out they were assigned to Ben Guerdane.[2] In both the ability to extract rents and their regulatory roles, however, there are also differences between different security services and between the case studies.

SMUGGLING RENTS AND SOCIAL PEACE

In both countries, government forces usually extract rent through the setting up of checkpoints along common routes on which smuggled goods are transported, eliciting a bribe for their passing. This is not limited to the police but also includes the (Tunisian) National Guard and customs agents, although police checkpoints appear to dominate.[3] This has at times led to a mushrooming of road checkpoints in the borderlands. In 2017 four different checkpoints could be observed on the road between Ben Guerdane and Ras Jedir, with a fifth just outside Ben Guerdane on the road to Zarzis. A Moroccan smuggler claimed to have counted even more on the small strip between Sidi Yahia and the Algerian border when the trade was booming in the early 2000s.[4] In Oujda, a formal entrepreneur complained that moving legally produced goods to Rabat was hugely difficult because police and customs officers along the road had begun to assume that all goods that were coming in from the Northeast were contraband.[5]

Locals generally noted the purpose of these checkpoints to be the extraction of rent from the smuggling trade. "They are not here for security, they just check your papers and ask for money," one resident of the Tunisian borderlands remarked: "It's a good place for them to work."[6] The rents here can be highly significant. A transporter moving contraband gasoline from Ben Guerdane to Djerba in early 2017, for example, would buy 20 liters of Libyan gasoline from a local wholesaler for around 10.5 TND, being able to sell it in Djerba for about 17 TND. As noted in the previous chapter, of the 6.5 TND profit, approximately 4 TND would have to be paid to the police checkpoint at the entrance to Djerba—almost a quarter of the final retail price, and a percentage that increases with the distance from the border, as transporters have to pass additional checkpoints.

Outside of checkpoints, there are occasional reports of police collecting sporadic bribes from roadside gasoline stations, especially in Morocco, but many vendors reported not having to pay any bribes to the police. Police forces often appeared to be careful and restrained in eliciting bribes from illegal survivalist activities. "The police tell you: when you have something to work, work, but don't make any trouble" a former Moroccan drug smuggler noted. "For the police, the most important thing is stability. They want no killings, no trouble, no violence."[7]

Across both case studies, this has typically been interpreted as officers balancing rent extraction with an interest in maintaining the social peace in the borderlands—which includes limiting their own exposure to a potential violent uprising or retaliation. Some of the other state actors in the borderlands echoed this sentiment when discussing their cooperation with local police forces: "Our goal is to fight contraband, the goal of the police is only security," a high official in the Moroccan customs complained.[8] Municipal officials in Tunisia complained that the police prioritize stability over law enforcement and are unhelpful in supporting formalization activities, or actively sabotage them.[9] In the words of a high-level bureaucrat in Ben Guerdane: "The police, however, only want things to stay quiet and stable, they don't care about the law."[10]

The role and importance of the military differ somewhat between Tunisia and Morocco. In Morocco the military has played a crucial role in securing the country's closed land border with Algeria. As discussed in chapter 3, Moroccan soldiers and their Algerian counterparts played a key role as coordinators, mediators, and screeners both at the regular meeting points for gasoline smugglers and at the gates across the border. The rent extracted here has been highly significant: while Moroccan soldiers largely stopped taking bribes from small-scale traders in 2010, they still collected them from large-scale traders, or traders operating in higher-value goods such as cigarettes. Gasoline smugglers report that the standard bribe per canister of contraband gasoline was 5Dh—a single wholesale trader would often move hundreds of canisters in a given night.[11] Similarly, transporting smuggled cigarettes through one of the gates manned with four soldiers could cost a smuggler up to 800Dh in total.[12]

Corresponding to the generally more marginal role of the military in Tunisian politics and security, which is traditionally dominated by the Ministry of Interior, Tunisian soldiers had long played a comparatively marginal role in Tunisian border security.[13] In recent years, however, and especially since the establishment of a militarized zone in southern Tunisia in 2013, their role has expanded. The trade that occurs through the territory controlled by the military is limited to those traders who have chosen to circumvent the smuggling structures through the border crossings. Based on the reports of smugglers operating in this area, their interaction with the military does not appear to be that different from their interaction with customs agents—they try to evade them whenever possible but are typically able to bribe them when they get caught.[14] As chapters 8 and 9 will highlight, new border infrastructure has made these routes more complicated.

SMUGGLING RENTS AND SOCIAL PEACE

In both Tunisia and Morocco, customs agents are and have long been among the most visible and active security forces to interact with smuggling networks. In Tunisia, they are typically involved in the misregistering of goods smuggled into the country and demand a fee from smugglers, generally in accordance with locally negotiated agreements, as discussed in chapter 3. A smuggler importing 10,000 TND worth of goods in early 2017 would pay 300 TND, approximately 3 percent of the goods' total value. Of the money collected from the smugglers, some of it is officially logged and hence directed toward the state's tariff income, while the rest is privately distributed among the customs agents. The distribution of this rent between state coffers and customs agents seems to have fluctuated with the different agreements that have been in force at the border crossing.

Particularly through their influence on which kinds of goods can be imported informally through the general agreement and which goods require additional payments or a particular relationship, customs officers are commonly situated directly between local smugglers and the interests of the central government or the formal business community. In this role, similar to police officers, there are references to customs officers not just extracting rents but also considering social stability in the borderlands. Indications of this come from a researcher who has run workshops with customs officers, describing their role as a "balancing act," and from smugglers themselves, with one large-scale wholesale smuggler from Ben Guerdane noting: "The customs are okay with all this, because they only want that it's calm."[15]

In Morocco, too, up until 2020 most bribes paid by smugglers operating through border crossings around the enclaves of Melilla and Ceuta were collected by customs agents. While the exact amount depended on the value of goods and the interlocutor, as discussed in chapter 3, the resulting amounts were highly significant. A fabric trader operating out of Oujda's Souk Melilla, for example, told me that if he was smuggling 1,000 euros worth of fabrics in 2017, he would typically pay a bribe of between 500 and 800 MAD, or 4–7 percent of the total value.[16] Although this may vary by goods, given that Castro and Alonso estimate that 332 million euros worth of licit goods were smuggled from Melilla to Morocco in 2007, this suggests that the overall size of rents collected by customs officers has long been a significant sum.[17] Contrary to the Tunisian case, Moroccan customs officers did not appear to use road checkpoints as opportunities to generate rents. Officers regularly checked cars along the roads for contraband, hailing from both Melilla and Algeria, and still do, but full legal fines and confiscations appear to have been more common than bribery here.[18]

Like all the security forces discussed in this section, Morocco's customs officers also appear to have balanced their rent-extraction activities with a concern for local stability and social pressure in the borderlands. At roughly the same time at which Moroccan soldiers stopped taking bribes from small-scale smugglers operating across the border with Algeria, Moroccan customs officials seem to have also stopped taking bribes from the small-scale independent smugglers operating through the Beni Ensar crossing with Melilla. A high official within the regional customs office confirmed that there was an effort to take some pressure off the "contraband viviere" due to its role in the local social fabric and the lack of alternative employment opportunities.[19]

This section has largely focused on rent streams generated through institutionalized arrangements. From a rentier perspective, it is worth noting that the existence of clearly communicated arrangements and standardized bribes—as outlined in chapter 3—is in fact likely a profit-maximizing strategy for customs officers. On the borders studied here where smuggling occurs through ports of entry, smuggled volumes have often been huge but typically transported in small units. Individual negotiations about bribe levels would hence slow down the trade and limit the number of traders from whom bribes can be extracted. At the same time, the limitation of these agreements to certain goods opens up opportunities for further—negotiated—illicit arrangements, "off the menu," so to say, for traders who can pay more.

It is worth noting that for perhaps all security forces discussed here, some rents have always likely flown through corrupt arrangements that have been individually negotiated outside of these institutions. While these are less systematic, some of them may explicitly build on political connections. In Tunisia, the extended family of former president Ben Ali, as well as his wife Leila Trabelsi, made a significant effort to insert themselves into the smuggling networks with Libya in the early 2000s.[20] Their connection to customs officials appears to have been crucial, as goods owned by the Trabelsis or their local collaborators would be waved through without control, fee, or question. It is, unclear however, how beneficial this arrangement was for local customs officers, and if it included a more centralized and direct rent stream through side payments by the Trabelsis. While the Trabelsi family has largely disappeared from Tunis with the 2011 revolution, networks of beneficial access, including some with connections high within the Tunisian state, are repeatedly mentioned by smugglers, politicians, and civil society actors.[21]

Municipalities

Apart from the security services, local municipalities are a central actor capitalizing on rent streams from the smuggling economy. Chapter 4 discussed how municipalities in both Morocco and Tunisia have managed to tax the distribution chains of smuggling networks trading in licit goods. This section demonstrates that rents derived from taxing informal rent streams have long been and still are a significant part of the municipal income in both Oujda and Ben Guerdane, giving municipalities a strong incentive to tolerate and organize the distribution networks of local smuggling economies. An expanding literature on taxation and informality has highlighted that this is not an unconventional relationship between local state authorities and informal economies.[22]

As in the case of the security services, there are also indications that municipalities balance rent incomes with an interest in maintaining social stability. At the same time, their rent extraction differs from that of the security services in notable ways. First, while security services extract rents at points where traders were moving, such as border crossings and road checkpoints, municipalities extract rents at points where traders are stationary, such as markets and roadside stalls. Second, the rent stream from informal cross-border trade to the municipalities examined here appears almost exclusively directed toward the municipalities as organizations rather than to the personal income of individual municipal agents, with some exceptions. Third, and again in contrast to security services, the strategies of municipalities need to be understood in the context of a traditionally weak actor within the national political structures of Tunisia and Morocco.

In Ben Guerdane, the Souk Maghrebi stands at the center of the municipality's income generation. Prior to 2011, the municipality received both payments from the vendors for each stall and fees from the receipts that they sold in order to allow customers an easier passage through the police checkpoints on the road.²³ In 2010, for example, the municipality made 215,000 TND off the market, 104,000 from the stalls, and 111,000 from the fees. The year before, they had made 347,000 TND off the market, 172,000 from the stalls, and 175,000 from fees.²⁴ While this may not immediately sound like a lot, it represented, respectively, 11.3 percent and 17.9 percent of the entire municipal budget.²⁵ It is worth noting that both 2009 and 2010 were not particularly good years for the market—a municipal official remembered that in the early 1990s the municipal income from the market was as high as 1.05 million TND, making up 60 percent of the municipal budget.²⁶

While the Souk Maghrebi represents the largest portion of the municipality's income from the smuggling trade, it also collected fees from other informal traders throughout the city, typically for the use of public space. In my conversations with municipal bureaucrats, they have been very clear and explicit about the fact that the municipality is dependent on directly taxing smuggling networks. When the events following the 2011 revolution threw the municipality's ability to tax the vendors in the market into question (see subsequent chapters), one of the alternatives discussed internally was, in fact, to start taxing the cars at the border crossing directly—to essentially set up their own checkpoint.²⁷

In Oujda, too, rent streams from the smuggling economy primarily reached the budget of the municipality through tax and rent income from the markets in which most of these goods were sold, most notably the Souk Melilla and the Souk Tanger, alongside the fees it collects from roadside vendors.²⁸ In 2017 the vendors in the Souk Melilla paid a monthly fee of 200 MAD to the municipality, adding up to a total yearly income of 2.6 MAD.²⁹ Vendors in the Souk Tanger paid a yearly fee of 504 MAD, adding up to a total yearly income for the municipality of over 268,000 MAD. The revision in 2008 of the law that allowed the municipality to directly collect fees from roadside vendors closed another significant rent stream, representing, in judgment of a senior municipal official, "an important loss for the municipality."³⁰

While these rent streams are highly significant for the municipal budgets of both Ben Guerdane and Oujda, the extent of the fees extracted from the vendors and conversations with a wide variety of municipal bureaucrats in both localities suggest that maximizing income is not the only consideration in how municipalities extract rents from smuggling networks. The stall fees that the municipality of Oujda and Ben Guerdane are charging are relatively small; when owners sublet the stalls to other vendors, the fees they charge, reflecting the market value of the property, are typically substantially higher.[31]

Municipal bureaucrats with a variety of ranks and responsibilities in both cities highlighted in interviews that their extraction of taxes and fees from the smuggling networks needs to be carefully balanced against concerns about social stability. A high official in Oujda's tax office highlighted the "security aspect" they needed to consider when deciding how and when to enforce the tax code, concluding that "this absorbs the rage and the unemployment . . . we are buying social peace."[32] In the words of one of his colleagues in the regional tax administration: "We cannot make these things disappear, and we cannot fight against them. The goal of the state is to stabilize, with our capacities."[33] The mayor of Oujda highlighted a similar point when I spoke to him: "We are afraid of the vendors, because there are things happening now, like with the Arab Spring, and you have to remember we are in a border region here. We have to build something here, or there will be trouble. So instead of forbidding it, we have tried to organize it a little bit."[34] In the words of a former high-level bureaucrat from Nador: "This is how this region lives. We tolerate this because there is also a social side to this. There are always protests, but there is a social side. Even the state cannot go against it. There is a security and a humanitarian side to this. This is a bomb that we cannot touch."[35] Their colleagues in Tunisia echoed a similar sentiment. Notably, the municipality of Ben Guerdane continued to support the market's cleaning and sanitation even once it became unable to extract any income from the Souk Maghrebi after 2011, as chapter 6 will discuss.

It is important to highlight here that within the state structures of Tunisia and Morocco, both pre- and post-2011, municipalities are relatively weak political actors. Despite recent decentralization programs, both countries have maintained centralized political systems.[36] Even in the context of engaging with the local smuggling economy, both the municipality of Oujda and the municipality of Ben Guerdane can be observed to have repeatedly been sidelined. In Ben Guerdane, the absence of an elected municipal council after the revolution further weakened the municipality. The process through which multiple agreements for the procedure at the Ras Jedir border crossing were negotiated between 2011 and 2017 included Libyan municipalities as well as multiple actors from the Tunisian state and civil society, but not the municipality of Ben Guerdane. Negotiators of the agreement generally referred to the municipality as "only administrative" and irrelevant.[37] This appears to have changed somewhat with the municipal elections in 2018, with disputes around the rules at the border crossing increasingly also occupying the newly formed municipal council.

While before the 2011 revolution in Tunisia the municipality was strongly perceived as a vehicle through which the ruling party exerted power, it was left without a clear political mandate and executive power in the years between 2011 and 2018. Municipal bureaucrats complained about endless delays as they had to run projects past Tunis. One municipal bureaucrat even went as far as claiming: "We are not the state, we are the municipality! The state is different. That's the central state."[38] It seems that when they attempted to take over Ben Guerdane in 2016, Islamic State fighters agreed with that assessment: while they attacked the office of the "Delegation," the local representation of the central state apparatus, they did not attack the municipality just across the street.

The dynamic in Oujda is similar. The budgets of Morocco's municipalities are relatively small and generally deal with the day-to-day management of communal activities, leaving little room for investment or larger projects. Investment typically comes from the regional level, or from development agencies like the Agence Oriental, which are closely tied to the political center.[39] While the municipality plays an important role in the day-to-day management of the Souk Melilla or Souk Tanger, the creation of these markets involved more direct investments from the regional level. In conversations with influential smugglers, the municipality very rarely comes up as a crucial interlocutor with the state. Instead, the local representatives of Morocco's centralized executive—the *qā'id*, and, most important, the *walī*—are the more active players here.

It follows that while rent streams from the smuggling economy to the municipalities in the borderlands of Tunisia and Morocco are of clear significance to municipal budgets, it is unlikely that the central features of state policy toward smuggling economies are formulated at a municipal level, or that the widespread toleration of smuggling in the borderlands of Tunisia and Morocco can be explained primarily through the contribution they make to municipal budgets. Instead, the instruments developed by local municipalities to organize and tax local smuggling networks are better conceptualized as adaptation strategies of a weak but locally embedded state actor. These, in turn, are tolerated by the central state in the context of its wider engagement with the smuggling economy and provide an informal replacement to more state funding for local governance.

Other States

This chapter focuses on the rent streams created and distributed in Tunisia and Morocco, and the two countries' political settlements. Still, in order to conclude the discussion of rents distributed to state actors, some mention should be made of the rent streams accrued by state actors foreign to those two countries. I will briefly review the key foreign state actors who benefit from this trade, while primarily asking whether these actors would be able to exert such a significant influence within the Moroccan or Tunisian state that they may provide an alternative explanation for the toleration and regulation of smuggling in these states.

The small Spanish enclave of Melilla has in many respects been a large profiteer of the smuggling economy across its border with Morocco. While the traffic at its border crossings is a nuisance in terms of clogging up roads, it is largely cordoned off from the rest of the city. There have been no indications of Spanish security forces taking systematic bribes from the trade in licit goods, but the introduction of frequent rotations of the police stationed in Melilla gives some support to suggestions that particular individuals in the security services may have been implicated in the trade in illicit goods.[40]

More important, there are multiple channels through which the city administration of Melilla has long benefited financially from the smuggling economy, mirroring what Igué and Soule in their analysis of Benin termed the "entrepot state."[41] First, while Melilla is a free port, the city still collects a small tax from the goods imported through its port, the IPSIE. If, as Castro and Alonso estimate, approximately half of the goods imported to Melilla are directed toward the smuggling economy, this suggests that it is responsible for a significant amount of Melilla's IPSIE income, in addition to the tax paid by the wholesalers and warehouse owners in Melilla, the tax paid by the supermarkets and stores through which some of the smaller traders supply themselves, and the tax paid by the various business activities through which money made in the illicit trade is recycled in Melilla.[42]

However, it is questionable how important these incomes are for the administration of Melilla. Due to its strategic importance for Spain, Melilla is largely supported through fiscal transfers from the mainland, which would likely make up for any budget shortfall created through decreases in IPSIE income.[43] The income generated by the IPSIE does not appear to be a priority for Melilla's administration—Spanish customs officials pointed to the fact that very little effort is made to adequately control, calculate, and enforce IPSIE payments in the port of Melilla, and that under- and misreporting of imports are rampant.[44]

More important for the subject of this chapter, there are no indications that the administration of Melilla or individuals within it are in a position to strongly influence the Moroccan government in its position on the smuggling economy. On the contrary, recent development projects in northern Morocco, such as a new port project, have positioned Morocco more as a commercial rival to Melilla. Alongside the de facto closing of much of the smuggling through the formal border crossings—discussed in chapters 7 and 8—Morocco's policy toward these networks cannot primarily be explained through the division of rent streams within Melilla.

The division of the rent streams from the smuggling economy in Algeria is at least as complex as that in Tunisia and Morocco, and its full discussion goes beyond the scope and purpose of this book. While the role of Algeria will be discussed again in the following chapters, to account for it as a potential explanation for Morocco's policy toward its smuggling economy, it is important to highlight a few key elements of this dynamic.

As discussed in chapter 3, elements of the Algerian security services have benefited directly from the smuggling economy.[45] At the same time, the smuggling economy has presented a significant drain on Algeria's resources once state subsidies, especially on gasoline, became one of the principal drivers of the trade. Much of the crackdown on the smuggling economy from the Algerian side in the past decade, and its increase in security infrastructure along the Moroccan-Algerian border, can be interpreted in this context.[46] At the same time, the smuggling economy also created economic opportunities for the populations of Algeria's borderlands—a fact that the state administration seems to have been aware of. During the run-up to the legislative elections in May 2017 in Algeria, a slight relaxation of the crackdown on smuggling along the Algerian-Moroccan border could be observed, likely reflecting an attempt by Algerian authorities to temporarily improve economic conditions in their borderlands.

The developments along the Moroccan-Algerian land border have largely mirrored the tense political relationships between the two countries more generally, signified most visibly by the closure of the land border in 1994. While the cooperation between Moroccan and Algerian soldiers has clearly played a role in the regulation of the smuggling economy along this border, it appears highly unlikely that the explanation for the wider Moroccan policy toward smuggling can be found in the distribution of rent streams from the smuggling economy within Algeria.

The most complex case in the distribution of foreign rent streams is perhaps Libya. Under the Gadhafi regime, the toleration of certain illegal economic activities, including human trafficking and the smuggling of contraband goods, was widespread and connected to the regime's political objectives—key positions in the country's illegal trade networks were given as rewards to individuals or groups loyal to the regime.[47] While Libya was under sanctions, smuggling networks provided the country with sparse goods while also creating mechanisms for the convertibility between the two currencies.[48] Tribes allied with the Gadhafi regime also benefited from the smuggling economy. While representing a significant simplification, Ben Guerdane's largest tribe, the Twazine, has widely been perceived to have been allied with the Gaddafi regime prior to 2011, causing significant complications for Twazine traders in Libya after the dictator's fall.[49]

While smuggling networks have been a part of the rent distribution in Libya, the smuggling of subsidized goods to Tunisia—gasoline, but also olive oil and other consumer goods—also represents a significant financial shortfall on the side of the Libyan state, especially as Libya, a major oil producer, still imports large volumes of its refined gasoline due to a scarcity of domestic refineries. As will be discussed in chapters 6 and 8, this has led to repeated pressure against these smuggling networks on the Libyan side in recent years.

Already complex under the Gaddafi regime, Tunisia's relationship with Libya has become increasingly fragmented following the 2011 uprising and the development of multiple competing governments within Libya. As before 2011, negotiations between state actors have played a critical role in the procedures that regulated smuggling along the Tunisian-Libyan border, as specific interests and power balances between involved actors changed repeatedly. However, while this interaction is important and will be discussed at length in the following chapter, it contains conflicts and common interests but does not indicate that the interests on the Tunisian side are fundamentally driven by or subservient to the interests or power of actors on the Libyan side. There appears to be no indication that, at least before 2011, elements of the Tunisian state have been systematically and strategically tolerating the smuggling of licit goods in order to sustain rent streams to allied groups in Libya.

Beyond State Actors

This section has briefly reviewed some of the principal rent streams that direct income to state actors through the institutions that regulate smuggling economies in Tunisia and Morocco. While some state agents benefit personally from the trade through individualized patron-client relationships, a range of state organs have been shown to benefit more systematically, through systematic income boosts to large sections of their personnel, or through the direction of rent streams into formal budgets through formal and informal taxation.[50]

This section has also noted, however, that by themselves, these rent streams do not offer a complete or even sufficient explanation of how and why huge smuggling economies are tolerated and informally regulated by the two North African states. Instead, we find security personnel in both countries forgoing potential bribe incomes from certain parts of the local smuggling economy, while state actors interviewed for this project, on both a local and a national level, continuously emphasize the importance of the smuggling economy for the stability of the borderlands, and some actors, such as the regional-level administrations, involve themselves in the toleration and regulation of these economies without receiving any rent streams. It is hence important to look at the remaining rent streams—those directed to nonstate actors, to understand the dynamic at play in these borderlands.

RENTS TO NONSTATE ACTORS

Like state actors, nonstate actors are not a homogeneous group—borderlands are complex social spaces, and there are myriad ways to distinguish between rent streams to different groups, tribes, classes, and constituencies. In addition, rent streams to private actors are not restricted merely to actors in the borderlands. As chapter 4 noted, in the language in which locals speak of the smuggling economy, the "barons," "big fish," and "bosses" are often contrasted with the "little guys," the "ants," the "youth." While this dichotomy naturally presents a simplification, it points to the enormous variety in the opportunities for accumulation presented by different positions within the smuggling economy, depending on capital or connections, barriers to entry, limits to social mobility, and the fundamental conditions for class formation.

This section cannot map this diversity exhaustively but focuses on the role that rent streams to nonstate actors play for the state and its relationship with the smuggling economy. It distinguishes, somewhat simplistically, between the effects of rent streams that allow for large-scale accumulation and those of more survivalist rent streams. While the former primarily relate to the management of national and local elites, the latter relates to wider dynamics around employment and stability in the borderlands.

The section argues that rent streams channeled to nonstate actors, and particularly borderland populations, constitute a key incentive for the Moroccan and Tunisian state in tolerating large-scale smuggling economies. While some barriers to entry, as well as the effects of capital accumulation, have created an environment in which a few actors accumulate high rents, large portions of local smuggling economies are deliberately structured to make them highly labor-intensive and reserve certain sectors with very low barriers to entry, hence functioning as a creator of accessible survivalist employment in otherwise marginalized regions. I argue that it is in these activities where one of the smuggling economy's primary roles in the political settlements of Tunisia and Morocco can be found.

Smuggling Rents and Elite Accumulation

Social mobility within North Africa's border economies has fluctuated with periods of boom and bust. In both borderlands, those who have benefited most from the smuggling economy appear as a relatively diverse mix of actors who, at the right moment, had access to the right connections or capital to take advantage of the opportunities that changing trade structures and political environments provided. The biographies and politics of these actors are complex and deserve a study of their own. Focusing on the distribution of rents and their relevance for states, this section aims instead to highlight three points: First, the trade in both licit and illicit goods has led to significant accumulations of capital by some individuals. Second, across both case studies, these actors do not exhibit a systematic overlap with traditional local elites or novel political movements. And third, the role of the state in the regulation of smuggling has put many of these actors in a position of dependency vis-à-vis some state actors, particularly the security services.

In Ben Guerdane, smuggling has provided locals who had the connections or the capital to enter or expand the business under the right conditions with opportunities for the accumulation of substantial amounts of wealth. While some of these opportunities lie in the smuggling of illicit goods, not all smuggling of licit goods is survivalist. For some, the provision of informal financial services has been highly lucrative.[51] The construction of some of the large new warehouses along Ben Guerdane's wholesale markets of smuggled licit goods provides an indication of significant capital accumulation within this sector, especially in the immediate post-2011 years.

While it is difficult to ascertain a comprehensive overview of the different individuals who have been able to accumulate large amounts of capital from the smuggling economy, they do not appear to constitute a homogeneous group. They include younger traders and some who were able to expand their business in the immediate post-2011 period. They do not appear to overlap with the elders of the city's tribal groups, the authority of which has often been framed as waning and limited in its reach into the informal economy.[52]

While local stories commonly connect some of these individuals with clientelist links to figures within the state security apparatus, they do not generally appear as political actors, or as representing a local political trend or movement. The members of parliament from Ben Guerdane since the 2011 revolution, while not all strangers to the business, do not appear to have been important players in the smuggling economy but primarily maintain relationships with those traders who are also active in civil society organizations.[53]

As mentioned earlier, not all actors who were able to extract high profits from Ben Guerdane's smuggling economy were from the city, or even from Tunisia's South. Beginning in the early 2000s, the Ben Ali regime increasingly inserted members of the family of President Ben Ali, as well as his wife Leila Trabelsi, into many of the country's successful businesses.[54] This extended to the country's smuggling economy. While the Trabelsi family was particularly active in smuggling through the port of Rades as well as along the Tunisian-Algerian border, they also became increasingly involved in Ben Guerdane in the early 2000s, cooperating with a few large-scale smugglers, while also leveraging their relationships with the customs authorities in order to import goods unchecked and untaxed.[55]

In Morocco's Oriental, too, opportunities for more significant accumulation of capital through the rent streams generated by the smuggling economy exist within the trade of both licit and illicit goods. Here, too, economies of scale in the wholesale trade appear to provide significant opportunities to actors with capital: there are cases of informal gasoline and electronics traders, for example, who were able to accumulate enough capital to launch large and successful formal business ventures.[56] In contrast to the Tunisian case, there appears to be less accumulation within the informal financial sector, and more connected to the exports of narcotics out of Morocco, particularly cannabis.[57]

As in Tunisia, the group of beneficiaries from these larger accumulations appears as a diverse set of actors and do not appear to be typically associated with more traditional elite groups: local tribal elders or the local leadership of the region's dominant political parties of the postindependence years have not been associated with the smuggling economy in any of the conversations for this project. As in Tunisia, there are no indications that the larger rent streams resulting from the smuggling economy have given rise to a local political elite that aims to present a challenge to either the state, the monarchy, or the current regime.

In contrast to the Tunisian case, there are also no clear indications that there has been a strategic insertion of national-level elites into the local smuggling economy, but it is impossible to rule this out entirely. More recently, however, a number of local businessmen who are perceived to have their origin in the region's smuggling economy, in both licit and illicit goods, have sought direct political office at local, regional, and even national levels. Notably, the entrance of local businesspersons into municipal and regional politics in the Oriental has frequently been connected with the rise of the PAM, a party that is closely associated with the monarchy and the central state.[58] This connects directly to the next point.

The role of the state in the toleration and regulation of smuggling implies that actors who have been able to accumulate larger amounts of rents maintain a form of dependency on state actors, and particularly the security services. In interviews, political operatives in northern Morocco have highlighted the state's ability to exert legal pressure on local actors who have their origins in the smuggling economy, including those who have since taken a role in formal politics. In the words of a regional political operative: "The state knows how to handle them. If they get close to making any trouble, the state can always say, oh, look, we have this nice police dossier here, why don't we take a look at that?"[59] While there have so far been no incidents of politicians from the region facing legal charges for their involvement in the smuggling economy, arrests of actors connected to smuggling activities with high profit margins are not without precedent.[60]

The same is true in Tunisia, which has repeatedly seen both arrests of local smugglers who had been operating with high profit margins, as well as the confiscation of some of their capital. As will be discussed more fully in the following chapter, Brigade Antiterrorisme (BAT) special forces raided the houses of multiple of the large financiers of Ben Guerdane's smuggling economy in 2017. While this triggered some protest and outrage within the city, it demonstrated the continued capacity of the Tunisian state to selectively target local actors.

A full discussion of the capital accumulations created by the smuggling economy is beyond the scope of this book, but the observations outlined here—diversity, a limited overlap with traditional political elites or markers of identity in the periphery, an absence of oppositional political activism, and dependency on security services—do not suggest that these groups have so far presented a political challenge to state structures in the region. In a sense, their dependency mirrors the preferred economic elite of an authoritarian regime: as the Ottoman Empire or the early North African states preferred the emergence of Jewish or Christian merchant classes that presented a smaller political threat, so may the modern states of Tunisia and Morocco have looked at the emergence of a smuggling nouveau-riche with less concern than some of the public statements suggested.[61] It is important to highlight, however, that the majority of borderland actors involved in the smuggling economy operate on significantly smaller scales.

The Masses: Regulation, Rent, and Access

As previous chapters have highlighted, distinctive features of the regulation of the smuggling of licit goods in Tunisia and Morocco are both its impersonal nature and the organization of the trade in a way that makes it highly labor-intensive, as thousands of people line up in cars or on foot to bring small bundles through border bottlenecks. Neither of these is a necessary condition of the smuggling networks' economic activity, illegal status, and informal regulation—one could easily imagine an illegal wholesale import business that maintains continuously high barriers to entry and is not labor-intensive. Both capital accumulation for elites and rent extraction by security services would still be feasible. In fact, the smuggling networks operated by the Trabelsi family in Tunisia in the early 2000s provide a prime example of this.

And yet these features are essential to the smuggling economy's ability to maintain opportunities to make a living for even some of the least connected and educated members of the borderland population, especially its young men. This does not appear coincidental—the smuggling economy's role in "feeding the borderlands" is constantly cited in conversations with smugglers, civil society members, bureaucrats, and politicians. When describing his priorities, one of the key negotiators of the agreement regulating smuggling at Ras Jedir after 2011 noted: "We want there to be a system in which everyone makes enough."[62]

The necessity of providing accessible jobs and income to borderlands populations has crucially shaped the way that smuggling of licit goods in Tunisia and Morocco is organized and regulated. More important, it provides a compelling explanation of the key political functions of the trade and one of the central drivers behind its toleration and organization. To illustrate, this section points to four features of North Africa's smuggling economies that highlight this relationship.

First, while incumbent actors have been able to erect significant barriers to entry to certain sections of the local smuggling economy, especially in the trade in illicit goods, and defended their monopolies in these trades through monopolizing supply chains, cooperation with security forces, or simple use of violence, barriers to entry in multiple large-scale sectors of the smuggling economy across both borderlands have remained very low. While these sectors might still contain a diverse mix of actors and a range of profit margins, no particular connections, few skills, and very little capital are required to join them. This has allowed a wide range of local actors to gain access to rent streams generated by the smuggling economies. In both borderlands, the smuggling of gasoline is a case in point. While wholesalers who transport significantly larger quantities of contraband gasoline exist in both countries and may maintain larger profit margins, they have generally made no efforts to limit the arrival of new entrants—in the words of one Tunisian scholar, "they leave that for the little man."[63]

In Tunisia, capital barriers to opening up a roadside contraband gasoline station have been extremely low. While some of the larger wholesalers may pay around 400 TND per month for a little roadside garage, many of the smaller vendors pay no rent at all, relying instead on simple wooden structures, a funnel with a filter placed next to the road, and some jerrycans, which cost around 5 TND.[64] Accessing the supply network also requires no particular social capital, as contraband gasoline is provided through a large network of transporters, who bring the gasoline across the border and sell it to local vendors.[65] Larger actors, wholesalers, and traders operating multiple gasoline stations do not appear to try to limit their competition through aggressive pricing, but they do still enjoy commercial advantages by being able to stockpile larger quantities and speculate on supply shortages. One gasoline trader in Ben Guerdane noted: "In gasoline, the big guys can't bully out the little guys. But they can still buy a really big quantity, and if there is a problem at Ras Jedir, they sell it at a high price."[66] Working as a transporter—both of gasoline but also of small consumer goods that can be bought at markets in Libya—similarly requires no particular connections, although it does call for a higher level of either capital or connections, as it requires access to a car.

In Morocco, during the heyday of the gasoline trade, setting up a roadside station similarly came with no significant barriers to entry. There was some segmentation of barriers to entry to the transport of gasoline: becoming a gasoline wholesaler present at the larger exchanges of Moroccan and Algerian gasoline traders required particular personal connections alongside significant capital, but becoming a transporter between a wholesaler and the many roadside vendors required only few connections and access to a car. If there was no money for a car, some made do with little motorcycles. A transporter in a rural community outside of Oujda explained to me how he could transport eight gasoline canisters on his small motorbike, allowing him to transport more than 160 liters at a time.[67] In certain areas of the rural borderland, local populations were engaging in the gasoline trade through donkeys, mules, or even by carrying the jerry-cans across by hand, hence necessitating very little start-up capital, and still producing significant income for the transporters.[68]

Even more than the gasoline trade, joining the transporters across the border with Melilla provided an easily accessible income stream. While working as a small independent trader requires start-up capital, working as a transporter required none and no significant connections.[69]

Across both case studies, gasoline was not the only smuggling network without significant barriers to entry, which also included a variety of consumer goods, such as (some) textiles and clothes, small quantities of processed foodstuffs, or kitchen equipment. These networks retained a diffuse structure, containing many vendors, buyers, and transporters, despite the fact that they passed through only a few small points at the border, which would have been an ideal environment for a single actor to enforce a monopoly or take a gate-keeper function, transforming the network into either a complete downstream monopoly or a classical double-funnel structure. Here, the impersonal nature of the regulatory institutions discussed in chapter 3 is a crucial factor: by building impersonal structures rather than empowering gate-keepers, they help maintain a diffuse structure of the network and low barriers to entry.

The same institutions are also relevant to the second point. As described in chapter 3, many of the institutions at the borders contained regulations that limited the size of the container or vehicle that could be used to smuggle goods through these nodes, thereby ensuring that the transport of these goods remained hugely labor-intensive. As they only allowed foot-traffic through Melilla's Barrio Chino crossing, the amount of goods that could be brought through in one trip was limited by the carrying capacity of the transporters and the size of the turnstiles, creating a huge demand for transporters. Similarly, large cars were typically unable to pass through the gates in the border fence between Morocco and Algeria. The size of the cars that could be used to smuggle goods through the Ras Jedir border crossing was commonly an element of the agreement that regulated this trade. In 2014, for example, the agreement included a stipulation that only small cars were able to partake in the trade, excluding transporters and large trucks. So, while some traders would order whole containers to be shipped into the ports around Tripoli, the load would then be divided onto multiple cars, employing a large number of transporters in the process. When an agreement in force between January and March 2017 further reduced the amount of goods that could be smuggled in a single car, wholesalers reported hiring significantly larger numbers of the local youth as transporters.[70] Notably, when restrictions on the type of cars disappeared from the agreement in 2017, negotiators from Ben Guerdane pushed repeatedly for its reinstatement, with the explicit purpose of maintaining the activity as labor-intensive.[71]

This restriction connects to a third feature of the local smuggling economy that contributed to the creation of accessible rent streams for the local population: barriers to the geographic distribution of some of these rents. Unsurprisingly, the less impersonal elements of the smuggling economies, such as the trade outside of border crossings in southern Tunisia that required drivers knowledgeable of the local terrain, created advantages for the local population. Importantly, however, even the impersonal institutions that regulated this trade often contributed to a regulatory structure that imposed a particular geographical distribution to the spread of some rent streams, focusing them on the borderlands. A transporter working between Tunisia and Libya would spend an enormous amount of time standing in line at the border, making the job less accessible for someone living far from Tunisia's borderlands. The same applies for transporters bringing goods over by foot or by donkey in northern Morocco, and advantaged farmers in the rural borderlands, who had natural storage space in their farms in a beneficial position. As chapter 3 highlighted, a system of checkpoints and crackdowns on transport restricted the contraband gasoline trade, and some of the distribution centers for nonflammable consumer goods largely to the borderlands.

These restrictions, however, have been partial and fluid. While a Nador residency card was needed in order to work as a transporter in the smuggling across the Melilla border, for example, these cards can be easily bought in the villages around Nador, and by the early 2010s traders working there were by no means exclusively from Nador anymore.[72] The number of external traders in Ben Guerdane is still comparatively limited, but there are increasing reports of traders from outside of Ben Guerdane beginning to work in the Souk Maghrebi. More important, Tunisians from all regions participated in the "Khat," the trade route that transported smuggled goods from Ben Guerdane to markets across Tunisia.[73]

A fourth and final factor that ensures the openness of various smuggling activities to small-scale actors from the borderlands is that the extraction of rents by the security services does not primarily draw on small-scale survivalist activities. The institutions at the borders described in chapter 3 in particular frequently contain mechanisms that allow small-scale actors to pass through nodes without having to pay regular bribes or informal fees. When discussing these structures, traders frequently interpreted this as an attempt to take pressure off smaller, survivalist activities. Here, however, two caveats are in order. First, these "bribe exemptions" have waxed and waned—in Morocco, it seems to be as recent as 2010–2011. In addition, this is not to imply that smaller actors are never coerced into paying bribes by individuals within the security services or are free from harassment, arrest, dispossession, or the many brutalities that can be part of the daily lives of the powerless in an illegal economy.[74]

In both northern Morocco and southern Tunisia, the importance of smuggling economies for local populations is amplified by the absence of alternative opportunities for income generation. As noted in chapter 2, formal economic development has been limited in both regions—there is little industry or manufacturing, while, agriculture, a traditionally strong employment creator, has not expanded its employment opportunities in line with demographic changes. In 2011 Ben Guerdane, a city of more than sixty thousand inhabitants, provided fewer than nine hundred jobs in industry and manufacturing.[75] Ben Guerdane's labor inspector estimated that its Souk Maghrebi alone employs around three thousand people, and that the wider smuggling economy is the largest employer in the city—an assessment shared by Mohamed Haddar.[76] In the words of one of the leading officials in the regional employer's association, working in the smuggling economy in Ben Guerdane is "not a choice—it is a necessity."[77] A senior figure in the Souk Maghrebi association put it this way: "It's the only source of life."[78]

The situation in northern Morocco is similar—with a population of more than 1.5 million, the region's industry and manufacturing sectors employ less than nine thousand.[79] A regional government official in Oujda named four rural areas in which his administration had determined that the majority of young men had been working as transporters in smuggling networks: Beni Khaled, Ahl Angad, Ain Sfa, and Ain Beni Mathar—most likely missing a fifth crucial one, Beni Drar, and multiple smaller areas closer to Oujda.[80] An official in a regional development office in Oujda summed up the region's development experience: "It was always the informal economy who created all this, both in the days when the border was open and in the days when it was closed. Everything we have created and developed here is thanks to the informal economy."[81] Across both case studies, many of those who were not themselves working in the networks were benefiting from the income through family connections, or through the smuggling economy's linkages to the formal economy. One textile smuggler in Oujda explained, "I have a whole chain of people working for me; think of the people who drive the taxis, who carry the goods. The government is thinking: What other jobs could we get for these people?"[82]

This is crucial for the politics of smuggling in North Africa. The scarcity of formal employment opportunities in the borderlands of Tunisia and Morocco makes the continuation, toleration, and institutional regulation of a labor-intensive smuggling economy essential for the stability of the Tunisian and Moroccan states and the survival of their ruling regimes. As the section on state security services and municipalities already hinted at, the role of the smuggling economy in maintaining stability in the borderlands through employment generation was ever-present in almost all interviews with smugglers, politicians, bureaucrats, or civil society analysts.

A high-level municipal bureaucrat in Ben Guerdane summed it up like this:

> Sometimes it is the law that secures the social peace. But here, we have a special situation. Here, it has never been just the law that secured this. Here it was always Libya that provided for people. People turn to Libya first, and they only turn to the state second, if there are problems with Libya. Then they turn to the state—and here we are the state—to provide for them. And the state needs to provide, for stability. Think, if Ben Guerdane is not stable, that is also the state of [Prime Minister] Youssef Chahed that is not stable.[83]

An official in local development spelled this out further: "This is a border zone and they want stability. Social peace is more important than the enforcement of the law."[84]

A smuggler in Morocco quoted a conversation he had with the governor of the Oriental mirroring the same sentiment. Explaining his tolerance for the smuggling economy in the smuggler's village, the governor told him: "I'd rather have them be active in front of the border than in front of my office!"[85] A local associational leader found a different image: "This is only to calm these people. You have to give them something to eat. There is an old French proverb: governing in Morocco is like raining. If it doesn't rain, and the people have nothing to eat they will riot. And there is still that relationship."[86]

In both case studies, concerns about public unrest in the case of a collapse of the smuggling economy were frequently expressed. In Morocco in 2017, the common concern was "a second Hoceima," referring to the city on Morocco's northern coast that in late 2016 had erupted into monthlong protests after the death of an informal fish-vendor, triggering a political crisis, protests across the country, hundreds of arrests, and the resignation of multiple ministers.[87] In Tunisia, of course, the concern is not a second Hoceima, but, after 2011, "a second revolution."[88] And, after ISIS attacked Ben Guerdane in 2016, failing in their attempt to "liberate" the city partly due to the resistance of its population, a local large-scale smuggler mused: "The government is scared of Ben Guerdane. It is a hot place. If they try to close everything, the people will fight for ISIS next time."[89]

The fear that a collapse of smuggling economies' ability to provide employment and income to local populations would lead to large-scale unrests that could seriously destabilize borderlands provides a strong explanation both for states' toleration of these economies and the engagement in institutional structures that regulate the trade in a fashion that makes them both labor-intensive and accessible to the local population. The quotes in this section, therefore, provide a first direct indication of the role of smuggling in the political settlements of Tunisia and Morocco.

THE INFORMAL AUTHORITARIAN BARGAIN

This chapter has highlighted the diversity of actors benefiting from rent streams generated through the smuggling of licit goods in the borderlands of Tunisia and Morocco. This has allowed some first inferences on why different actors engage in these activities—or why state actors tolerate them. The importance of smuggling for the sustenance of the wider borderland population in the absence of sufficient formal development structures has already emerged as a critical dynamic, and one that is frequently overlooked in favor of popular narratives that focus on corruption as a key driver.

Tracing rents, however, not only contributes to tracing the incomes and interests of different actors but also helps to map how smuggling and its regulation shape the wider distribution of resources and resource-generating opportunities in the borderlands and beyond. Consequently, it provides an indication of where smuggling sits within the wider political settlements of Tunisia and Morocco. Deepening this provides a first answer to one of the larger questions of this book: Does smuggling in these borderlands undermine the states that have decided to tolerate and regulate it?

As discussed in chapter 1, political settlement approaches analyze stability and institutional performance as dependent on the congruence of (formal and informal) institutional structures, the distribution of resources, and the distribution of power.[90] In a political settlement framework, and in contrast to, for example, New Institutional Economics, informal institutions, even if they are in direct contradiction to formal institutions, do not necessarily undermine stability and development. Consequently, the existence of informal and hybrid regulation of smuggling that was outlined at length in chapters 3 and 4 is not in itself a decisive indication of smuggling's relationship to state-building. The key question, from this angle, is whether these institutions allocate rents in a way that brings the overall distribution of resources in line with the balance of power.

Khan describes a clientelist political settlement as a situation "when significant holding power is based on sources outside the incomes generated by formal institutions."[91] The stability of these settlements, then, depends on the ability of informal institutions to channel rent streams to those groups who do not benefit from the formal institutions relative to their holding power in order to keep them from defecting from the settlement. In scholarship on political settlements, this is commonly viewed in terms of informal "side payments" to elites who could otherwise act as spoilers. In the case of Tunisia and Morocco, both of which broadly fit the description of clientelist political settlements for most of their postindependence history, this logic is more commonly found in analyses of elite management or state-military relationships. Rather than evaluating the systematic breaking or subversion of the formal law by smugglers as a subversion of the state, a political settlement perspective invites an examination of whether the rent streams generated in this way are motivating actors to accept the wider political settlement, what kind of settlement this is, and whether all relevant actors could have been committed with rent streams from formal institutions alone.

As this chapter has noted, in both case sites, security services and municipalities as well as different elite groups have been able to benefit from the trade alongside significant portions of the borderland population. The rents extracted by local and national elites and by security services might fit the most classical conception of "side payments" within clientelist political settlements in developing countries, especially given the important position of security services in both countries.[92] This largely dovetails with the literature on the political economy and business-state relationships in Tunisia and Morocco, which has similarly highlighted the role of crony capitalists and well-connected families close to the ruling regime.[93]

At the same time, however, the chapter has highlighted not only that rents are distributed to elite groups but that a key element of the structure of regulatory institutions appears designed to provide an impersonal and relatively accessible informal rent stream to wide sections of the borderland populations. In the context of a political settlement analysis, these rent streams suggest a side payment to a larger group of the population that is relatively excluded from formal rent streams. Its impersonal nature and access structures here distinguish it from an individual-level patron-client relationship, likening it more to a form of broad-based clientelism like urban bias or geographically or industry-specific subsidies.[94]

More so than the interests of security services, local elites, or local norms, these rents provide a compelling driver not just of the toleration of the smuggling economy more widely, but also the structures of its institutional regulation. As this chapter has examined, members of security services, local state bureaucrats, and civil society actors all noted that their participation in the toleration and regulation of smuggling is also shaped by the concern that the absence of this rent stream to wide sections of the borderland population would likely trigger widespread unrest and severely threaten the ability of formal state institutions to continue functioning in the borderlands. In the context of a clientelist political settlement, the rents generated through the regulation of smuggling via impersonal informal institutions thereby provide an essential side payment to a group that would otherwise likely threaten the stability of the settlement itself: the borderland population.

Highlighting rents to borderland populations as an essential political function of smuggling economies provides an argument against one of the most popular claims about informal trade in the region: namely, that it is primarily caused by corruption among state enforcement agents. While security agents have been able to extract significant rents from smuggling economies, their extraction is balanced with concerns about the stability of the settlement as dependent on rents channeled to the wider borderland population—to the degree that we see cases of state agents not taking bribes at all. Even where it is substantial, it therefore does not provide a convincing explanation of the primary driver or primary political function of the tolerated and regulated smuggling economy. Similarly, the role of smuggling as an important stabilizing aspect within wider political settlements provides a powerful explanation for the continuity of the smuggling economy in the region, its often-observed persistence, and ability to adapt to change, to survive countless proclaimed "crackdowns," anticorruption campaigns, border walls, and civil wars. Here, its resilience is not rooted in its ability to hide itself, to escape the state, or to bend state policies to their will, but because in the borderlands, its continuity is fundamental to the stability of the political settlement as a whole and thereby also in the interest of actors who do not directly benefit from the distribution of rents.

This reading of smuggling in the Maghreb, then, built on the feature and function of the regulation of smuggling and the rents that emerge from it, does not support the common claim that it "undermines" the state. On the contrary, it suggests that it is a central part of the institutional structure on which the state itself rests and a feature of the form of state-building that these two states have pursued. While the regulation that structures smuggling in these locations stands in direct contradiction to the formal law, it has also become necessary for the maintenance of a distributional structure on which the effectiveness of that very formal law itself depends. The focus of formal state investment on the coastal centers in both countries, as noted in chapter 2, would have been more directly politically destabilizing in the absence of accompanying informal rent streams channeled to the periphery through smuggling economies. Here, the analysis connects to a common framing in the wider political economy literature of the region.

SMUGGLING RENTS AND SOCIAL PEACE

The idea of an "authoritarian bargain" has become a commonly used shorthand to describe the wider postindependence citizen-state relationships in much of the Middle East and North Africa. It describes a "sort of implicit deal between authoritarian regimes and politically significant groups to provide them with well-compensated jobs in the bureaucracy and the security forces, among other privileges such as access to subsidized commodities, housing and services, in exchange for political quiescence, if not loyalty."[95] While it typically makes some allowance for the role of corruption, especially in generating commercial opportunities for crony capitalists, the political economy scholarship on authoritarian bargains and social contracts in the region typically focuses on methods to channel rent streams and privileges that are rooted in formal institutions.[96] It also typically lacks a discussion of the geographic distribution of these rents and thereby remains fundamentally incomplete.

The analysis presented here offers a corrective to the traditional take on the authoritarian bargain, by suggesting that in the region's borderlands and economic periphery, there existed another, an *informal authoritarian*, bargain. It describes implicit arrangements between authoritarian regimes and a variety of groups in their political and economic periphery, to allow them to engage in technically illegal survivalist and accumulative activities such as smuggling, hawking, and the sale of contraband goods, in exchange for political quiescence and assistance with the provision of security. While the employment opportunities provided by informal and smuggling economies provide a certain complementarity to the provision of public-sector employment, the cheap goods provided through the smuggling economy provided a similar complementarity to the state provision of subsidized goods. These arguments are not limited to smuggling—the list of these activities could be expanded to include, among others, the cultivation and sale of cannabis in the case of Morocco and irregular migration to Europe in the case of both Tunisia and Morocco.

This is not to say that the economic periphery did not also benefit from the formal elements of the classical authoritarian bargain, but to highlight that the postindependence distribution of resources and opportunities across the region contained a highly uneven distribution of formal and informal rent streams. In addition, it is interesting to note that this uneven distribution related not only to rent streams that were accessible to the citizenry more widely but also to state institutions, as municipalities in the peripheries of Tunisia and Morocco also drew on informal and hybrid institutions to generate funds.

As noted in chapter 2, the geography of an uneven distribution of formal rents predates the modern structure of smuggling in the region as well as the postindependence political settlement. Both the Tunisian South and the Moroccan Northeast suffered intense political repression during the colonial era, alongside limited and primarily extractive economic development. Both regions also remained underrepresented among postindependence political elites, while finding themselves on the losing side of postindependence political conflicts, as much of Tunisia's southeastern borderlands supported the Youssefist uprising and successive revolts in Morocco's Rif Mountains provoked the scorn of King Hassan II.[97]

In both countries, state investments into formal-sector development remained highly uneven, overlapping with the geographic areas from which most of the political elites hailed, and unable to overcome the structural disadvantages of the economies of the periphery. As the postindependence development model concentrated formal state investment in coastal cities in both countries, the notion of "useless" ("inutile") regions became common parlance and is still widely cited in both regions.[98] This chronology is important in order to note that smuggling economies—at least in their modern structure—caused neither the clientelist national political settlement nor the borderlands' economic marginalization. Instead, they appear as a feature of the settlement that developed—and yet their role is not logically inevitable. A more geographically even division of formal rent streams and the development of an independent and competitive private sector might have similarly provided income to border regions. However, this would have implied a lower income, at least temporarily, for the main elites of the postindependence political settlements while also creating another business elite that could create a power base independent of the regime.

This suggests that the role of the political center in setting the structural conditions of the smuggling economy must be further examined. While the income channeled to borderland populations is essential for the stability of the political settlement, it does not follow that these populations themselves have demanded or engineered this particular mode of incorporation within the settlement. So far, the analysis provided does not indicate that North African states are being "remade" at their borders through the bottom-up order-making of local smuggling economies, as has been suggested in other regions.[99] Neither does it appear that local elites or corrupt local state agents have forced this arrangement on national-level elites, nor that a more authentic, historically or locally embedded form of order is emerging out of local traditions, tribal structures, or moral conceptions. While state agents and institutions point to constraints to their actions through the risk of local mobilization and unrest, smugglers themselves frequently note the control that remains with the central state, both in its economic choices and in its ability to control and change existing arrangements through arrests and confiscations. Both positions connect directly to a longstanding debate about whether informal and illicit economies and the incomes generated by them primarily constitute a "weapon of the weak" outside of the regulation of the state or a "weapon of the strong" in which elites can instrumentalize disorder to enrich themselves.[100]

While this section has laid out the first part of the book's answer to the question of whether smuggling subverts the states of the Maghreb, it also provokes new questions. Does the fact that the population of the borderlands has received rent streams in the context of the national political settlement imply that they are included in it, in any real sense of the word, or does this require additional power over the architecture of the settlement? What happens if the settlement or the underlying distribution of power changes, if the state is either unable to continue the distribution of rents through the smuggling economy or refuses to do so? And what are the mechanisms through which pressure is exerted and negotiated?

All these questions demand a closer analysis of how power is distributed and exercised in this context, how the regulation discussed so far is negotiated, how different groups compete to influence it, and how they navigate its consequences. This, then, is the focus of the remainder of this book. Here, the various local, national, and regional pressures that have led to a renegotiation of the role of smuggling in Tunisia and Morocco, as noted in chapter 2, become a key asset for this analysis. As Khan has pointed out, observing and predicting power in political settlements is a difficult task but can be approached by observing them change over time.[101] To observe how institutions and rent streams have reacted to changes in the distribution of power, the following two chapters therefore focus on tracing the changes in the two borderlands studies in the past decades. Chapter 6 begins by analyzing the developments in Tunisia's southern borderlands since 2010. In the years that followed, the 2011 revolution, the civil war in Libya, and the Islamic State attack against Ben Guerdane all brought challenges and changes to the balance of power in the borderlands, prompting a renegotiation of the role of smuggling in the wider political settlement. Chapter 7 then turns to northern Morocco. While southern Tunisia experienced revolution, the role of smuggling in Morocco's political settlement and the balance of power in Morocco's northern borderlands were challenged through reforms by a new king, alongside the subsequent collapse of large sections of the local smuggling economy. Chapter 8 then compares the experiences of different smuggling networks through these years. It asks what allowed some to thrive and saw others collapse, and it seeks to understand the effects of these negotiations and changes on the local population, asking if they are not, in the end, the ones who were "undermined."

Chapter Six

TUNISIA

Smugglers and Revolution

On January 14, 2011, Tunisian president Ben Ali joined his family on a flight to Jeddah, Saudi Arabia, having dissolved his government and declared a state of emergency after weeks of protests against his rule. He never returned to Tunis—the next morning Tunisian state television announced that he had resigned his position, marking the first Arab dictator to step down in what became to be known as the "Arab Spring."

In the stories of southern and central Tunisia, the 2011 revolution has many homes. Its origin in the country's interior, in the protests that erupted in Sidi Bouzid in 2010 after the self-immolation of Mohamed Bouazizi, has become a part of the popular narrative. In the mining towns of Gafsa, people frequently refer to a local protest movement in 2008 as the real beginning of a revolution three years in the making.[1] In the stories told in Ben Guerdane, too, the revolution has a prologue. In the Ramadan of 2010, protests and strikes rocked the border town, as locals were protesting against a border closure that hurt the local smuggling economy. Just a few months later, revolution swept the country.

At a national level, Tunisia's revolution led to some clear changes in the country's political settlement. It gave the country new institutional structures, including a constitution that was, until its suspension in the summer of 2021, generally considered democratic and progressive by outside observers and many Tunisians, and that had been the grounding of a series of free and fair elections in the following years.² For the decade that followed 2011, this institutional structure was largely underpinned by consensus politics among a group of actors that had also changed since 2011, now no longer including the personal network of the former president Ben Ali, but including the previously persecuted moderate Islamist movement.³ At the same time, the continued existence of crony networks, regional economic inequalities, IFI-aligned monetary policies, and a series of economic crises in the following years cast doubt over the degree to which distributional structures had really changed, as continuously high unemployment, high inflation, and regional inequalities spurred new protests in the following years.⁴

The combination of parliamentary consensus politics, protracted crises, and economic inequality both eroded the trust in Tunisia's postrevolutionary political settlement and became part of the backlash that swept a seeming political outsider, Kais Saied, into power in 2019. Without the support of a party apparatus, the constitutional law scholar won the second round of the presidential elections in a landslide, positioning himself as a challenge to the postrevolutionary political order. In 2021 he would go on to suspend parliament alongside large sections of the constitution and consequently mark the end of an era of postrevolutionary Tunisian politics. In his rise and his discourse, the question of how inclusive this postrevolutionary political arrangement was to those at its margins became a critical part of the question that Saied's rise posed to Tunisia's political elite. This is thus another reason to examine this settlement from the perspective of one of these margins.

This chapter follows the changes that Tunisia's political settlement has undergone since 2010 from the perspective of its southern borderlands. The years since those 2010 protests have been dramatic and eventful in Ben Guerdane: the revolution brought the complete collapse of the local state enforcement capacity, followed by negotiations for its gradual return, the installation of new security infrastructure, the emergence of legal civil society organizations representing smugglers, an ISIS invasion attempt, and the escalation of the civil war in Libya. It began with huge new opportunities for smugglers and closed with increasing pressures on smuggling networks, even before the advent of Covid-19. But the purpose of the chapter is not merely to analyze these tumultuous years, but to ask what these events can teach us about the role of smuggling in post-2011 democratic

Tunisia. Following on from a regime that had relied on an informal authoritarian bargain that included the toleration of smuggling, how did the democratizing state negotiate its continuation or replacement? And what can this teach us about how these arrangements were negotiated, and between whom?

The chapter begins by arguing that while the 2010 protests in Ben Guerdane were not a trigger of the revolution, they were an indication of a wider dynamic of the late Ben Ali regime—a continual testing of the limits of the existing political settlement that ultimately led to his downfall. It then traces how changes in the relative balance of power between smugglers and state agents, the changing institutional structure of the Tunisian state, and the volatile security situation have shaped the renegotiation of the role of the smuggling economy in Tunisia. It notes that despite all these events, by the end of the decade, the central role of the smuggling economy had remained relatively stable: still a central source of income for the borderlands, it was as fundamental to the political settlement of democratic postrevolutionary Tunisia as it had been to the Ben Ali regime. The renegotiation reveals a continued willingness by the Tunisian state to tolerate and manage smuggling, alongside an interest by smugglers themselves to reinstitutionalize their relationship with state structures after the disruption of 2011, albeit on revised terms. Interestingly, new democratic institutional structures have facilitated formalized collective action among smugglers and contributed to a restructuring of the intersection between smugglers and state agents. When pressures on smuggling increased, largely driven by external factors, smugglers explicitly turned to the Tunisian state to facilitate alternative arrangements.

THE RAMADAN PROTESTS AND THE REVOLUTION

Before discussing the changes that the 2011 revolution brought to Tunisia's politics from the perspective of Ben Guerdane, it is important to start with the observation that the pre-2011 political settlement was not stable, but also that it was not Ben Guerdane that led to its collapse.

While Ben Ali had come to power in 1987, it was primarily the second phase of his reign, beginning in the early 2000s, that was marked by an increasingly predatory insertion of members of his family into positions of power within the national economy, thereby displacing more established recipients of rent streams.[5] The years leading up to the 2011 revolution also were accompanied by the repeated flaring up of popular protest movements in the region's periphery, most prominently the protests in Gafsa in 2008.[6] While Ben Ali won the presidential elections in 2009 with almost 90 percent of the vote, and the idea of a popular revolution sweeping away his regime would have seemed outlandish to most analysts, there were dynamics of contestation and the testing of the limits of the current political settlement.

These national dynamics were mirrored in Ben Guerdane in the summer of 2010. The past decade had been good to the city's smuggling economy, as traders from around the country were supplying themselves with cheap goods in Ben Guerdane. While there had been some tension between the municipality and the vendors in the Souk Maghrebi over the municipality's experiment with tax farming in 2008, this had been revoked by 2009.[7] The Trabelsi family had somewhat inserted themselves into the local smuggling economy, as discussed in chapter 5, but this insertion had remained relatively limited compared to their more extensive control over smuggling on the Algerian border.[8] Some of the Trabelsis' business ventures even represented a form of synergy with the local smuggling economy, such as the role of a bus company commonly associated with the Trabelsi network in providing transport for customers to the Souk Maghrebi.[9] And yet 2010 was to serve as a serious test of the importance of Ben Guerdane's smuggling rents for the wider stability of the region, and an indication of the deep distrust between the town and the Tunisian state—two themes that were to remain hallmarks of the coming years.

While the proximate causes for the Ramadan protests in Ben Guerdane in 2010 are clear, their deeper political dynamics are highly contested. Starting in late 2009, the Libyan state imposed a fee of 150 LYD for Tunisian traders entering Libya, which slowed down the local smuggling economy but could still be managed through Libyan intermediaries, before the Libyan authorities completely closed the border for Tunisian traders in August 2010.[10] The effect on the local economy was devastating: as the smuggling economy through Ras Jedir ground to a halt, thousands were missing their main income stream, and the town's cafés began to fill with unemployed young men.

Partly because the Libyan side never provided a full explanation for this closure, different stories existed about the motives for it. Kamel Morjane,

Tunisia's foreign minister at the time, suggested the origins for this decision were entirely Libyan:

> The decision to close the border was not at all coming from the Tunisian side. Gaddafi took this decision in order to impose a fee on each truck that was crossing into Libya, which prompted a negative reaction by the traders. I was then asked to go into Libya, with the minister of interior and the minister of commerce, to solve this problem during Ramadan. The Libyan prime minister received us around 11 p.m., then went to see Gaddafi, and then came back with his decision to open the border. Gaddafi always closed the border when he wanted to punish Tunisia for policies that he didn't like. When you meet with Gaddafi, that's always difficult, because you never know if you have succeeded or not.[11]

In Ben Guerdane, however, much of the anger was not directed at Gaddafi, but at the Tunisian state. Almost everyone I spoke to in Ben Guerdane believed that the origin of the border closure lay with the Tunisian regime, that Gaddafi's actions were in fact "whispered to him" by Ben Ali.[12] In this version of events, Ben Ali either secretly requested or provoked the border closure by the Libyan regime, in order to directly hurt the smuggling economy of Ben Guerdane. In one version, the Ben Ali regime wanted to block the southern smuggling economy as a result of pressure from the well-connected formal business community. In the more common version, however, the Ben Ali clique was motivated to crack down on the Ben Guerdane smuggling networks because these were competing with multiple other smuggling networks in which the Trabelsi clan had a significantly larger stake, most important, one operating through the port of Rades and Sfax, as well as the market at El-Jem. It is difficult at this point to conclusively determine which version of events is correct. However, the absolute dominance of the second version of events in Ben Guerdane is a telling indication of the skepticism toward the Ben Ali regime, and the conception of that regime as increasingly pushing Ben Guerdane out of the fragile distribution of access and resources, working instead in the service of northern business elites, legal or illegal. Beyond Ben Guerdane, these narratives have been staples of the political discourse in the Tunisian South.

More important, the events demonstrate how essential the rent streams from the smuggling economy were for stability in the South in prerevolutionary Tunisia and evidence the power of traders in the borderland community to mobilize and put pressure on state institutions if their trade was threatened. The month after the border closure saw massive protests—both peaceful and violent—in Ben Guerdane, including hundreds of arrests, burning of tires and police cars, and the posting of more than one thousand riot police in Ben Guerdane and its surroundings.[13] The protests saw heavy participation by the younger generation and the making of some local political activists who would later come to play a role in the democratic Tunisia: in 2011 Nafti Mahdhi, who had been one of the leaders of the protests, was elected to the newly formed National Constituent Assembly.

Locally, many people draw a connection between the 2010 protests and the 2011 revolution, highlighting the frustration with the Ben Ali regime that was at the center of both protest movements, claiming that the summer 2010 riots were "the first time that the police was defeated in Tunisia."[14] However, the two events did not directly merge into each other. Once the border was reopened in September 2010, calm returned to Ben Guerdane.[15] When protests began in Sidi Bouzid on December 17, they first spread in the country's interior, reaching Ben Guerdane only on December 26 and Medenine the next day.[16] So rather than viewing the Ramadan 2010 protests as a trigger or beginning of the 2011 revolution, they are better conceptualized as an indication of how essential smuggling rents were to the ability of the Tunisian state to control and stabilize its southern borderlands, and as one of a wider set of instances of a regime noting the limits of its political settlement—before being swept out of power just a few months later.

For the smugglers of Ben Guerdane, the 2011 revolution meant not only the end of the Ben Ali regime, but the swift suspension of informal regulations of smuggling that were dependent on the participation and enforcement by state agents amid the complete collapse of state enforcement capacity at the border. Police, municipal agents, border guards, and customs had all largely abandoned their posts, and local civilians took over control of the border crossing.[17] What followed for much of 2011 and 2012 was a form of gold rush for the local smuggling economy, as any controls on the quantity of goods that could be brought through disappeared alongside any tariffs or bribes. Goods that were previously monopolized by networks connected to the Trabelsi clan, such as sportswear or tuna, could also be traded by everyone.[18] In the words of one smuggler in Medenine: "During the revolution, we brought in everything. There was no state. We brought in cannabis, everything."[19]

In Ben Guerdane, the period immediately after the 2011 revolution allowed a variety of local actors to profit. While those who had significant amounts of capital available could benefit from bringing in huge quantities at no cost, smaller actors could benefit from the increasing volumes as well as the expansion of the distribution network for gasoline. As the mechanisms that had contained the sale of contraband gasoline to the borderlands collapsed, informal roadside gas stations could increasingly be found around the country. According to an employee at a large international gasoline supplier to Tunisia, internal analysis suggested that in the years between 2011 and 2014, providers of formally imported gasoline recorded losses of up to 80 percent in some areas in the South and Northwest of the country and up to 60 percent in its center.[20] In the period after 2011, the local economy also benefited from the influx of Libyan refugees and travelers, supplying informal money exchange booths with a cheap and expansive supply of Libyan dinar. Still, while the smugglers of Ben Guerdane were happy to make hay while the sun was shining, some that I spoke to also recalled an awareness that this situation would not last for long.[21]

NEGOTIATING NEW SETTLEMENTS

Apart from initiating changes to the national-level institutional structure and governing coalition, the 2011 revolution also changed the balance of power between smugglers and agents of the state in the southern borderlands in ways that would prove to be important for the negotiations of the role of smuggling in the new political settlement. The revolution temporarily weakened the enforcement capacity of the central state as well as the local state apparatus, as police, soldiers, customs officers, and tax collectors were only slowly returning to their postings and unsure about their new status, orders, and power in the postrevolutionary state. As I will discuss later, this weakening lasted longer for some state actors than others: while the municipalities remained without local enforcement services for years, this weakening was more temporary for the centralized security services.

A more permanent change was the dramatic increase in the freedom of expression and association following the 2011 revolution, as the development of civil society organizations that could increase the ability of citizens to organize, coordinate, and put pressure on state institutions was to play a crucial role in the renegotiation of Ben Guerdane's smuggling economy post-2011. Two negotiations provide particularly interesting illustrations of this dynamic. Both concern the reinstatement of the informal regulatory system in Ben Guerdane after the disruption of the revolution: one around the procedures at the Ras Jedir border crossing, and one around the taxation of the Souk Maghrebi. One involves smugglers negotiating with the central state; the other, with the local municipality.

Negotiating the Procedure at the Ras Jedir Crossing

While the large wholesale smugglers operating through the Ras Jedir border crossing had profited significantly from the lack of regulations and control after the 2011 revolution, some of the traders sensed that a backlash was coming.[22] Tunisian media outlets were running stories about the increase in smuggling, accusing the smugglers of supporting terrorist organizations, and politicians began to jump on the topic. Short, temporary closures of the Ras Jedir crossing became more frequent.

In early 2012 the Organisation of Tunisian Libyan Brotherhood (OTLB) was founded by a group of wholesale smugglers of consumer goods from the Ras Jedir market, a schoolteacher, and four men working as transporters on the Ras Jedir route. The expressed purpose of the group was to act as an intermediary between the traders in Libya, the traders of Ben Guerdane—the Souk Ras Jedir in particular—and the Tunisian government. Since its founding, this group has been a key element in the smuggling networks' bargaining with the central state. The group's ability to form itself and seek a legal, organized, and structured rather than clientelistic relationship with the state was a direct result of the revolution, as its own leadership highlighted.[23] While the group is in no form a democratic representation of Ben Guerdane's wholesalers, the past years have demonstrated their ability to negotiate arrangements that have been accepted by local traders.

One of the primary concerns of the OTLB in the immediate postrevolutionary phase was the rhetoric, expressed by politicians and media alike, that claimed that smuggling networks were similar to or cooperating with terrorist groups. When the president of the OTLB had the opportunity to meet Tunisia's president at the time, Moncef Marzouki, together with other civil society leaders from Ben Guerdane, this characterization of smuggling on national television was one of their main talking points. Their suggestion was the creation of a TV show that would clarify the difference between smuggling and terrorism and express that "the border is a resource for us."[24] At the same time, the group offered advice to the president on whom the Tunisian state should interact with in the confusing and rapidly changing postrevolutionary political environment in Libya.

While taking a formal meeting with an association that was de facto representing smugglers is an unusual decision for a politician, it was not uncharacteristic for President Marzouki, a lifelong human rights activist and political maverick. When I spoke to him about the meeting in Tunis in 2017, he had lost the presidency to Beji Caid Essebsi, and his political rivals had accused him of being a "terrorist sympathizer" for his criticism of a lack of accountability of the security forces. Asked why he decided to take the meeting, he answered: "Half of Tunisia's economy is informal. If you want to call them criminals, you can do that, but that does not help. The informal economy must become part of Tunisia's structural economy. I know that the president believes that they are all criminals. But don't forget that these people also called me a terrorist."[25]

Crucially, aside from seeking to address their reputation, the OTLB also expressed their willingness to reinstate a regulatory arrangement for the procedures at Ras Jedir that would end the ability of smugglers to pass through without any payment. They approached the regional head of customs as well as the governor of Medenine with the proposal to reintroduce a fee to be paid by smugglers at the border crossing, beginning with 50 TND, approximately one-third of the rate that was typical before the revolution, to perhaps be increased slowly over time. One of the negotiators of the proposal recounted to me that the deal was proposed in a meeting with a delegation of the regional governor and a regional customs official on the phone.[26] After two months of deliberations by the governor's side and customs, this fee was in fact introduced at the Ras Jedir border crossing. It appears to have been generally accepted by the local traders, and it rose to between 100 and 150 TND by the summer of 2014.

Slightly lower than the prerevolutionary rate, the new fee reflected, in the view of the traders, the weakened bargaining position of the post-2011 state, but also the unsustainability of the 2011 "free-for-all."[27] In this same time frame, other elements of regulation also returned: the old prohibition against large trucks, providing an advantage for local traders, was also reintroduced at the border crossing. Given the position of the governor and regional customs head in a highly centralized Tunisian state, it is highly unlikely that this decision was made on a local or regional level. Instead, it is best interpreted as the first indication that the postrevolutionary democratic Tunisian state would continue to tolerate and regulate its southern smuggling economy.

Negotiating the Rules in the Souk Maghrebi

Similar to the agreement at the Ras Jedir border crossing, the hybrid institutional structures that had regulated the relationship between the municipality of Ben Guerdane and the vendors at the Souk Maghrebi had also collapsed with the 2011 revolution. Three developments had changed this relationship.

First, the enforcement capacity of the municipality had decreased drastically. The municipal agents, who had usually collected the market fees as well as a variety of other municipal taxes, had suffered a particularly harsh blow to their image through the revolution, as it was one of them, Faida Hamdy, who had confiscated the scale of Mohamed Bouazizi, the informal vendor whose self-immolation had become a symbol of the revolution.[28] When municipal agents refused to leave their offices, the government reassigned them to the police, leaving them answerable to the local police chief and out of the control of the municipality.[29] The police, who had, before the revolution, occasionally helped in collecting municipal taxes, were generally unwilling to support the municipality in these activities in the years following 2011.[30]

Second, the municipality's lack of the ownership rights of the land on which the market was built was exposed to the vendors. As mentioned in chapter 4, that land belonged to the Ministry of Defense, leaving the municipality unable to either sell or rent the land to the vendors and leading to the hybrid regulatory arrangement that had existed before the revolution. In 2011, through proceedings in a local court, the vendors learned about the illegality of this procedure and consequently refused payment to the municipality.[31] Here, the national institutional changes that came with the 2011 revolution were crucial, as they both increased the local population's access to information and made it impossible for the weakened municipality to continue with, and enforce, an illegal form of fee collection.

Third, the expansion of the freedom of expression and association after 2011 facilitated the organization of vendors in the market. With the assistance of the municipal labor inspector and a national-level NGO, the Tunisian Inclusive Labour Initiative, a group of vendors from the market founded a market association, the Association of Ben Guerdane's Traders, in 2012.[32] The explicit goal of the association, as expressed by its leadership, was to formalize and legalize its relationship with the municipality and negotiate a new procedure for the organization and taxation of the market. At the same time, this formalization would not entail the payment of the full tax rates—instead, the association was arguing for the creation of a free-trade zone, covering all of Ben Guerdane. Apart from the municipality, the association had approached regional and national-level politicians and claims to have met with the governor.[33] As with the OTLB, the Association of Ben Guerdane's Traders was talked about with skepticism by some of the local vendors I spoke to, but it did become the de facto main interlocutor for the market.[34]

The confluence of these three factors dramatically weakened the bargaining power of the municipality vis-à-vis the vendors of the Souk Maghrebi. In line with classical political settlement analysis, a shift in the balance of power directly affected institutional performance. After the revolution, the vendors refused to pay any fees to the municipality until a new agreement had been reached. The municipality, on the other hand, was unable to offer any form of legal agreement until it had acquired the land on which the market stood, which was formally owned by the Ministry of Defense. In the turbulent context of postrevolutionary politics and frequent cabinet changes, this proved to be a difficult exercise.

In 2014, as confirmed by municipal officials, the market association and the municipality reached an agreement.[35] It suggested that in exchange for paying a yearly fee of 240 TND—equivalent to the rate that had been paid in 2008—the vendors would be willing to sign contracts with the municipality, which in turn guaranteed that the vendors would gain access to electricity, the absence of which had been a long-standing grievance in the market.[36] On September 11, 2014, more than two hundred vendors provided copies of their identity cards in order to have contracts with the municipality set up. The deal failed in the end, however: the municipality was unable to follow through on its end of the bargain, as it still did not own the land.[37]

TUNISIA

For the municipality, the loss of these income streams was catastrophic. By 2012, the municipality's market income had fallen to less than a quarter of its 2008 level. While a superficial look at its total budget indicates an increase following 2011, this was primarily due to a rise in transfers from the central state in order to sustain the higher expenses that came with the increases in government salaries after the revolution. The budget without state interventions had been almost halved (fig. 6.1). In addition, the continuous postponing of municipal elections after the revolution had left the municipality without elected political leadership for years.[38] Consequently, the primary local state organ responsible for articulating a vision of economic development remained sidelined in the postrevolutionary years. Furthermore, in 2015 any hope for an engagement with Ben Guerdane that was not primarily security-focused was quickly derailed by two tragedies.

SETTLEMENTS UNDER ATTACK

In the summer of 2015, two terrorist attacks shocked Tunisia. In March an attack on the Bardo Museum in Tunis left twenty-four dead. In June a gunman killed thirty-eight people at a tourist resort near the city of Sousse.[39]

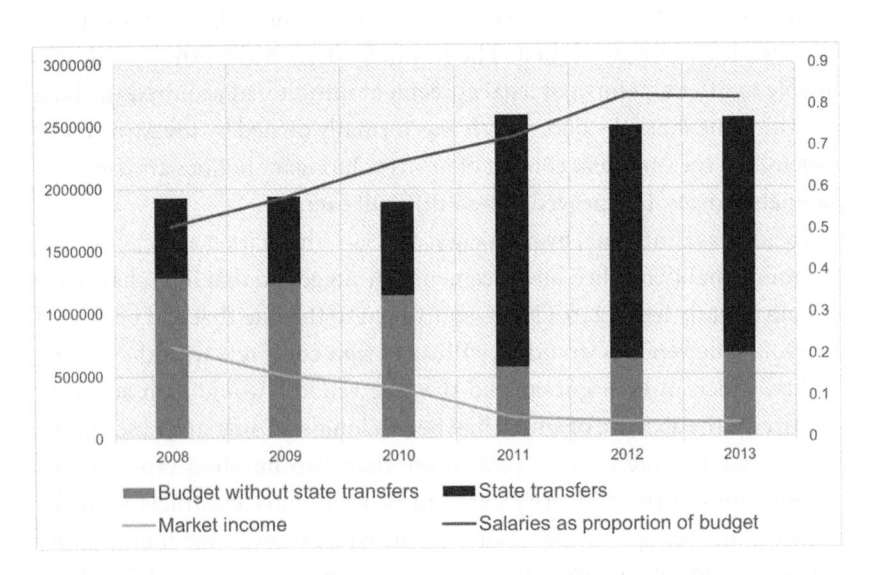

FIGURE 6.1 Budget data for the municipality of Ben Guerdane, 2008–2013, accessed by the author in 2014. Graph by author.

ISIS claimed responsibility for both attacks. Swiftly, terrorism returned to the top of the Tunisian political agenda. Targeting largely foreigners, the attacks also served to cripple the country's tourism industry for years to come and refocused international attention in Tunis from democracy promotion to security issues. As some of the men involved had been trained in camps in Libya, and more than three thousand Tunisians were still estimated to be among the ranks of extremist groups operating in Syria and Iraq, the issue of Tunisia's border security became a national and international preoccupation.[40] In 2016, construction began on a trench across the Tunisian-Libyan border, accompanied by new surveillance infrastructure funded jointly by the United States and Germany.[41] A new scanner was installed at the Ras Jedir border crossing, and police presence in the town increased significantly.[42] These dynamics accelerated dramatically in March 2016.

On the morning of March 7, a group of around one hundred IS militants that had been training in Libya launched an attack on Ben Guerdane that was aimed at "liberating" the city and establishing a foothold for the Islamic State in Tunisia.[43] Apart from simultaneously attacking key strategic points of the Tunisian military and National Guard, the fighters also seized a local mosque, broadcasting a message to the local population through its loudspeakers and encouraging them to join the Islamic State. With the Medenine region functioning as one of the largest per capita suppliers of foreign fighters to the Islamic State, Ben Guerdane has long occupied a prominent position in the region's jihadi imaginary—Al Qaeda's leader in Iraq, Abu Musab Zarqawi, is commonly cited as saying about the town that "if it was located next to Fallujah, we would have liberated Iraq."[44]

Counting on local support ended up being a serious miscalculation on the side of the IS fighters. Not only did Ben Guerdane's population refuse the call to support the attacking Islamic State fighters, but many locals took up arms themselves and fought side by side with the Tunisian military.[45] A comparatively high number of local IS recruits, economic marginalization, and dissatisfaction with the Tunisian state did not translate into wider support for the Islamic State. As discussed in chapter 4, the moral and religious landscape that surrounded the smuggling economy is frequently characterized by conservatism and disillusionment with the central state but does not necessarily dovetail with violent jihadism.[46] After a few hours, the IS fighters began to be pushed back; by the end of the day, their failure was apparent. In the end, forty-nine militants, thirteen Tunisian security forces, and seven civilians lost their lives.[47] While the Tunisian government celebrated the victory and Ben Guerdane buried its dead, Prime Minister Essid also announced a "thorough evaluation" of the local security structure.[48] The return of the security apparatus to Ben Guerdane was in full force.

Smugglers, activists, and administrators I spoke to all agreed that the March 2016 attack fundamentally changed their relationship with the Tunisian state, as the presence of police, National Guard, and military forces once again increased significantly. In the immediate aftermath of the attack, many locals, including smugglers, welcomed this change.[49] In the words of one local resident, "After the revolution, there was a lot of freedom, but then there was too much freedom, and it was dangerous, and people wanted the police to come back. And it is only a small group of people here who really want the freedom—not the families."[50] Almost everyone I spoke to expressed the need for a larger security presence in the city. However, the changes did not only bring security. In the words of one prominent local human rights activist: "We have gained security, but we have lost much, in terms of commerce, in terms of our standard of living.... Before these events, two to three thousand of our youth could make a trip to Libya every day and earn 100–150 dinar—now they don't make that in a month, and that affects the families that they are going to feed." He added: "the margin of liberty in Ben Guerdane is now much reduced."[51] This sentiment was mirrored by a police officer giving me an involuntary ride to the Ben Guerdane police station. Explaining to me that the attitude of the Tunisian police had changed since the revolution, he noted: "You must know that we are now all for freedom of expression. Just not in Ben Guerdane."[52]

This new situation naturally affected the continuous negotiations around the procedures at the Ras Jedir border crossing. A local wholesale smuggler involved in the negotiations for the agreement complained: "After March 7, people who talked against the new arrangements were threatened with being arrested as terrorists."[53] Smuggling through the Ras Jedir border crossing continued, as security forces largely emphasized calm and stability. When I asked one large-scale smuggler why there had not been more resistance against the increase in security force presence, he cited the continuation of the trade through Ras Jedir as a crucial reason: "Because for Ben Guerdane, if the border is open, they accept anything."[54]

Bit by bit, however, the costs of smuggling, through payments at police checkpoints, the informal fee at the border crossing, and limitations on the quantities that could be transported, increased. The state had returned, and the balance of power shifted. By early 2017 the informal fee to be paid to the Tunisian customs agents at Ras Jedir had reached 300 TND, six times the value with which the OTLB-led negotiation had originally reintroduced the fee.[55] In the months leading up to the 2016 attack, a scanner had already been installed at the Ras Jedir crossing. Following a concern from the Tunisian government that weapons were smuggled through the border crossing, the quantity of goods that could be smuggled under the prevailing procedures dropped significantly, eating further into the traders' profit margins.[56]

Fundamentally, the year after the IS attacks saw an increase in state enforcement personnel at the Tunisia-Libya border, once again somewhat altering the underlying distribution of power in the borderlands. As would be expected, it saw a renegotiation of the institutions that regulated the smuggling economy, shifting toward higher expenses for smugglers and higher presence of and side payments to security personnel as well as some concessions toward the interests of the central state with respect to the quantity of goods that could be smuggled. The fundamental necessity of these income streams in the political settlement, however, had not changed.

POPULAR DIPLOMACY

The years following the 2016 attack also once again highlighted that the Tunisian state was not the only actor with whom the regulation of the smuggling economy had to be negotiated. The fall of Gaddafi in 2011 set in motion a struggle for authority in Libya, which quickly took on a highly localized dimension, with different cities, militias, and tribal groups vying for resources and influence.[57] As the postrevolutionary political agreement unraveled in 2014, this dynamic intensified.[58] For external actors, including the Tunisian state, engaging with a variety of rapidly changing local interlocutors became increasingly difficult. At the same time, rent streams generated from smuggling economies, including human trafficking, the trade in drugs and weapons, but also licit goods such as foodstuffs, gasoline and crude oil had become crucial resources for competing groups in the Libyan war economy.[59] The Ras Jedir border crossing, in particular, had turned into a valuable resource in the power struggle for western Libya. As control of the border crossing became increasingly contested, the fragility of Tunisia's political settlement, being dependent on the toleration of illicit trade networks by one of its neighbors, became more visible, giving rise to significant unrest and a process of "popular diplomacy" led by smugglers, especially from 2016 on. This provides another example of the centrality of the rents from the smuggling economy to the stability of the Tunisian South, the willingness of the Tunisian state to recognize this necessity, and the continuous renegotiation of its regulation after 2011.

During the 2011 revolution in Libya, brigades from the coastal city of Zuwara quickly seized control of the Ras Jedir border crossing, and they have remained an important presence at the crossing for the years that followed.[60] Ethnically Amazight, Zuwara had been marginalized during Gaddafi's rule and maintained a tense relationship with the largely Arab tribes that surrounded the town from the South, as well as the Arab coastal town of Zawya.[61] In the years since 2011, Zuwara has developed a reputation as a comparatively well-governed city, organized largely through its municipal council.[62] While the city gained some international attention in 2015 for expelling migrant smugglers, it has benefited from other smuggling routes running through its territory, most important, the gasoline smuggling route running from the refinery in Zawya to the coast of Zuwara and from there on to Malta and southern Europe, and the route at the center of this chapter, running from the Ras Jedir crossing to the ports of western Libya.[63]

In the years since 2011, conflicts in western Libya around the control of this smuggling route caused significant difficulties for the traders of Ben Guerdane. Attempts by other actors in western Libya to gain control of these smuggling routes not only caused uncertainty for smugglers but also often multiplied the number of checkpoints on their routes, increased the costs of passage, and often left them at the mercy of untrained and unruly militias.[64] Most prominent among the actors challenging the control of Ras Jedir by Zuwara was the Brigade of the Martyr Jamal Ghaeb, a militia formed in 2011 south of Zawya. The expanding role of the group from 2016 onward represented one facet of a new phase of competition around the control of the smuggling routes, making the situation increasingly untenable for Tunisian traders.

Following a series of disagreements around the fees that different groups were demanding from traders, as well as multiple incidents between smugglers and armed groups operating checkpoints in Libya, the conflict began to escalate throughout 2016. In April the groups manning the Libyan side of Ras Jedir closed down the traffic of goods, citing "harassment" of Libyan travelers and the damage that fuel smuggling inflicted on the Libyan economy.[65] Protests and strikes followed in Ben Guerdane. As in 2010, the focus of the anger was not just against the groups in Libya but against the Tunisian state, which people felt was not being sufficiently supportive of the town. The crossing was reopened, before another closure in August following a skirmish between armed groups on the Libyan side, and then again in September, when smugglers from Ben Guerdane blocked the road to the border crossing following the killing of a young man in the military zone near the border.[66]

Finally, in November 2016 traders of Ben Guerdane, smugglers, and civil society organizations blocked off the border crossing under the slogan "Let Ben Guerdane live," citing the high costs of smuggling and the poor treatment that some of them had undergone at the hands of armed groups in Libya.[67] By entirely cutting off their own income streams, the smugglers managed to signal how seriously they saw their livelihoods threatened and put pressure on the Tunisian government to find a solution for the city. In a sense, this indicated a rejection of the political settlement, which they saw as having slipped to including them on terms that were not sufficient to maintain their livelihoods.

While Tunisian authorities were alarmed and eager to resolve the situation, they also frequently pointed out that they lacked the connections and local knowledge to broker a deal with the groups on the Libyan side.[68] Instead, the situation at the Ras Jedir crossing was resolved through a series of locally driven informal negotiations, in what became known as the "popular diplomacy process." This—the closing of the border, the direct challenge to the Tunisian state to resolve the situation, and the centrality of the locally driven informal negotiations—would become a pattern that has characterized a range of conflicts and negotiations at this border from 2016 to the present day.

Throughout 2016, a group of local smugglers, including the head of the OTLB and the Association of Traders of Ben Guerdane, the spokesman of the sit-in, local civil society leaders, and a member of parliament had built channels of communication with different groups on the Libyan side and had begun to provide the main negotiation channel with actors in the borderlands of western Libya.[69] While the sit-in continued, these communications intensified. As reported by its participants, meetings between the affected parties took place, first in Ben Guerdane, then in Zuwara. They included the aforementioned local traders as well as representatives of the Tunisian police and customs, representatives of the Libyan customs, and nine different municipalities on the Libyan side of the border, along with, as a document produced through the process indicates, members from multiple Libyan armed groups, including the Jamal Ghaeb brigade.[70]

By January 2017, these talks had led to an agreement on the procedures under which smuggling was to be conducted through the Ras Jedir border crossing. When I spoke to them, some of the participants in these negotiations claimed that they had the full support of the Tunisian government to informally negotiate a procedure for the Ras Jedir border crossing that was in violation of Tunisian law as long as it did not endanger the state's security.[71] While I was not able to verify this, by January 2017, informal support of the Tunisian government for these negotiations is indicated through direct meetings between members of the cabinet and members of the "popular diplomacy" negotiation team.[72] In exchange, the negotiators report to have assured them that the procedures would still maintain a no-tolerance policy toward "terrorism, drugs, and weapons."[73] Still, officially, the Tunisian state never endorsed the agreement—the member of parliament who signed the agreement made clear in his conversations with me that he did so as a member of Tunisia's civil society, justifying this rather unconventional step as the only solution to avoiding larger unrest, and finding employment for the young men of the region, in the absence of formal employment opportunities.[74]

The agreement that was finally reached contained tight limits on the amount of goods that could be brought through but was soon renegotiated for more permissive agreements, as outlined in chapter 3. While the "popular diplomacy" was not without its critics and was accused of being personalistic, ideological, or an undermining of the state's role in diplomacy, it did manage to negotiate a new agreement for the border crossing that was broadly acceptable to all main parties.[75] It supported the mediation between a variety of actors on the Libyan side, specifying how different rent streams would be divided among different Libyan groups, and established a channel of negotiation that became increasingly institutionalized, as meetings between the popular diplomacy participants continued after the opening of the border.

The popular diplomacy negotiations show the degree to which the postrevolutionary state had, after initial suspicion, come to accept that stability in the South remained dependent on rent streams from the smuggling economy. Its willingness to rely on local smuggling networks to negotiate the procedures at Ras Jedir with Libyan interlocutors highlights the fact that in their understanding of the necessity of these rents, smugglers and the state were largely pulling in the same direction.

The process also demonstrated, however, a deep and commonly unacknowledged dependence on Tunisia's eastern neighbor. Discussions around the challenges that the Libyan revolution and the ongoing civil war have brought for Tunisia's economy typically focus on the effects of Libya's instability, highlighting issues such as migrant streams, poor border control, and the illicit arms streams.[76] What is usually left unconsidered is that a new postwar power structure in Libya could also create a Libyan national political settlement that may not be compatible with the presence of a vast smuggling economy on its border with Tunisia and consequentially cut off rent streams that even the post-2011 state has come to expect and rely on.

A preview of such a scenario occurred in the spring of 2017. Libya's civil war had led to a deterioration of the domestic economy, triggering a liquidity crisis, a booming black market, high inflation, and increasing scarcity of many essential goods in Libya. Gasoline, which had traditionally been cheap due to the generous subsidy policies of the oil-rich state, had become increasingly expensive, as large volumes were smuggled onto oil tankers off the coast of western Libya, and criminal networks began to redirect gasoline from the official supply networks and sell it off at more expensive prices.[77]

As a result, the public acceptance of gasoline smuggling to Tunisia dropped sharply, and civil society groups in western Libya began organizing demonstrations against the practice.[78] For those who had been looking to put pressure on the smuggling networks, gasoline, which was also consumed locally and smuggled by a diffuse and not particularly well-connected network, was an ideal target. In the words of one Libyan activist, "Our pressure is on gasoline, but our real intent is on the oil. You can't blame the small guys, but we start with these because it's the easier part."[79] Local authorities, including the city council of Zuwara, quickly began to express to their Tunisian partners that in order for the trade of Ras Jedir to continue, the gasoline trade had to stop.[80]

Consequently, in the summer of 2017, the procedure at Ras Jedir changed again, and limits on the amount of gasoline that could be brought through were strictly enforced. The amount of gasoline that was allowed to come through was now limited to what a normal-sized tank could hold. According to local traders, even the contraband gasoline trade through the desert had collapsed, demonstrating the enforcement capacity of these informal arrangements.[81]

The effect of this shortage on the local gasoline networks was devastating. While most informal gasoline stations remained open, prices skyrocketed. By mid-July the price of 20 liters of contraband gasoline had almost tripled, and at times it rose beyond the price charged at formal gas stations. Most vendors remained stoically optimistic, hoping that more gasoline would come through again soon.[82] Others were more pessimistic. I spoke to a gasoline vendor who had opened his store just a few months earlier. When I told him I admired his patience, he smiled, then paused. "Soon" he replied, "there will be an explosion."[83]

NEW PRESSURES

In the years that followed, the popular diplomacy process continued, benefiting from training for its civil society actors through international donors and establishing a relationship with the newly elected Municipal Council in Ben Guerdane. However, their activity was designed to navigate conflicts between different actors *within* these local arrangements and not necessarily deal with pressures *on* them. The years since have continuously introduced new pressures on the system as a whole, threatening, again and again, the ability to maintain a negotiated and tolerated system of smuggling that could supply Ben Guerdane. Three episodes in particular stand out: the anticorruption campaigns of successive governments, the effects of new infrastructure along the border, and the Covid-19 pandemic.

The "War on Corruption"

On May 23, 2017, Chafik Jarraya, a businessman with a reputation for his political connections, was arrested on charges of "attacking the integrity of the state."[84] In the weeks and months that followed, other businessmen and customs officers were also arrested, kicking off a highly publicized national anticorruption campaign of Prime Minister Chahed.[85] Corruption and the links between politicians and business elites had been a talking point since before the revolution and have maintained a staple of the postrevolutionary discourse up to the present day. The combination of publicized but uninstitutionalized anticorruption initiatives and some suggestions that these might provide an opportunity to boost fragile state budgets more recently were again heavily used by President Kais Saied.

In 2017 it did not take long for the war to reach Ben Guerdane. A week after Jarraya's arrest, an infamous large-scale smuggler in Ben Guerdane, known by his nickname "Washwasha," was arrested on charges of supporting a terrorist organization.[86] Three weeks later, thirteen of Ben Guerdane's *sarraf*, the providers of informal financial services, were arrested in their houses in the middle of the night by special forces and charged with financing terrorism. Allegedly, three million dinar in cash were confiscated.[87] Most of the men were released quickly after their arrests, and the arrests did not affect the general tolerance by the government with respect to the popular diplomacy agreements or the procedures at Ras Jedir.[88] And yet the campaign, and especially the fashion in which it was conducted, left a deep impression on Ben Guerdane.

The accusations of terrorism, the use of specialized antiterror units, and the boasts about the large confiscations of cash all were typical features of the war on corruption. But for Ben Guerdane, they also once more reinforced the image of a state that, on the one hand, tolerated smuggling networks as alternatives to economic development, but, on the other hand, freely used force against them whenever it was convenient, especially to habitually raid them for cash, like a modern-day *mallah*, the military expeditions during the Beylical period that used to collect taxes from remote tribes.[89] Locals were particularly frustrated by the fashion in which the arrests had been conducted. Most used the word "attack" rather than arrest. Almost everyone mentioned the fact that they had been arrested at night, and in front of their families. In the words of one smuggler: "With this campaign, there are no longer any rights, they can even rob the gold of the women, there is no law in this. This is against human rights, to attack these houses, at midnight, for no reason."[90]

Nobody I spoke to believed that any of the traders were actually connected to terrorist groups. A high-level source in a ministry involved in the war on corruption confirmed that the accusation of terrorism and the special antiterror unit had primarily been used because it did not include much judicial supervision: "This use was based on a level of procedure—it was easier to do this way. It is also quicker. The police don't have the means to prove academically that these people are connected to terrorism. And there is also the risk of the judiciary. And there is a risk of arresting the innocent, that's true. But in every operation there are risks. And these people are antistate."[91] The same source also confirmed that the arrests did not change the government's wider attitude toward the role of the smuggling economy in ensuring stability in the South but was merely "conjunctural" rather than structural, "aiming to reinstate an equilibrium."

After the tumult and negotiations of the postrevolutionary period, these events were a harsh reminder—and one of many to come—of what it meant to be included "informally" in a political settlement, and of the means that the new—increasingly recovered and allegedly democratic—state still possessed in exerting pressure on the smuggling networks.

Infrastructure

Plans to increase security infrastructure along the Tunisia-Libya border predated the IS attack on Ben Guerdane and were already visible in the establishment of a military zone along parts of the border in 2013. Especially in the context of the conflict in Libya, the security and observability of Tunisia's land border had increasingly become a concern not just in Tunisia's national politics but among international funders as well. Germany and the United States in particular have provided substantial funds for border security infrastructure in Tunisia since 2016.[92] The impact of these was not instantaneous, however. Even though a trench and an earthen wall were in place along large parts of the northern sections of the Tunisia-Libya border by early 2016, they had no noticeable impact on the smuggling activity across this route in 2016 and early 2017. In the words of a high-ranking local police commander, "I've been here for three years. That wall? We built a tiny ditch and put a bit of sand on one side, and that's it."[93] Indeed, most of the smugglers operating on that route either put wooden boards over the ditch and drove across it or threw their goods across.[94]

Over time, however, this began to change. From late 2017 onward, reports about more difficulties for smugglers across the desert route increased. Conversations with bureaucrats involved in the provision of the security infrastructure suggest that the effectiveness of the new infrastructure, based on technological equipment and training, may have only increased gradually. At the same time, further escalations of the conflict in Libya heightened Tunisian fears about a spillover and led to the deployment of further military units to the area and an increase in patrols.[95] As a consequence, trade across the desert route appears to have first become more expensive and then increasingly infeasible for many of the traders operating here. This not only affected smugglers, but also pastoralists operating in the area. It is unclear to what degree the tightening across the "desert route" represented a conscious policy or primarily a side effect of the conflict in Libya and wider national and international concerns about mobility across this border. Nonetheless, its effects were clear. On one level, it created new points of conflict between security forces and local communities, especially around the use of force across this border. In particular, repeated killings of smugglers along the desert route gave rise to protests by local community groups and additional demands on local mediation. On another level, in the years between 2017 and 2020, it refocused attention on those smuggling routes that were still viable—through the formal border crossings, and in particular the Ras Jedir crossing. By 2020, however, a new wave of disruptions would also reach the border crossings themselves.

Covid-19

The arrival of the Covid-19 pandemic in Tunisia was not primarily a borderlands story. It presented first and foremost a national health crisis and a substantial disruption of the country's entire economic structure, formal and informal. By the end of 2021 the pandemic had cost over twenty-five thousand Tunisian lives and substantially deepened the country's already severe and overlapping economic crises. While the effect on its border economy was not unique to the sector, the pandemic did add further pressures on its smuggling economy. From March to November 2020, both border crossings were closed—a particularly serious situation given the restrictions already imposed on the border routes. Other public health measures, such as brief periods of lockdown and Covid tests, presented further barriers—and further costs—on local traders.

While the pandemic has affected sectors and regions across Tunisia, research on informal work and the pandemic has highlighted that informal economic activities, including smugglers, have faced particular vulnerabilities in its context.[96] These have included barriers to accessing state support and loans as well as a substantial personal vulnerability to lockdowns and global supply shocks—both of which directly affected the traders of Ben Guerdane.

Most important, however, the pandemic represented a further pressure on a community of traders that had already endured a range of pressures in the preceding years. It is worth nothing that these pressures did not displace the larger attempt to sustain a tolerated and informally regulated smuggling economy through the Ras Jedir border crossing. Even in 2021, both key aspects of the popular diplomacy process and the informal arrangements that regulated smuggling through the Ras Jedir border crossings still existed. There is no indication that either the repeated wars on corruption or the increase in security infrastructure were intended to put an end to these arrangements. However, in conjunction, these different pressures have caused repeated disruptions and as a consequence a substantial narrowing of their ability to maintain their key function: feeding the borderlands.

For Tunisia's southern borderlands, these pressures highlighted the fragility of their informal mode of incorporation into the wider distribution of resources and put emphasis on new strategies of adaptation, including switching to formal activities, switching to different forms of illegal activities, drawing on savings and social connections, and, in many cases, migration. The ability to adjust to these pressures, however, was not evenly distributed across the borderlands—a challenge that will be at the center of chapter 8.

"I'M WITH THE SUSPECT": BEN GUERDANE IN TUNISIA

This chapter has traced the renegotiation of the role and regulation of smuggling in Tunisia's political settlement after its 2011 revolution from the perspective of its southern borderland. It has demonstrated that under the surface of these tumultuous years, the rent streams generated by the smuggling economy have remained fundamental to the stability of the postrevolutionary political settlement. At the same time, the process of this renegotiation itself has revealed some of the workings of these arrangements. It has allowed the chapter to trace the importance of the relative balance of power between different local state structures and smugglers. Critically, it has observed a willingness, if not eagerness, by both smugglers and state actors to reinstitutionalize their relationship after the events of 2011. Yet alongside this continuity, the changes that came with Tunisia's democratization had a direct effect on the negotiations between smugglers and state representatives. As expansions in freedom of speech and association allowed traders to form official associations, this has both strengthened their ability to bargain collectively and formalized some of their interactions with the state.

Despite these developments, the relationship between the central state and Ben Guerdane after 2011 and particularly after 2016 was characterized primarily by security problems and security solutions, rather than economic development. The primary representatives of the Tunisian state in its southern borderland were still the policeman and the soldier. The tolerations and negotiations by the state outlined earlier remained informal, within the cracks of security objectives, while public statements on smuggling were often aggressive. Developmental projects for the historically marginalized regions remained a talking point but failed to materialize.

Incorporation is not inclusion, and negotiations do not necessarily imply an equal footing—a situation that many people involved in these discussions were deeply aware of. Noting this provides an important addition to a chapter that has traced negotiations between smugglers and the state. It is to highlight that, in order to explain the deepening resentment toward the central state that can often be felt in the Tunisian South today, looking at rent streams alone is insufficient: the modes of interaction are similarly critical. And so before concluding, it is worth briefly returning to Ben Guerdane one more time, to a few symbolically charged days, to explore how the city's relationship with the postrevolutionary state was perceived locally.

It is March 2017. For the first anniversary of the IS attack on Ben Guerdane, a committee of local civil society associations, in cooperation with the Ministries of Culture and Youth, had put together a week-long program of celebrations, including concerts, poetry readings, seminars, and sports events, that was to culminate in a visit by Prime Minister Youssef Chahed to the municipality. The theme of the week, remembrance, was endowed with a double meaning. Apart from remembering the martyrs of the 2016 attack, the celebrations were explicitly designed to remind the Tunisian state of Ben Guerdane, and of past promises to take a more developmental approach toward the city. "The first goal was to remember: remember the battle and how people died, and to remind the government about Ben Guerdane, which was forgotten," one of the main organizers argued. "We want to remind the state of Ben Guerdane—for sixty years, people have waited for development in Ben Guerdane, and that is what we want to remind them of." This argument was not separate from the local smuggling economy: "The relationship between the state and Ben Guerdane depends on Ras Jedir; if it is open things will go well, and if it is closed there will be difficulties. So we hope that one day the state will find a replacement for this gate."[97]

The events also showed an awareness by the organizers and volunteers that despite having been the scene of a victory against a terrorist group, they were still associated with terrorism in public discourse. In the words of a local activist: "We want to show a good image for Ben Guerdane, show that we are against terrorism, that terror can never win here. We want to show people a good image for the South. And we want to give young people hope so that they do not turn to terrorism."[98] One of the organizers mirrored this sentiment: "These events are to show people many things. We are not the factory of terrorists, we are the grave of terrorists. The sons of Ben Guerdane, these youth here, they like life."[99] Many of the events also tried to highlight the city's economic potential. A run to the beach aimed to remind its audience that Ben Guerdane was close to the sea, and that a tourism industry could be developed there.

Not everyone in Ben Guerdane was behind this project, however. While some enjoyed the events and noted the chance to present a better image of Ben Guerdane to national media, others took issue with the concerts and poetry readings on religious grounds or found them inappropriate in the context. Others opposed the costs, arguing that the money should instead be spent on development projects, or found the event to take a too conciliatory tone with respect to a state that had failed to make good on its promises to deliver economic development.

Two public plenary discussions on "youth" and "economic development" also illustrated the difficulties of the local civil society in addressing these topics. While the invited speakers at the seminar on economic development struggled to apply their lectures to the circumstances of Ben Guerdane, the discussion that followed quickly foregrounded popular grievances. "The government locally exists only as police and security forces, not as investment," one of the contributors concluded. "The government has said to Ben Guerdane: 'You have Ras Jedir, work as much as you want, but we are watching you.'"[100] Multiple speakers expressed frustration that the wealthiest smugglers, when choosing to diversify into the formal sector, would invest in the country's North rather than in their city. Comments included calls for action directed at the state, especially with respect to investment, alongside complete disillusionment with the state. "The government has always been absent here," another participant argued; "the only thing it gives us is Dolopran," comparing the toleration of the local smuggling economy with a popular painkiller. As the question-and-answer session went on, disagreements among members of the audience became increasingly heated, and a fist-fight ensued.

The next day's event was a seminar on youth. Organized by a civil society organization, the event was held in front of a full audience—but, apart from the few young women who were paid to work at the event, I was the youngest person in the room, by a significant margin. Ben Guerdane's youth had chosen to be entirely absent from the seminar that was advertised to discuss its future. The first of three invited middle-aged speakers launched directly into a discussion of jihadi radicalization, assuming that this was such an obvious prism through which to see the local youth that it did not warrant an explanation. The other two, a French academic and a former government minister, entirely ignored the issue of youth in their talks. "Oh, thank God they flew in a French professor to tell me I'm not a terrorist," one participant scoffed as we walked out. At the same time, many of the younger civil society activists were near the youth house and the sports fields, practicing a performance to be presented to the prime minister.

Prime Minister Chahed's visit represented an encounter between the government of a postrevolutionary state that was still developing its policies toward Ben Guerdane and a city that was divided and unsure about what to expect from this new state that had so far very much felt like the old one. On the morning of the visit, Ben Guerdane woke up to the number of local police checkpoints having multiplied. Security force presence on the street was overwhelming, and moving around was difficult. From the early morning on, fighter jets flew over the town at a low altitude and at regular intervals. People were livid, interpreting the jets as an intimidation tactic and the security presence as a sign that the prime minister felt that he needed to be protected from the people of Ben Guerdane—the exact people who were expecting his praise for having protected Tunisia against the Islamic State.

When Chahed gave a televised speech in the city center, angry protesters could be heard throughout, chanting "get out," or "Marzouki," the name of the former president and one of Chahed's political rivals. The visit contained important promises, designed to raise the prospect of a more positive and developmental engagement between the city and the central state. They included the development of a local industrial zone, a water desalination project, compensation for the martyrs' families, and the transfer of the land of the Souk Maghrebi to the municipality. And yet after the early tones of this encounter, the substance of the speech had become irrelevant. Instead, the local reaction was quickly characterized by mistrust. I watched the speech together with a group of traders and vendors in the Souk Maghrebi market. Most of the vendors agreed with the sentiments of the protesters. After the speech, a little joke made the rounds, based on the prime minister's last name also being the Arabic word for "witness." "Are you with Chahed?" one vendor asked the other. "No," the other replied, "I'm with the suspect."

Before the end of the day's festivities, and before the presentation of a show rehearsed by the city's Youth House, the prime minister had already left Ben Guerdane. Among the things he left behind was a statue commemorating the martyrs of the 2016 attack, which had been the center of much controversy in the week leading up to his visit. Rumors about enormous costs of the statue had given rise to accusations of corruption and waste; others were frustrated with its location in a square that had become commonly used for protests and demonstrations. Now, as it was supposed to be unveiled by the prime minister, it turned out that the statue was still not finished. It would remain unfinished for another year.[101]

Youssef Chahed's day in Ben Guerdane, on the anniversary of the 2016 attack, had been a microcosm of the complex relationship between Tunisian state and the city. Despite some optimism in the run-up, and despite lofty development promises, it had been characterized by frustration and mistrust—both as the result of previous broken promises and because the logistics of the visit once again served as a reminder of the security focus that had long been the lowest common denominator of this interaction. Mirroring the discussion of smuggling within moral perceptions at the end of chapter 4, this also acts as a reminder for this book, which largely focuses on the materialistic aspects of the relationship between smugglers and states, that the local reliance on these rents and relationships does not necessarily imply that they are perceived as legitimate, desirable, or dignified. In the years that followed the 2017 visit, however, the maintenance of these rent streams and their partial collapse took center stage. With this came the challenge of adapting to these changing circumstances—a challenge that had begun a few years earlier in Morocco.

Chapter Seven

MOROCCO

Smugglers and Reform

July 2013 was a fateful month for the mayor of Oujda, Omar Hajiira. At the beginning of the month, he had attended a popular Moroccan talk show and voiced some of the challenges that came with governing a city dependent on smuggling economies.[1] Drugs were coming into the country; expired foodstuffs were affecting the health of the local population. In the standard move of a Moroccan politician looking for applause, Hajiira turned the conversation to Algeria: "Why are our neighbors doing this to us?" Just a few days later, it looked like Algeria was replying. In late July, soldiers began digging a trench along the northern section of its border with Morocco, the dramatic beginning of a larger effort to fortify its western border, which in the following years would include a larger trench, and finally a wall.[2] Much of the local smuggling trade, and in particular the gasoline trade, began to collapse. Omar Hajiira returned to a city in crisis.

While it's still a popular local talking point that Hajiira's TV appearance directly caused these developments, the increase in border fortification is, in fact, more consistent with a wider Algerian strategy, mirrored on the border with Tunisia and Mali, of fortifying its borders in the context of security concerns.[3] The previous chapter described how the closures of the Ras Jedir border crossing in Tunisia, even for a few weeks, have set off significant protest movements, directly threatening state control in the borderlands. Morocco's Northeast, traditionally no less dependent on its smuggling economy, now faced a permanent closure. A rent stream that had been fundamental to its informal integration into the national political settlement had dried up, almost overnight. And yet, against expectations, the collapse of the local smuggling economy did not cause a major destabilization of Morocco's Northeast. The region did experience an economic crisis, but protests were generally small and sparse. What had happened?

While the previous chapter has argued that, underneath a flurry of dramatic events, the fundamental dependence of Tunisia's political settlement on smuggling rents has remained constant in the past decade, this chapter argues the opposite for Morocco. It demonstrates that in the decade before the smuggling economy's collapse, a series of political and economic reforms, sparked largely by the ascendancy of a new king and Morocco's response to the 2011 uprisings, reduced the importance of the rents generated by the smuggling economy, restructured the intersection between state and traders, and created alternative strategies for key local elites and merchants. These changes, together with the acceleration of formal state investment in the region after the border closure and the continuation of the smuggling economy on the border with Melilla, at least until 2019, provided a context for the restructuring of income streams in the northeastern borderlands. While the Tunisian case represents the continuation of an informal integration into the political settlement of its borderlands in the context of the transition from authoritarianism to democracy, the Moroccan case describes the increased formalization of the incorporation of the borderlands into the wider political settlement in the context of the maintenance of the authoritarian political structure.

This chapter traces the changes in Morocco's political settlement from the perspective of its northeastern borderlands. Like the previous chapter, it examines the negotiations and changes that maintained the combination of formal and informal rent streams, institutions, and power structures that characterize political settlements. As in the Tunisian case, it also observes a restructuring of the intersection between state and informal actors. Contrary to the Tunisian case, however, which noted the strengthening of the organizational capacities of informal actors to articulate demands from the bottom up, albeit without breaking free of the confinements of an informal incorporation into the political settlement, organizational changes within the border economy in Morocco were more actively shaped by the state in a top-down fashion.

The chapter begins with the reforms enacted in the early years of the reign of Mohamed VI, a new development plan for the Oriental, and the reforms that followed the 2011 uprisings. It discusses how these reforms have changed the situation and opportunities of those involved in the local smuggling economies before 2013. Finally, it examines the effects of the new border fortifications from 2013 onward, as well as the support programs for borderland communities that were introduced by the Moroccan state and their ripple effects until the end of the decade, when further restrictions were placed on smuggling in Ceuta and Melilla.

A NEW KING, AND A NEW START FOR THE NORTH

For Morocco, the new millennium began with a new monarch. In July 1999 Hassan II, who had shaped Morocco's postindependence development for almost four decades, passed away, leaving his crown prince to become King Mohamed VI. As is common in monarchical transitions, the new ruler was publicly framed as a reformer, breaking with some of the policies of his father. In his speeches, he promised to tackle corruption and create jobs for the country's youth. In 2004 he created a commission to investigate human rights abuses committed under his father's rule, pursued new international trade agreements, and passed a new family code, which was framed as advancing women's rights in the largely conservative country. Particularly prominent was his public positioning as an advocate for the poor and the disadvantaged.[4] While the real effects of many of these reforms have been questioned, they represent an effort to solidify the king's position at the center of the country's political equation, employing reforms to balance demands for political and economic liberalization and strengthen links with new constituencies.[5]

One corollary of this was the reshaping of the palace's relationship with the country's Northeast. Hassan II had an infamous scorn for the region after having played a key role in putting down the Rif rebellion in 1958, publicly referred to its people as "thieves" and "savages" during the 1980s bread riots, and refused to visit it for much of his reign[6]. His son did not appear to have inherited these prejudices. The region's historic economic neglect not only made it a logical candidate for a demonstration of the king's pro-poor policies but also highlighted the need for local investment in order to counter risks of local unrest and illegal emigration.

And so, on March 18, 2003, Mohamed VI gave a speech in Oujda that outlined the palace's new development program for the region, launching the "Royal Initiative for the Development of the Oriental." Aiming to stimulate investment, youth employment, and especially the small and medium enterprise (SME) sector, the initiative was initially endowed with 30 million MAD, to be supplemented by funds from other institutions. Its propositions were representative of the general thrust of the king's social and development policies at the time, institutionalized in 2005 in the National Initiative for Human Development. They were was also typical in their symbolic and practical proximity to the royal palace and the central state—up until 2014 the headquarters of the agency tasked with developing the Oriental was still located in Rabat, 500 kilometers away.

Beyond underlining the image of the king as a pro-poor reformer, his speech also hinted at the program's political logic. It put the investments in the context of the fight against "poverty, marginalization, and all the fancies of extremism," praised the region's "loyalty and allegiance," mentioned its crucial role for Morocco's stability and security, describing it as a "bulwark providing the Moroccan state protection," and twice referenced its ability to provide "immunity."[7] From the early 2000s onward, the state's increasing involvement and investment in the Northeast already noted an awareness of the risks of social unrests in its periphery, reacting with a conscious, though slight, adjustment of a distribution of formal resources.

The importance of this dimension was to be repeatedly reinforced in the years that followed. In 2004 an earthquake in the region again exposed the degree to which public infrastructure had been neglected. Media coverage emphasized the role that the repeated visits of the king and promises of intense economic support played in dampening local protests following the tragedy.[8] The larger test, however, came in 2011. Unlike Tunisia, Morocco did not experience a revolution in 2011, but it did not remain unaffected by the uprisings sweeping the region. On February 20 thousands protested in the capital city of Rabat, decrying corruption in the country's political system as well as high unemployment, staggering inequalities, rising living costs, and police brutality. Large protests followed in most of the country's major cities.[9]

Similar to the other monarchies in the region, the Moroccan state reacted to the protests by promising social and political reforms, paired with promises of higher social spending and selective opposition crackdown.[10] On May 9 King Mohamed VI announced constitutional reforms in a televised speech. In July they were accepted by a popular referendum, followed by new parliamentary elections. The reforms included—formally—strengthening the authority of parliament and the prime minister, making Tamazight an official language of the country, and committing to a decentralization agenda.[11]

While they did not topple the regime, the events of 2011 did bring the protest potential of economic inequality back to the attention of the country's administration. Albeit less dramatically than in Ben Guerdane, the region around Oujda had already seen sporadic protests in 2010 and saw additional protests in 2011.[12] While the development initiative for the Northeast predates the 2011 uprisings, many of the larger projects in the region, such as the expansion of formal market structures for street vendors or the promotion of a national program to formalize informally self-employed workers, fell into the post-2011 period. In the words of Oujda's mayor: "We are afraid of the vendors, because there are things happening now, like with the Arab Spring, and you have to remember we are in a border region here. We have to build something here, or there will be trouble. So instead of forbidding it, we have tried to organize it a little bit."[13]

A large focus of the new programs launched between 2003 and 2013 was on infrastructure development, picking up on previous grievances and symbolically and practically addressing the region's marginalization. Multiple projects strengthened the region's connection to the rest of the country through investments in transport links, including an extension of the highway between Oujda and Fez, the construction of a large port in Nador, the extension of Oujda-Angad airport, and the completion of a large highway along the Mediterranean between Tangier and Saidia.

Further projects included industrial parks, the extension of Oujda's hospital, a thermal solar station in Ain Beni Mathar, and two large tourist developments along the Mediterranean coast in Saidia and Nador. The INDH, launched by the king in 2005 with a budget of 10 billion MAD over its first five years, was aimed at improving living conditions in selected cities and rural municipalities throughout the country—many of which were situated within the Oriental.[14] Its activities ranged from the provision of new carts for street vendors to cultural activities to the reconstruction of some of Oujda's large informal markets: the Souk Tanger, the Souk Quds, and the Souk Melilla. Between 2005 and 2016 the INDH reports having invested 391 million MAD in the prefecture of Oujda-Angad alone.[15]

The past few years have seen an academic debate on whether the reforms of the early years of Mohamed VI's reign, as well as particularly the constitutional changes from 2011 onward, represent a genuine change of Morocco's political and economic structure or should primarily be interpreted as window dressing by an autocratic regime.[16] While these discussions lie beyond the scope of this book, a full evaluation of the development interventions in the Northeast is complicated by the fact that in some cases not a lot of time has elapsed since their completion. Still, two wider statements can be made based on the research conducted for this project.

First, among the members of the local business community, politicians, administrators, and those involved in the development projects in the Oriental interviewed for this project, a significant consensus emerged that many of the local development projects have not yet delivered as hoped. While most agreed that the infrastructure upgrade was real and helpful, there was significant disappointment with the small amount of private investment it had generated. So far, private investments had been "very, very limited," one high official in the Agence Oriental summarized: "We still cannot compete."[17] The industrial zones, in particular, had trouble attracting businesses. Oujda's "Technopole," designed to create fifteen thousand jobs and originally limited exclusively to companies working on "clean tech" and renewable energies, quickly dropped these conditions, ultimately taking on automobile vendors to fill its space.[18] The absence of a strategy that integrated local labor in the construction of these projects, with some construction companies drawing on expat labor instead, caused significant tension.[19] While a newly created program to give a new "self-employed" legal status to informal own-account workers attracted over 100,000 applications in a few years, those were mainly in coastal areas, with the Oriental vastly underrepresented.[20]

Second, despite these shortcomings, some of the reforms and developments did contribute to a diversification of the income streams of some of the actors in the local smuggling economy. More important, both by decreasing the local reliance on rent streams from the smuggling economy and effecting the restructuring of the intersection between smugglers and state structures, these changes contributed to the absence of large-scale protest or destabilization following the border closure. The next section will elaborate on this.

CHANGING RENT STREAMS IN THE ORIENTAL

Interviews with a variety of officials involved suggest that development activities in the Oriental between 2003 and 2013 were not designed to substitute smuggling rents or make them less important to the political settlement, at least in the short to medium term. In the words of a leading administrator in the Agence Orientale, the plan was not to replace the smuggling economy, but "to formalize the contraband, to make it visible."[21] Nevertheless, at least three features of the 2003–2013 reform agenda directly influenced the Oriental's smuggling economy: Morocco's free-trade agreements, the construction of new markets in the city center alongside the creation of new market associations, and the investment opportunities provided by construction projects and the real estate sector. All these would influence how the region reacted to the border closure in 2013.

Free-Trade Agreements

Opening Morocco up to the international market has become a hallmark of Mohamed VI's trade policy, including new free-trade agreements with Turkey (2003), the UAE (2003), Egypt, Jordan, and Tunisia (2004) and the United States (2005), and an Advanced Status Agreement in the context of the European Neighbourhood Agreement with the European Union (2008).

For informal trade networks, these meant new competition. Two of their traditional competitive advantages vis-à-vis the country's formal import sector were slowly eroded: the cheaper price of their goods due to tariff avoidance, and the availability of goods that had not before been formally imported, especially from the European Union. Many vendors noted that the demand for their goods had begun to decrease, as "people used to come from Casablanca to Oujda to buy things, and now that is just not happening anymore."[22] Imports from Melilla, too, decreased in importance. While Morocco's total imports from Spain increased by 289 percent between 2000 and 2012, Melilla's imports—as a proxy for the goods smuggled to Morocco—increased by only 18 percent in the same time frame.[23]

The origin of the goods sold in Oujda's city markets began to change. While almost all goods sold in the Souk Melilla had been smuggled in from the Spanish enclave in the early 2000s, a decade later many vendors had started to also legally import their goods via the port of Casablanca or buy from wholesalers who had done so.[24] Turkish and Chinese textiles, in particular, became increasingly important, but this was not limited to textiles—vendors in the Souk Fellah who had traditionally been supplied through smuggling networks with Algeria also mentioned that they had begun to buy more from Casablanca.[25] One of these adjustments had become a treasured story of a formal sector entrepreneur and former politician in Oujda:

> When I was still head of the [redacted to ensure anonymity], there were two young men who would sell in front of my office, some canned food product. They had imported it from Algeria, it was smuggled good, but originally it came from Turkey. I could see that those were bright young men, so I talked to them. And I asked them: "Why do you bring this in from Algeria. We have a free-trade agreement with Turkey—just bring it in legally!" And they didn't know that they could do this, and now they bring in whole containers from Casablanca.[26]

The effects of this were not homogeneous. For example, when I spoke to fabric vendors smuggling through Melilla who had specialized in a high-end market and were well-acquainted with their clientele, they remarked that they did not feel the competition as much as their colleagues working in a lower price segment.[27] Access to capital also determined whether traders were able to capitalize on new opportunities. While smaller vendors would buy from wholesalers in Casablanca, transporting the goods to Oujda themselves and becoming increasingly uncompetitive, wholesalers could build relationships directly with producers in China or Turkey, ordering goods by the container. A clothes vendor in Nador who had originally imported his goods from Melilla and Algeria told me about his visit to China in 2011. He had visited a trade exhibition in Guangdong Province and recalled having been amazed at the large contingent from northern Morocco: "You'd be sitting at a restaurant, in China, speaking Tamazight, and people would come up to you and say 'Oh, you're from Nador, too!'"[28] Building relationships with suppliers in China, Turkey, or Casablanca helped some of the traders to rebuild a competitive advantage by obtaining better rates or monopoly access to certain goods.[29] For those who couldn't, it has meant a weakening of their competitiveness. For both, it has meant a decrease in their reliance on informal cross-border commerce.

New Markets and Market Associations

One of the cornerstones of the INDH's activities in Oujda was the construction of new markets for the city's informal vendors. The markets fall into two categories. The first includes twenty-eight comparatively small markets built in the urban periphery as part of the "program against social exclusion in the urban space." Most of them, as their administrators confirm, have not been successful: located in the city's periphery, they do not provide commercial spaces that are attractive enough to motivate street vendors to give up their spots on the busy roads of the city center.[30]

This differentiates them from the second category of the new markets—the big ones in the city center already described in chapter 4, largely representing a formalization of formerly informal markets in the same locations, and including significant investments from the municipality, the region, and the vendors themselves. They are significantly larger, hosting several hundred vendors, in some of the best commercial space in the city. The main markets here are the Souk Tanger, the Souk Quds, and the Souk Melilla.[31] While the reconstruction of the Souk Tanger involved the initiative of Oujda's mayor and the temporary relocation of the vendors during its construction, the initiative for the reconstruction of the Souk Melilla came from a fire that destroyed large sections of the original, informal market in 2011.[32] By the summer of 2017, a new market for the Souk Fellah had also been constructed, but the vendors had not moved to their new location yet.

As discussed earlier, these markets had been a central part of the distributional network for licit contraband goods in the region. This was unaffected by their renewal. The new markets did not introduce any controls over the origin or legality of the goods sold, supporting the argument that the purpose of these projects was not the replacement of the smuggling economy, but its structuring and organization by the state. "By constructing a market, they won't make the contraband stop, but this market currently doesn't look legal, it doesn't look nice, it just doesn't," the head of a vendor's association said about the plans for a new market. "The government doesn't care about whether the products are legal, it's whether the market looks legal."[33] An official within the INDH program tasked with the construction of the new markets described their primary mission not as the replacement, formalization, or legalization of the smuggling economy, but as the "embellishment of the city."[34] Here, the markets mirror a wider national strategy of the "sedentarization" of informal and roadside vendors.[35]

Still, the new markets had distinct effects on the distribution networks of the local smuggling economy. Three main points stand out here: First, they provided a new, and significantly improved, infrastructure for the vendors. Aside from aspects such as the security of tenure that came with the legality of the new arrangements, particularly relevant for vendors interested in renting out, selling, or passing on their stores, vendors mentioned the quality of the new infrastructure.

Second, the new markets drew the local vendors' finances into closer contact with both the formal banks and the municipality. The agreements between vendors and the various state entities involved in the markets' construction around the sharing of the construction costs of the ownership structure of the market stalls required some vendors to open bank accounts.[36] Similar to the Tunisian case, the agreements formalized and regularized their fiscal relationships with the municipality, while also clearly assigning the latter responsibilities toward the vendors, such as the maintenance of the market structures.

Third, the construction of the new markets transformed the intersection between the vendors and local state institutions by elevating the role of market associations. Since the early 2000s the number of associations has increased dramatically across the country, having become a preferred tool of the Moroccan state to structure its intersection with civil society, their legal status striking a balance "between an opening up toward civil society and the maintenance of 'soft' state control."[37] All market constructions and reconstructions in Oujda, alongside other development and social projects, were conditional on the creation of an association representing the local vendors. In many cases, local state representatives appear to have been critical in the creation of these associations. Many heads of local associations mentioned having been originally encouraged to form their association by a local politician or state representative.[38] For the creation of many of the new markets, INDH employees themselves organized meetings for the local vendors so that an association president could be elected.[39]

Associations played an important role not only in providing input into the market construction but also in generating the lists of vendors who would benefit—a point that, according to local administrators, commonly sparked conflict.[40] The heads of the associations became the main mediators both between the vendors and the local state structures and among the vendors themselves. Thereby they were replacing the previous informal mediators in the markets, the *Amin Tujjar*, typically older male vendors who had previously represented vendors and craftsmen but had largely disappeared by the time of the market reconstruction.[41] Contrary to the *Amin Tujjar*, the heads of the market associations quickly became members of the local chamber of commerce and, rather than mere technical mediators within the market, began to function as local political entrepreneurs.

The foundation of formal civil society organizations presents a key similarity in the restructuring of the intersection between state and informal traders in both Tunisia and Morocco in the context of the negotiation of the institutional regulation of smuggling. As demonstrated in the previous chapter, even if not all vendors are members, or broadly supportive of these associations, the organizational capacity of traders, legal status, freedom of expression, and access to information can have a direct impact on the balance of power between traders and state structures. However, there are distinct differences between the politics of local associations around informal trade in Tunisia and Morocco.

Contrary to their Tunisian counterparts, none of Oujda's market associations seems to engage in, or in any way associate with, radical politics, public protests, or strikes. While the associations themselves are, like in the Tunisian case, not typically associated with political parties, their presidents largely are. As one association president highlighted, an association with a party is particularly beneficial for their role within the chamber of commerce, where it not only provides political allies and instant access to a full political program.[42] Heads of market associations in Oujda with whom I spoke, however, do not seem to cluster around any particular party but are associated with parties across the entire Moroccan political spectrum.

Unsurprisingly, association presidents in their discourse also largely follow the typical "red lines" for accepted politics in Morocco—they are not openly critical of the king and largely share the state's discourse on development politics. As a result, many of the vendors perceive the market associations as associated with the Moroccan state. "Associations are part of the municipality," one textile vendor complained. "They don't do much for the vendors, and they don't do much for us. It's all political."[43]

The reasons for this can be found in the wider political context of the associations' work. Three points are worth highlighting here. First, in contrast to the Tunisian case, the influence of the leadership of the market associations in Oujda was derived less from their ability to leverage popular protest against the state, which they at no point threaten or participate in, than from being able to monopolize the intersection between local administration and vendors. In this position, they are also dependent on the state itself. While there are no laws prohibiting the founding of multiple associations in one market, there is typically only one association that functions as a link to local state authorities.[44] In the case of multiple associations, one of the local representatives of the INDH explained, "the authority has to pick the most credible association," adding that they "let the associations at first do their thing, but if that doesn't go well the authorities will intervene."[45]

Second, while Tunisia's transition from authoritarianism to democracy significantly expanded the organizational capacities of civil society associations, this was not equally the case in Morocco. The number of civil society associations increased in the early 2000s, but they remained constrained in their possibilities by Morocco's authoritarian political structure and the risks of arrests or crackdowns.

Third, the interactions between civil society associations in Tunisia in the immediate post-2011 era were precipitated by a shift in the balance of power toward local traders, but the same cannot be said in the Moroccan context. As a result, the restructuring of the intersection between traders and state in the Moroccan context was shaped more through top-down preferences than through bottom-up pressures, resulting in the dominance of associations that—both before and after the 2013 border closure—remained largely conservative in their engagement with the Moroccan state. I will return to this point below.

It is important to note that the construction of these markets did not benefit everyone equally. Spaces were typically assigned based on the locations of the vendors in the previous market, primarily benefiting vendors who were already established in attractive city-center locations. This left some of the vendors outside the market structure altogether, and others with poor locations within the new structures.[46] Some vendors in the old informal markets were unable to pay the financial contribution that came from the vendors for the move to the new market or couldn't afford the rent. At the same time, some suffered from the construction of another form of new, formal market. In 2007 Marjane, a Moroccan supermarket chain owned by the king's holding company, opened the first large supermarket in Oujda, with a space of 6,500 square meters.[47] In the two years that followed, Asswak Essalam, Metro, and Carrefour followed suit. A study conducted by the Chamber of Commerce in 2009 found that more than 75 percent of vendors polled attributed a decrease in their sales to the new markets, with foodstuffs, cosmetics, cleaning products, and "white electronics" most severely affected.[48]

The Real Estate Market

One final change in income opportunities began before the new economic programs in the Oriental but has interacted with and expanded through them. It involves the increasing diversification of the income of some of the members of smuggling networks through investments in the formal sector, particularly the real estate market.

One of the most notable differences between the investment strategies of large-scale informal traders in Tunisia and those in Morocco lies in the relative ease with which traders in Morocco appear to be able to manage their income through the formal banking system, the trust that they have developed toward the system, and their propensity to invest in formal projects. While some of the large-scale traders in Ben Guerdane have pursued formal sector investments, this has been comparatively limited, as many of the vendors and informal financiers still hold significant amounts of their money in cash.[49] Some of this may be attributable to more rigid enforcement of anti–money laundering mechanisms in Tunisia, but it is likely just as much affected by a general mistrust of both the state and the formal banking system. Traders have largely ignored attempts at legal amnesties to encourage the formalization of black-market cash. One administration official in the Tunisian South went to meet with a variety of traders to encourage them to formalize their assets. "We even showed them the law. I had brought an accountant with me, but people just say 'yeah, okay, it is written here, but who knows what the state will do,'" he recalls.[50]

In Morocco, there are strong indications that the movement of informally generated income into the formal economy, and hence the diversification by large-scale informal traders, is significantly more widespread. Regional bureaucrats are relatively transparent about this in interviews. "These people are not forbidden from investing in the formal economy here," a regional representative of the Ministry of Commerce confirmed to me. Asked about inquiries on where the money originated, he replied: "No, absolutely not, that is not a problem. We will take their capital, no matter where it is from. It's the same with bank accounts. These people, they are great merchants, when they put a lot of money in the bank, nobody will ask them where it comes from."[51] Statistics support these accounts: even though Nador records a lower per capita income than the Moroccan average, it registers a high level of bank accounts, containing deposits that are on average twice as high as the national average.[52]

A full discussion of the drivers of this difference in engagement with the formal banking system lies beyond both the scope and focus of this chapter. Nevertheless, it is notable that remittances from Moroccans living in Europe have historically played a significant and systematically encouraged role in developing the Oriental, especially in its real estate sector. "People who went to Europe always thought they'd come back here, so they invested here. The banks here got a lot of capital from this," a local city planner remembers.[53] As many remittances entered the local market informally, a structure of toleration of these transactions around remittances would be easily accessible for informal traders as well. Other interviews have speculated that the toleration of these activities may be more strategic. "There is a chain, and the state is the weakest link in it, and it knows that, and otherwise there would be no investment anyway," one local political operative argued.[54]

As a result, the decade before the fortification of the Algeria-Tunisia border already saw significant investments from informal trade networks in formal businesses and the real estate sector in the Oriental.[55] This included chic cafes that can be found across Oujda and Nador, lavish wedding spaces outside of the cities, and residential real estate.[56] While investments from traders involved in the drug economy played a particularly large role here, this has also included wholesale traders in licit goods and rural actors who had invested in land.[57] A high official in Oujda's center of urban development reports that 10,428 requests for new construction projects were submitted in 2011: "There is a lot of construction going on where you see people who made their money in contraband."[58] Officials I spoke to in the centers for urban development and local development agencies in both Oujda and Nador, as well as the regional administration, also directly connected a boom in real estate purchases and prices in recent years to investment coming from the smuggling economy.[59] As a former drug smuggler argued, the limited visibility of real estate ownership made it attractive: "So people mainly bought houses, like the houses over there, but if they had a nice car, that would show how much money they have."[60]

While it is unclear whether hopes to capitalize on investments from the region's informal economy played a role in the conception of the development projects that were implemented in the Oriental after 2003, there was a concerted effort to attract private capital from the region, and especially its diaspora. An UNCTAD report outlining investment opportunities in the Oriental region highlights that "the diaspora is an essential source of foreign capital, which regional governments are above all aiming to channel into productive sectors."[61] What is certain is that the investment in infrastructure, roads, and transport that came with the post-2003 projects also benefited the local real estate sector. In addition, it created direct investment opportunities. While the extent to which these have been taken up by members of smuggling economies is difficult to estimate, a high-ranking official in the Agence Oriental explicitly confirmed that many of the new houses built in the Marchica project, a large-scale tourism project on the region's Mediterranean shore, had in fact been bought by local investors in order to launder money.[62]

The opportunities for economic diversification presented by the expanding real estate market and the new development projects were of course not equally relevant for all members of the local smuggling economy but primarily benefited those with larger capital reserves. This includes large-scale wholesalers of licit goods, wholesalers in the gasoline trade, and those trading in illicit goods, especially narcotics.

Before the Closure

Contrary to southeastern Tunisia, northeastern Morocco has not witnessed large-scale protests, a revolution, strikes, fleeing police, or the effects of a civil war across its border in the past decade.[63] At the same time, not all development projects outlined in King Mohamed VI's 2003 visit or the constitutional reforms of 2011 materialized quite as planned, or to everyone's benefit. As this section has outlined, however, the free-trade agreements, the construction of new market infrastructures, the rise of market associations, and the opportunities for diversification created by the real estate market and the new development projects all had an impact on rent and income structures in the borderlands. They decreased the reliance of some local actors on income streams generated through smuggling across the Algerian border, as they either supplied alternative sources of income or provided the infrastructure that would make it easier to gain access to new sources of income outside of the smuggling economy. At the same time, they restructured the intersection between local state structures and smugglers in a way that—contrary to the Tunisian case—did not coincide with a shift in the underlying power relations, largely following top-down reforms. Both dynamics became crucial when, beginning in 2013, the fortification of the Algerian-Moroccan border led to the collapse of various local smuggling activities and removed one of the central rent streams that had integrated the region into the wider political settlement.

CONNECTING THE BORDERLANDS

While the land border between Morocco and Algeria had been officially closed since the Atlas Hotel attack in Marrakesh in 1994, it had remained highly porous in the two decades that followed, as discussed in chapter 3. Initiated by Algeria, this porosity decreased rapidly from 2013 onward due to a set of border fortifications, beginning with a trench dug by Algeria, followed by an electronic surveillance structure added by Morocco in 2014, followed by the construction of a wall by Algeria.[64] The construction of this infrastructure came hand in hand with an end of the general toleration of the local smuggling economy by members of the Algerian security services.

The collapse of the cross-border trade with Algeria made the old informal inclusion of northern Morocco into the country's political settlement untenable, as a crucial rent stream was cut off. Previous sections have argued that the time between 2003 and 2013 created opportunities for diversification for some local actors, but the years following 2013 put these to the test. In fact, despite the collapse of one of the central rent streams that had informally incorporated Morocco's Northeast into the wider political settlement, no protest movements emerged that were comparable to the ones observed in Tunisia during periods of border closures. There are no indications that

Morocco was in any serious danger of losing control over its northern border regions between 2013 and 2021.

This was largely due to two mechanisms through which rent streams were restructured after 2013, thereby altering the integration of the region into the wider political settlement. The first was the adjustment of local traders to the new situation by rerouting their supply streams through Melilla or Casablanca or relying more heavily on formal income streams. Second was an aid program provided by the Moroccan state. I argue that the changes introduced between 2003 and 2013, together with the projects launched by the state to support the borderlands after 2013, led to a formalization of the political settlement, in which rent streams from Algeria were no longer fundamental to local stability and the local economy was more directly connected to the Moroccan state.

Adapting

The border fortifications came as a surprise for local traders. Many told me that they had expected that porosity would increase again soon. Small protests in the border region led local authorities to offer reassurances that the situation was temporary.[65] It was not. The increase in border fortifications dramatically decreased the ability of different smuggling networks to bring in goods from Algeria, especially those trading in licit goods and survivalist activities. A study conducted by Oujda's chamber of commerce estimated that of the informally traded goods in Oujda in 2004, 40 percent of textiles, 72 percent of electronic goods, 73 percent of pharmaceuticals, and 91 percent of home appliances had come in from Algeria, but goods brought in from Algeria had become a rarity by 2016.[66] The gasoline trade almost entirely collapsed. While whole villages in the borderlands had spent their nights bringing thousands of canisters across the border, by 2016 only a few traders reported managing to bring across small quantities, in rare windows of opportunity every few weeks.[67]

Following the fortification of the Algerian border, some of the traders who had originally worked on the Algerian border began to supply themselves through Melilla or seek employment as carriers across the border of Melilla.[68] Others constructed more complicated routes to Algeria: some Moroccan-made goods, including shoes, underwear, and jeans, that used to be carried directly across the border were now brought to Melilla, then shipped to the harbor of Malaga and moved to ships headed for the port of Ghazaouet in Algeria, where they are being imported and underdeclared in exchange for a bribe.[69] Algerian dates, which were commonly smuggled across the border and sold in the markets of Beni Drar and Oujda, were reported to have been rerouted via Melilla.[70]

More commonly, however, traders chose to resupply via Casablanca instead. This was exacerbated by the wider effect of the economic crisis, as it decreased the local demand for the commonly more high-end products coming in from Melilla. In the words of a senior figure of a local market association: "People are not buying and not selling, many cannot afford to go to Melilla and buy things, so people prefer to go to Casablanca and get Turkish products, because they are cheaper."[71] For many of the textile traders, preexisting commercial connections to Casablanca and the formalized market infrastructure established before 2013 eased this transition.[72] Even for traders who had to change their supply structure or even their field of trade—some switched to electronics, which were still in relatively high demand—the new markets supplied an infrastructure and a well-located place of sale. While many of the gasoline vendors left the occupation entirely, others sought to also restructure their supply networks, buying from formal gas stations or independent suppliers.[73]

Large-scale traders who had some capital available or had already invested in the formal sector, especially in the real estate sector and the hospitality and gastronomy sector before 2013, were able to build more extensively on these incomes. In one case, a former electronics trader in one of the city's formerly informal markets built up a chain of formal stores. In another case, a former gasoline wholesaler built one of the sixteen new formal gas stations that were opened in Oujda in 2016 alone.[74]

Still, opportunities to adjust were unevenly distributed. Large wholesale traders and some of the traders based in the formalized markets had some forms of capital savings, but many of the traders from rural borderland communities, especially young men involved in the gasoline trade that I spoke to, appear to have had little or no savings, despite at times significant incomes, or found their savings swiftly eaten up waiting for the border to reopen.[75] At the same time, the connections to their former bosses and wholesalers was typically not strong enough to find employment through them. Some of the rural communities along the border, which had been buzzing hubs of exchange in 2013, faced abject poverty just a few years later and found themselves, for the first time in decades, reliant on state support.

The Emergency Program for the Border

The fact that the new border fortifications had deprived borderland communities of their income was not lost on the Moroccan administration. In the context of an "Emergency Program for Development of the Borderlands," a variety of projects were launched over the following years under the leadership of the regional delegation of the central state.[76] While a comprehensive budget for the program was never published, local media reported a budget of 271 MAD for its first round, the majority of which was provided by the Ministry of Interior, with a potential 600 million for its second phase.[77]

While the post-2003 reform agenda in the region was not aimed at creating a formal economic structure in the borderlands to replace the smuggling economy, this had become the stated goal after 2013. "We cannot for ages leave a border with an informal economy and then all the sudden when it closes not help them," a local MP phrased it.[78] A high official in the regional administration spoke of a "replacement" strategy.[79] Others were more explicit. "A key goal is to create an infrastructure that will keep people in the borderlands, as we have already suffered enough from rural exodus," a senior official in a municipal organization argued. "If they come here, they will build something anarchic that will not be good for the city," he expanded, explicitly raising urbanization and informal settlements in the periphery of the region's cities as a central state concern.[80] A high official in the Agence Oriental struck a similar tone: "If we do not do this, these people will move to Casablanca, or to Tanger, or they will steal."[81] An exodus from the borderlands had already begun. "A lot of people have abandoned their houses here and moved to the city, because they couldn't survive out here when the border closed," a resident of a borderland community noted "When the border closed, I sold the two chickens that I had, just to feed my children."[82]

Given the concern about a rural exodus, it is unsurprising that the development project for the borderlands focused on rural projects and primarily included agricultural projects, and those aimed at the so-called social and solidarity economy. Key projects included the provision of irrigation for agricultural land in the border area, the encouragement of almond and olive cultivation, and government support for local, small-scale agricultural projects focused in particular on animal rearing.[83] The programs focused explicitly on fourteen districts along the border that had been judged as most affected by the collapse of the smuggling economy, with priority given to Beni Drar, Beni Khalid, and Angad.[84]

Crucially, like the 2003–2013 reforms, these programs not only aimed to provide aid but also took the opportunity to reorganize the intersection between the state and local communities. Development associations played a key role in managing the interaction with communities and negotiating access to state projects, and it was clearly communicated to borderland communities that aid would exclusively be provided to cooperatives. Agents from development agencies and local state administrations visited the borderlands and advised the formation of cooperatives. According to ODECO, the relevant administration, between August 2016 and 2017 alone, Angad saw seventy-five new cooperatives, Beni Khalid eighty, and Beni Drar ninety.[85]

At the same time, local state agencies began the process of integrating borderland settlements into the regional infrastructure network and land-use plans. While many of the settlements near the border had been built informally and without permission, *plans de redressement* were created to retrospectively formalize their creation.[86] Roads and water lines were extended—quite literally, borderland settlements were connected to the formal infrastructure of the Moroccan state. By 2015, borderland settlements near Oujda began to be connected to the national electricity grid, as a senior official in the Office National de l'Électricité (ONE) confirmed that despite the high costs, their inclusion had become a "political priority."[87] "Social stability and economic stability were the key concerns here," a senior official in a local planning office argued. "If things are going well, quiet, that is what matters."[88]

While proponents of the emergency program praised its strategic vision, many practitioners interviewed have expressed skepticism with respect to its feasibility and sufficiency. A senior official tasked with the implementation of some of the key agricultural axes of the program summed up commonly expressed doubts on the feasibility of agriculture as an alternative to smuggling: "Agriculture is, of course, the dominant sector here, but can it really absorb this unemployment? We have proposed projects to the youth, but so far very little has been taken up. To change the activity of someone who did contraband before, that is difficult. They are not ready for agriculture. Agriculture takes time, you need years to see the profit, that is hard for these youth that are used to immediate profit. Changing a mentality is hard."[89]

Many of the newly founded cooperatives expressed significant frustration with the support that they were receiving through the program. Implementation was slow—the first round of animals was given out to cooperatives in May 2017, years after the border closure. The number of animals given out frequently appeared to have been insufficient as a sustainable source of income.[90] In addition, with savings run down, many of the new cooperatives struggled to afford food for the animals, and while there was a restriction on selling any of the animals, this was not always followed. "The program is ineffective, because of the distribution problems, and because of the small quantities," the head of a local cooperative argued.[91] The connections to the electricity and water grid also faced difficulties locally, as the costs for individual households to connect to the network were often prohibitive.

The rural communities along the border were connected to a new, formal and legal, income stream, but the connection was tenuous, slow, and often confusing. At the mercy of a formal structure that was just developing, new to them, and characterized by state mismanagement and scarcity, many of the local communities were struggling to adjust to the new situation. The following chapter will return to this issue at length.

STABILITY AND FRAGILITY

This chapter has followed the quiet restructuring of rent streams in the Moroccan Northeast and their effect on local actors' abilities to adapt to the collapse of smuggling networks that traded with Algeria. Contrary to the experience of southern Tunisia, northeastern Morocco saw a reduction of the role of smuggling rents even before 2013, and after 2013 a conscious and targeted attempt through state programs to replace informal rent streams with formal ones. As a result, while a complete collapse of smuggling activities along the Tunisia-Libya border for a similar period would most likely pose a serious threat to the stability of southern Tunisia, the stability of the Oriental was not threatened. A smuggler of fabrics working through Melilla succinctly summed up the lack of large-scale unrest after the collapse of the Algeria routes: "They found alternatives."[92]

To a degree, the resilience of the Oriental to the border closure can hence be traced to the formalization of its incorporation into the wider political settlement. However, important caveats remain. The formalization of rent structures in Morocco's Northeast was partial. Until 2019 trade through Melilla still existed. Narcotics trafficking appeared to have been substantially less affected by the border fortifications.[93] And although the supply network had shifted more toward legal trade, the regulatory structure around the city markets remained of a hybrid nature, as discussed in chapter 4.

Notably, the decreasing role of smuggling rents was originally not the result of a strategic choice by the Moroccan government. It was first a side effect of a range of policies that were not aimed to replace smuggling, and it became a conscious aim of development engagement in the region only after 2013, when external pressures had led to the collapse of a range of local smuggling activities and raised the prospect of widespread starvation, unrest, and rural exodus in the borderlands without a replacement strategy. Even then, replacement was costly and fragile. The situation led the Moroccan state to undertake significant investments in infrastructure and agricultural projects in the borderlands that it had not been willing to undertake while smuggling rents were still high—and that the Tunisian state has not been willing to undertake until now.

However, there is one exception to this dynamic. While contractions in the role of smuggling rents along the Morocco-Algerian border were not directly triggered by the Moroccan state, recent restrictions on smuggling along the borders with the two Spanish enclaves of Ceuta and Melilla were likely more intentional. In 2019 and 2020 avenues to smuggle through regulated entry points between Morocco and the Spanish enclaves were increasingly shut down. This primarily affected the small-scale *portadores* carrying goods through the iron turnstiles in the border crossings. While many of the border closures with the enclaves following 2019 have overlapped with border closures motivated by the Covid-19 pandemic, the first crackdowns seem to predate the pandemic. They appear more rooted in tense Moroccan-Spanish relationships and unease that came with the image of the activities of poor small-scale traders illegally carrying goods across an EU frontier.

There are some indications that the Moroccan state's experience with the years following the 2013 closure has also influenced or at least informed their approach to the closures at Melilla and Ceuta. The analyses published by Morocco's Economic, Social and Environmental Council (CESE) provide a relevant source of state-sanctioned analyses of the impacts of the closure. As noted earlier, border fortifications along the Algerian border had not provided an insurmountable challenge to more highly capitalized actors, particularly in the narcotics trade. Similarly, CESE reports highlight that the new fortifications will likely not interdict all smuggling and will not be a substitute for addressing the deeper causes of smuggling.

The group most imminently affected by the closure and most vulnerable to it were the independent and contracted transporters carrying goods across for meager incomes. While the closures on the Moroccan-Algerian border saw the Moroccan state scrambling to put together projects to support the most vulnerable among those who had been put out of work, such programs seemed to have come in earlier and in a slightly more targeted manner along the Ceuta and Melilla crossings. Whether these have been successful in providing alternative livelihoods is too early to tell, in particular as the Covid-19 pandemic still weighs heavily on the region. The same is true for the wider effects of this closure on the formal and informal economy of northeastern Morocco. Here the decisive factor is likely whether large-scale operators and wholesale smugglers are able to find substitutes for the collapse of the "turnstile routes." While the closure brings serious risks to traders on both sides of the border—and in particular wholesalers in the two Spanish enclaves—it is worth noting, as discussed in this chapter, that the importance of smuggled goods through these enclaves for the retail markets of Northern Morocco had already decreased for years, in particular in competition with goods imported legally through Casablanca.

If the 2019 and 2020 closures further mirror the dynamics set in place in 2013, they double down on the wider dynamic that has characterized the Oriental in the past decade: the uneven replacement of informal rent streams with new income streams. "Uneven" is the central term here. While they have likely contributed to less social unrest following the border closures, access to these new income streams was not uniform and not always sufficient, still leaving the region in a severe economic crisis. As the following chapter will discuss, pockets of poverty and disconnection developed especially in rural borderland communities. Many of the people interviewed for this project expressed serious concerns about the future of the borderlands. "This place is like a hidden bomb that nobody sees, and that is ready to explode," a volunteer in a development association in a borderland community near Oujda argued.[94] "If we don't employ these people in the next five years, something really bad will happen," an Oujda resident made a similar point.[95] In the words of the head of an association in Nador: "The money here needs to reach the people before it is too late. And actually, it is too late. Too many of them have died already in the ocean, on the way to Europe."[96]

A sense of pressure and an uncertain look into the future unite the two case studies of this book. For both regions, this comes at the end of years of transformation of the intersection between the informal economy and state structures. In both countries, negotiations around the regulation of smuggling and distribution of rents alongside nationwide changes in the legal framework for civil society organizations have led to the establishment of more institutionalized channels of negotiation between state representatives and informal traders. However, in the nature and result of these lie critical contrasts. In Tunisia, these negotiations and institutionalizations coincided with a shift in the underlying balance of power away from a temporarily weakened state, alongside new space for civil society organizations in a democratizing national institutional structure. This allowed traders to establish organizations that were less dependent on the state or directly co-opted by it and at least momentarily leverage organizational capacity and local knowledge to shape regulation through bottom-up demands, albeit within the constraints of the still primarily informal integration into the political settlement. Following 2011, Morocco saw reforms rather than a revolution. Contrary to the Tunisian case, the restructuring of the intersection between smugglers and state in Morocco occurred in a context in which their integration into the political settlement was increasingly reliant on formal rent streams, and where the state had maintained a high enforcement capacity as well as a clearly authoritarian context. While traders in the borderlands frequently expressed understanding and desire for collective action and public protests, concerns about state crackdowns against protesters were common: "We are scared of prison. Everyone watches each other, everyone is afraid, if someone is planning something, they will catch them, because someone will have told the police."[97] As a result, the restructuring of the intersection between state and traders was significantly shaped by top-down state preferences about organizational forms and became increasingly populated with political entrepreneurs whose authority is at least partially dependent on their relationship with the state, mirroring the discussion of rents and elite management in chapter 5. Contrary to smugglers' organizations in Tunisia, their Moroccan counterparts have not engaged in strikes or roadblocks, public mobilization, or civil disobedience. In further contrast to the Tunisian case, the ability of local state structures to extract revue from the traders has not suffered despite the economic crisis in the Oriental, and despite the increasing need for traders to shift their supply chains to legal imports.

Together, the previous chapter and this chapter have provided case studies in change and continuity in the role of smuggling in the political settlements of Tunisia and Morocco. Tracing negotiations of the regulation of smuggling in the context of changing national and regional politics, these chapters have highlighted the importance not only of the underlying balance of power and the wider political and institutional context but also of the structures at the intersection between smugglers and states. Crucially, these discussions suggest that in order to understand how borderlands are incorporated into political settlements, it is not sufficient to ask whether they are primarily reliant on formal or informal rent streams, or under which terms these rents are distributed. Instead, crucial questions remain around who shapes and negotiates the terms themselves, how different groups influence these negotiations, and how they manage to adapt to different and changing forms of incorporation. As the following chapter will discuss, a focus on these issues provides an important corrective to the discussions of stability and incorporation by pointing toward dynamics of fragility and exclusion.

Chapter Eight

THE VALLEY AND THE MOUNTAIN
Lived Political Settlements

We are in Oujda, Morocco, in early 2017. The border with Algeria, open terrain just a few years ago, is now flanked by a fence, a ditch, and a wall. The nights along the border, which used to be buzzing with activity, have become quiet. I'm in the car with Ali, a former smuggler of prescription drugs.[1] When the fences went up, Ali used his savings and connections to start a small enterprise. Later in the evening, in a house not too far from the border and surrounded by his family, he proudly presented some of his inventory and paperwork. He was a "formal" man now—Ali managed to adapt to the changing times.

But not everyone did. As the evening falls, we are driving out of Oujda to a small field on a hill, overlooking the borderland. Ali still comes out here sometimes, looking at his former place of work. He is not the only one: when we arrive, there are about ten other cars parked, young men in the front seats, interspersed on the field, smoking, facing Algeria. Many of them are former gasoline smugglers. They have little to do these days—their trade has all but disappeared. While many of their families started formal cooperative projects that the state encouraged in the borderlands to ease the crisis, many of the young men did not get involved.

"Look at them," Ali begins, "they were born here, and when they were born, they were oriented toward the border. And now they sit here, still watching it."[2] In the cars on this field, as with many conversations with young men in Morocco's borderlands, there is an uneasy sense of a group suspended in time—waiting for the border to reopen, for smuggling to resume, without any real hope that it ever will.

Chapters 3, 4, and 5 described the stabilizing role that smuggling economies can play by informally including peripheral regions into North African political settlements, and how institutional rule-based arrangements contributed to structuring and regulating them. Chapters 6 and 7 presented evidence of continuity and change in the borderlands of Tunisia and Morocco, as the role of smuggling economies in these political settlements was challenged, renegotiated, and restructured in the first two decades of the twenty-first century. This was done primarily with a look at the wider structural dynamics, at how the role of smuggling in changing settlements has changed while actors sought to maintain the stability of the wider settlement. This chapter now takes a closer look at how the people in these borderlands have adjusted to these changing settlements, to changing rules and changing political regimes, and how they have mustered different resources in order to manage to influence the rules of the game or prosper under them.

At the heart of this story is another comparison—not between the two case sites, but between the experiences of two different smuggling networks across both countries: gasoline and textile smugglers.[3] Despite experiencing very different challenges and changes, textile smugglers in both Morocco and Tunisia have fared relatively well in recent years: they have frequently been able to formalize their status in ways they found beneficial, have maintained or gained access to well-organized market structures, have been able to adjust to changing regulatory environments relatively well, and have established associations and intermediaries with local and regional state institutions. At the same time, those involved in gasoline smuggling in both Tunisia and Morocco have fared considerably worse. They have been unable to establish associations to engage in negotiations with the state. Struggling to be able to influence their environment or to adapt to or diversify to changing environments, they have been hit hardest by changing rules and new border fortifications. By the end of the second decade of the twenty-first century, gasoline networks in Tunisia were facing collapse, and this had already happened in Morocco. Here, former gasoline traders were also struggling, more than other groups, to adapt to a more formal economic existence.

THE VALLEY AND THE MOUNTAIN

While textile networks were largely able to formalize on their own terms, the experience of gasoline smugglers, in northern Morocco in particular, more closely resembles what is commonly referred to as "adverse incorporation": an integration into new structures that they had no say in designing and found difficult to navigate. What has driven this difference? The chapter argues that differences in organizational capacity, capital, and institutional history have left smugglers with heterogeneous abilities to set the terms of their inclusion into these changing settlements. All three factors affected their ability to engage with state institutions. And, critically, even in the context of smuggling, the chapter finds that being able to negotiate their relationship with the state has been a key factor in determining success and failure for these networks.

The divergent experiences of gasoline and textile smugglers also highlight the diverse effects of inclusion through informal institutions that have stood at the center of much of this book vis-à-vis formal institutions or more personalistic forms of clientelism. In the case of textile networks, informal regulatory systems were accompanied by processes of negotiation that allowed the building up of resources, connections, organizational capacity, and respectability. All these eventually contributed to the negotiation of more formal forms of inclusion on their own terms. In contrast, gasoline networks did not see their informal inclusion accompanied by these processes. Consequently, they were at risk of becoming completely unconnected once the original institutions changed or collapsed.

All this builds to a wider observation that this chapter seeks to make: it argues that the key question at the margins of political settlements is not about who is included and who is excluded from these arrangements, or whether they are included formally or informally. The critical dynamic is how networks can organize access to the resources that allow them to negotiate inclusion on their terms, and to adapt when the terms of their inclusion change. Rather than formality or informality, it is these terms of inclusion and access to their negotiation that determine the inclusiveness of a political settlement. An analysis of these terms requires a close examination of the microdynamics of how people engage with and navigate the institutions that structure their lives—an analysis of what I call here "lived political settlements."

This chapter seeks to present an example of such an analysis. Its remainder is made up of three sections. The first section traces the recent history of gasoline networks in Tunisia and Morocco. The second examines how textile smuggling networks have fared in the same context. The third section builds on comparative elements between the two networks and two localities to draw out comparative insights and what they can teach us.

GASOLINE

The experience of gasoline smugglers in Tunisia and Morocco over the past two decades provides lessons on the challenges of both formal and informal inclusion, and on the difficulties that groups face in both negotiating and affecting their position in political settlements. To trace the experience of gasoline traders under changing political settlements, it is important to first note some of the central features of this network.

Features of the Gasoline Networks

As the previous chapters have noted, in both Tunisia and Morocco, gasoline smugglers are among the least organized, centralized, or coordinated smuggling networks. Their points of sale are more geographically dispersed than those of the vendors operating in market structures in the city center. In both cases, points of import are numerous, and the points of supply on the other side of the border are diffuse, involving a large number of gas stations and informal suppliers.

The gasoline trade does not necessitate extensive cross-border connections, as traders typically buy from formal retail petrol stations across the border.[4] As a result, gasoline traders in both countries often work by themselves or with direct members of their family. Even if traders work alongside one another in companionship, economic partnerships are rare. "You don't want someone else to get the profits that you are getting," a Moroccan gasoline trader notes. "If you are in a partnership, someone else will get half of the profit, but you want all of the profit."[5] The most common units of organization are either families or wholesalers who employ a range of transporters who function effectively as self-employed subcontractors.

While gasoline traders are not an entirely homogeneous group, the network's ease of access and low capital requirements have attracted sections of the borderland populations that had difficulty accessing other networks. In Tunisia, ease of access and low capital requirements have made gasoline smuggling one of the most attractive employment options for young men in the borderlands.[6] The years following 2015 also appear to have seen a significant group of entrants who had been pushed out by competition in more lucrative networks, such as informal money exchange, where market power was increasingly monopolized by larger players.[7] While the gasoline trade in Morocco shares these characteristics, it also maps on a rural-urban distinction, as large sections of gasoline traders and vendors hail from the rural borderlands.[8] During the trade's heyday, entire villages relocated closer to the border to take advantage of it.[9] Here, too, low barriers to entry, especially with regard to information and training, appear crucial. As one rural gasoline smuggler recalled: "We lacked the knowledge for other things. If you trade other things you need to know them, about the quality, how to sell them, where to sell them. We didn't have that."[10] Smugglers in rural areas often reported starting work on the border together with their family at young ages, leading to widespread concern about the educational levels of many of the traders in rural areas.[11] No similar geographic pattern was discernible in Tunisia, likely due to the fact that the immediate borderland is almost entirely uninhabited.

Inclusion Dependent on Institutions

In summary, the easy access to the gasoline trade has shaped the profile of many of its traders: many have entered the networks with little social or economic capital, and, in Morocco, frequently with little experience of life in the city. The loosely networked structure of the trade and its geographic dispersal have left it without larger organizational structures. Both aspects have characterized the sense in which the gasoline traders were informally included in the political settlement in Tunisia and Morocco up until 2014. Essentially, their inclusion was entirely reliant on informal institutions through which they were able to access rent streams. The income of gasoline smugglers in Tunisia was dependent not on relationships or skill, but on the existence of an agreement at the Ras Jedir crossing that allowed them to import subsidized gasoline into the country with low bribe rates. For the gasoline traders of northern Morocco, the same was true for the institutions that regulated the trade along the closed border, as discussed in the previous chapter.

While the impersonal nature of these institutions and low barriers to entry ensured that access to these arrangements remained open for everyone, they also contributed to a form of inclusion that did not foster economic networks or skills, thereby creating enormous dependence on these institutions themselves—institutions over which the traders typically had little control. In the case of Morocco, many of the gasoline traders I spoke to remained unsure of how these institutions had emerged. When bribe levels for many traders dropped sharply in 2011, traders speculated about the king having heard about their hardship but did not have any firm sense of how these agreements were negotiated.[12] Tunisian gasoline traders usually had a sense of who was negotiating these arrangements, but they were themselves entirely excluded from the negotiations. As discussed in chapter 6, the negotiation process for the agreements at Ras Jedir included civil society leaders, wholesale traders of licit consumer goods, and representatives of the vendors in the Souk Maghrebi, but no gasoline traders.

In both cases, the exclusion of gasoline traders from the negotiations appears closely related to the structure of their trade, with both the lack of larger organizational forms and the lack of connections with traders across the border and government officials making it difficult to be recognized as a relevant negotiating partner, be informed about negotiations, or force inclusion in the negotiations. As gasoline traders lacked associations, they lacked both obvious intermediaries that could negotiate with state agents and the capacity for collective action to support their demands. In addition, they had no privileged access to political figures or to information on changing political and economic environments across the border that they would have been able to leverage with state agents. I will expand on this when examining the case of textile traders.

Lower organizational capacity and lack of cross-border connections were not the only reasons for the traders' exclusion from these negotiations. Lower barriers to access had made gasoline smuggling attractive for groups with lower socioeconomic backgrounds, which traders of other networks viewed with some suspicion. Throughout the interviews conducted with bureaucrats, civil society, and or traders from other smuggling networks, gasoline smugglers were commonly framed as simple, unruly, or cognitively inferior. Gasoline traders themselves recognized their "image problem" but framed it as an issue of communication and education.

In Tunisia, one of the negotiators of the agreements for the Ras Jedir border crossing, himself a wholesale trader of consumer goods, argued that there were no gasoline traders represented in the Organisation for Tunisian Libyan Brotherhood, or at the negotiations, because "if we had a gasoline trader, they would only use their position to advance their own interests."[13] A civil society activist involved in the negotiations argued that there were no gasoline traders because "this is a different type of communication, it's a different language. They haven't been taught the discourse of politics."[14] Gasoline traders themselves highlighted difficulties with both access and communication: "Talking to the state? That is just for the bourgeois, not for us. The poor always suffer," one trader argued. "There is no occasion for us to talk to them; if we talk, they will just not listen."[15]

These discourses were closely mirrored in Morocco. The leadership of the market association of the Souk Melilla highlighted that their educational status was a crucial reason that they had been better able to organize and negotiate.[16] "If the gasoline traders get an association, who will represent them? They do not have anyone who could represent them," a vendor in the same market argued. "They are used to sitting in the street, if you give them a proper place, they will still sit in the street."[17] A regional government official asserted that "we need to work on their mentality, on their culture, on their psychology ... they need to be better educated ... right now, they are just not logical."[18] Others identified a problem of "culture," "mentality," and "spirit."[19] As in Tunisia, Moroccan gasoline traders themselves pointed to their lack of connections and similarly highlighted educational differences and a lack of knowledge of the region's urban centers.

Tunisia: Facing Changing Institutions

As their inclusion in the political settlement rested on the functioning of specific informal institutions, rather than personal networks or specific skills in the trade, the dependence of gasoline traders in North Africa on these institutions was substantial. Their breakdown, then, directly threatened their livelihoods. Without access to negotiations, their options to react to a deterioration of the arrangements that determined their livelihoods were limited. To the detriment of gasoline traders, breakdowns of these informal institutions can be observed in both case sites in recent years, largely triggered by deteriorating economic situations in Algeria and Libya.

The smuggling of gasoline in Tunisia had expanded significantly after the 2011 revolution, as state security forces withdrew from the borderlands and the fall of the Gaddafi regime opened spaces for new actors in Libya. By 2016, however, years of civil war had put significant strains on Libya's economy, and gasoline smuggling stood at the heart of increasing public concern about the looting of the country's resources.[20] As discussed in chapter 6, activists had targeted gasoline smuggling across the border with Tunisia as it was seen as a relatively weak trade that was politically unconnected and had not forged relationships with actors that had access to means of violence.[21] Tunisian negotiators confirmed that by early 2017 the reduction of gasoline smuggling had become the main demand from their Libyan counterparts.[22] By mid-2017 both the agreement governing the Ras Jedir border crossing and the structures along the desert routes had changed in a way that dramatically reduced the quantities of gasoline that could be brought across. Gasoline traders remained excluded from these negotiations, which had now become primarily about their trade. Once the agreements changed, many gasoline smugglers adopted a wait-and-see attitude, hoping that the agreement would change again in their favor.

When this did not work, their options were limited. Within a short period, not only had they become factually excluded from the political settlement but they also lacked means to communicate with state interlocutors. As a result, gasoline traders were instrumental in supporting a roadblock at the Ras Jedir border crossing in 2018, restricting commercial traffic in an attempt to get their message heard.

Two things are noteworthy here. First, their demands were not just in reference to smuggling but also called for state investments to generate alternative economic opportunities to the smuggling economy. Second, even though their difficulties primarily stemmed from Libya, their demands were aimed at and communicated toward the Tunisian state, demanding recognition, support, and intercession.[23] The first two demands, in fact, called for the adoption of their positions by the recently formed municipal council, as well as the opening of negotiation channels by the central state. These suggest the recognition of their current exclusion from the political settlement and their dependence on a fragile situation in Libya, alongside a desire to build modes of inclusion that contained more stable relationships with the Tunisian state. This sentiment was echoed throughout the research for this project and is mirrored by the textile networks discussed later.

The sit-in was largely unsuccessful. While renewed negotiations over the procedures at the border crossing took place, their demands were not met, and the reopening of the border was accompanied by altercations with security forces and further violent unrest in the city.[24] In the years that followed, gasoline trade remained increasingly restricted. Even during times when trade through Ras Jedir was open and not disrupted by the Covid-19 pandemic, traders did not see a substantial increase in the amounts of gasoline that could be brought through the informal arrangements at the border crossing. Gasoline smugglers remained largely shut out of the political settlement in which they had been informally included and were facing an uncertain future.

Morocco: Informal Exclusion, Formal Incorporation

A similar situation, albeit perhaps even more dire, had faced their Moroccan counterparts a few years earlier. As discussed in chapter 7, Algeria began fortifying its border with Morocco in 2013, reacting in part to the loss to the national income caused by the smuggling economy, which had become harder to sustain in the context of low oil prices. Dependent on moving large quantities of goods across the border, endowed with low capital or technological capacities, and unable to reroute their supply via Melilla, gasoline networks were hit hardest by the new fortifications. They represented—by design—a collapse of the regulatory arrangements, structured by a set of local informal institutions that had included Morocco's gasoline vendors in the larger political settlement.

The features of the gasoline network, once conducive to the inclusion of poor rural youth with minimal barriers to entry, now actively hindered their ability to adapt to the new situation, and to navigate their reinclusion in the political settlement. While there were some small attempts at protesting the border fortifications, the geographic spread of the traders, their lack of connection with other networks or political allies, the authoritarian context, and Algeria's determination to eliminate the gasoline trade all limited the effectiveness of protest as a strategy.[25]

Most of the members of the borderland focused on finding a new income. The lack of strong links between suppliers, transporters, and wholesalers meant that most members of the gasoline trade were looking by themselves and were not typically employed by their former bosses. Their rural origins and the lack of connections to commercial actors across the border, which had not been a problem under the old political settlement and in the case of a location close to the border even presented an asset, had now become a hindrance to inclusion in the new settlement. Their limited knowledge of the city as a commercial space, lack of connections across the border, and lack of experience with business environments made finding other work difficult.

A former gasoline trader from the borderlands who had actually managed the transition to a stall at the Souk Melilla observed the benefits for those gasoline traders who made a larger effort in building connections across the border: "Some of the people who were working at the time, they would have interactions with lots of people, they would go to Algeria, talk to people about the price, then take the gasoline to Nador, even Casa[blanca]. And the people who did that, they also saved, and they are in a better position now." He argued that his having spent some of his youth in the city was a crucial factor for his relative success: "I know how the city works, how to talk to people, to customers. The people in the border they don't know the city, they don't know how to get people to buy things." He continued: "They don't know how to communicate with people. They wouldn't know how to talk to people in a shop. They look different, too, their haircut, the way they dress."[26] One of his colleagues also emphasized the importance of connections over formal education: "The people who worked with Melilla, they may not be very educated, but they know how things work, they got into the city, they could contact, they knew how to adapt. But these people who stayed in the countryside, they don't know how to work here, they are struggling."[27]

As chapter 7 noted, the Moroccan state swiftly realized that the political settlement that had informally included its northeastern border population had become untenable, and that it needed to react in order to avoid unrest in its borderlands. Algerian fortifications put the continuation of a key element of the previous settlement, smuggling rents, beyond the control of the Moroccan authorities. In the following years, the Moroccan state set about building the structures to include the borderlands in the formal political settlement, through new formal development programs and initiatives, new roads, water lines, and electricity grids.

These programs represented a restructuring of the political settlement from above—they were designed and implemented by state institutions in relation to a population with which they previously had little engagement. Despite references by state officials to "participatory approaches," borderland communities interviewed for this project often did not feel consulted.[28] The speed with which the programs were deployed in conjunction with the limited contact between state institutions and these communities prior to the crisis made a real negotiation of these programs unlikely. To rural borderland communities, their new inclusion in the political settlement was largely presented as a "take it or leave it" offer. These dynamics created winners and losers in Morocco's borderlands. Many former gasoline smugglers, for whom many of these projects were originally designed, struggled with the new situation. With respect to three key dimensions—connection, organization, and legibility—they found themselves sidelined in the new political settlement, with little sense of any genuine inclusion.

As gasoline traders were primarily connected to the previous political settlement through a set of now defunct informal institutions, their inclusion in a new formal political settlement and the implementation of development projects in the borderlands necessitated the creation of new structures of communication and new interlocutors. State institutions held meetings in the borderlands and encouraged the formation of local development associations, on which they drew alongside local political representatives. "Before there was no contact. The administration didn't want to have any contact, and the youth also, they are illegal, they don't really want to talk," one local bureaucrat recalled.[29] The creation of new connections, then, "was very difficult, because there was no understanding."

The role that local politicians and administrators played here is notable: the origin story of almost every local developmental association in the borderlands that I spoke with began with a local or regional politician speaking to them, suggesting the formation of an association, and offering access and support.[30] This offered opportunities for civil society activists and political entrepreneurs, but only for very few of the former gasoline smugglers. "We try to connect them," the head of a local association recounted, "because they are not used to working with the state."[31] The success of this was limited: the dominant impression among the borderland population was one of disconnection.

With new projects also came a reshaping of the organizational structure of the borderlands according to the preferences of state institutions. While organizational structures of gasoline traders had been limited prior to the crisis, state institutions providing economic assistance in the borderlands after 2013 categorically required recipients of any support to fit into a new organizational form—the cooperative. Again, local politicians and administrators visited borderlands, encouraging the formation of cooperatives. The formation of family-based cooperatives and female-led cooperatives, in particular, was advocated as particularly desirable. "The Jiha (the regional-level administration) came here and said that you need to set up cooperatives, and we will help you," a borderland resident remembers. "Ideally, you should be a family, because that will be well organized. Make groups of five and form cooperatives."[32] "They prefer working with women," a border resident argued, "because they feel that women are more truthful and that they are easier to work with."[33]

Various bureaucrats involved in these projects directly confirm this observation. "If we work with women, we are sure to get good results," a leading official at the Agence Oriental told me, because "women are more serious."[34] "For me, right now, it's the women that do the work," an official who is leading agricultural projects affirms, highlighting the utility for the state of restructuring rent streams in the borderlands toward women: "The push toward women here is logical, they look for work, not for profit. They are ready to work to get out of the house. For me, it is the women that change a bit the situation here, especially the young women. The women are ready to work for cheaper, they are looking to develop themselves. For the men, the priority is money."[35] One of his colleagues agrees: "It is easier for us to work with women because they are more reliable and more durable. They last for longer, they don't quit, while the men, they quit more quickly. Women are more satisfied with a small profit, while the men, they want larger profits, and they want it more quickly."[36]

The shift toward working with women was not limited to cooperatives. A collaboration between a textile manufacturer and the regional administration saw the planning of a factory aimed specifically at employing female labor from the immediate borderlands. A senior official argued that the focus had shifted from looking to create jobs for former smugglers to creating employment for someone in their family, "maybe their sister."[37] The focus on women in these development initiatives represents the creation of a new intersection between the Moroccan state and its borderland communities based on the explicit preferences of the state. By encouraging female intermediaries, Moroccan state agents consciously selected actors who had lower expectations of income or benefits and thereby effectively lowered the costs of organizing the survival of borderland communities and avoiding rural flight.

Through these development initiatives, the gendered structures of organization and income in the rural borderlands have been partially reversed. During the heyday of the smuggling trade, access to income streams was largely restricted to men. "The women, back then, they were princesses, they got their money from their husbands," a borderland resident remembers. "It is known in the rural areas that women stay at home."[38] The new development initiatives not only provided women with incomes but also put them in charge of many of the newly created cooperatives—employing the former (male) traders. "Their sisters and mothers are the ones doing the jobs, they make bread and sell it, they are feeding their husbands and sons," the (female) head of a development agency in the rural borderland argues. "The government is trying to focus on women, but while doing that, they have forgotten everything about men. This will create problems here, because now the men in this region, many of them are on drugs, and they are stealing things now."[39] While some female heads of cooperatives worried that the changes in gendered responsibilities would lead to frustrations and tensions within the communities, others were more optimistic. Almost all of them, however, commented on the fact that the new organizational structures had left their male family members not only with low motivation but also with little to do, and they expressed concern about their situation.[40]

Finally, the new institutional structures brought new challenges of legibility. Many borderland residents struggled to understand the institutions they were now required to interact with, mistrusted them, or lacked the literacy to comply with them. In the words of a regional member of parliament: "These people are not educated to work with rules, to work with the formal economy, they are now in a system that is new for them. We need to accompany them on this and encourage them."[41] Heterogeneous ability to navigate these institutions had profound influences on who managed to gain access to the formal rent streams made available through development projects.

Once again, especially former gasoline smugglers were in a difficult situation. In early 2017 I frequently visited the local ODECO office, the agency that processed the applications for cooperatives. Every time I visited, the office was packed, with lines leading out of the office and down the staircase. The intern at the front desk was trying to field requests from all angles, as the crowd became increasingly frustrated with the wait and the complexities of the administrative process. Almost every time I found the agency's head in a shouting match with a disgruntled applicant. Frequently, visitors from rural borderlands complained that they had to make multiple expensive trips to the city. Another time, they were struggling to understand that their application had been rejected—they had been told by local officials in the borderlands that they would be helped and provided with an income.[42]

"People were afraid of getting into cooperatives, but the government encouraged them," one borderland resident remembered. They were scared "because they also had to pay some money to get these documents done, there is the transport to the city that you had to go to." On top of that, illiteracy—prevalent in the rural borderlands where access to education was limited and many started working on the border at a young age—provided additional problems in navigating administrative hurdles: "When I go somewhere, I don't know if it is the right office, or if I have signed the right form."[43] From this, the impression swiftly spread that in order to successfully set up a cooperative, contacts were needed. "If you don't know someone, they will throw out your file," some worried. "The help doesn't reach the people who are in need, it reaches the people who already have enough."[44]

Their challenges in building contacts, their dislocation in the rearranging of the organizational structures of the borderland, and their difficulties in navigating new formal institutions all left many of the former gasoline traders entirely alienated from a novel political settlement that was claimed to have been designed for their very inclusion. While bureaucrats often cited the previously high pay of smugglers as the central challenge in integrating them into the formal labor market, smugglers themselves highlighted their lack of education and connections as fundamental barriers in an extremely competitive low-skilled labor market.[45]

When I was speaking to former gasoline smugglers across the Moroccan-Algerian border, there was a sense of a group struggling to find its place in the new settlement, while being aware that there was no real role for them. While some had found small formal sector jobs in construction or gardening, others were relying on small temporary activities. Many remained outside the labor market. A sense of idleness, of limbo, of waiting was prevalent, especially among the younger men. Many described their existence as one of "waiting," waiting for the border to open again, for opportunities to emerge. And yet few professed any real hope that this would happen. There was a parallel here to what Alcinda Honwana described as "waithood"—of having grown out of childhood but rendered unable by their economic position to reach the independence and fulfill the social expectations associated with adulthood.[46]

Borderland communities and law enforcement officials spoke with concern about increasing drug consumption in the borderlands.[47] Some smugglers tell tales of wild nights partying in the nearby coastal city of Saidiyya when business was still booming, with girls and alcohol.[48] In recent years, consumption trends appear to have shifted toward cheaper and harder narcotics, such as different varieties of synthetic psychotropics, commonly referred to as *karkoubi*. Borderland residents, as well as former smugglers, typically connect the influx of the highly addictive drugs with the rise in petty crime, theft, and violence in the borderlands. Police statistics and newspapers have reported rising levels of violent crime and increasing seizures of psychotropics.[49]

After 2013, gasoline smugglers in Tunisia and Morocco moved from being informally included in the wider political settlement to being either left uneasily on the margins of a changing settlement or adversely incorporated into a new settlement that did not offer them a real role, income, or sense of purpose. Their experience suggests two insights into inclusion and informal political settlements.

First, it highlights that a more formal political settlement is not necessarily a more stable one. In Morocco, the years after 2013 have seen a decrease in the number of people in the borderland community who are dependent on illicit economies for their income, and an increase in income streams directly administered formally and legally by state institutions. There has also been some investment by state institutions, shifts to legal economic activity, and an increase in state-connected organizational forms such as associations and cooperatives, alongside an inclusion of borderlands into spatial management plans, road networks, and water and electricity networks. It is reasonable to say that the inclusion of the borderland in the political settlement has become more formal.

Despite these programs, and the absence of large-scale unrest in the borderlands, the previous sections have pointed to serious pockets of vulnerability that remain. While smuggling has gone down, other forms of crime have increased, and a large group of unemployed young men excluded from local income streams alongside expanding concerns about drug consumption and criminal activity spell serious risks for the stability of the region. As an increasing body of work on supply-side eradications in illicit economies has highlighted, eradication of illicit economies can have severely destabilizing effects.[50] As the previous sections have noted, even if new formal rent streams are being created, organizing them at the intersection between state and former smugglers brings significant challenges. This highlights the importance of inclusive development programs and the difficulties with formally including those who were previously informally included.

This leads directly to the second point: for informal gasoline traders, the experience of being included in a political settlement through informal institutions that they could not influence came with serious risks and undermined their ability to adapt to changing settlements. While the impersonal nature of informal regulatory institutions and low barriers to entry ensured their access to the rent streams generated by the smuggling economy, they created a reliance on these institutions and did not facilitate the creation of associational structures, the skills, the diversification of economic activities in the borderlands, or the development of contact networks either across the border or with local state structures. This left gasoline traders in an extremely challenging position once their inclusion through the smuggling economy collapsed and the institutional landscape changed to their disadvantage. This highlights the importance of organizational forms and connections—especially the institutional channels of negotiation with the state, even for smuggling networks.[51] But what drives the development of these channels and their success? To develop these issues, it is useful to look at the contrasting experience of textile smugglers.

TEXTILES

Textile smuggling networks in Tunisia and Morocco stand in clear contrast to gasoline smugglers with respect to the features of their networks and their experience in recent years. They demonstrate how, in a different context, the inclusion through informal institutions can be compatible with the formation of associations, formal negotiations with the state, and a strong ability to adjust to changing settlements. Their success highlights the role of organizational structures and stresses the importance that connections with state structures can still have in determining success within the informal economy.

Features of the Textile Networks

One of the most notable differences between the networks smuggling gasoline and networks trading smuggled textiles examined here is that the latter have, in both case sites, established points of retail where lots of traders operate close to one another in formal and informal markets that contain hundreds of vendors, wall to wall. There is little disagreement among textile traders that the concentration of their retail structures in a small urban space has been a factor in their ability to influence the terms of their relationship with the state. "When we are on the road, there is only one of us," a vendor in Oujda's Souk Melilla observes. "Here, we are over a thousand people. They can't just come here and take the products."[52]

While most markets studied here did not form formal market associations until the last decade, there are strong indicators that their clustering also helped foster organizational structures. For years before formal organizations were founded, loose communal structures for the payment of security staff or the resolution of disputes were in place. Communication, travel of information, and coordination all likely facilitated organization—all but one trader-based associations observed in both case sites that were formed since 2011 have been based in, and been limited to, a market structure.

The fact that textile traders were able to cluster in a small urban space was a feature of their trade, which they shared with other traders of non-flammable licit consumer goods of low to medium value, such as foodstuffs, kitchenware, or white electronics. The traders of these markets also typically shared broadly similar longstanding occupational practices—apprenticeships, or the coordination through an *Amin Tujjar* in the Moroccan case. In those markets that were formalized enough to have rent contracts, such as the Souk Libya in Medenine, the sale of gasoline was explicitly prohibited. But concerns about the flammable nature of their product was not the only thing that kept gasoline vendors out of these markets. The way in which consumers purchase gasoline likely contributed to a more diffuse distributional pattern, alongside the absence of institutional precedence for municipal taxation of gasoline.

The features of their business also made textile traders more likely to develop in-depth contacts with other traders, both domestically and abroad. While gasoline traders could buy from any gas station across the border and would get the same product, textile traders reported that building relationships with suppliers improved their knowledge of the produce, lowered prices, or gained them preferential access to specific products—significant advantages in a crowded market. These networks also communicate information about other products or supply routes and thereby make it easier for traders to adjust in the case of changes to the regulatory structure. In the case of Tunisia's "popular diplomacy" process, as discussed in chapter 6, traders directly sought to leverage their contacts across the border to improve their relationships with the state at home.

As with gasoline, the textile trade is not controlled by any tribal group or family, and the informal institutions that regulate the smuggling of these goods are impersonal. Still, there are barriers to entry, as access to market infrastructure, experience, and capital are crucial. Across both case studies, many of the traders working in textiles received all three from their family, typically because they took over the stalls and learned the trade from family members who were already working in the same markets. Textile traders, alongside other market vendors, often highlighted the importance of this experience for their commercial success.[53]

Market stalls in both case sites were typically allocated based on lists of vendors who had been in similar locations before. In Morocco, this created windows of opportunity in the 1970s and 1980s—when informal market spaces expanded—and a path dependency, in which families were able to maintain their position in the market. As the value of the market stalls rose, some left the market altogether but rented out their stall at competitive rates. In some markets, such as Ben Guerdane's Souk Maghrebi, stalls were assigned by the municipality, directly benefiting politically well-connected families. Here, too, as some of the vendors began building larger stores outside of the market, they either left stalls to their family or rented them out at a profit.[54]

Barriers to entry, such as capital, access to market infrastructure, training, and connections, have not formed textile traders into a homogeneous group. But they have shaped their occupational characteristics and contributed to a social makeup that is somewhat different from that of gasoline traders: textile traders appear more literate and more frequently have at least finished school. They typically have higher levels of capital, and in the Oriental they are typically from an urban background. The discourse around a problematic "mentality" and unruliness discussed in the section about gasoline traders is not heard about textile traders.

Textile Traders in Changing Political Settlements

These features—higher organizational capacity, the more cohesive character of their occupational institutions, and the typically more affluent and educated background—all contributed to textile networks weathering the challenges of recent years comparatively well in both Tunisia and Morocco. A closer examination of their success also highlights another factor: their ability to build and maintain structures of negotiation with state structures.

In both case sites, textile networks—alongside other vendors trading in the same markets—have maintained or gained access to well-organized market structures and attracted state investment in their infrastructure. In Tunisia, the traders based in the Souk Maghrebi have made inroads toward gaining formal contracts for their stalls and access to electricity, as discussed in chapter 6. In Morocco, the past decade has seen the construction of various smaller, formal market structures in the urban periphery alongside the formal reconstruction of larger markets in Oujda's city center with significant state investment, including the Souk Melilla. It is also worth noting that the process of the construction and reconstruction of these markets was largely conducted through conversation and negotiation with vendors in the markets. For most of the vendors, the changes in the market infrastructure were generally seen as positive.[55]

The input of traders into the development of market infrastructure closely relates to the development of associations among the markets. In both case sites, textile traders have heavily participated in the formation of legally recognized associations and have gained access to local and national-level decision-makers, as highlighted in chapters 6 and 7. In Tunisia, textile traders were represented in the Association of the Traders of the Souk Maghrebi, which gained legal status as an association and was involved in direct negotiations around market infrastructure and the legal status of its traders with local, regional, and national cabinet-level decision-makers.[56] In Morocco, textile traders were represented in multiple associations, such as the association of the Souk Melilla in Oujda or the association of the Commercial Complex in Nador, which gained both legal status and membership in the regional chambers of commerce and secured access to local and regional-level politicians and administrators.[57] While gasoline traders commonly complained that getting access to state interlocutors was a challenge, associations of textile traders were generally enthusiastic about the access they received, boasting of the high-level politicians that they spoke with, and how quickly they could get an appointment.[58]

In both case studies, textile traders have seen, or made significant progress toward, the partial formalization of their enterprises. In both cases, facilitating the formalization of textile smugglers increasingly became official government policy, at least on a local level. Stable hybrid institutions taxing the markets built an incentive for local administrations to support the trade, while the presence of associations established clear interlocutors. State investments in market structures and the creation of hybrid institutions that regulated an increasing amount of their distribution networks further accompanied the trade's increasing formalization. In crucial contrast to gasoline traders, however, textile traders saw their relationship with the state formalized through terms that they largely either found acceptable or had specifically lobbied for. Their formalization was largely one of the same occupational structure, rather than, as in the case of Morocco's gasoline traders, their integration into different activities. Crucially, they understood the new structures that they were engaging in and had input—albeit at times limited—into their formulation.

These changes contributed to traders' ability to weather some of the larger challenges that their businesses faced in recent years. As discussed in chapter 7, traders in Morocco faced the permanent collapse of their traditional business model as a consequence of the fortification of the Morocco-Algeria border and the proliferation of free-trade agreements. Textile traders adjusted by diversifying their supply networks, drawing on legal imports and using their expertise, knowledge of the market, and expanding connections with producers to stay afloat.[59] Crucially, the existence of formalized market structures and associations and the influx of state development programs helped traders transition into more formal and legal enterprises as the smuggling economy fell into crisis.

Inclusions and Exceptions

The experience of textile networks suggests two clear contrasts to the experience of gasoline networks. First, while the experience of gasoline networks demonstrated that the formalization of a political settlement is not necessarily stabilizing, or in the interest of the affected informal networks, the case of textile traders shows that it can very well be. Despite the significant challenges that textile smugglers faced in the past few years, they were one of the least likely networks to become a significant source of wider instability within the political settlement. They were more capable of adapting to new settlements and formalizing some of their activities and, crucially, had established organizational structures that were able to mediate and negotiate with local state structures. As noted in chapters 6 and 7, much of these negotiations focused on setting the terms for further formalization, concerning issues such as access to electricity, market infrastructure, and competition from less formalized vendors. In both countries, local heads of associations collaborated with a diverse set of political parties and at no point supported political positions that could be categorized as radical or destabilizing within the national context. While there was some concern in the formal business community when vendors associations in Morocco were first admitted to the local chambers of commerce, the unease quickly proved unfounded.[60] The vendors' association in Ben Guerdane supported some local protests, such as the 2016 protest movement in the city, as most civil society associations in Ben Guerdane did, but they were not generally advocating political tactics that included mass mobilization. Neither were their equivalents in Morocco.

This closely relates to the fact that traders did not perceive their more formal status to be disadvantageous and generally understood the new structures and institutions by which they were regulated. They generally perceived their new position as more dignified, as it typically included an improvement in infrastructure. The increasing formalization of textile traders in both case sites included changes in their organizational structure that made the networks more accessible for state institutions, through the rise of associations. Contrary to the case of Morocco's gasoline traders, however, this reorganization was more limited in depth and scope, was easier to navigate, and did not lead to the exclusion or dislocation of large numbers of traders.

Second, the experience of textile traders shows, in contrast to that of gasoline traders, that the inclusion through informal institutions can be advantageous in preparing networks for shifts in the political settlement. In the case of gasoline, their inclusion through impersonal informal institutions did not foster the creation of organizational resources or connections, leaving them disconnected and marginalized as the informal institutions changed or collapsed. For textile traders, however, a history of bargaining and contact with state officials through the negotiation and maintenance of the institutional regulation of city markets had built relationships that helped with the negotiation of formalization and made formal structures more legible and manageable. It also established for the state a familiarity in dealing with informal textile traders and a financial reliance on the income generated by these markets, which facilitated negotiations around the formalization of the trade.

In conversations with textile traders and local bureaucrats, the effects of this history of institutional interaction were frequently referenced. As a result of the different informal institutional mechanisms that had been created to informally tax the markets in the city center, these markets were commonly framed locally as "less informal" than the activities in the borderlands, even as their operation was still entirely illegal. "Souk Melilla, even before the new market was built, this was formal," a senior figure in the vendor's association argues, referring explicitly to the informal tax that the municipality had collected from local vendors prior to the creation of the new market.[61] As chapter 7 noted, even Oujda's mayor struck a similar tone.[62] In the words of another local bureaucrat: "Souk Melilla is the valley of contraband; the border region is the mountain. In the valley, they are happy to work with the authorities, but on the mountain, they don't. In the valley, there are less problems."[63]

Before concluding, it is worth noting again that the work in the value chains of textile smuggling and gasoline smuggling is not homogeneous. While this section has focused on many members and central dynamics within these trades, there are instructive exceptions to these wider dynamics. Some of the gasoline wholesalers who amassed significant amounts of capital found it easier to adjust to more formal arrangements than their transporters. Similarly, diversity within textile smuggling is critical. This section has focused on textile smugglers, wholesalers, and vendors who operate in markets, but the trade has also long employed some of the most vulnerable individuals in Morocco's smuggling economy: the transporters at the gates of Melilla.[64] Before the increasing closures and constraints on their movements from 2019 onward, they were typically employed ad hoc by wholesale traders to carry goods through the turnstiles discussed in chapter 5. While the wholesalers, larger traders, and market vendors benefited from the various dynamics discussed in this section, transporters did not see their mode of inclusion fundamentally change before it collapsed. Much of the procedure at the border around them was formalized—the police taking a larger role in organizing their queues, for example—but they did not witness a formalization of the institutions under which they worked.

Even when trade through Melilla was still open, in the years between 2013 and 2019 traders on this border already saw their pay diminished while working conditions remained harsh. As a result of the economic crisis, a growing number of locals have sought work as transporters, increasing competition, while changes in the hours at the border crossing had repeatedly narrowed their time window.[65] Alternative sources of income remained rare—many transporters are indebted to wholesalers and dependent on their daily income to survive. Carrying heavy goods and standing in the sun for hours has often done serious damage to the health of the transporters, many of whom are older women. Worse yet, the pushing of many of the transporters into small spaces as they stream into Melilla has caused stampedes and suffocation. Repeatedly, transporters have died.[66]

Consequently, although formalizations, associations, and an ability to navigate changing institutional contexts have been key features of the past years for most textile traders, they have not necessarily spread to all sections of the trade's value chain. Instead, pockets of particularly vulnerable individuals within the trade largely mirror the experience of many gasoline smugglers. This does not come as a surprise if we consider that their social and economic resources, connections, and organizational structures mirror those of gasoline smugglers. Poorly paid, brutal, dangerous, and not requiring particular skills or connections, the gates of Melilla attracted workers from across Morocco who often had limited capital or alternatives and did not share social bonds or places of assembly. While wholesalers in Melilla formed official associations and market associations developed on the Moroccan side of the border, transporters did not manage to create similar connections. In the early 2020s, as smuggling through the turnstiles in Melilla became increasingly impossible, transporters also shared the fate that many gasoline smugglers had experienced since 2013—needing to learn out how to engage with formal state relief and support programs.

LIVED POLITICAL SETTLEMENTS

This chapter has shifted the focus from the changing arrangements that have incorporated the Maghreb's borderlands into its wider political settlements in the past two decades. It has sought to examine how different groups seek to mobilize connections and resources to affect them from below and to adjust as they are changing. It has moved from the wider political settlements, commonly analyzed at a relatively macro- and top-down level, to what I call "lived political settlements," by analyzing the experiences of different smuggling networks in navigating these changing settlements. Most of the book has been dedicated to discussing whether smuggling economies have undermined the states of Tunisia or Morocco, but this chapter has highlighted that while the borderlands have not necessarily undermined the state, the form of their inclusion into the national political settlement has, in a sense, undermined some groups within border communities while providing opportunities for others. It has given rise to economic structures that, while regulated, have created real vulnerabilities for those sections of the local population that were dependent on institutions they had no direct influence over and that could be revoked or collapse at any time. There are both conceptual and critical practical consequences of these considerations.

The chapter speaks to a wider discussion of the role of "inclusion" of borderlands. The term is omnipresent in state approaches to developing borderlands, and yet, as we see here, its effects are heterogeneous. Recent years have seen increasing critiques of the widespread use of inclusion as a development goal, from financial inclusion to digital inclusion to the inclusion in value chains. At the heart of many critiques has been the idea of "adverse incorporation": of contexts where the origins of economic marginalization lie not in exclusion but in the terms of inclusion.[67] This observation is particularly relevant to informal economies, where development and formalization typically manifest as inclusions in new regulatory systems. As Kate Meagher and Ilda Lindell have pointed out, while arguments for the inclusion of informal economic actors often sound consensual and uncontroversial, they are "obscuring the role of struggles for and against inclusion, and divisions or alliances unleashed by it."[68] This chapter has extended some of these discussions to the borderlands of the Maghreb. It has noted that being incorporated into a political settlement through rents connected to informal institutions can be both a catalyst to formalization and further inclusion and a recipe for excessive dependency and exclusion. Following from this, it has shown that formalization—inclusion in new formal regulatory systems—can itself create divisions, winners and losers, among informal actors and consolidate or fragment informal forms of political organization.

By noting that these effects were contingent on features of networks, the analysis has further unpacked, for the context of informally incorporated groups, what political settlement analysis describes as "holding power." This fills a critical gap in this field of scholarship, which, due to its common focus on elite bargains and ruling coalitions, has seen comparatively little work that examines how more marginalized groups manage and navigate their position in changing political settlements.[69] Consequently, the holding power of informal organizational structures, in particular, is underdiscussed. This chapter has highlighted that aside from more classical elements of holding power such as capital and organizational capacity, the history of negotiating local institutional regulation with state structures has been an important factor. This connects again to the issue of inclusion itself. Meagher has pointed out that "the ability to foster inclusive economic relations from below is not a product of popular agency per se, but of the specific informal institutional repertoire of a particular locality."[70]

The chapter has traced the importance of intersections with state actors in these processes. It has shown that even when analyzing the fate of smugglers, at the periphery of their countries' territories, laws, and political settlements, the intersection with the state still retains importance. While previous chapters have pointed to the role of state structures in maintaining and enforcing informal regulatory institutions, this chapter has noted their role in shaping the intersection between themselves and different smuggling networks and consequently affecting the structure and fate of these networks in recent years. The experiences of the networks discussed have highlighted the importance of recognizing heterogeneity not only in the power to affect a settlement, negotiate, or force inclusion, but also in the ability to adjust to changing institutional structures. The analysis has described how changing settlements and institutional structures bring changes of legibility, especially for marginalized groups, as understanding and navigating new institutions may require skills and resources that they do not have at their disposal.

All these observations have taken on an even larger practical importance in recent years. This is in part because they have provided some critical clues to the pockets of vulnerability that have already developed within seemingly stable arrangements, such as Morocco's northeastern borderlands. These vulnerabilities are likely to deepen. While smuggling has decreased, other forms of crime have increased, and the adverse incorporation of former gasoline smugglers, and particularly young men, alongside increased drug consumption and a deeper sense of alienation in the immediate borderlands suggests serious threats to the region's stability in years to come.

This will become more important in the context of likely further renegotiations of these settlements. As the previous chapters have highlighted, both Tunisia's and Morocco's borderlands have already had to navigate substantial economic pressures even before the double hit of new border fortifications and the Covid-19 pandemic at the end of the second decade of the new century. It appears likely that the 2020s will continue to bring further pressures on North Africa's smuggling economies and limit their ability to fulfill the political and economic functions they have served in the past decades. From this follows a call for more formal state engagement and development plans for peripheral regions in the coming years.

Given the role of these regions for the region's stability, these programs will likely emerge, in one form or another, as they have in Morocco in recent years. But for these, too, this chapter has lessons. As states seek to restructure their relationship with smuggling economies in the region, it will be important to recognize that both formalization and the continuation of previous strategies of structured and segmented toleration do not necessarily imply stability and real inclusion. Inclusive politics will require close attention to how and by whom the terms of inclusion are negotiated, how different groups adjust to them, and what forms of economic and organizational structures they give rise to. As exemplified by the gendered changes in Morocco's borderlands, there is a need to consider the effects of different forms of inclusion on social structures within groups, looking beyond the distribution of rents themselves and toward nonmaterial factors such as dignity, working conditions, social status, and how borderland populations themselves view, understand, and navigate changing political settlements.

CONCLUSION
Remaking the Maghreb

This book began with vignettes of two places in Tunisia in 2014: one, the country's parliament in Tunis, where MPs debated increasing the legally mandated punishments for smugglers and decried it as "economic terrorism"; the other, the border town of Ben Guerdane and its Souk Maghrebi, where the local municipality still contributed to the organization of the sale of smuggled goods and was hard at work to make sure it would soon be able to tax them again. These pages have traced the relationship between smugglers and the states of the Maghreb beyond these seeming contradictions. They have examined the economic and political function that smuggling has fulfilled in the region, how this has been negotiated, and the vulnerabilities it has caused.

In early 2023 we find these same places in crisis. In Tunisia, the parliamentary chamber in which the book started stands empty. The parliament's suspension in July 2021 by President Kais Saied marked the end of an era of postrevolutionary politics in Tunisia, the nascent democracy facing an uncertain future. The first round of parliamentary elections in late 2022 was conducted in an authoritarian context and saw the lowest popular turnout anywhere in modern history. Further south, the situation is looking similarly uncertain. The conflict in Libya, a protracted economic crisis, and repeated border closures amplified by the Covid-19 pandemic have eroded the incomes of many traders in the Souk Maghrebi. This book does not

CONCLUSION

provide a complete account of these crises, nor does it offer a prediction or roadmap of where they will go next. But as the renegotiation of Tunisia's political settlement and the possibility of a new "authoritarian bargain" once again stands at the center of its political discussion, it is a critical reminder that the changing character of governance in Tunisia is not just negotiated in Tunis. It provides an important addition to our understanding of the full scope and the tools of the "real governance" that Tunisians engage with every day and has always gone beyond the county's formal laws and institutions.

Across the Maghreb, citizen-state relationships are in a process of renegotiation and will continue to be for years to come, as postindependence social contracts and the remaining or revamped authoritarian political settlements have revealed their fragilities and are further challenged by concurrent crises. As Marc Lynch has noted, there are "simply too many drivers of political instability for even the most draconian regime to stay in power indefinitely."[1] This book contributes to our understanding of these changes in critical ways. Looking back, it provides a corrective to incomplete descriptions of what the previous social contract and mode of governance have looked like for many citizens of the Maghreb. Alongside more formal issues such as employment and social protection, the strategic toleration of illegal activities, "forbearance," and informal rent streams have long shaped citizen-state relationships in the region and are a starting point for much of their renegotiation. If previously informal or illegal activities are closing down, be it as a result of changing geopolitics, "formalization," or "law and order" politics, those who relied on them will demand alternatives. The informal authoritarian bargains discussed in this book go beyond the borderlands: they are relevant to the other informal businesses that employ the majority of the region's labor force, to the planned legalization of cannabis cultivation in Morocco's Rif Mountains, to informal mining in Jerada, to informal construction, mobility, and remittances.[2] But it is here that they can be observed particularly well, in a space where so many of the key political themes of the day interact: insecurity and cross-border mobility; informal employment and fragile livelihoods; protests and resistance; legacies of inequality, authoritarianism, distrust, and indignity; demands for new development models; and conflicts about who they will include. As such, they provide lessons on the real relationships between the actors involved. They can offer insights into why actors who engage in

CONCLUSION

activities that are technically illegal, from smugglers to street vendors, may see it as the responsibility of the state to address challenges to these activities and engage in protests to demand support. They can help us understand why these same actors might both engage in illegal activities and still see corruption as one of the main challenges facing their countries and livelihoods. But they also help us understand the difficulties in the road ahead as citizen-state relationships are renegotiated and borderlands remade.

Morocco's story in particular is instructive here. The past decade in its northern borderlands illustrates the challenges in transforming how populations and regions are incorporated into the national economic and political structures. Going far beyond the borderlands, these challenges stand at the heart of political and economic agendas across the regions in years to come. This book examines crucial complications of the common narratives of inclusion and subversion and offers concrete examples of what has and has not worked. This final chapter seeks to draw out the wider relevance of these analyses. It begins by summarizing the key themes of the book before drawing out their theoretical and concrete practical implications, within and beyond the Maghreb.

REGULATION, INCORPORATION, AND VULNERABILITY

The questions at the heart of this book have emerged out of a tension between contemporary discourses around smuggling and state-building, and empirical observations of smuggling activities in the Maghreb. What has been described as hidden can often be found in plain sight; what has been described as unregulated often follows clearly communicated rules. What has been described as nonstate often saw state involvement; what has been described as destabilizing has frequently coincided with periods of public unrest whenever it decreased. Why did states tolerate these activities or contribute to their regulation? What are the consequences—is smuggling undermining state institutions or contributing to alternative forms of state-building?

To answer these questions and apparent contradictions, the preceding chapters have focused on the interactions between the two entities so frequently framed as antagonists in the struggle for order—smugglers and states. Tracing the past decade in the borderlands of Tunisia and Morocco, examining the effects of political shifts and external shocks in both

CONCLUSION

countries, they have found plenty of these interactions between smugglers and states. Their key findings cluster around three main themes: regulation, incorporation, and vulnerability.

This book began its examination of the relationship between smuggling and state structures with an analysis of its *regulation*. It observed that smuggling economies in North Africa trading in licit goods are primarily regulated through informal institutional arrangements. It presented detailed descriptions of these institutions, highlighting that while they were mainly informal, they were neither small-scale nor personalistic. They were not dependent on personal characteristics or connections of traders, and they contained third-party enforcement through the active and systematic involvement of local state agents. They were able to regulate the quantity and price of smuggled goods. And, critically, they were able to segment different types of smuggled goods. This provided a counterpoint to the common narrative that licit smuggling networks subvert states by generating a form of general unregulated porosity through which more harmful actors—smugglers of illicit goods or terrorists—can slip.

Institutions, however, are not the only element of regulation that is worth noting. Chapter 4 also highlighted how understandings of moral appropriateness and legitimacy affect attitudes toward the trade and the participation of borderland populations. It noted that while the trade is regulated through local informal institutions, this does not necessarily imply that local populations see these institutions as legitimate. Furthermore, while informal institutions have contributed to the widespread presence of networks with low barriers to entry, access to capital and connections have also shaped smuggling networks by molding higher barriers to entry to more profitable networks or positions. Notably, both dynamics are not entirely divorced from the state, either. Different moral evaluations of various smuggling activities were frequently connected to evaluations of the role of the state. And, as the comparison between gasoline and textile networks has foregrounded, relationships with state institutions remained a crucial factor in determining the ability of different smuggling networks to prosper, build capital, and diversify. This analysis of the regulation of smuggling thereby provided a first entry into a discussion of its political economy: it emphasized that states need to be considered as playing an important role in the regulation of smuggling, not merely as an enforcer or occasional nonenforcer of formal laws.

CONCLUSION

Any analysis of regulation generates questions about regulators. Questions emerge about why states tolerated and regulated smuggling networks in their periphery, and who benefited from the resulting rent streams. This led large parts of this book to focus on an analysis of *incorporation*—of the role that rents generated by smuggling economies have had in informally incorporating different groups into wider political settlements, to incentivize them to accommodate wider distributions of resources. Having traced the incomes generated by smuggling economies and their regulation, chapter 5 argued that while the notion of an authoritarian bargain, or trading political acquiescence for formal rents through subsidies and state employment, has been a staple of the analysis of the political economy of the Middle East and North Africa, it has existed alongside another arrangement. The toleration and regulation of the smuggling needs to be understood in the context of an informal authoritarian bargain in the region's borderlands. Here, informally generated rent streams provided income opportunities to borderland populations and compensated them for the concentration of formal rent streams and state investment in the coastal centers. Borderlands are thereby incorporated—but, crucially, only informally so—into national political settlements. Notably, borderland communities are not the only ones whose access to resources is organized through smuggling economies. State institutions, including security services and local municipalities, have found ways to access smuggling rents through bribes and informal taxation, and politically connected elites have been able to use clientelist relationships in order to insert themselves into the smuggling economy.

This incorporation of borderlands through smuggling economies has been challenged in recent years in the context of broader changes in the region. The Tunisian revolution not only removed a set of politically connected actors with interests in the smuggling economy but also led to a renegotiation of the role of smuggling in the postrevolutionary order. While the years following the revolution saw bargaining between smugglers and states on a variety of levels over the terms of their incorporation, it also saw the reconstituted democratic Tunisian state once again rely on the smuggling economy to incorporate its borderlands.

Morocco, on the other hand, saw a soft realignment of its political settlement with the ascendancy of a new king and the expansion of formal state investment in the northeastern borderlands. However, this did not primarily aim to replace the smuggling economy but to further structure it,

CONCLUSION

and build on its economic role in the region. Once Algeria began to reinforce its land border, effectively cutting off networks smuggling gasoline and other licit goods, further formal state investment in the borderlands was needed to make up for the shortfall in informal rent streams.

This analysis of both regulation and incorporation has generated a first answer to the question about whether networks smuggling licit goods in North Africa have been subverting the region's states. It suggests that most smuggling activities are not subversive to the region's states but in fact closely regulated by them, and, most crucially, fundamental to supporting the wider political settlements, by supporting the distribution of resources on which the stability of the state itself rests. Rather than as a remaking of the state by the periphery or a return of traditional, tribal, or nonstate organizational forms, the politics of smuggling must be analyzed with a consideration of wider modes of governance that involve the state itself.

There are, however, deep cracks within this stability. The analysis is incomplete without also noting various *vulnerabilities* that are inherent to this arrangement, and particularly to the groups informally incorporated into it. As the final chapters have highlighted, these arrangements are vulnerable insofar as they are dependent on economic and political conditions in the region that are not always within the control of the respective states themselves. In Tunisia and Morocco, smuggling economies were thrown into crises in recent years as a result of the civil war in Libya and Algeria's construction of new border fortifications, as well as more recent restrictions of movement caused by a global pandemic. In addition, they are dependent on a heterogeneous regional subsidy and tariff regime in the region, which is increasingly under threat in the context of expanding free-trade agreements and subsidy reforms in the region.

As the previous chapter highlighted, the limitation of smuggling and formalization of the settlement do not necessarily increase stability and inclusion but may lead to new sources of instability and adverse incorporation of those who lack the power to engage with the terms of inclusion offered. Here, vulnerability extends to the populations informally incorporated into these political settlements. Smugglers commonly experience insecurity and structural violence as a result of their extralegal enterprise and working conditions, even if those are generally tolerated. As the comparison between gasoline traders and textile traders has highlighted, the effects of an incorporation through informal institutions are highly context-dependent. They can be a stepping stone to a formalization on terms that are acceptable to traders or lead to complete dependence on these institutions and disconnections in the event of their collapse. As the chapter noted, connections to state structures and other traders, organizational capacity, and institutional history are crucial in shaping the ability of informal economic actors to influence the terms on which they are incorporated into political settlements, and, crucially, not all incorporation is genuinely inclusive.

STATE-BUILDING, INFORMAL INSTITUTIONS, AND POLITICAL SETTLEMENTS

At the core of this book has been the argument that the politics of the Maghreb's periphery is closely tied to that of its center. In parallel to that, it has tried to demonstrate that the politics of the Maghreb's periphery holds important lessons for the study of politics more broadly: for our understanding of state-building and its relationship with smuggling, of informal institutions, and of political settlements.

This book has sought to extend scholarship on the relationship between smuggling and state-building by combining a structured political economy approach with the focus on local dynamics of order-making in borderlands that has been a hallmark of contemporary work in African borderland studies.[3] In arguing that smuggling can be embedded in particular modes of state-building rather than subverting states, but at the same time noting that these modes of state-building are not necessarily driven by bottom-up dynamics, it has mapped out a middle ground in a central discussion on the politics of borderlands.

The analysis of smuggling in Tunisia and Morocco presented here has provided evidence against the portrayals of states and smugglers as inherently antagonistic that can be found in both the work of critical scholars like James C. Scott and neo-Weberian accounts of state-building.[4] At the same time, however, it also urges a more cautious approach toward claims that these processes of order-making have made borders the frontlines of the renegotiation of states, that states are reshaped and molded at their borders and "engulfed by legal pluralism."[5] Scholars such as Thomas Hüsken and Georg Klute have argued that governance processes in borderlands require an analytical approach that looks beyond the state as the primary

CONCLUSION

actor in order-making.[6] This book takes a contrary position. Alongside scholars such as Kate Meagher and Gregor Dobler, it points to the continuous, though at times hidden, role of actors from the political center in the borderlands.[7]

While there may have been plenty of action in the borderlands, this should not obscure the ways in which this action has been shaped, organized, and even regulated by the state. Crucially, this book has noted that the state's role in the borderlands does not have to be confined to the actions of local state agents who may be following different interests from those of the central state far off in the capital, but that it can be closely connected to the fundamental distributive and institutional basis of the state itself. It has developed this argument by tracing the role of the state as a regulator and enforcer even in informal regulatory arrangements that at first sight may easily be considered outside of its remit. It has highlighted the role of state agents in negotiating informal institutions, as well as the degree to which locally negotiated institutions and even normative perceptions were subject to the wider structural conditions of national political settlements.

A large part of the book has been focused on describing a particular—seemingly exotic—set of institutional arrangements. It has argued that in the features of these arrangements lies a fundamental challenge to the common characterization of *informal institutions* in mainstream political economy. Theories across the spectrum have typically assumed that informal institutions are incapable of creating impersonal structures of regulation or third-party enforcement.[8] This book has supported and expanded critiques of this characterization through its analysis of informal institutions in the regulation of smuggling.[9]

First, it has shown that informal institutions are capable of establishing impersonal structures of regulation. The informal regulation of smuggling at the Ras Jedir border crossing, for example, the procedures at the Melilla border crossings, or those at the gates alongside the Algerian border with Morocco are all largely impersonal. Participation in the activities regulated by these institutions may require certain characteristics of the people involved in them, such as a residency card for Nador, but this is not untypical for impersonal institutions. Crucially, they are not tied to particular personal identities or relationships.

Second, it has shown that informal institutions are not necessarily "rules in force" but can contain third-party enforcement—which may include state actors.[10] The intuition behind the idea that informal institutions cannot regulate impersonally builds on the assumption that they lack third-party enforcement and are self-enforcing, thereby requiring them to operate on a basis of trust.[11] In the context of the institutions observed here, this does not hold: soldiers, customs agents, and police forces illegally but systematically act as enforcement agents for these institutions. While in some cases they appear as corrupt patrons, we also observe them enforcing informal rules and not collecting any bribe at all, or collecting a fixed payment that has been agreed as part of the institution itself. Crucially, they create interactions that are large-scale, are predictable, and necessitate neither trust nor evasion.

This does not imply, however, that the two categories—formal and informal institutions—completely collapse into each other. The fact that informal institutions are created, communicated and enforced outside the officially sanctioned channels remains analytically meaningful and should be retained as the primary substantive feature of informal institutions.[12] This analysis, however, has suggested that other features cannot be inferred from the institutional type alone but are embedded in and conditional on their political environment. The third-party enforcement of informal institutions around smuggling by state agents is tied to the political choice to tolerate some forms of smuggling. The impersonal nature of these institutions is closely related to the political necessity of maintaining low barriers to entry for certain networks in order to generate employment in the borderlands. Consequently, this book has highlighted that to provide a meaningful discussion of the features of informal institutions, an analysis of their political context—their political economy—is indispensable.

The analysis presented here also support Frances Cleaver's observation that regulatory institutions do not typically emerge as rational solutions to collective action problems, but as the results of historical patterns of "bricolage."[13] An empirical example includes the development of informal and increasingly formalized taxation of the distributional networks of textile smuggling through traditional market taxes. Crucially, however, this process of institutional development and bricolage is not a random walk but deeply embedded in historical arrangements and power relations.[14] As noted in the previous chapter, the ability of different groups to affect the development of institutions and navigate changing institutional structures is highly heterogeneous and related closely not only to capital and

CONCLUSION

organizational capacity but also to the ability to structure the intersection with state structures.

On a related point, this book also urges caution with respect to the local legitimacy and developmental nature of informal and hybrid institutions. An expanding literature on "development with the grain" has emphasized that institutions that are informal or hybrid in nature and embedded in local practices and negotiations are perceived as particularly legitimate by local populations and, being adapted to local circumstances, can be particularly efficient or developmental.[15] Discussions with borderland populations outlined in chapter 4, however, have supported the perspective that local participation in informal and hybrid institutions, or even their involvement in their negotiation, is not necessarily an indication of their moral legitimacy.[16] Borderland populations and smugglers themselves commonly view smuggling critically and evaluate it in a wider economic context that is characterized by a lack of alternatives. Views on the legitimacy of these institutions are heterogeneous, and participation is not always perceived as entirely voluntary.

This book has drawn on political settlements as an analytical framework to bring institutions, rents, and changing balances of power into its analysis of state-building. Tied to a precise and structured theory of political economy, it has found this a more productive structure than leaning more broadly on social contracts or authoritarian bargains. As Abdul Raufu Mustapha, Kate Meagher, and Nicholas Awortwi have noted, "The political settlement approach provides an analytical tool for moving beyond the routine pathologizing of African states with a view to understanding them in terms of what they are, not in terms of their failure to replicate ideal-typical Weberian states."[17] Similarly, and joining recent work by Jonathan Goodhand, this book has found a political settlement approach productive for viewing commonly pathologized systems of borderland governance in terms of what they are, not in terms of a priori assumptions about smuggling and state subversion.[18]

In the process of its empirical analysis, this book has made multiple theoretical contributions to the literature on political settlements more widely: First, it has contributed to our understanding of the role of informal institutions and illegally generated rent streams in the stabilization of political settlements. As noted by Mushtaq Khan, the role of informal institutions marks a central contribution of political settlement approaches to modern political economy.[19] And yet the conception of informal institutions in political settlement scholarship is still underdeveloped. Political settlement approaches so far do not apply their central assumption, the dependence of institutional performance on the political context, to the features of informal institutions, relying instead on their characterization as personalistic. Noting that informal institutions can be impersonal or contain third-party enforcement does not clash with any of the central assumptions of the political settlement framework but generates new research questions on the role of informal institutions and organizational structures in political settlements.

Second, this book has contributed to the spatialization of political settlements. Goodhand and Meehan have pointed to political settlement analysis's focus on the nation-state as its sole frame of reference as its most fundamental limitation, as it "underplays international and regional dimensions" and "lacks an explicit analysis of space and territory."[20] This book has sought to provide such an analysis. It has noted that political settlements, while often conceptualized within the boundaries of the nation-state, are deeply embedded in cross-border relationships. This introduced new sources of fragility into the political settlements of Tunisia and Morocco, as changes in the political settlements of their neighbors directly affected the stability of their own. At the same time, the preceding chapters have highlighted the territorial unevenness of North Africa's national political settlements and the relationships and overlaps of local, national, and borderland settlements—its domestic territorial politics. Currently, such relationships are not clearly conceptualized within political settlement approaches. Mirroring conceptions of vertical inclusion, there appears to be an assumption that subnational settlements are integrated into national settlements through subnational elites, which then connect local populations. As the cases of both Medenine and the Oriental have highlighted, however, borderland populations are not universally "delivered" or included through local elites but engage with local, regional, and national elites, as well as local and national institutions.

Third, this book has contributed to the study and conceptualization of inclusion, and particularly informal inclusion in political settlements. While political settlement approaches commonly frame inclusion through informal rents as a side payment to powerful groups, their application to

CONCLUSION

smuggling has shown that it can also incorporate relatively powerless groups. Such informal incorporation can generate challenges for the affected groups that differ from more formal modes of incorporation. Consequently, there is a need to reframe the debate on inclusivity and stability in political settlements: the formalization of political settlements does not necessarily increase their stability or inclusivity, and discussions of both horizontal and vertical inclusion are insufficient if they do not also include an analysis of the terms of inclusion. Chapter 8 has demonstrated that political settlement analysis can productively be connected to an expanding discussion on inclusive economies and adverse incorporation in the study of African politics.[21]

REMAKING THE MARGINS

At the time of writing, North Africa's borderlands face a larger accumulation of pressures than they have at any other point in the postindependence period. The combination of new border fortifications, the Covid-19 pandemic, trade agreements, violent conflict, supply-chain disruptions, and protracted economic crises all have curbed their ability to fulfill the role that they have for most of the past decades. Some of these pressures may be reduced in the coming years, while the consequences of others are continuing to accumulate. One way or the other, the Maghreb is facing another renegotiation of its relationship with its borderlands. This will almost inevitably happen in a domestic and international policy context that is shaped by continuous unease about mobility in the region and suspicion of its borderlands. As the early examples of Morocco already highlight, these renegotiations will most likely include some form of formalization of further state engagement. For this to be successful, they will need precise tailoring to the political, social, and economic particularities of borderlands that have been shaped by smuggling economies.

This book does not provide a masterplan for these engagements and how to make them successful. Indeed, it is inherently skeptical of the ability to formulate these plans outside of the communities that are affected by them. However, there are important lessons in these accounts that can provide some guidance, and that stand at odds with how many policy makers, in and outside of the region, tend to think about smuggling. I will highlight three themes here—porosity, corruption, and development. While I will discuss these in the empirical context of Tunisia and Morocco, their applicability is not limited to North Africa.

First, the analysis has suggested that the conception of border porosity in North Africa that underlies contemporary policy discourses in the region is fundamentally incorrect. Policy discussions and reports typically begin from the assumption of a form of general border porosity, where different actors can move across borders outside the view of the state.[22] Occasionally, the argument is made that small-scale smuggling of licit commodities has created these paths, which can now be used by weapons smugglers or terrorists.[23] As this discussion of the institutions that regulate smuggling in North Africa has shown, this is fundamentally incorrect. Not only do small-scale commodity smuggling and the smuggling of drugs or weapons occur along different paths, but the paths that the former uses are highly regulated through informal institutions that are partially enforced by state agents and contain limits on the quantity and types of goods that may pass through them.

The policies that typically follow from this assumption of general porosity include the construction of new formal regulatory institutions to counter the perceived absence of regulation, and improvements in state enforcement capacity to counter its perceived weakness. Most prominently, this has included the construction of new border fortifications: the past decade has seen increased fortifications along the Melilla-Morocco border, the Algeria-Morocco border, and the Tunisia-Libya border. The effects of these fortifications, however, have been mixed. While the new fortifications on the Melilla-Morocco border coexisted with huge amounts of smuggling until 2019, the new fortifications on the Morocco-Algeria border almost entirely wiped out networks smuggling licit goods, while confiscation data suggests that they have had a relatively limited effect on networks trading in illicit goods and particularly in drugs.[24]

With respect to the efficiency of border walls and fortifications, the analysis presented in this book urges caution. It notes that new regulatory institutions are not constructed in an institutional vacuum, but that their effect is determined by their interaction with preexisting informal regulatory arrangements and power structures. Furthermore, it highlights that the effects of border fortifications on different networks are heterogeneous. Preliminary experience from the region suggests that new infrastructure

CONCLUSION

frequently risks restricting the smuggling of licit goods without seriously disrupting networks trading in illicit goods. Meanwhile, the creation of new border infrastructure risks disrupting rent streams that are crucial for local communities and may thereby lead to a destabilization of the borderlands and undermine previous informal security arrangements.[25]

Second, this book has suggested that a reevaluation of the role of corruption in organized crime and illegal cross-border trade in North Africa is needed. Much of the policy literature on the issue has identified corruption among security services and state officials as a root cause of smuggling and transnational organized crime in the region.[26] Commonly, anticorruption training and improvements of institutional oversight are suggested to address this issue.[27] However, an analysis of the borderlands of Tunisia and Morocco suggests that as smuggling is deeply embedded in the distributional politics and political settlements of the region, the role of corruption as a root cause has likely been overstated. While it commonly accompanies the phenomenon of smuggling—and is both essential and a constant nuisance to the smugglers themselves—we have seen evidence in these borderlands of smuggling that is facilitated by security forces without the collection of any bribes at all. It suggests that corruption is a feature of the politics of smuggling but not its cause. In the absence of corruption, smuggling would not necessarily halt.

While this raises serious doubts as to the effectiveness of anticorruption measures in tackling smuggling in North Africa, it does not mean that the issue is not worth further exploration. Corruption likely plays a larger role in the smuggling of goods outside of the regulatory structures discussed here and represents a set of rent streams to powerful constituencies in the security services that may act as veto-players to any reform programs for the borderlands. It does, however, suggest a need for more targeted thinking about corruption. As with border infrastructure, policy making needs to consider the wider politics and institutional dynamics of smuggling rather than just respond to predetermined normative concepts of best practice in order to anticipate the real effects of its interventions.

Third, the analysis presented suggests that development initiatives need to play a larger role in policy engagement with borderlands and are in serious need of innovation and expansion. While this book has highlighted some negative side effects that disrupting smuggling economies can have for borderland populations, this does not imply that the reliance on smuggling economies is sustainable. As noted throughout, smuggling economies contain real risks for those involved, have been associated with lower incentives to pursue education, and are subject to changes in regional politics, subsidy regimes, free-trade agreements, and state crackdowns. What is needed is an alternative economic plan for the region's borderlands that goes beyond law-and-order approaches but emphasizes historic neglect and the need for investment and development.

As the experience of Morocco's emergency program for the borderlands has shown, there are unique challenges in creating formal opportunities for borderland communities reliant on smuggling. As many young men have quit school to join smuggling networks, low educational levels require a tailored approach to employment creation. The flexibility and independence that in many cases came with working in smuggling networks present additional challenges to integration into a different sector. Finally, the lack of credible intersections and the lack of trust between particularly younger and lower-level members of smuggling networks and local state institutions need to be urgently addressed in order to build more successful development policies for borderlands in the region.

The analysis provided here suggests why two of the approaches frequently proposed—agricultural projects and special economic zones—are not without problems. Agricultural projects in Morocco commonly failed to engage young male smugglers, due to both the challenges in transitioning to a different sector and the absence of a vision of work that connected to desires for dignity and perspective. This was closely related to the programs' failure to create an intersection with the local population that was easy to navigate and capable of fostering trust, cooperation, and a sense of genuine inclusion.

While special economic zones as a formal alternative to smuggling are either suggested or already in place in Tunisia and Morocco, there is a need for caution. As demonstrated, access to capital, connections, and the ability to restructure businesses among former smugglers are highly heterogeneous. While special economic zones offer opportunities for some smugglers, they do not necessarily replicate the low barriers to entry that many subsections of the local smuggling economy rely on. At the same time, they represent yet another regulatory regime to navigate or manipulate, opening up opportunities for already well-capitalized or well-connected actors, with limited oversight over the conditions of employment they may generate.

CONCLUSION

Both examples point to a need for a significant expansion not only of development-oriented policy making in North African borderlands, but also in innovation in these approaches themselves, requiring an explicit study of the terms of inclusion for different social groups. To create alternatives to the low barriers to entry that were essential to many smuggling networks, programs should be designed explicitly with marginalized sections of the borderland population in mind, putting genuinely inclusive employment initiatives at their center. Programs need to build on precise studies of border economies, not only to be able to target networks that are most in need of support, but also to recognize the political structures they are engaging with. If they create new regulatory structures, programs should be designed, negotiated, and communicated in a way that facilitates adaptation and considers local understandings of dignified work, while building an intersection with borderland populations that doesn't marginalize already powerless actors. Otherwise, there is a real risk that programs designed to include borderland economies end up perpetuating exclusion, alienation, and eventually deeper instability.

BEYOND LAW AND ORDER

> We are the children of this republic, we believe in the state, and we will reinforce the state. And the informal economy is a phenomenon that risks striking the state at the heart of its existence.
>
> —MEHDI JOMAA, FORMER PRIME MINISTER OF TUNISIA, 2014

This book began with a quote from Tunisia's former prime minister, noting the contrast between the language with which states in North Africa often frame smuggling economies as subversive threats to their existence and how in practice they commonly tolerate, regulate, and tax them. The book has sought to resolve this contrast by demonstrating states' continuous reliance on illegal economies to support political settlements and the maintenance of order on which the formal institutions of the state depend. While arguing against a portrayal of smuggling as inherently subversive, it has also sought to highlight the fragilities inherent in this form of order by noting the heterogeneous experiences of different networks and the vulnerabilities that borderland communities face. There are still good reasons not to throw out the idea of subversion from the study of smuggling and border economies, but it needs to be complemented by a question: Who is subverting whom?

By approaching smuggling through the lens of politics and development rather than from a law and order perspective, this book has aimed to suggest a political contextualization of both law and order. It has highlighted that while the economies of North Africa's borderlands are more likely to routinely operate outside the law of the political center, they are shaped by rules and structures that cannot be entirely separated from the politics of the center. The order that emerges is neither new nor necessarily subversively encroaching on the state in the periphery but is the result of a specific model of inclusion that purposefully placed the region's borderlands in economic dependence on tolerated illegal activity in a context of formal state neglect. It does not "strike the state at the heart of its existence"—it has long been an element of how it navigated and supported its very existence. It is not a threat to reinforce against, but a legacy to be addressed.

Appendix 1

STUDYING SMUGGLING IN NORTH AFRICA

STUDYING SMUGGLING

As noted in chapter 1, researching smuggling comes with a particular set of methodological challenges. At the heart of this often stands the task of making visible something that does not always desire to be visible, recording something that is frequently beyond the realm of typical bureaucratic methods of recording. At the same time, the study of illegal activities and the interaction with often vulnerable populations require particular attention to research ethics, risk, positionality, and triangulation.[1] This appendix has been added with two goals in mind: First, to trace how this project's data was collected in order to support and explain its use in the empirical chapters of this book as well as highlight its limitations. And second, to contribute to a still relatively small but expanding discussion on the methodological challenges and opportunities in studying illegal trade, as well as illegal activities more widely.

The history of scholarship on cross-border trade has seen a huge methodological variety in approaching the challenges inherent in studying smuggling. Quantitative scholarship has typically focused on macrodynamics, measuring the scope and composition of smuggled goods.[2] Methodologies here have varied from observing and inspecting cars on crossing points, to analyzing satellite images, to estimating the volume of smuggling streams through indicators of the consumption of smuggled goods.³ Multi-indicator models have used wider ranges of variables, including black-market premiums, consumption, and price indices, to construct estimates of informal cross-border trade.⁴ With many of these methods, there is a trade-off between the breadth and depth of insight produced and a focus on estimating the size of smuggling flows. While Friedrich Schneider and Dominik Enste's seminal paper aims to estimate the "size, causes, and consequences" of shadow economies in seventy-six different countries, their approach provides little detail on subnational processes.⁵

Qualitative and mixed methods scholarship on smuggling have both focused on mapping macrostructures and sought to unpack more microdynamics in borderlands.⁶ Here, too, methodologies have been diverse and frequently encompass multiple approaches, including extensive ethnographic work in and on borderland communities, detailed studies of markets and social networks, archival work, court documents, and legal scholarship.⁷ Some scholarship has productively combined both survey work and more focused interviews with smugglers and key stakeholders.⁸ As Stephen Ellis and Janet MacGaffey have highlighted, what unites different methodological approaches toward the study of smuggling is that the challenges involved in data collection and triangulation often make research on these issues particularly consuming of time and resources and consequentially limit the scope of each study.⁹ In this context, matching a methodological approach and its limitations with a project's question and theoretical framework is of particular importance.

This study's methodological approach has been shaped by its interest in the position of smuggling in the region's politics. In its analytical approach, it is therefore closely connected to structural analyses of politics, the natural methodological focus of which has usually been country-level political economy analyses, accompanied by small-n country-level comparative approaches.¹⁰ As Jonathan Goodhand and Patrick Meehan have noted, the methodological nationalism embedded in this type of scholarship has led to a scarcity of work on subnational and transnational politics within larger national structural political settlement, explicitly limiting its ability to account for the role of borderlands in its political analyses.¹¹

Chapter 1 described how this project's interest in the role of smuggling in the wider political economy of Tunisia and Morocco requires an empirical focus on informal institutions, their associated rent streams, negotiation,

APPENDIX 1

and effects on different communities. Work on informal institutions, including in a borderland context, has been dominated by in-depth ethnographic work, which appears uniquely suited to tracing and understanding patterns of behavior and regulation that are unwritten, embedded in everyday practice, or hidden and requires an in-depth understanding of local contexts.[12] This has included both single case studies and, given the transnational character of cross-border trade, increasingly multisite ethnographies.[13]

As this project's analysis seeks to place frequently hidden forms of regulation and negotiation within larger political dynamics, its methodological challenge lies in combining both structural-comparative and ethnographic methods.[14] Consequently, it has built on elements of political ethnography in order to provide in-depth analyses of the informal institutions that regulate smuggling in North Africa, their relationship to local moral perceptions, and their effects on border communities. To generate insights into wider structural dynamics, it relies on cross-case comparisons both between two field sites, where it traces the changes and renegotiations of smuggling economies in recent years, and in-case comparisons between two different smuggling networks in each field site.

The remainder of this appendix consists of two sections: The first lays out the wider theoretical grounding of the project's comparative and ethnographic approach. The second section discusses the project's data collection, noting relevant challenges with respect to access, positionality, ethics, and risk, and how these have influenced the project.

POLITICAL ETHNOGRAPHY, COMPARISON, AND CHANGE

Political Ethnography

A number of political science scholars have in recent years advocated for the renewed and extended use of ethnographic methods within the discipline.[15] While ethnographic work has historically been a foundational part of the study of politics from Tocqueville's 1835 *Democracy in America* to the work of James Scott, political science and anthropology have increasingly diverted, whereas "ethnographic work, to the extent that it existed in political science, tended to be trimmed down to fieldwork interviews and/or subordinated to game theoretic models."[16] A central point in this critique has been an edited volume on "political ethnography" in 2009 that highlights the utility of ethnographic work particularly in the context of micropolitics, in testing and fleshing out generalizations produced by other methods, providing epistemic innovation, and expanding the boundaries of what is commonly considered "political." There is significant disagreement across disciplines on the definition of an ethnography, but the volume points to two general features: participant observation and an ethnographic sensibility—"an approach that cares—with the possible emotional engagement that implies—to glean the meanings that the people under study attribute to their social and political reality."[17]

Although a large section of this project's data comprises interviews, the project has sought to approach its interviews with an ethnographic sensibility and to contextualize and understand them alongside extensive participant observation conducted during fieldwork in the two case sites.

Lisa Wedeen has argued that ethnography can be uniquely useful to fill in the gaps between official demonstrations of obedience and ordinary experiences of unbelief and resistance.[18] In its examination of informal institutions and smuggling, this study in a sense attempts the reverse, by using ethnographic approaches to trace structures of regulation in the seemingly disobedient. As Edward Schatz has noted, political ethnographies are, in a sense, partial ethnographies that focus on the exercise of power. They represent "a distancing from the attempts to represent *holistically* a culture, society, group, or locale that earlier generations of ethnographers offered" while highlighting contextual factors, mapping "the part (politics) in relation to the whole (the socio-political context, both in its temporal and locational sense)."[19]

If a political ethnography is partial in its focus, ethnographic work on cross-border trade similarly faces challenges in its geographic limits. This project follows a range of studies on cross-border trade by drawing on fieldwork at multiple sites.[20] As Judith Scheele has highlighted, fieldwork on cross-border trade in wide spaces imposes further linguistic and logistic challenges for the researcher and hence limits on the ethnography as a whole.[21] The claim of a political ethnography of cross-border trade in North Africa hence cannot be to be a complete analysis of its varying social and cultural contexts, but primarily of the way in which these contexts connect to the politics of smuggling. Crucially, however, this provides opportunities for comparison.

APPENDIX 1

Paired Comparisons and Observing Change

In addition to using ethnographic approaches in order to trace and highlight informal regulatory structures around smuggling, this book relies on comparative approaches and process tracing in order to connect them to questions around state-building and changing power relationships.

While having been a central part of qualitative research ranging back to the work of John Stuart Mill, there has been little theoretical work on paired comparisons until recently, as it was commonly assimilated into single-case studies or regarded as a degenerate form of multicase analysis.[22] More recent work advocates the combination of paired comparisons with process tracing.[23] As Tarrow argues and is demonstrated by both Putnam et al. and Linz and Valenzuela, paired comparison can be particularly useful in institutional analysis.[24] Furthermore, it provides a fitting intermediary step in theory building, between a single case study and multicase analysis that tests the hypotheses created by the theory. It hence appears to be an appropriate next step for the development of a theory of the political economy of informal trade.

Paired comparisons face a range of methodological challenges. Degrees of freedom are typically low, and atypical case selection has commonly weakened analytic insights. Following Gisselquist and Moller and Skaaning, this project seeks to tackle these issues through careful case selection and by combining multiple levels of comparison.[25] Different chapters and arguments draw on both in-case and cross-case comparisons in order to highlight central structural dynamics in the political economy of smuggling in North Africa.

The first level of paired comparisons, "in-case," examines two informal trade networks operating in the same location. A wide variety of factors—political systems, geography, and local social and economic structures—can be held constant, while key variables of interest, such as the structure of the networks and their role in the local enforcement environment, can be examined. The in-case comparisons therefore follow a most-similar systems logic.[26] This book draws on in-case comparisons both in highlighting how informal institutions heterogeneously regulate different smuggling networks and how different networks have adjusted to and been able to influence wider changes in their regulatory environment.

APPENDIX 1

The second level of paired comparison compares across cases. This allows the tracing of how the different structural conditions in the two case sites—more specifically, variations in political and institutional history—have shaped the renegotiation of the role of smuggling in the political settlements of the region. In addition, as the project conducts a similar in-case comparison in both case sites, thereby adding a second set of paired comparisons, with two networks trading in the same goods but in a different country, it can trace how case-specific conditions have affected the in-case comparison, pointing to similarities of networks' experiences across different contexts and shared underlying dynamics.

Especially in the context of these dynamics, it is important to note that a central comparison here is also between processes—the project traces the renegotiation of the role of smuggling in the political settlements of the two case sites in order to understand both its role and how it is created and maintained through the relationship between different actors. In addition, it also draws on disruptions and changes in political settlements and observes their effects. To think through causal directions between the variables and to explain dynamics of change in the institutional environment, constructing an account of the changing local institutional environment is an important feature of this project, approximating what Tarrow called "dual process tracing" within a paired comparison.[27] The project has been informed by recent work on process tracing that has sought to systematize both the way that process tracing aids the triangulation of information and its application to comparative.[28]

Case Selection

As noted in chapters 1 and 2, the case selection for this project then needs to consider both two geographical case sites and two products and the informal trade networks associated with them. In addition to the discussion in chapters 1 and 2, this section briefly reviews the technicalities of the case selection. The necessary data to conduct this selection had been collected through three months of preliminary fieldwork in 2014, as well as the study of the preexisting literature, media coverage, and policy reports.

The two networks that I have chosen are gasoline and fabrics. As chapter 2 has noted, they are two of the most widely traded licit goods, having had a strong influence on shaping the macrostructures of trade in the region, with perhaps the most significant effects on borderland employment, and being present in a range of borderlands, thereby increasing the wider applicability of the findings. At the same time, the goods form part of a different macrostructure within the region and require different connections and skills from their traders, giving rise to points of differentiation between the networks that provide opportunities for comparison. I have focused on fabrics in order to narrow down the "nongasoline licit goods produced outside the region" category to one of its most common items, but at times I draw on other items from the category to demonstrate that it remains representative for a wider set of goods. This sets two conditions for the selection of the two case sites: active networks trading in both gasoline and fabrics must be present. To improve the comparison, they should furthermore occupy a similar position within the regional macrostructure in the trade of the relevant goods.

The two case sites that I selected are the Medenine region in Tunisia and the Oriental region in Morocco. As required, smuggling networks that import subsidized gasoline from neighboring countries and smuggling networks that import textiles while avoiding tariffs are present in both regions. The two cases share a range of contextual and historical factors that echo wider themes in the history of North Africa's borderlands. In addition, both have seen a recalibration of a primarily clientelist political settlement in recent years, which has included a renegotiation of the role of smuggling. Crucially, these have occurred under somewhat different structural conditions—following a revolution and a dip in state capacity in one case and following top-down reforms with continually strong state capacity in the other, as well as a relatively heterogeneous national history of statebuilding, as chapter 2 has noted. Chapters 6–8 draw on these differences in particular.

In addition, the two case sites offer three rather diverse borderlands. The border between Tunisia and Libya is both formally open and largely rural. The border between Morocco and Algeria is also largely rural but has been formally closed since 1994. The second border in the Oriental region, that between Morocco and the Spanish enclave of Melilla, is open but located in an urban environment. Chapter 3 in particular draws on these differences.

APPENDIX 1

DATA COLLECTION AND CHALLENGES

Alongside conversations and materials that cover a wider time frame, the vast majority of the data for this project was collected during eleven consecutive months of fieldwork in Tunisia and Morocco in 2016 and 2017. This also built on three consecutive months of fieldwork in Tunisia conducted in 2014. During these periods I conducted more than 230 semistructured interviews with members of smuggling networks, local bureaucrats, civil society leaders, politicians, journalists, academics, and formal sector actors. I also conducted a small number of focus group discussions, primarily of informal traders, alongside one group of unemployed university graduates and local civil society activists engaged in formalization projects. Appendix 2 contains a complete list of these interviews and the codes that are used throughout this book to cite particular interviews.

The data collected through interviews has been complemented by extensive participant observation throughout the fieldwork period, which included observing informal markets, roadside vendors, border crossings, local administrations, public discussions, and festivities. The following sections outline some of the central features, challenges, and limitations of the data collection.

Access

Gaining access presents the first methodological challenge of research in informal cross-border trade. The time-consuming process of building trust with traders limits the number of people researchers can speak to, and all access comes with its own biases, as the willingness of traders to engage with researchers correlates with a variety of important variables, such as the type of goods they trade in or their social class.

Of the people I spoke to for this project, politicians, civil society leaders, and street-level bureaucrats presented few challenges in terms of access, as they were generally identifiable and approachable, and I was able to engage with people in a range of positions and political backgrounds.

Geographic access was also manageable—with the exception of brief interruptions due to periods of violence and in one case the temporary revocation by the local security forces of my permission to be present there, I was able to move freely in Ben Guerdane, Medenine, and surroundings for

APPENDIX 1

the entire duration of the data collection period for this project. The same was true for Oujda and Nador. While my access to the village of Beni Drar near Oujda was limited due to the preferences of the local administration, I was still able to conduct a small number of interviews there.

Members of gasoline and textile networks, who stand at the center of this study's paired comparison, were largely generous with their time and their willingness to talk. Despite their illegality, their businesses were normalized in the local community and, as chapter 3 discusses, tolerated by law enforcement to such a degree that talking to me constituted no major risk for them. While the traders most active in the negotiation with state institutions were specifically selected for interviews because of their position, there was also an element of snowball sampling in the selection of some of the interview partners, which has been commonly associated with serious selection biases.[29] This has been mitigated, however, by the large number of different "snowballs" accrued over a long fieldwork period, as well as a concerted effort to speak to members representing different socioeconomic groups. At no point during this project was money or any material benefit offered in order to gain access or interviews.[30]

To gain a wider understanding of the different local smuggling networks and the rules by which they operated, I also interviewed members from a diverse range of licit and illicit networks in both locations, covering a wide variety of activities, including, among others, the smuggling of foodstuffs, car parts, drugs, cigarettes, kitchenware, shoes, electronics, and human trafficking. As some of these networks are less normalized and identifiable than gasoline and fabrics, some of the access challenges identified earlier were exacerbated but could be mitigated over time through building relationships and approaching different members of these networks. Interestingly, even drug smugglers were not the most difficult people to gain access to for this project—obtaining formal interviews with military personnel was impossible, while interviews with members of the police remained informal. This limits the project's insights into the dynamics within the armed forces in both countries, but a significant amount of information about their role can still be obtained through participant observation, informal interviews, and the accounts of those interacting with them.

There is a relatively even split in the interviews conducted between the two case sites but a huge gender discrepancy across both case studies, and only a few of the women interviewed are involved in smuggling networks.

APPENDIX 1

This is primarily a consequence of the fact that and smuggling networks in both case sites are predominantly male. The thirty-three interviews conducted with women were the result of a concerted effort to include female voices. This brought particular challenges, given women's packed schedules in the face of the double burden of professional work and housework, and the conservative social structures in both field sites. Overcoming these difficulties typically involved interviewing women in their home or near their place of work, being mindful of their schedule, as well as the help of a female research assistant.

The methodology used here, focusing on a broad set of members of two crucial networks, alongside purposefully selected representatives of a wide set of other networks and politicians, civil society leaders, and street-level bureaucrats, allows this study to provide detailed descriptions of the structures and dynamics of networks as well as their interaction with state structures but prohibits it from making statistical estimations, such as the precise percentage of women among the fabric transporters in Morocco.

Interviews

As previous scholarship on cross-border trade has noted, interviewing smugglers, in particular, comes with unique challenges.[31] Processes of building trust and establishing rapport that are central to gaining access do not end when interviews start, bringing in additional considerations and limitations.

Given the sensitive content of the conversations, most interviews were conducted under the condition of anonymity. While recording interviews electronically was not feasible in the context, almost everyone was comfortable with me taking written notes on a small notepad, which further reaffirmed my positioning as a student. This allowed me to obtain detailed notes, which I later typed and thematically coded for analysis. I was able to note down verbatim quotes, but their length tends to be limited to two or three sentences.

I conducted most interviews in French, English, or German alone, and research assistants and friends acted as translators in interviews conducted in local Arabic dialects. I did engage in Arabic language training as part of this project and have been learning Arabic for years, but the substantial differences between dialects and in particular the dialects of the borderlands

APPENDIX 1

in question did not leave me confident to conduct interviews in Arabic by myself. Still, Arabic did help build rapport in interviews and everyday encounters, while the ability to conduct interviews in French, particularly with bureaucrats, helped to frame interviews in the language of technocracy and development, in which bureaucrats felt more comfortable speaking about the local smuggling economy.

The structure and content of interviews differed hugely dependent on the participant, though interviews with informal cross-border traders commonly included a life history element, which has been found to be particularly productive in studying cross-border trade, followed by thematic questions on the trade.[32] Recent scholarship has highlighted the interactional nature of interviews as a form of data collection, noting that interview content cannot be taken as a "snapshot" of what is going on in a person's head but is instead created through the encounter of the interviewed with the researchers, with the researchers' positionality deeply affecting the content of the interview.[33]

In many cases, the interviews were the first sustained interaction I had with the people I was interviewing. Apart from the introductions and the features of my position that interviewees picked up on immediately—my ethnicity (white), gender (male), age (younger than many interviewees), and nationality (foreign)—the interviews were also a process through which my respondents were trying to gather information about me. I provided an introduction to my work at the beginning of a meeting, though this was not always sufficient to dispel preconceptions of what I might "really" be doing, the most common assumptions being that I intended to collect information on behalf of my government, its secret service, or its military, that I was a journalist, or that I was interested in buying or selling drugs or arms. These assumptions were potentially damaging not only to the content of the interview but also to my security. I was particularly careful to not ask any questions, at least in the early parts of interviews, that might shed doubt on my identity as a "student interested in the economic structures and regulatory environments of borderlands," and I usually started with the more economics-centered questions. I made sure not to disclose advance knowledge of illicit trade networks and adopted a more naïve persona when the issue came up. I almost never asked overtly political questions of nonpoliticians, although respondents typically brought up politics unprompted.

Still, there were more meaningful ways in which this limited the questions I was able to ask. My knowledge of illicit trade networks is built on a more limited sample of interviews than my knowledge of licit trade networks, as I had to reduce these discussions to the interviews in which either my opposite would bring them up or I would feel comfortable enough to ask. I also was unable to construct any quantitative social network analyses of the different connections among traders, as systematic questions about the specific names of their suppliers or interlocutors would have been viewed as highly suspicious.

My positionality also had effects on the answers I received. My position as a foreigner commonly led people to feel like they should behave as an ambassador and present their environment in the best light. Fortunately, this tended to decrease over the duration of the interview. In interviews with people of relatively low social status, despite my assurances to the contrary, answers would occasionally be characterized by a belief that I would be able to organize help. Still, this remained less prevalent than I had originally anticipated, likely because my characterization as a student and the lifestyle and demeanor I adopted were clearly separate from foreign NGO workers or foreigners in a position of power.

Naturally, the fact that the subject matter discussed included sensitive subjects and illegal activities significantly affected interviews. As Sanchez has noted, if smuggling activities are normalized and socially accepted locally, conversations become easier, particularly if embedded in local discourse.[34] I learned to phrase questions in this context, typically referring to "trade" and "business" rather than smuggling. Learning from research assistants and experience to phrase questions in a nonjudgmental manner and breach sensitive subjects appropriately was an important process. All this was facilitated by the fact that many of my questions were about institutions and about rules and structures of interaction that many shared. As a result, I was able to pose questions that could imply less personal responsibility, asking more about "how are things done" before asking "how you specifically are doing things."

Nevertheless, incentives toward misreporting need to be considered in the evaluation of the interview data. The initial step was for me to treat each interview first and foremost as what it was—a conversation affected by positionalities, interests, and discourses, rather than statements of objective fact. I then tried to piece these together through careful triangulation, using

APPENDIX 1

some of the logics of Bayesian process tracing described by Fairfield and Charman, considering people's incentives and positionalities.[35] A large number of interviews, along with a collection of documents, some secondary literature, and most crucially the experience gained through participant observation, allowed me to triangulate information in order to generate robust data on informal institutions around smuggling in North Africa. To give an example, the change of the procedure at Tunisia's Ras Jedir border crossing, mentioned in chapter 3, was confirmed to me by three separate sources, each of whom have intimate knowledge of the procedure and did not know one another, not having any motive, or in this case the ability, to coordinate a precise and elaborate lie. Additionally, I did not receive any information contradicting their stories.

There is a worrying tendency in academic and journalistic writing on smuggling to make arguments based on one single, anonymous source, frequently with no discussion of its positionality or credibility. Thankfully, due to the length of the fieldwork period for this project, there are very few instances in this project where I have to rely on a single anonymous source. None of them is fundamental to the argument I present, but they offer interesting detail, and I have included them only where I believe them to be credible, to have detailed knowledge of the processes they are describing, and to have no incentive to misrepresent them.

Participant Observation

Participant observation has been an important part of the data collection for this project. Observing the distribution networks of informal cross-border trade in markets across the region, buying contraband gasoline, accompanying a Moroccan NGO on trips where they gave seminars to formalize informal workers, attending the festivities for the anniversary of the IS attack on Ben Guerdane and the demonstrations in Al-Hoceima, walking time and time again through the border crossings of Melilla, driving through checkpoints every day and having one too many run-ins with the local police, and holding late-night discussions with friends and their families all provided context and information beyond the rather artificial boundaries of interviews. It also helped me build contacts and provided me with the understanding of local social structures that would help me behave appropriately toward my respondents.

APPENDIX 1

Again, my ability to participate was mediated through my identity. As a foreigner (and someone requiring research ethics approval), participating in smuggling myself was impossible. However, my positionality also brought advantages: even once I had spent significant time in my field sites, the assumption was still that my understanding of local processes was nil, providing me with an ongoing commentary on my surroundings by those around me. A reputation as a researcher working on the economy also created a certain interest by local bureaucrats and businesspeople to discuss the local economy, which provided valuable insight and context.

Finally, my positionality within the local community was crucially influenced and supported by three people who at one time or another worked as my research assistants, and whose local embeddedness and kind character helped us to find access and build trusting relationships. All three were close to me in age and fluent in English, as well as French and local Arabic dialects. In Tunisia, I began working with Mohamed in 2014, when he introduced himself to me in the street. It was a fortunate encounter, as he would become a competent translator and quasi-bodyguard for years to come. His coming from a local family but not being particularly well-known proved hugely valuable, as it made him able to reassure respondents while at the same time not placing us in the context of any political or social group. In Morocco, I began working with Jaouad in 2016, after his university professor had recommended him to me, and Mawya in 2017, after her tutor had recommended her. Having different genders and different social backgrounds—one from a rural, one from an influential urban family—while both maintaining involved links with local civil society, they provided me with a rich perspective on their surroundings and allowed me to in some cases pick a translator who I felt was most suited for the context of a particular interview.

Ethics and Risk

I have complied with the ethics guidelines of the institutions I was based at throughout this project—for the fieldwork conducted in 2014, this was the University of Oxford, and for the fieldwork conducted in 2016 and 2016, it was the London School of Economics and Political Science. Due to widespread illiteracy and heightened concerns about confidentiality and security, I have relied on an oral consent procedure, which I developed for my

APPENDIX 1

2014 fieldwork in coordination with the research ethics committee at the University of Oxford and consequently adapted for the 2016 and 2017 sections of this project.

Conducting interviews with smugglers brought two sets of additional ethical challenges: one regarding my acting lawfully myself, and one regarding my responsibility toward those with whom I was interacting. With respect to lawfulness, my research did not require me to break any laws but put me in a position to witness illegal activities. This is a common ethical issue, particularly in criminology.[36] Given the nonviolent nature of these activities, their institutionalization, and the awareness of law enforcement agencies, siding with the responsibility to protect the confidentiality of the participants of this study was a straightforward choice.

With respect to my responsibility to those I was interacting with, apart from ensuring informed consent, ensuring anonymity has been particularly important. I had a conversation about anonymity before every interview, adopting an opt-out system where anonymity was the assumed standard. Aside from anonymizing all these interviews, I have also anonymized multiple interviews in which my opposite had explicitly consented to be cited by name because they did reveal information that I believed could potentially be harmful to them, and I preferred to err on the side of caution. All interview transcripts and notes have been saved and transmitted in encrypted form.

Finally, the project involved some risk to my own security. The security situation, particularly in the Tunisian South, has been volatile for the past years, and Ben Guerdane once again became a red zone on the FCDO's map a few days after I completed my fieldwork there. The nature of my research necessitated additional caution in both field sites. In cooperation with LSE Health and Safety, the security strategy for this project was based on a low profile, surveillance detection, irregular patterns of movement, and close cooperation with local partners. While in Ben Guerdane additional measures included tracking through my phone and regular check-ins, and, from 2016 onward, all nights spent outside of the city. Fortunately, no incidents occurred that suggested that this strategy was insufficient, but this did limit my flexibility and the number of interviews I could do in a day. Although the length of my fieldwork made this less problematic, the low-visibility aspect of these security strategies ensured that these issues were not present in the immediate interview environment.

Appendix 2

INTERVIEW LISTS

Interview descriptions have been anonymized, with the exception of a very few instances (M60, T45, and T49, for example) in which the interview was agreed to be conducted on the record. Smaller localities have similarly been anonymized.

Interview List Tunisia

Code	Anonymized description	Interview date	Interview location
T1	Tunisian academic	19 July 2014	Jendouba
T2	Senior politician, economist	24 July 2014	Tunis
T3	Local resident	25 July 2014	Tabarka
T4	Gasoline smuggler	28 July 2014	Jendouba
T5	Gasoline smuggler	29 July 2014	Jendouba
T6	Senior administrator, state-owned enterprise	30 July 2014	Jendouba
T7	Tunisian academic	30 July 2014	Jendouba
T8	Tunisian academic	12 August 2014	Tunis
T9	Tunis-based political analyst	12 August 2014	Tunis
T10	Member of parliament	14 August 2014	Tunis
T11	Analyst, formal sector gasoline importer and distributor	15 August 2014	Tunis
T12	Member of parliament	15 August 2014	Tunis
T13	Midlevel local bureaucrat	19 August 2014	Djerba (Houmt Souk)
T14	Civil society activist focused on local economic issues	20 August 2014	Ben Guerdane
T15	Small-scale informal vendor of household items, Souk Maghrebi	20 August 2014	Ben Guerdane

(continued)

APPENDIX 2

Interview List Tunisia (Continued)

Code	Anonymized description	Interview date	Interview location
T16	Local journalist	20 August 2014	Ben Guerdane
T17	Senior official, local employers' association	21 August 2014	Ben Guerdane
T18	Local civil society actor focused on agriculture	21 August 2014	Ben Guerdane
T19	Civil society activist focused on local economic issues	22 August 2014	Ben Guerdane
T20	Vendor, Ras Jedir wholesale market	22 August 2014	Ben Guerdane
T21	Small-scale gasoline smuggler	22 August 2014	Ben Guerdane
T22	Civil society activist	22 August 2014	Ben Guerdane
T23	Midlevel local bureaucrat	25 August 2014	Djerba (Houmt Souk)
T24	Representative of regional employer's association	26 August 2014	Medenine
T25	Senior official, regional development organization	26 August 2014	Medenine
T26	Midlevel municipal bureaucrat	27 August 2014	Medenine
T27	Senior municipal bureaucrat	27 August 2014	Medenine
T28	Senior official, regional employment office	27 August 2014	Medenine
T29	Senior official, formal textile production and export	28 August 2014	Djerba (Houmt Souk)
T30	Formal-sector exporter of fabrics	29 August 2014	Djerba
T31	Senior Tunisian academic	2 September 2014	Medenine
T32	Senior municipal bureaucrat	3 September 2014	Ben Guerdane
T33	Local labor activist	3 September 2014	Ben Guerdane
T34	Resident, former gasoline smuggler	3 September 2014	Ben Guerdane
T35	Senior municipal politician	4 September 2014	Ben Guerdane
T36	Senior municipal-level bureaucrat	4 September 2014	Ben Guerdane
T37	Small-scale informal money exchange operator	5 September 2014	Ben Guerdane
T38	Small-scale smuggler and transporter of car parts	9 September 2014	Ben Guerdane
T39	Senior municipal bureaucrat	9 September 2014	Ben Guerdane
T40	Wholesale smuggler of licit goods, civil society activist	10 September 2014	Ben Guerdane
T41	Senior municipal bureaucrat	11 September 2014	Ben Guerdane
T42	Tunisian senior academic	19 September 2014	Hammamet
T43	Policy analysts working on border security	23 September 2014	Tunis
T44	Senior official, national employers' association	3 January 2017	Tunis
T45	Senior politician, former president of Tunisia	4 January 2017	Tunis
T46	Civil society actor, focused on economic and security issues	6 January 2017	Tunis
T47	Civil society activist, focused on informality	6 January 2017	Tunis
T48	Senior economist, politician	6 January 2017	Tunis
T49	Senior politician, former foreign minister	7 January 2017	Tunis
T50	Civil society activist, focused on corruption issues	8 January 2017	Tunis

APPENDIX 2

Code	Anonymized description	Interview date	Interview location
T51	Civil society activist, focused on decentralization	8 January 2017	Tunis
T52	Journalist	8 January 2017	Tunis
T53	Official, Tunisian stock exchange	10 January 2017	Tunis
T54	Journalist	14 January 2017	Tunis
T55	Tunisian academic	17 January 2017	Tunis
T56	Civil society activist, focused on informality	20 January 2017	Tunis
T57	Member of parliament	20 January 2017	Tunis
T58	Member of parliament	30 January 2017	Tunis
T59	Member of parliament	30 January 2017	Tunis
T60	Transporter for wholesale smuggler of licit goods	5 February 2017	Ben Guerdane
T61	Senior figure, local association of informal traders	6 February 2017	Ben Guerdane
T62	Labor inspector	8 February 2017	Ben Guerdane
T63	Local union leadership figure	8 February 2017	Ben Guerdane
T64	Senior municipal-level bureaucrat	8 February 2017	Ben Guerdane
T65	Formal sector small-scale businessman and activist	9 February 2017	Ben Guerdane
T66	Civil society activist and small-scale smuggler of gasoline and smaller licit goods	10 February 2017	Ben Guerdane
T67	Local resident, former gasoline smuggler	11 February 2017	Ben Guerdane
T68	Wholesale smuggler of licit goods, civil society activist	11 February 2017	Ben Guerdane
T69	Local resident, former gasoline smuggler	13 February 2017	Ben Guerdane
T70	Textile smuggler	13 February 2017	Ben Guerdane
T71	Senior municipal bureaucrat	14 February 2017	Ben Guerdane
T72	Small-scale gasoline smuggler	16 February 2017	Djerba (Houmt Souk)
T73	Senior Tunisian academic	17 February 2017	Medenine
T74	Informal vendor in city market	18 February 2017	Medenine
T75	Young local resident	18 February 2017	Medenine
T76	Cigarette smuggler	19 February 2017	Medenine
T77	Smuggler, licit goods, originally from Hama	19 February 2017	Medenine
T78	Smuggler of fruit and vegetables on desert route	19 February 2017	Medenine
T79	Senior Tunis-based researcher and policy analyst	22 February 2017	Tunis
T80	Tunis-based academic working on Tunisian politics	28 February 2017	Tunis
T81	Tunisian academic and policy analyst	28 February 2017	Tunis
T82	Midlevel municipal bureaucrat	3 March 2017	Ben Guerdane
T83	Civil society activist	3 March 2017	Ben Guerdane
T84	Senior municipal-level bureaucrat	3 March 2017	Ben Guerdane
T85	Civil society activist, local cultural organizer	3 March 2017	Ben Guerdane
T86	Local resident	4 March 2017	Near Tataouine

(continued)

Interview List Tunisia (Continued)

Code	Anonymized description	Interview date	Interview location
T87	Large-scale smuggler of various goods, coordinator of multiple transporters	4 March 2017	Rural borderland between Ben Guerdane and Tataouine
T88	Senior municipal bureaucrat	4 March 2017	Ben Guerdane
T89	Former high-level municipal bureaucrat, formal sector businessman	5 March 2017	Ben Guerdane
T90	Senior local civil society organizer	5 March 2017	Ben Guerdane
T91	Senior civil society activist	5 March 2017	Ben Guerdane
T92	Wholesale smuggler of licit goods	5 March 2017	Ben Guerdane
T93	Official in regional economic infrastructure development activities	5 March 2017	Ben Guerdane
T94	Wholesaler of smuggled gasoline	6 March 2017	Ben Guerdane
T95	Wholesaler of smuggled gasoline, former informal financial services provider	6 March 2017	Ben Guerdane
T96	Wholesale smuggler of licit goods, civil society activist	6 March 2017	Ben Guerdane
T97	Large-scale smuggler of various licit goods	7 March 2017	Ben Guerdane
T98	Small-scale informal vendor of household items, Souk Maghrebi	7 March 2017	Ben Guerdane
T99	Senior municipal bureaucrat	7 March 2017	Ben Guerdane
T100	Civil society activist, specializing in corruption	9 March 2017	Tunis
T101	Member of parliament	11 July 2017	Tunis
T102	Member of parliament	12 July 2017	Tunis
T103	Academic working on migration	14 July 2017	Tunis
T104	Local resident, former gasoline smuggler	17 July 2017	Ben Guerdane
T105	Wholesale smuggler (licit goods), civil society activist	17 July 2017	Ben Guerdane
T106	Wholesaler of smuggled gasoline	18 July 2017	Ben Guerdane
T107	Senior civil society activist	18 July 2017	Medenine
T108	Small-scale vendor, contraband gasoline	19 July 2017	Zarzis
T109	Large-scale smuggler of various licit goods	20 July 2017	Ben Guerdane
T110	Local resident, former gasoline smuggler	20 July 2017	Ben Guerdane
T111	Former pharmaceutical smuggler, formal sector entrepreneur	20 July 2017	Ben Guerdane
T112	Senior municipal bureaucrat	20 July 2017	Ben Guerdane
T113	Senior municipal-level bureaucrat	20 July 2017	Ben Guerdane
T114	Civil society activist in Western Libya	25 July 2017	Tunis
T115	Policy analyst	26 July 2017	Tunis
T116	Policy analyst working on border security	26 July 2017	Tunis
T117	Tunisian academic and policy analyst	28 July 2017	Tunis

APPENDIX 2

Code	Anonymized description	Interview date	Interview location
T118	Tunis-based researcher	28 July 2017	Tunis
T119	Senior official, relevant Tunisian ministry	28 July 2017	Tunis
T120	Minister, Ministry of Commerce	28 July 2017	Tunis
T121	Senior official, local employment bureau	5 September 2017	Ben Guerdane
T122	Medium-scale smuggler, bags and textiles, vendor	5 September 2017	Ben Guerdane
T123	Textile smuggler and vendor in city market	5 September 2017	Ben Guerdane

Interview List Morocco

Code	Anonymized description	Interview date	Interview location
M1	Moroccan academic	14 October 2016	Ifrane
M2	Small-scale informal vendor in city market	30 October 2016	Oujda
M3	Vendor of kitchen equipment in city market	10 November 2016	Oujda
M4	Senior official, regional administration, Oujda-Angad	11 November 2016	Oujda
M5	Informal vendor (electronics) in city market	15 November 2016	Oujda
M6	Civil society activist	16 November 2016	Oujda
M7	Former large-scale gasoline smuggler	19 November 2016	Oujda
M8	Formal sector entrepreneur and consultant	28 November 2016	Oujda
M9	Local senior official in position connected to commerce	29 November 2016	Oujda
M10	President, development association	30 November 2016	Oujda
M11	Senior official, local environmental agency	30 November 2016	Oujda
M12	Midlevel municipal bureaucrat	2 December 2016	Oujda
M13	Head, formal business association	4 December 2016	Oujda
M14	Local official, INDH	5 December 2016	Oujda
M15	Moroccan senior academic	6 December 2016	Oujda
M16	Moroccan senior academic	7 December 2016	Oujda
M17	Senior municipal official	7 December 2016	Oujda
M18	Moroccan economist	14 December 2016	Rabat
M19	Senior Moroccan academic	15 December 2016	Mohammedia
M20	Journalist	15 December 2016	Casablanca
M21	Diplomat	3 April 2017	Rabat
M22	Civil society activist	9 April 2017	Oujda
M23	Moroccan academic	11 April 2017	Oujda
M24	Director, local development association	12 April 2017	Nador
M25	Local resident, teacher	12 April 2017	Nador
M26	Midlevel political operative and civil society activist	12 April 2017	Nador
M27	Formal sector entrepreneur	12 April 2017	Nador
M28	Activist at local development association	13 April 2017	Nador

(continued)

APPENDIX 2

Interview List Morocco (Continued)

Code	Anonymized description	Interview date	Interview location
M29	Head of local development association	13 April 2017	Nador
M30	Moroccan academic	13 April 2017	Nador
M31	Midlevel political operative and civil society activist	18 April 2017	Nador
M32	Vendor and senior figure in informal vendors associations	18 April 2017	Nador
M33	Former senior official, urban development	18 April 2017	Nador
M34	Vice-president, informal market association	20 April 2017	Oujda
M35	Former gasoline smuggler, now vendor in a city market	20 April 2017	Oujda
M36	Textile smuggler and vendor in city market	20 April 2017	Oujda
M37	Vendor, alimentary products, city market	20 April 2017	Oujda
M38	Vendor, textiles, informal city market	20 April 2017	Oujda
M39	Informal electronics vendor in city market	21 April 2017	Oujda
M40	Entrepreneur, former pharmaceutics smuggler	23 April 2017	Oujda
M41	Small-scale smuggler and transporter of alimentary goods from Melilla	23 April 2017	Oujda
M42	Small-scale smuggler of licit goods from Melilla	23 April 2017	Oujda
M43	Vendor of shampoo, city market	23 April 2017	Oujda
M44	Vendor of electronics, city market	23 April 2017	Oujda
M45	Vendor of iron goods, city market	23 April 2017	Oujda
M46	Head of informal market association and textile trader	25 April 2017	Nador
M47	Regional official, Ministry of Commerce	26 April 2017	Nador
M48	Senior figure in local market association, informal vendor	27 April 2017	Oujda
M49	Textile smuggler, activist, local market association	27 April 2017	Oujda
M50	Vendor, smuggled underwear in city market	27 April 2017	Oujda
M51	Moroccan academic	28 April 2017	Oujda
M52	Former textile smuggler, textile vendor, city market	29 April 2017	Oujda
M53	Small-scale vendor, informal city market	30 April 2017	Oujda
M54	Former gasoline smuggler, civil society activist and community leader	30 April 2017	Small rural community near Algerian border
M55	Small-scale smuggler and transporter of alimentary goods from Melilla	30 April 2017	Oujda
M56	Small-scale smuggler of licit goods from Melilla	30 April 2017	Oujda
M57	Informal vendor of smuggled pharmaceuticals	30 April 2017	Oujda
M58	Vendor of smuggled textiles in city market	30 April 2017	Oujda
M59	Vendor and market association activist, city market	30 April 2017	Oujda

APPENDIX 2

Code	Anonymized description	Interview date	Interview location
M60	Mayor, municipality of Oujda	2 May 2017	Oujda
M61	Senior official, regional tax office	3 May 2017	Oujda
M62	Local politician	4 May 2017	Oujda
M63	Senior regional customs official	4 May 2017	Oujda
M64	Civil society actor and senior academic	4 May 2017	Oujda
M65	Head of regional development association and municipal bureaucrat	4 May 2017	Oujda
M66	Former senior regional bureaucrat in commerce-related position	6 May 2017	Nador
M67	Midlevel political operative and civil society activist	8 May 2017	Nador
M68	Emigrated resident returning for an investment conference	8 May 2017	Nador
M69	Local midlevel bureaucrat in a position connected to commerce	8 May 2017	Nador
M70	Official, chamber of commerce	11 May 2017	Oujda
M71	Midlevel bureaucrat, agricultural development agency	12 May 2017	Oujda
M72	Bureaucrat, agricultural development agency	12 May 2017	Oujda
M73	Midlevel bureaucrat, regional agricultural development agency	12 May 2017	Oujda
M74	Midlevel bureaucrat, regional agricultural development agency	12 May 2017	Oujda
M75	Senior figure, local market association, and informal vendor	14 May 2017	Oujda
M76	Medium-scale textile smuggler with a stall in a city market	14 May 2017	Oujda
M77	Vendor of smuggled sneakers in city market	14 May 2017	Oujda
M78	Senior bureaucrat, urban planning agency	15 May 2017	Oujda
M79	Local microcredit provider	15 May 2017	Oujda
M80	Senior local administrator, development agency	15 May 2017	Oujda
M81	Senior figure in local market association and informal vendor	16 May 2017	Oujda
M82	Local bureaucrat closely connected to emergency program for border regions	16 May 2017	Oujda
M83	Informal vendor of sneakers in city market	16 May 2017	Oujda
M84	Small-scale smuggler of alimentary goods between Melilla and Oujda	17 May 2017	Oujda
M85	Informal vendor of sneakers in city market	17 May 2017	Oujda
M86	Researcher, journalist	18 May 2017	Rabat
M87	Official in public body connected to the Auto-Entrepreneur Programme	26 May 2017	Rabat
M88	Local midlevel bureaucrat in a position connected to commerce	30 May 2017	Nador
M89	Senior regional official connected to electrification of borderland settlements	1 June 2017	Oujda

(continued)

APPENDIX 2

Interview List Morocco (Continued)

Code	Anonymized description	Interview date	Interview location
M90	Small-scale transporter of smuggled goods between Melilla and Oujda	3 June 2017	Oujda
M91	President, informal trade and market association	4 June 2017	Oujda
M92	Small-scale smuggler/transporter between Melilla and Oujda	4 June 2017	Oujda
M93	Senior figure in local informal market association	5 June 2017	Oujda
M94	Head and staff of local development association	6 June 2017	Suburb of Oujda
M95	Member of parliament	7 June 2017	Oujda
M96	Head of small agricultural cooperative of former gasoline smugglers	7 June 2017	Rural community near Algerian border
M97	Vendor of smuggled textiles in city market and head of a market association	7 June 2017	Oujda
M98	Women's cooperative near Algerian border benefiting from emergency borderland program and its local administrator	8 June 2017	Rural community near Algerian border
M99	Small-scale smuggler and transporter of alimentary goods from Melilla	11 June 2017	Oujda
M100	Former gasoline smugglers, current family agricultural cooperative	14 June 2017	Small rural community near Algerian border
M101	Former gasoline smuggler	14 June 2017	Urban community near Oujda
M102	Former gasoline smuggler, head of agricultural cooperative	15 June 2017	Small urban community near Oujda
M103	Former gasoline smuggler, member of agricultural cooperative	15 June 2017	Small urban community near Oujda
M104	Head of agricultural cooperative, former smuggler	15 June 2017	Small urban community near Oujda
M105	Midlevel administrator, regional administration	15 June 2017	Oujda
M106	Local politician and formal sector entrepreneur	20 June 2017	Oujda
M107	Member of parliament	23 June 2017	Oujda
M108	Senior official, Agence Orientale	23 June 2017	Oujda
M109	Head of agricultural cooperative near Algerian border	6 July 2017	Oujda
M110	Former gasoline smuggler	7 November 2016	Oujda suburb
M111	Former human trafficker	7 November 2016	Oujda suburb

APPENDIX 2

Interview List Melilla

Code	Anonymized description	Interview date	Interview location
ML1	Formal sector businessman and consultant	7 May 2017	Melilla
ML2	Academic	28 May 2017	Melilla
ML3	Three members of Spanish riot police	29 May 2017	Melilla
ML4	Spanish customs official	30 May 2017	Melilla
ML5	Academic	25 July 2017	Melilla

Focus Group List

Code	Focus group description	Date	Location
FG1	Vendors, Souk Maghrebi	4 September 2014	Ben Guerdane
FG2	Vendors, Souk Maghrebi	4 September 2014	Ben Guerdane
FG3	Vendors, Souk Maghrebi	10 September 2014	Ben Guerdane
FG4	Former gasoline smugglers, Morocco	26 October 2016	Small rural community near Algerian border
FG5	Local unemployed university graduates	9 February 2017	Ben Guerdane
FG6	Civil society activists working on informal vendors	17 February 2017	Medenine
FG7	Former gasoline smugglers, Morocco	30 April 2017	Small rural community near Algerian border

NOTES

1. ON THE RADAR

1. Jomaa refers to the words for smuggling (*tahrīb*) and terrorism (*irhāb*). While they contain the same three consonants, they stem from entirely different linguistic roots and are not etymologically related.
2. Louise I. Shelley, *Dirty Entanglements* (New York: Cambridge University Press, 2014).
3. Jamie Prentis, "Zuwara Feels the Effect of Petrol Smuggling," *Libya Herald* (blog), February 13, 2018, https://www.libyaherald.com/2018/02/14/zuwara-feels-the-effect-of-petrol-smuggling/.
4. David A. McMurray, *In and out of Morocco: Smuggling and Migration in a Frontier Boomtown* (Minneapolis: University of Minnesota Press, 2001).
5. By locating its cases in North Africa, this book also aims to close a gap by expanding debates on African borderlands into a region that so far has been widely neglected. A wealth of studies are closely networked and in conversation with one another on border economies in West Africa (Chalfin 2001; Meagher 2014; Nugent 2003, 2007; Tandia 2010; Walther 2012), South Africa (Dobler 2011, 2014; Englund 2001; Coplan 2001; Hughes 2008; Zeller 2009, 2010), and East Africa (Feyissa and Hoehne 2010; Little 2007; James 2009; Titeca 2012, 2009; Titeca and Herdt 2010), to name just a few, but there has been comparatively less research on borderlands and smuggling in North Africa. While there are some notable exceptions to this scarcity primarily coming from ethnographic accounts, such as Meddeb (2012) or Scheele (2012), which will be discussed in the following chapter, they are often relatively unconnected to the literature on African borderlands more widely and are entirely unconnected to the broader political economy literature in the region (Malik and Gallien 2020). This book aims to connect these fields of inquiry more effectively.

1. ON THE RADAR

6. World Bank, "Impact of the Libya Crisis on the Tunisian Economy" (Washington, D.C.: World Bank, 2017), https://openknowledge.worldbank.org/handle/10986/26407.
7. Lotfi Ayadi et al., "Estimating Informal Trade Across Tunisia's Land Borders," World Bank Report, Policy Research Working Paper (World Bank, December 1, 2013), https://documents.worldbank.org/en/publication/documents-reports/documentdetail/856231468173645854/estimating-informal-trade-across-tunisias-land-borders.
8. Moncef Kartas, "On the Edge? Trafficking and Insecurity at the Tunisian–Libyan Border," Security Assessment in North Africa Working Paper (Geneva: Small Arms Survey, 2013); Tom Blickman, "Morocco and Cannabis: Reduction, Containment or Acceptance," Drug Policy Briefing (Amsterdam: Transnational Institute (TNI), March 2017); Inkyfada, "تونس-أمراء-الحدود-مسالك-تهريب-السلاح," December 8, 2017, https://inkyfada .com /ar /2017 /12 /08 /%D8%AA%D9%88%D9%86%D8%B3-%D8%A3%D9%85%D8%B1%D8%A7%D8%A1 -%D8%A7%D9%84%D8%AD%D8%AF%D9%88%D8%AF-%D9%85%D8%B3%D8%A7%D9%84%D9%83-%D8%AA%D9%87%D8%B1%D9%8A%D8%A8 -%D8%A7%D9%84%D8%B3%D9%84%D8%A7%D8%AD/; Mark Micallef, "Shifting Sands—Libya's Changing Drug Trafficking Dynamics on the Coastal and Desert Borders," background paper commissioned by the EMCDDA for the EU Drug Markets Report 2019 (European Monitoring Centre for Drugs and Addiction, 2019).
9. Marc Lynch, ed., *The Arab Uprisings Explained: New Contentious Politics in the Middle East* (New York: Columbia University Press, 2014); Eva Bellin, "Reconsidering the Robustness of Authoritarianism in the Middle East: Lessons from the Arab Spring," *Comparative Politics* 44, no. 2 (January 1, 2012): 127–49, https://doi.org/10.5129/001041512798838021; Yahia H. Zoubir and Gregory White, *North African Politics: Change and Continuity* (London: Routledge, 2015).
10. Ragui Assaad, "Making Sense of Arab Labor Markets: The Enduring Legacy of Dualism," *IZA Journal of Labor & Development* 3 (April 25, 2014): 6, https://doi.org/10.1186/2193-9020-3-6; Suzi Mirgani and Suzi Mirgani, eds., "An Overview of Informal Politics in the Middle East," in *Informal Politics in the Middle East* (Oxford: Oxford University Press, 2021), 4, https://doi.org/10.1093/oso/9780197604342.003.0001.
11. Mirgani and Mirgani, "Informal Politics in the Middle East"; Khalid Mustafa Medani, *Black Markets and Militants: Informal Networks in the Middle East and Africa*, new ed. (Cambridge: Cambridge University Press, 2021); Asef Bayat, "Un-Civil Society: The Politics of the 'Informal People,'" *Third World Quarterly* 18, no. 1 (March 1, 1997): 53–72, https://doi.org/10.1080/01436599715055; Asef Bayat, "Activism and Social Development in the Middle East," *International Journal of Middle East Studies* 34, no. 1 (2002): 1–28.
12. Aside from the work that is specifically on borderlands, such as Hamza Meddeb's account of smuggling under Ben Ali, "Courir ou mourir: Course à el khobza et domination au quotidien dans la Tunisie de Ben Ali" (PhD thesis, Institut d'études politiques, Paris, 2012), one notable exception to this scarcity is Medani's *Black Markets and Militants*, a study of informality in the development of Islamist movements in Egypt and Sudan.

2. SMUGGLING IN NORTH AFRICA

13. For Tunisia, see World Bank, "Tunisia—Breaking the Barriers to Youth Inclusion" (World Bank, November 1, 2014), https://www.worldbank.org/content/dam/World bank/document/MNA/tunisia/breaking_the_barriers_to_youth_inclusion_eng.pdf; for Morocco, Tara Vishwanath et al., "Promoting Youth Opportunities and Participation in Morocco" (World Bank, June 1, 2012), http://documents.worldbank.org/curated/en/681321468276890567/Promoting-youth-opportunities-and-participation-in-Morocco.
14. Advocats Sans Frontières, "The Kasserine 'Region as a Victim' Petition: A First in Transitional Justice in Tunisia" (Tunis: Advocats Sans Frontières, 2015), https://www.asf.be/wp-content/uploads/2015/11/20160615_DossierRegion_Victim_ENG.pdf.
15. Soufan Group, "Foreign Fighters—An Updated Assessment of the Flow of Foreign Fighters Into Syria and Iraq" (Soufan Group, December 2015).
16. Max Gallien and Matthew Herbert, "Out of the Streets and Into the Boats: Tunisia's Irregular Migration Surge" (Atlantic Council, November 27, 2017), http://www.atlanticcouncil.org/blogs/menasource/out-of-the-streets-and-into-the-boats-tunisia-s-irregular-migration-surge.
17. Stephen Ellis and Janet MacGaffey, "Research on Sub-Saharan Africa's Unrecorded International Trade: Some Methodological and Conceptual Problems," *African Studies Review* 39, no. 2 (September 1996): 19–41; Sami Bensassi and Jade Siu, "Quantifying Missing and Hidden Trade: An Economic Perspective," and Nikki Philline C. de la Rosa and Francisco J. Lara, "Lorries and Ledgers: Describing and Mapping Smuggling in the Field," both in *The Routledge Handbook of Smuggling*, ed. Max Gallien and Florian Weigand (Abingdon, UK: Routledge, 2021).
18. For an excellent introduction to scholarship on gender and smuggling, see Caroline E. Schuster "Gender and Smuggling," in Gallien and Weigand, *Routledge Handbook of Smuggling*.
19. At least in the case of Tunisia, there is outstanding work on these dynamics in the pre-2011 period, most notably Kamel Laroussi, "Commerce informel et nomadisme moderne," Ecole des Hautes Études en Sciences Sociales Paris, 2007; Rafaâ Tabib, "Effets de la frontière tuniso-libyenne sur les recompositions économiques et sociales des Werghemmas: de la possession à la réappropriation des territoires" (thèse de doctorat, Cités Territoires Environnement et Sociétés, 2011); and Meddeb, "Courir ou mourir."
20. "Inofficial" or "unstructured" trade would be potential alternative translations here.
21. The definition given does not address the issue of trade in the absence of formal regulation and trade channels. However, as this does not arise in the empirical context of this book, I do not discuss it here. For brevity, I use "informal trade" as a synonym for informal cross-border trade.

2. SMUGGLING IN NORTH AFRICA

1. Jean-Pierre Cassarino, "Approaching Borders and Frontiers in North Africa," *International Affairs* 93, no. 4 (July 1, 2017): 883–96, https://doi.org/10.1093/ia/iix124; Daniel Meier, "Introduction to the Special Issue: Bordering the Middle East,"

2. SMUGGLING IN NORTH AFRICA

Geopolitics 23, no. 3 (July 3, 2018): 495–504, https://doi.org/10.1080/14650045.2018 .1497375.

2. Max Gallien and Florian Weigand, "Studying Smuggling," in *The Routledge Handbook of Smuggling*, ed. Gallien and Weigand (Abingdon, UK: Routledge, 2021).
3. Fortunately there has been, since the publication of Peter Andreas's "Dirty Entanglements: Corruption, Crime, and Terrorism, by Louise I. Shelley," *Political Science Quarterly* 130, no. 2 (2015): 350–51, some outstanding political science scholarship on smuggling in mainstream publications, including the monographs reviewed in his paper; Aisha Ahmad's discussion of the relationship between smuggling and nonstate actors in Afghanistan and Somalia in *Jihad & Co.: Black Markets and Islamist Power* (Oxford: Oxford University Press, 2017); as well as multiple chapters in the volume edited by Gallien and Weigand, *Routledge Handbook of Smuggling*. Nevertheless, as this section notes, these are comparatively recent interventions in a field traditionally dominated by anthropology, sociology, and history.
4. Kate Meagher, "Smuggling Ideologies: From Criminalization to Hybrid Governance in African Clandestine Economies," *African Affairs*, 2014, http://afraf .oxfordjournals.org/.
5. Gallien and Weigand, "Studying Smuggling."
6. R. I. Rotberg, ed., *When States Fail: Causes and Consequences* (Princeton, NJ: Princeton University Press, 2004), 5–9.
7. Ulrich Schneckener, *States at Risk—Fragile Staaten Als Sicherheits- Und Entwicklungsproblem* (Berlin: Stiftung Wissenschaft und Politik, 2004), 7.
8. Volker Boege et al., "On Hybrid Political Orders and Emerging States: What Is Failing—States in the Global South or Research and Politics in the West?" *Berghof Handbook for Conflict Transformation Dialogue Series*, no. 8 (April 9, 2009): 15–35; Christoph Heuser, "The Effect of Illicit Economies in the Margins of the State—the VRAEM," *Journal of Illicit Economies and Development* 1, no. 1 (January 14, 2019): 23–36, https://doi.org/10.31389/jied.7.
9. Catherine Boone, "Trade, Taxes, and Tribute: Market Liberalizations and the New Importers in West Africa," *World Development* 22, no. 3 (March 1994): 453–67.
10. Judith Scheele, *Smugglers and Saints of the Sahara: Regional Connectivity in the Twentieth Century* (Cambridge: Cambridge University Press, 2012).
11. Kate Meagher, "A Back Door to Globalisation? Structural Adjustment, Globalisation & Transborder Trade in West Africa," *Review of African Political Economy* 30, no. 95 (2003): 57–75.
12. J. Collin et al., "Complicity in Contraband: British American Tobacco and Cigarette Smuggling in Asia," *Tobacco Control* 13 Suppl 2 (December 2004): ii104–11, https:// doi.org/10.1136/tc.2004.009357; Max Gallien, "Cigarette Smuggling: Trends, Taxes and Big Tobacco," in Gallien and Weigand, *Routledge Handbook of Smuggling*; Max Gallien and Florian Weigand, "Channeling Contraband: How States Shape International Smuggling Routes," *Security Studies* 30, no. 1 (March 12, 2021): 1–28, https://doi.org/10.1080/09636412.2021.1885728.
13. Jean-Francois Bayart, Stephen Ellis, and Beatrice Hibou, *The Criminalization of the State in Africa* (Oxford: Boydell & Brewer, 1999).
14. Querine Hanlon and Matthew Herbert, "Border Security Challenges in the Grand Maghreb" (Washington, D.C.: United States Institute of Peace Press, 2015).

2. SMUGGLING IN NORTH AFRICA

15. Louise I. Shelley, *Dirty Entanglements* (New York: Cambridge University Press, 2014).
16. Andreas, "Dirty Entanglements."
17. William Reno, "Clandestine Economies, Violence and States in Africa," *Journal of International Affairs* 53, no. 2 (2000): 433–59; James D. Fearon and David D. Laitin, "Ethnicity, Insurgency, and Civil War," *American Political Science Review* 97, no. 1 (February 2003): 75–90, https://doi.org/10.1017/S0003055403000534.
18. Peter Andreas, *Blue Helmets and Black Markets: The Business of Survival in the Siege of Sarajevo* (Ithaca, N.Y.: Cornell University Press, 2008).
19. See Meagher, "Smuggling Ideologies," on changing narratives on smuggling and conflict in West and East Africa. I keep the discussion on the relationship between smuggling and violence in conflict settings relatively limited here, as my focus is not on fragile or conflict environments, and I do not intend to limit the discussion of the political meaning of the relationship between smugglers and states to the occurrence of violence.
20. For state actors, see Richard Snyder and Angelica Duran-Martinez, "Does Illegality Breed Violence? Drug Trafficking and State-Sponsored Protection Rackets," *Crime, Law and Social Change* 52, no. 3 (September 1, 2009): 253–73, https://doi.org/10.1007/s10611-009-9195-z; Luca Raineri and Francesco Strazzari, "Drug Smuggling and the Stability of Fragile States: The Diverging Trajectories of Mali and Niger," *Journal of Intervention and Statebuilding* 16, no. 2 (May 17, 2021): 1–18, https://doi.org/10.1080/17502977.2021.1896207; Matthew Herbert, "From Contraband to Conflict: Links Between Smuggling and Violence in the Borderlands of Meso-America and North Africa," PhD diss., Fletcher School of Law & Diplomacy, Tufts University, 2019. On nonstate actors, see Ahmad, *Jihad & Co.*; David Brenner, "Rebels, Smugglers and (the Pitfalls of) Economic Pacification"; Shalaka Thakur, "Checkpost Chess: Exploring the Relationship Between Insurgents and Illicit Trade"; and Peter Andreas, "The Illicit Trade and Conflict Connection: Insight from US History," all in Gallien and Weigand, *Routledge Handbook of Smuggling*.
21. Jonathan Goodhand, "From War Economy to Peace Economy? Reconstruction and State Building in Afghanistan," *Journal of International Affairs* 1, no. 58 (2004); "Frontiers and Wars: The Opium Economy in Afghanistan," *Journal of Agrarian Change* 5, no. 2 (April 1, 2005): 191–216, https://doi.org/10.1111/j.1471-0366.2005.00099.x; "Corrupting or Consolidating the Peace? The Drugs Economy and Post-Conflict Peacebuilding in Afghanistan," *International Peacekeeping* 15, no. 3 (June 1, 2008): 405–23, https://doi.org/10.1080/13533310802058984; and "Bandits, Borderlands and Opium Wars in Afghanistan," in *A Companion to Border Studies*, ed. Thomas M. Wilson and Hastings Donnan (Chichester, UK: Wiley, 2012), 332–53, http://onlinelibrary.wiley.com/doi/10.1002/9781118255223.ch19/summary.
22. Goodhand, "Corrupting or Consolidating the Peace?" 414.
23. Richard Snyder, "Does Lootable Wealth Breed Disorder? A Political Economy of Extraction Framework," *Comparative Political Studies* 39, no. 8 (October 1, 2006): 943–68, https://doi.org/10.1177/0010414006288724.
24. Goodhand, "Bandits, Borderlands," 334.
25. James C. Scott, *The Art of Not Being Governed: An Anarchist History of Upland Southeast Asia* (New Haven, Conn.: Yale University Press, 2009), 4, x.

2. SMUGGLING IN NORTH AFRICA

26. Thomas Hüsken and Georg Klute, "Political Orders in the Making: Emerging Forms of Political Organization from Libya to Northern Mali," *African Security* 8, no. 4 (October 2, 2015): 320–37, https://doi.org/10.1080/19392206.2015.1100502.
27. Ann Dryden Witte, Kelly Eakin, and Carl P. Simon, *Beating the System: The Underground Economy* (Boston: Praeger, 1982); Friedrich Schneider, "The Size of the Shadow Economies of 145 Countries All Over the World: First Results Over the Period 1999 to 2003," IZA Discussion Paper, Institute for the Study of Labor (IZA), 2004, https://ideas.repec.org/p/iza/izadps/dp1431.html; Friedrich Schneider and Dominik H. Enste, "Shadow Economies: Size, Causes, and Consequences," *Journal of Economic Literature* 38, no. 1 (March 2000): 77–114, https://doi.org/10.1257/jel.38.1.77; Yair Eilat and Clifford Zinnes, "The Shadow Economy in Transition Countries: Friend or Foe? A Policy Perspective," *World Development* 30, no. 7 (July 1, 2002): 1233–54, https://doi.org/10.1016/S0305-750X(02)00036-0; Bruno S. Frey and Hannelore Weck-Hanneman, "The Hidden Economy as an 'Unobserved' Variable," *European Economic Review* 26, no. 1–2 (1984): 33–53; Ana María Oviedo, Mark Roland Thomas, and Kamer Karakurum-Özdemir, *Economic Informality: Causes, Costs, and Policies: A Literature Survey* (World Bank Publications, 2009).
28. Paul Nugent, *Smugglers, Secessionists and Loyal Citizens on the Ghana-Togo Frontier: The Lie of the Borderlands Since 1914* (Oxford: James Currey, 2002), 7, 232.
29. Johny Egg and Javier Herrera, *Échanges transfrontaliers et intégration régionale en Afrique subsaharienne* (Paris: Éditions de l'Aubes, 1998); Judith Vorrath, "On the Margin of Statehood? State-Society Relations in African Borderlands," in *Understanding Life in the Borderlands: Boundaries in Depth and in Motion*, by I. William Zartman (Athens: University of Georgia Press, 2010), 102.
30. Kristof Titeca, "Tycoons and Contraband: Informal Cross-Border Trade in West Nile, North-Western Uganda," *Journal of Eastern African Studies* 6, no. 1 (February 1, 2012): 59, https://doi.org/10.1080/17531055.2012.664703.
31. For comprehensive discussions of this literature as a whole, see Gregor Dobler "The Green, the Grey and the Blue: A Typology of Cross-Border Trade in Africa," *Journal of Modern African Studies* 54, no. 1 (March 2016): 145–69, https://doi.org/10.1017/S0022278X15000993; Meagher, "Smuggling Ideologies."
32. T. Hagmann and D. Peclard, "Negotiating Statehood: Dynamics of Power and Domination in Africa," *Development and Change*, no. 41 (2010): 539–62.
33. Thomas Hüsken, "Die Neotribale Wettbewerbsordnung Im Grenzgebiet von Ägypten Und Libyen," *Sociologus* 59, no. 2 (April 1, 2009): 117–43, https://doi.org/10.3790/soc.59.2.117; Hüsken, "The Practice and Culture of Smuggling in the Borderland of Egypt and Libya," *International Affairs* 93, no. 4 (July 1, 2017): 914, 913, https://doi.org/10.1093/ia/iix121.
34. Kristof Titeca and Tom de Herdt, "Regulation, Cross-Border Trade and Practical Norms in West Nile, North-Western Uganda," *Africa* 80, no. 4 (November 2010): 573–94, https://doi.org/10.3366/afr.2010.0403.
35. Meagher, "Smuggling Ideologies."
36. Béatrice Hibou, "The 'Social Capital' of the State as an Agent of Deception: Or the Rules of Economic Intelligence," in *The Criminalization of the State in Africa*, ed. Jean-Francois Bayart, Stephen Ellis, and Beatrice Hibou (Oxford: Boydell and Brewer, 1999); William Reno, *Warlord Politics and African States* (Boulder, Colo:

2. SMUGGLING IN NORTH AFRICA

Lynne Rienner, 1998); Reno, "Clandestine Economies, Violence and States in Africa," *Journal of International Affairs* 53, no. 2 (2000): 433–59.
37. Timothy Raeymaekers, "African Boundaries and the New Capitalist Frontier," in *Companion to Border Studies*, ed. Thomas M. Wilson and Hastings Donnan (Chichester, UK: Wiley, 2012), 318, 324.
38. Titeca and de Herdt, "Regulation, Cross-Border Trade, and Practical Norms," 573–94, Tom de Herdt and Jean-Pierre Olivier de Sardan, eds., *Real Governance and Practical Norms in Sub-Saharan Africa: The Game of the Rules* (London: Routledge, 2015)..
39. Meagher, "Smuggling Ideologies," 14. Notably, in addition to the question of a shift of the locus of regulatory power between the domestic center and periphery, the question also emerges whether the embedding of regulatory arrangements around cross-border informal trade within international trade structures moves the locus of power beyond the periphery and into the sphere of international value chains and global trade structures. Meagher, "A Back Door to Globalisation?"; Timothy Raeymaekers, "Reshaping the State in Its Margins: The State, the Market and the Subaltern on a Central African Frontier," *Critique of Anthropology* 32, no. 3 (September 1, 2012): 334–50, https://doi.org/10.1177/0308275X12449248.
40. Peter Andreas, *Smuggler Nation: How Illicit Trade Made America* (Oxford: Oxford University Press, 2014); Andreas, *Blue Helmets and Black Markets*.
41. Peter Andreas, "Smuggling Wars: Law Enforcement and Law Evasion in a Changing World," in *Transnational Crime in the Americas*, by Tom Farer (New York: Routledge, 1999), 87–100.
42. Peter Andreas and Ethan Nadelmann, *Policing the Globe: Criminalization and Crime Control in International Relations* (Oxford: Oxford University Press, 2008).
43. Nathan Brown, "Brigands and State Building: The Invention of Banditry in Modern Egypt," *Comparative Studies in Society and History* 32, no. 2 (April 1990): 258–81, https://doi.org/10.1017/S0010417500016480; Karen Barkey, *Bandits and Bureaucrats: Ottoman Route to State Centralization* (Ithaca, N.Y: Cornell University Press, 1994).
44. Scott, *The Art of Not Being Governed*.
45. Meagher, "Smuggling Ideologies."
46. Thomas Bierschenk and Jean-Pierre Olivier de Sardan, eds., *States at Work: Dynamics of African Bureaucracies* (Leiden: Brill, 2014); de Herdt and Oliver de Sardan, *Real Governance and Practical Norms*.
47. Filip Reyntjens, "Legal Pluralism and Hybrid Governance: Bridging Two Research Lines," *Development and Change* 47, no. 2 (March 1, 2016): 346–66, https://doi.org/10.1111/dech.12221; Franz von Benda-Beckmann, "Who's Afraid of Legal Pluralism?" *Journal of Legal Pluralism and Unofficial Law* 34, no. 47 (January 1, 2002): 37–82, https://doi.org/10.1080/07329113.2002.10756563.
48. Kristof Titeca and Rachel Flynn, "'Hybrid Governance,' Legitimacy, and (Il)Legality in the Informal Cross-Border Trade in Panyimur, Northwest Uganda," *African Studies Review* 57, no. 1 (April 2014): 71–91, https://doi.org/10.1017/asr.2014.6; Thomas Bierschenk and Jean-Pierre Olivier de Sardan, "ECRIS : Enquête Collective Rapide d'Identification des conflits et des groupes Stratégiques . . .," *Bulletin de l'APAD*, no. 7 (July 1, 1994), http://apad.revues.org/2173.
49. Titeca and de Herdt, "Regulation, Cross-Border Trade and Practical Norms," 579.

50. Raeymaekers, "Reshaping the State," 345.
51. Titeca, "Tycoons and Contraband," 49.
52. Jonathan Goodhand, Jan Koehler, and Jasmine Bhatia, "Trading Spaces: Afghan Borderland Brokers and the Transformation of the Margins 1," in Gallien and Weigand, *Routledge Handbook of Smuggling*; W. Prichard and V. van den Boogaard, "Norms, Power and the Socially Embedded Realities of Market Taxation in Northern Ghana," ICTD Working Paper (International Centre for Taxation and Development, 2015).
53. Jonathan Goodhand, "Epilogue: The View from the Border," in *Violence on the Margins*, ed. Benedikt Korf and Timothy Raeymaekers, Palgrave Series in African Borderlands Studies (New York: Palgrave Macmillan, 2013), 247–64, https://doi.org/10.1057/9781137333995_10.
54. Gregor Dobler, "Localising Smuggling," in Gallien and Weigand, *Routledge Handbook of Smuggling*.
55. Douglass C. North, *Institutions, Institutional Change and Economic Performance* (Cambridge: Cambridge University Press, 1990).
56. Rafael La Porta and Andrei Shleifer, "Informality and Development," working paper (National Bureau of Economic Research, June 2014), http://www.nber.org/papers/w20205; Hernando De Soto, *The Other Path* (New York: Basic Books, 1989), 180; Michael Bratton, "Formal Versus Informal Institutions in Africa," *Journal of Democracy* 18, no. 3 (July 31, 2007): 96–110, https://doi.org/10.1353/jod.2007.0041.
57. Federico Varese, *The Russian Mafia: Private Protection in a New Market Economy* (Oxford: Oxford University Press, 2001); Diego Gambetta, *The Sicilian Mafia: The Business of Private Protection* (Cambridge, Mass.: Harvard University Press, 1996).
58. Soto, *The Other Path*; Hernando De Soto, *The Mystery of Capital*, new ed. (London: Black Swan, 2001); Daron Acemoglu and James A. Robinson, *Why Nations Fail: The Origins of Power, Prosperity and Poverty* (New York: Profile Books, 2012).
59. Charles Tilly, *Coercion, Capital and European States, A.D. 990–1990*, new ed. (Cambridge, Mass.: Wiley-Blackwell, 1993); Tilly, *Trust and Rule*, Cambridge Studies in Comparative Politics (Cambridge: Cambridge University Press, 2005).
60. Tom Goodfellow, "Political Informality: Deals, Trust Networks, and the Negotiation of Value in the Urban Realm," *Journal of Development Studies* 56, no. 2 (March 4, 2019): 1–17, https://doi.org/10.1080/00220388.2019.1577385; Lant Pritchett, Kunal Sen, and Eric Werker, eds., *Deals and Development: The Political Dynamics of Growth Episodes* (Oxford: Oxford University Press, 2017).
61. Kate Meagher, "Introduction: Special Issue on 'Informal Institutions and Development in Africa,'" *Africa Spectrum* 42, no. 3 (2007): 405–18; Meagher, Kristof Titeca, and Tom de Herdt, "Unravelling Public Authority: Paths of Hybrid Governance in Africa," Justice and Security Research Programme Policy Brief, 2014.
62. Frances Cleaver, *Development Through Bricolage: Rethinking Institutions for Natural Resource Management* (Abingdon, UK: Routledge, 2012); Frances Cleaver, "In Pursuit of Arrangements That Work: Bricolage, Practical Norms and Everyday Water Governance," in *Real Governance and Practical Norms in Africa: The Game of the Rules*, ed. Tom de Herdt and Jean-Pierre Olivier de Sardan (London: Routledge, 2015); Max Gallien and Vanessa van den Boogaard, "Formalization and Its Discontents: Conceptual Fallacies and Ways Forward," *Development and Change* 54, no. 3 (2023): 490–513, https://doi.org/10.1111/dech.12768.

2. SMUGGLING IN NORTH AFRICA

63. Kellee S. Tsai, "Adaptive Informal Institutions and Endogenous Institutional Change in China," *World Politics* 59, no. 1 (October 2006): 116–41, https://doi.org/10.1353/wp.2007.0018; Lily L. Tsai, "Solidary Groups, Informal Accountability, and Local Public Goods Provision in Rural China," *American Political Science Review* 101, no. 2 (May 2007): 355–72, https://doi.org/10.1017/S0003055407070153; Alena V. Ledeneva, *How Russia Really Works: The Informal Practices That Shaped Post-Soviet Politics and Business* (Ithaca, N.Y.: Cornell University Press, 2006); Matt Andrews, *The Limits of Institutional Reform in Development: Changing Rules for Realistic Solutions* (Cambridge: Cambridge University Press, 2013); Henry E. Hale, "Formal Constitutions in Informal Politics: Institutions and Democratization in Post-Soviet Eurasia," *World Politics* 63, no. 4 (October 2011): 581–617, https://doi.org/10.1017/S0043887111000189.
64. Gretchen Helmke and Steven Levitsky, "Informal Institutions and Comparative Politics: A Research Agenda," *Perspectives on Politics* 2, no. 4 (2004): 725–40.
65. Mushtaq Khan, *Rents, Rent-Seeking and Economic Development: Theory and Evidence in Asia* (Cambridge: Cambridge University Press, 2009); Khan, "Political Settlements and the Governance of Growth-Enhancing Institutions," draft paper, Research Paper Series on Growth-Enhancing Governance, 2010; Hazel Gray, *Turbulence and Order in Economic Development: Institutions and Economic Transformation in Tanzania and Vietnam* (Oxford: Oxford University Press, 2018); Gray, "Access Orders and the 'New' New Institutional Economics of Development," *Development and Change* 47, no. 1 (2016): 51–75, https://doi.org/10.1111/dech.12211; Lindsay Whitfield et al., *The Politics of African Industrial Policy: A Comparative Perspective* (Cambridge: Cambridge University Press, 2015). Although they share a common theoretical project, the amount of scholarship published on political settlements in recent years makes it increasingly difficult to pin down one singular definition or approach. Edward Laws, "Political Settlements, Elite Pacts and Governments of National Unity: A Conceptual Study," DLP Background Paper, 2012, finds sixteen different distinct definitions of "political settlements" in the current literature. For a wider discussion of some of this diversity, see Gray, "Access Orders"; Gray, *Turbulence and Order in Economic Development*; Gray, "Understanding and Deploying the Political Settlement Framework in Africa," in *Oxford Research Encyclopedia of Politics*, ed. Hazel Gray (Oxford: Oxford University Press, 2019), https://doi.org/10.1093/acrefore/9780190228637.013.888; and Pritish Behuria, Lars Buur, and Hazel Gray, "Studying Political Settlements in Africa," *African Affairs* 116, no. 464 (July 1, 2017): 508–25, https://doi.org/10.1093/afraf/adx019. I stay closest here to the original formulation by Khan in "Political Settlements," although the discussion in this book does not depend on the particulars of this formulation.
66. Gray, "Political Settlement Framework in Africa."
67. Khan, "Political Settlements," 3.
68. David Booth, "Political Settlements and Developmental Regimes: Issues from Comparative Research," Roundtable Seminar: The Ethiopian Developmental State and Political Settlement (Addis Ababa: Ethiopian International Institute for Peace and Development, 2015); Jonathan Goodhand and David Mansfield, "Drugs and (Dis)Order: A Study of the Opium Trade, Political Settlements and State-Making in Afghanistan," working paper (London: Crisis States Research Centre, 2010);

2. SMUGGLING IN NORTH AFRICA

Tom Goodfellow, "Seeing Political Settlements Through the City: A Framework for Comparative Analysis of Urban Transformation," *Development and Change* 49, no. 1 (2018): 199–222, https://doi.org/10.1111/dech.12361; Tobias Hagmann, *Stabilization, Extraversion and Political Settlements in Somalia* (London: Rift Valley Institute, 2016); Tim Kelsall, "Thinking and Working with Political Settlements," ODI Briefing Papers (ODI, January 2016); Oliver J. Walton et al., *Borderlands and Peacebuilding: A View from the Margins* (London: Conciliation Resources, 2018), https://researchportal.bath.ac.uk/en/publications/borderlands-and-peacebuilding-a-view-from-the-margins.
69. Goodhand, "From War Economy to Peace Economy?"; "Frontiers and Wars"; "Corrupting or Consolidating the Peace?"; "Bandits, Borderlands."
70. Jonathan Goodhand and Patrick Meehan, "Spatialising Political Settlements," in *Accord Insight 4: Borderlands and Peacebuilding*, by Sharri Polanski and Zahbia Yousuf (London: Conciliation Resources, 2018).
71. Scheele, *Smugglers and Saints of the Sahara*; Judith Scheele and James McDougall, eds., *Saharan Frontiers: Space and Mobility in Northwest Africa* (Bloomington: Indiana University Press, 2012); Laroussi, "Commerce informel et nomadisme moderne" (Paris: Ecole des Études en Sciences Sociales, 2007); Hüsken and Klute, "Political Orders in the Making"; Fatiha Daoudi, *Vécu frontalier algéro-marocain depuis 1994: quotidien d'une population séparée* (Paris: Éditions L'Harmattan, 2015).
72. Laroussi, "Commerce informel et nomadisme moderne."
73. Scheele, *Smugglers and Saints of the Sahara*; Matthew H. Ellis, *Desert Borderland: The Making of Modern Egypt and Libya* (Stanford, Calif.: Stanford University Press, 2018).
74. Ibn Khaldûn, *The Muqaddimah—An Introduction to History*, 1377.
75. Ellis, *Desert Borderland*.
76. Laroussi, "Commerce informel et nomadisme moderne," 62; Lisa Anderson, *The State and Social Transformation in Tunisia and Libya, 1830–1980* (Princeton, N.J.: Princeton University Press, 1987), 66.
77. Meier, "Introduction to the Special Issue"; Cassarino, "Approaching Borders and Frontiers."
78. I. William Zartman, "States, Boundaries and Sovereignty in the Middle East: Unsteady but Unchanging," *International Affairs* 93, no. 4 (July 1, 2017): 937–48, https://doi.org/10.1093/ia/iix118.
79. Ibn Khaldûn, *The Muqaddimah*. This conception in parts resembles that in Igor Kopytoff's *The African Frontier: The Reproduction of Traditional African Societies* (Bloomington: Indiana University Press, 1987), a classic account of African borderlands.
80. Zartman, "States, Boundaries and Sovereignty," 938.
81. Anderson, *The State and Social Transformation*, 138.
82. Laroussi, "Commerce informel et nomadisme moderne"; Yvette Katan, *Oujda, une ville frontière du Maroc (1907–1956): Musulmans, juifs et chrétiens en milieu colonial* (Paris: Éditions L'Harmattan, 2000).
83. Laroussi, "Commerce informel et nomadisme moderne."
84. Corinna Mullin and Brahim Rouabah, "Decolonizing Tunisia's Border Violence: Moving Beyond Imperial Structures and Imaginaries," *Viewpoint Magazine* (blog),

2. SMUGGLING IN NORTH AFRICA

February 1, 2018, https://www.viewpointmag.com/2018/02/01/decolonizing-tunisias-border-violence-moving-beyond-imperial-structures-imaginaries/.
85. Laroussi, "Commerce informel et nomadisme moderne."
86. Zartman, "States, Boundaries and Sovereignty"; Cassarino, "Approaching Borders and Frontiers"; Louise Fawcett, "States and Sovereignty in the Middle East: Myths and Realities," *International Affairs* 93 (July 1, 2017): 789–807, https://doi.org/10.1093/ia/iix122.
87. Michael J. Willis, *Politics and Power in the Maghreb: Algeria, Tunisia and Morocco from Independence to the Arab Spring* (London: Hurst, 2012), 64.
88. Willis, 38; al-Saghir Salihi, *Al-Isti'mār al-Dākhilī Wa-al-Tanmiyah Ghayr al-Mutakāfi'ah: Manẓūmat al-Tahmīsh Fī Tūnis Namūdhjan*, al-Ṭab'ah al-ūlá (Tunis: al-Ṣaghīr al-Ṣāliḥī, 2017); Nazih N. Ayubi, *Over-Stating the Arab State: Politics and Society in the Middle East*, new ed. (London: Tauris, 1996), 117–21; David E. Long and Bernard Reich, eds., *The Government and Politics of the Middle East and North Africa*, 3rd ed. (Boulder, Colo.: Westview Press, 1995), 464.
89. Akbar Ahmed and Harrison Akins, "The Plight of the Rif: Morocco's Restive Northern Periphery," *Al Jazeera*, September 28, 2012, https://www.aljazeera.com/indepth/opinion/2012/09/2012924103333182505.html; Kenneth Perkins, *A History of Modern Tunisia*, 2nd ed. (New York: Cambridge University Press, 2014), 135–55.
90. Safwan M. Masri, *Tunisia: An Arab Anomaly* (New York: Columbia University Press, 2017), 210; Mounira M. Charrad, "Central and Local Patrimonialism: State-Building in Kin-Based Societies," *ANNALS of the American Academy of Political and Social Science* 636, no. 1 (July 1, 2011): 55, https://doi.org/10.1177/0002716211401825.
91. Charrad, "Central and Local Patrimonialism," 60.
92. Willis, *Politics and Power in the Maghreb*, 265.
93. Masri, *Tunisia*, 207.
94. Willis, *Politics and Power in the Maghreb*, 287.
95. Adeel Malik and Bassem Awadallah, "The Economics of the Arab Spring," *World Development* 45 (May 2013): 296–313, https://doi.org/10.1016/j.worlddev.2012.12.015; Alexei Kireyev et al., "Economic Integration in the Maghreb: An Untapped Source of Growth" (Washington, D.C.: IMF, 2019), https://www.imf.org/en/Publications/Departmental-Papers-Policy-Papers/Issues/2019/02/08/Economic-Integration-in-the-Maghreb-An-Untapped-Source-of-Growth-46273.
96. Lofti Ayadi et al., "Estimating Informal Trade Across Tunisia's Land Borders," World Bank Report, Policy Research Working Paper, December 1, 2013. https://documents.worldbank.org/en/publication/documents-reports/documentdetail/856231468173645854/estimating-informal-trade-across-tunisias-land-borders.
97. Scheele, *Smugglers and Saints of the Sahara*; Thomas Hüsken, *Tribal Politics in the Borderland of Egypt and Libya* (New York: Palgrave Macmillan, 2018); Laroussi, "Commerce informel et nomadisme moderne."
98. Laroussi, "Commerce informel et nomadisme moderne."
99. Kate Meagher, "Informal Integration or Economic Subversion? Parallel Trade in West Africa," in *Regional Integration and Cooperation in West Africa: A Multidimensional Perspective*, by Real Lavergne (Ottawa: IDRC, 1997).
100. Hamza Meddeb, "Courir ou mourir: Course à el khobza et domination au quotidien dans la Tunisie de Ben Ali," PhD thesis, Institut d'études politiques, 2012.

2. SMUGGLING IN NORTH AFRICA

101. Cassarino, "Approaching Borders and Frontiers"; Anouar Boukhars, "The Potential Jihadi Windfall from the Militarization of Tunisia's Border Region with Libya" (Washington, D.C.: Carnegie Endowment for International Peace, January 26, 2018), https://carnegieendowment.org/2018/01/26/potential-jihadi-windfall-from-militarization-of-tunisia-s-border-region-with-libya-pub-75365.
102. Nate Rosenblatt, "All Jihad Is Local—What ISIS' Files Tell Us About Its Fighters," New America International Security Program (Washington, D.C.: New America, 2016).
103. Riccardo Fabiani, "The Multiple Types of Interaction Between Jihadists, Criminals and Local Communities," in *Transnational Organized Crime and Political Actors in the Maghreb and Sahel*, by Jihane Ben Yahia et al., Mediterranean Dialogue Series 17 (Berlin: Konrad Adenauer Foundation, 2019); International Crisis Group, "Tunisia's Borders: Jihadism and Contraband," Middle East and North Africa Report (Geneva: International Crisis Group, 2013), http://www.crisisgroup.org/en/regions/middle-east-north-africa/north-africa/tunisia/148-tunisia-s-borders-jihadism-and-contraband.aspx.
104. Mohamed A. El-Khawas, "North Africa and the War on Terror," *Mediterranean Quarterly* 14, no. 4 (December 4, 2003): 176–91; Ruben Andersson, *Illegality, Inc.* (Berkeley: University of California Press, 2014).
105. Hanlon and Herbert, "Border Security Challenges"; Sofian Philip Naceur, "Decrypting ICMPD" (Tunis: Forum Tunisien pour les Droits Economiques et Sociaux, 2011), https://ftdes.net/en/decrypting-icmpd.
106. Max Gallien and Matthew Herbert, "Divided They Fall: Frontiers, Borderlands and Stability in North Africa," North Africa Report (Pretoria, South Africa: Institute for Security Studies, March 3, 2021).
107. Amaney A. Jamal and Michael Robbins, "Social Justice and the Arab Uprisings," American University of Beirut Working Paper Series, April 2015, https://scholarworks.aub.edu.lb/bitstream/handle/10938/21216/20150401_sjau.pdf.
108. Shantayanan Devarajan and Lili Mottaghi, "Towards a New Social Contract," World Bank, April 1, 2015, http://documents.worldbank.org/curated/en/202171468299130698/Towards-a-new-social-contract; Elena Ianchovichina, "Eruptions of Popular Anger: The Economics of the Arab Spring and Its Aftermath," MENA Development Report (Washington, D.C.: World Bank, 2018), https://openknowledge.worldbank.org/handle/10986/28961; Steffen Hertog, "The Political Economy of Distribution in the Middle East: Is There Scope for a New Social Contract?" *International Development Policy | Revue internationale de politique de développement* 7, no. 7 (February 1, 2017), https://doi.org/10.4000/poldev.2270.
109. Magdi Amin et al., *After the Spring: Economic Transitions in the Arab World* (Oxford: Oxford University Press, 2012); Assaad, "Making Sense of Arab Labor Markets."
110. Hertog, "The Political Economy of Distribution"; Steffen Hertog, "Is There an Arab Variety of Capitalism?" Working Papers, Economic Research Forum, June 12, 2016, https://ideas.repec.org/p/erg/wpaper/1068.html; Assaad, "Making Sense of Arab Labor Markets."
111. Ragui Assaad and Mongi Boughzala, eds., *The Tunisian Labor Market in an Era of Transition* (Oxford: Oxford University Press, 2018); Ragui Assaad and Caroline Krafft, "Labor Market Dynamics and Youth Unemployment in the Middle

2. SMUGGLING IN NORTH AFRICA

East and North Africa: Evidence from Egypt, Jordan and Tunisia," Economic Research Forum Working Paper, Cairo, April 2016; Amirah El-Haddad and May Gadallah, "The Informalization of the Egyptian Economy (1998–2012): A Factor in Growing Wage Inequality?" Economic Research Forum Working Paper, Cairo, 2018.

112. Adeel Malik and Max Gallien, "Border Economies of the Middle East: Why Do They Matter for Political Economy?" *Review of International Political Economy* 27, no. 3 (May 3, 2020): 732–62, https://doi.org/10.1080/09692290.2019.1696869.
113. Boukhars, "The Potential Jihadi Windfall"; International Alert, "Marginalisation, Insecurity and Uncertainty on the Tunisian–Libyan Border," 2016, http://www.international-alert.org/sites/default/files/TunisiaLibya_MarginalisationInsecurityUncertaintyBorder_EN_2016.pdf; Gallien and Herbert, "Divided They Fall."
114. John O. Igue and Bio G. Soule, *L'etat entrepot au Benin: Commerce informel ou solution a la crise* (Paris: Karthala, 1992); Dobler, "The Green, the Grey and the Blue"; Meagher, "Informal Integration or Economic Subversion?"
115. This has been convincingly connected to the protection of politically connected business elites by Ferdinand Eibl and Adeel Malik, "The Politics of Partial Liberalization: Cronyism and Non-Tariff Protection in Mubarak's Egypt," CSAE Working Paper Series, Centre for the Study of African Economies, Oxford University, 2016, https://ideas.repec.org/p/csa/wpaper/2016-27.html.
116. Ayadi et al., "Estimating Informal Trade," 7.
117. Tim Eaton, "Theft and Smuggling of Petroleum Products," in Gallien and Weigand, *Routledge Handbook of Smuggling*; Tim Eaton, *Libya's War Economy: Predation, Profiteering and State Weakness* (London: Chatham House, 2018), https://www.chathamhouse.org/sites/files/chathamhouse/publications/research/2018-04-12-libyas-war-economy-eaton-final.pdf; Francesca Manocchi, "How Libya's Oil Smugglers Are Bleeding Country of Cash," *Middle East Eye*, January 29, 2019, https://www.middleeasteye.net/news/how-libyas-oil-smugglers-are-bleeding-country-cash.
118. Tim Eaton, "Libya—Rich in Oil, Leaking Fuel," Chatham House Shorthand Story (London: Chatham House, 2019), https://chathamhouse.shorthandstories.com/libya-rich-in-oil-leaking-fuel/index.html.
119. This dynamic has been particularly important in the context of Libya during the height of the sanction regime following the Gulf of Sidra incident in 1981 but has been less relevant in recent years.
120. Laroussi, "Commerce informel et nomadisme moderne"; Ayadi et al., "Estimating Informal Trade"; Idriss Houat, *Dhahirat At-Tahreeb* (The phenomenon of smuggling) (Oujda, Morocco: CCIS Oujda, 2004); Meddeb, "Courir ou mourir."
121. Igue and Soule, *L'etat entrepot au Benin*.
122. Interviews ML4, ML1.
123. World Bank, "Impact of the Libya Crisis on the Tunisian Economy;" Ayadi et al., "Estimating Informal Trade."
124. Although technically free ports, the Spanish enclaves of Ceuta and Melilla do collect a small fee on imported goods, the IPSIE (see chapter 7).
125. Ayadi et al., "Estimating Informal Trade"; Houat, *Dhahirat At-Tahreeb*; KPMG, "Illicit Cigarette Trade in the Maghreb Region," 2017.
126. Scheele, *Smugglers and Saints of the Sahara*.

2. SMUGGLING IN NORTH AFRICA

127. Harriet Sherwood Hazem Balousha in Gaza City, "Palestinians in Gaza Feel the Egypt Effect as Smuggling Tunnels Close," *Guardian*, July 19, 2013, https://www.theguardian.com/world/2013/jul/19/palestinians-gaza-city-smuggling-tunnels; Nicolas Pelham, "Gaza's Tunnel Phenomenon: The Unintended Dynamics of Israel's Siege," *Journal of Palestine Studies* 41, no. 4 (July 1, 2012): 6–31, https://doi.org/10.1525/jps.2012.XLI.4.6.
128. Georgios Barzoukas, "Drug Trafficking in the MENA—The Economics and the Politics," EISS Brief Issue, European Institute for Security Studies, 2017; Tom Blickman, "Morocco and Cannabis: Reduction, Containment or Acceptance," Drug Policy Briefing (Amsterdam: Transnational Institute (TNI), March 2017); Kenza Afsahi and Salem Darwich, "Hashish in Morocco and Lebanon: A Comparative Study," *International Journal on Drug Policy* 31 (2016): 190–98, https://doi.org/10.1016/j.drugpo.2016.02.024; Max Gallien and Matthew Herbert, "GITOC Report on Drugs in North Africa" (London: Global Initiative Against Transnational Organised Crime, 2019).
129. Gallien and Herbert, "GITOC Report on Drugs."
130. Gallien and Herbert.
131. Moncef Kartas, "On the Edge? Trafficking and Insecurity at the Tunisian–Libyan Border," Security Assessment in North Africa Working Paper (Geneva: Small Arms Survey, 2013).
132. N. R. Jenzen-Jones and Ian McCollum, "Web Trafficking—Analysing the Online Trade of Small Arms and Light Weapons in Libya," Small Arms Survey Working Paper (Geneva: Small Arms Survey, 2017).
133. Lorena Gazzotti, "The 'War on Smugglers' and the Expansion of the Border Apparatus," in Gallien and Weigand, *Routledge Handbook of Smuggling*.
134. Isabelle Werenfels, Anette Weber, and Anne Koch, "Profiteers of Migration? Authoritarian States in Africa and European Migration Management," SWP Research Paper (Berlin: Stiftung Wissenschaft und Politik, July 2018); Matthew Herbert, "At the Edge—Trends and Routes of North African Clandestine Migrants," ISS Paper (Pretoria, South Africa: Institute for Security Studies, November 2016).
135. Max Gallien and Matthew Herbert, "Out of the Streets and Into the Boats: Tunisia's Irregular Migration Surge," Atlantic Council, November 27, 2017, http://www.atlanticcouncil.org/blogs/menasource/out-of-the-streets-and-into-the-boats-tunisia-s-irregular-migration-surge; Althai Consulting, "Leaving Libya—Rapid Assessment of Municipalities of Departures of Migrants in Libya," June 2017, http://www.altaiconsulting.com/wp-content/uploads/2017/08/2017_Altai-Consulting_Leaving-Libya-Rapid-Assessment-of-Municipalities-of-Departure-of-Migrants-in-Libya.pdf; Mark Micallef, "The Human Conveyor Belt: Trends in Human Trafficking and Smuggling in Post-Revolution Libya" (Geneva: Global Initiative Against Transnational Organised Crime, March 2017).
136. Matthew Herbert, "Rising Irregular Migration and Its Complicated Politics in the Maghreb," ISS Report (Pretoria, South Africa: Institute for Security Studies, 2019); Laia Soto Bermant, "Consuming Europe: The Moral Significance of Mobility and Exchange at the Spanish–Moroccan Border of Melilla," *Journal of North African Studies* 19, no. 1 (January 1, 2014): 110–29, https://doi.org/10.1080/13629387.2013.862776; Andersson, *Illegality, Inc.*

2. SMUGGLING IN NORTH AFRICA

137. Rosenblatt, "All Jihad Is Local."
138. Mohammed Masbah, "Transnational Security Challenges in North Africa: Moroccan Foreign Fighters in Syria 2012–2016," *Middle Eastern Studies* 55, no. 2 (March 4, 2019): 182–99, https://doi.org/10.1080/00263206.2018.1538972; J. Peter Pham, "Foreign Influences and Shifting Horizons: The Ongoing Evolution of al Qaeda in the Islamic Maghreb," *Orbis* 55, no. 2 (January 1, 2011): 240–54, https://doi.org/10.1016/j.orbis.2011.01.005; International Crisis Group, "How the Islamic State Rose, Fell and Could Rise Again in the Maghreb" (Geneva: International Crisis Group, July 24, 2017).
139. Thomas Renard, ed., *Returnees in the Maghreb: Comparing Policies on Returning Foreign Terrorist Fighters in Egypt, Morocco and Tunisia* (Brussels: Egmont—Royal Institute for International Relations, 2019).
140. For examples of this, see Meagher, "Informal Integration or Economic Subversion?"; and J. Igué, *Le Commerce de contrebande et les problèmes monétaires en Afrique occidentale* (Cotonou: CEFAP, Université Nationale du Benin, 1977), on smuggling in West Africa.
141. Meddeb, "Courir ou mourir."
142. For more information on hawala banking, see Edwina A. Thompson, "An Introduction to the Concept and Origins of Hawala," *Journal of the History of International Law* 10 (2008): 83; Mohammed El Qorchi et al., *Informal Funds Transfer Systems: An Analysis of the Informal Hawala System* (Washington, D.C.: International Monetary Fund, 2003); Matthias Schramm and Markus Taube, "Evolution and Institutional Foundation of the Hawala Financial System," *International Review of Financial Analysis*, special issue, 12, no. 4 (January 1, 2003): 405–20, https://doi.org/10.1016/S1057-5219(03)00032-2.
143. The structural similarities between the Moroccan Northeast and the Southeast of Tunisia have been the subject of recent academic attention. See Noureddine Bouammali, "Emigration internationale de travail et mutations socio-spatiales d'une ville frontalière: Cas d'Oujda (Maroc)" (PhD diss., Tours, Fr., 2006), http://www.theses.fr/2006TOUR1502; M. Elloumi, *Développement rural, environnement et enjeux territoriaux: Regards croisés Oriental marocain et Sud-Est tunisien*, ed. P. Bonte, Henri Guillaume, and M. Mahdi (Tunis: Cérès, 2009), http://www.documentation.ird.fr/hor/fdi:010050190.
144. Laroussi, "Commerce informel et nomadisme moderne."
145. Jean-François Martin, *Histoire de la Tunisie contemporaine: De Ferry à Bourguiba 1881–1956* (Paris: Éditions L'Harmattan, 2003), 77; Catherine Coquery-Vidrovitch, *Frontières, problèmes de frontières dans le tiers-monde* (Paris: Éditions L'Harmattan, 2000).
146. Henri Guillaume, *Entre désertification et développement: La Jeffara tunisienne* (Tunis: Cérès Éditions, 2006), 198; Laroussi, "Commerce informel et nomadisme moderne," 62; Anderson, *The State and Social Transformation*, 66.
147. Laroussi, "Commerce informel et nomadisme moderne," 77, 78.
148. International Alert, "Marginalisation, Insecurity and Uncertainty," 9.
149. Long and Reich, *Government and Politics of the Middle East and North Africa*, 463; Salihi, *Al-Istiʿmār al-Dākhilī Wa-al-Tanmiyah Ghayr al-Mutakāfiʾah*.
150. Hamed El-Said and Jane Harrigan, "Economic Reform, Social Welfare, and Instability: Jordan, Egypt, Morocco, and Tunisia, 1983–2004," *Middle East Journal* 68,

2. SMUGGLING IN NORTH AFRICA

no. 1 (2014): 113; Caroline Freund, Antonio Nucifora, and Bob Rijkers, "All in the Family: State Capture in Tunisia," World Bank, March 1, 2014, http://documents.worldbank.org/curated/en/440461468173649062/All-in-the-family-state-capture-in-Tunisia; Leila Baghdadi, Hassan Arouri, and Bob Rijkers, "How Do Dictators Get Rich? State Capture in Ben Ali's Tunisia," in *Crony Capitalism in the Middle East: Business and Politics from Liberalization to the Arab Spring*, ed. Ishac Diwan, Adeel Malik, and Izak Atiyas (Oxford: Oxford University Press, 2019); Willis, *Politics and Power in the Maghreb*, 60.

151. Ali Abaab, Mohamed Haddar, and Aida Tarhouni, "Plan Régional d'environnment et de Développement Durable (PREDD) Du Governorat de Médenine" (Tunis: Deutsche Gesellschaft für Internationale Zusammenarbeit, 2014), 8.
152. International Alert, "Marginalisation, Insecurity and Uncertainty"; Anderson, *The State and Social Transformation*.
153. Meddeb, "Courir ou mourir"; Laroussi, "Commerce informel et nomadisme moderne"; Rafaâ Tabib, "Effets de la frontière tuniso-libyenne sur les recompositions économiques et sociales des Werghemmas: de la possession à la réappropriation des territoires" (PhD diss., Cités Territoires Environnement et Sociétés, Tours, Fr., 2011).
154. Katan, *Oujda, une ville frontière du Maroc*, 21.
155. Katan, 360; Max Gallien and Yasmine Zarhloule, "Moroccan Farmers' Protests Highlight the Human Toll of Border Dispute," *Middle East Eye*, April 5, 2021, https://www.middleeasteye.net/opinion/morocco-farmers-protests-highlight-human-toll-algeria-border-dispute.
156. Kamel Laroussi, "Mutations de la société nomade et du commerce caravanier dans le sud-est Tunisien à la fin du XIXe siècle," working paper, 2008, 10, http://www.academia.edu/25965603/Mutations_de_la_soci%C3%A9t%C3%A9_nomade_et_du_commerce_caravanier_dans_le_Sud-Est_tunisien_%C3%A0_la_fin_du_XIXe_si%C3%A8cle; Jean Ganiagé, *Les origines du protectorat francais en tunisie (1861–1881) jean ganiage*, 1957, 120, http://archive.org/details/OriginesProtectoratFrancaisEnTunisie.
157. Mohamed Berriane and Andreas Kagermeier, *Remigration Nador I: Regionalanalyse der Provinz Nador* (Passau, Ger.: Passavia, 1996), 29.
158. Berriane and Kagermeier, 82; Katan, *Oujda, une ville frontière du Maroc*, 108.
159. Daoudi, *Vécu frontalier algéro-marocain depuis 1994*, 27.
160. Gallien and Zarhloule, "Moroccan Farmers' Protests."
161. Willis, *Politics and Power in the Maghreb*, 41–44.
162. John Waterbury, *The Commander of the Faithful: The Moroccan Elite: A Study in Segmented Politics* (London: Weidenfeld and Nicolson, 1970), 269.
163. Willis, *Politics and Power in the Maghreb*, 62; El-Said and Harrigan, "Economic Reform, Social Welfare, and Instability," 108; Mohammed Said Saadi, *Moroccan Cronyism: Facts, Mechanisms, and Impact* (Oxford: Oxford University Press, 2019), https://www.oxfordscholarship.com/view/10.1093/oso/9780198799870.001.0001/oso-9780198799870-chapter-6.
164. Karine Bennafla and Montserrat Emperador Badimon, "Le 'Maroc inutile' redém couvert par l'action publique: les cas de Sidi Ifni et Bouarfa," *Politique africaine* 120, no. 4 (2010): 67–86.
165. Bouammali, "Emigration internationale de travail," 31.

3. REGULATING SMUGGLING AT THE BORDER

166. Bouammali, 123; Berriane and Kagermeier, *Remigration Nador I*; OECD, *Interactions entre politiques publiques, migrations et développement au Maroc* (Paris: OECD Publishing, 2017), 47.
167. Hanlon and Herbert, "Border Security Challenges."
168. Gallien and Herbert, "GITOC Report on Drugs."
169. Receiving most of its budget from the Spanish state and held largely as a strategic settlement, Melilla is not dependent on tax income and is allowed to maintain extremely low tariffs in its ports. At the same time, these tariffs are commonly evaded (interview ML4).
170. Houat, *Dhahirat At-Tahreeb*.
171. Berriane and Kagermeier, *Remigration Nador I*.
172. Miguel Ángel Pérez Castro and Miguel Ángel Montero Alonso, "Estudios economicos sectorales de la Cuidad Autónoma de Melilla" (Melilla: Consejería de Economía y Hacienda de la Ciudad Autónoma de Melilla, December 2014), 98.

3. REGULATING SMUGGLING AT THE BORDER

1. Querine Hanlon and Matthew Herbert, *Border Security Challenges in the Grand Maghreb* (Washington, D.C.: United States Institute of Peace Press, 2015).
2. William F. S. Miles, "Jihads and Borders—Social Networks and Spatial Patterns in Africa, Present, Past and Future," in *African Border Disorders*, by Olivier Walther and William F. S. Miles (London: Routledge, 2018), 201; Carolyn Nordstrom, *Global Outlaws: Crime, Money, and Power in the Contemporary World* (Berkeley: University of California Press, 2007).
3. Hanlon and Herbert, "Border Security Challenges," 6.
4. Jamie Prentis, "Zuwara Feels the Effect of Petrol Smuggling," *Libya Herald* (blog), February 13, 2018, https://www.libyaherald.com/2018/02/14/zuwara-feels-the-effect-of-petrol-smuggling/.
5. As mentioned earlier, "irregular" bribes occasionally occurred, for example, if customs agents purposefully caused a traffic jam and then charged cars a fee to bypass it. Conversions to British pound sterling (GBP) are based on official exchange rates in 2019 and throughout this book have been included for the convenience of the reader only. This is not meant to indicate the availability of GBP locally at this rate and at the time at which the respective institution was in force. It is also important to highlight that there are significant differences between the black-market rate and the official exchange rate for the Libyan dinar.
6. While this might appear very high, it's worth noting that many traders import goods with values significantly beyond 2,000 LYD.
7. Triangulated through multiple interviews with different traders as well as informants involved in negotiating this agreement
8. Given this section's focus on Tunisia and the complexity of Libya's competing legal structures in 2014, I focus on Tunisia here.
9. There are legal exemptions for the import and export of some goods, but these are usually specified for personal consumption and set at a lower threshold, such as two hundred cigarettes or 250 ml of perfume.

10. Memorandum of Understanding, signed in Zuwara on the first Sunday of January 2017. This was confirmed to me by one of its negotiators (interview T102). (Throughout this book, interviews are cited by a code assigned to each. The full list of interviews can be found in appendix 2.)
11. Interview T68; Sami Ghorbal, "Tunisie: aux origines de la chute de Chafik Jarraya, l'homme qui personnifiait l'impunité de la corruption," *JeuneAfrique.com* (blog), June 16, 2017, https://www.jeuneafrique.com/mag/444630/politique/tunisie-aux-origines-de-chute-de-chafik-jarraya-lhomme-personnifiait-limpunite-de-corruption/.
12. Interviews T40, T96.
13. Douglass C. North, *Institutions, Institutional Change and Economic Performance* (Cambridge: Cambridge University Press, 1990); Mushtaq Khan, "Political Settlements and the Governance of Growth-Enhancing Institutions," draft paper, Research Paper Series on Growth-Enhancing Governance, 2010.
14. For a full text, contact author.
15. Memorandum of Understanding, January 2017.
16. Many Libyans, both civilians and soldiers, travel to Tunisia for medical services, commonly crossing through the Ras Jedir crossing. Many health centers in southern Tunisia, especially Djerba and Sfax, routinely cater to Libyan medical tourists. This became of added importance throughout recent conflicts in Libya.
17. The group names are my translations.
18. Quotes from interviews T57, T96.
19. Interview T60.
20. Ruben Andersson, *Illegality, Inc.* (Berkeley: University of California Press); Peter Andreas, *Border Games: Policing the U.S.-Mexico Divide*, Cornell Studies in Political Economy (Ithaca, N.Y.: Cornell University Press, 2009), 135; Laia Soto Bermant, "The Myth of Resistance: Rethinking the 'Informal' Economy in a Mediterranean Border Enclave," *Journal of Borderlands Studies* 30, no. 2 (April 3, 2015): 263–78, https://doi.org/10.1080/08865655.2015.1046993.
21. Miguel Ángel Pérez Castro and Miguel Ángel Montero Alonso, "Estudios economicos sectorales de la Cuidad Autonoma de Melilla" (Melilla: Consejería de Economía y Hacienda de la Ciudad Autónoma de Melilla, December 2014).
22. David A. McMurray, *In and Out of Morocco: Smuggling and Migration in a Frontier Boomtown* (Minneapolis: University of Minnesota Press, 2001), 123.
23. Interview M36.
24. Interview ML3. It is worth noting that this frequently involves violent altercations among traders, and between traders and the police. As hundreds of transporters shuffle for access to small spaces, recent years have seen serious injuries and fatalities. "The Moroccans are making it easy, the Spanish authorities though, they are rude, they treat us badly, they hit us," traders commonly complain, usually indicating that this is a more serious issue at Barrio Chino than in Beni Ensar (interviews M41, M42).
25. Interviews M55, M56.
26. Interviews M41, M42.
27. Interviews M41, M42.
28. Exact times can change according to season.

3. REGULATING SMUGGLING AT THE BORDER

29. Interview ML3.
30. Interview M36.
31. The regulation discussed here ceased to be in effect with the construction of significant border fortifications by both Algeria and Morocco from about 2015 onward. This is discussed in detail in later chapters.
32. Interviews M7, M102, M103, M104.
33. Interview M7.
34. Interview M111, M35, M80.
35. Interview M35.
36. Interview M35.
37. Interviews M102, M103, M35.
38. Interview M80.
39. Focus Group 4, interviews M110, M111, T9.
40. Interview T111.
41. Andreas, *Border Games*; Max Gallien and Florian Weigand, "Channeling Contraband: How States Shape International Smuggling Routes," *Security Studies* 0, no. 0 (March 12, 2021): 1–28. https://doi.org/10.1080/09636412.2021.1885728.
42. Interview T87.
43. Interview M111.
44. Focus Group 4, interview M111.
45. Gretchen Helmke and Stephen Levitsky, "Informal Institutions and Comparative Politics: A Research Agenda," *Perspectives on Politics* 2, no. 4 (2004): 725–40.
46. One exception to this are the members of the Spanish police, who help structure the trade in Melilla in their official function. However, while the traders are in Melilla and throughout their interactions with the Spanish police, they are not breaking any laws, suggesting that their interaction with the police is secondary to the regulation of smuggling "at the border" discussed in this chapter.
47. Khan, "Political Settlements," 12.
48. Elinor Ostrom, *Understanding Institutional Diversity* (Princeton, N.J.: Princeton University Press, 2005); Avner Greif, *Institutions and the Path to the Modern Economy: Lessons from Medieval Trade* (Cambridge: Cambridge University Press, 2006).
49. Alisha C. Holland, "Forbearance," *American Political Science Review* 110, no. 2 (May 2016): 232–46, https://doi.org/10.1017/S0003055416000083; Holland, "The Distributive Politics of Enforcement," *American Journal of Political Science* 59, no. 2 (April 2015): 357–71; Judith Tendler, "Small Firms, the Informal Sector, and the Devil's Deal," *IDS Bulletin* 33, no. 3 (2002): 1–15, https://doi.org/10.1111/j.1759-5436.2002.tb00035.x.
50. Frances Cleaver, *Development Through Bricolage: Rethinking Institutions for Natural Resource Management* (Abingdon, UK: Routledge, 2012); Kate Meagher, "Beyond the Shadows: Informal Institutions and Development in Africa—Introduction," *Afrika Spectrum* 43, no. 1 (2008), http://hup.sub.uni-hamburg.de/giga/afsp/index. See Max Gallien, "Informal Institutions and the Regulation of Smuggling in North Africa," *Perspectives on Politics* 18, no. 2 (June 2020): 492–508, https://doi.org/10.1017/S1537592719001026, for an expansion of this argument based on this chapter.

4. REGULATING SMUGGLING IN THE BORDERLANDS

1. Luca Raineri, "Cross-Border Smuggling in North Niger: The Morality of the Informal and the Construction of a Hybrid Order," in *Governance Beyond the Law: The Immoral, the Illegal, the Criminal*, ed. Abel Polese, Alessandra Russo, and Francesco Strazzari, International Political Economy Series (Cham, Switz.: Springer International, 2019), 227–45, https://doi.org/10.1007/978-3-030-05039-9_12; Judith Scheele, *Smugglers and Saints of the Sahara: Regional Connectivity in the Twentieth Century* (Cambridge: Cambridge University Press, 2012); Thomas Hüsken, *Tribal Politics in the Borderland of Egypt and Libya* (New York: Palgrave Macmillan, 2018).
2. Laurence Michalak, "The Changing Weekly Markets of Tunisia: A Regional Analysis" (University of California, Berkeley, 1983); Donna Perry, "Rural Weekly Markets and the Dynamics of Time, Space and Community in Senegal," *Journal of Modern African Studies* 38, no. 3 (September 2000): 461–85; R. J. Bromley, Richard Symanski, and Charles M. Good, "The Rationale of Periodic Markets," *Annals of the Association of American Geographers* 65, no. 4 (1975): 530–37.
3. Max Gallien, "Beyond Informality: The Political Economy of Illegal Trade in Southern Tunisia" (MPhil thesis, University of Oxford, 2015).
4. Mongi Azabou and Jeffrey B. Nugent, "Chapter 6—Tax Farming: Anachronism or Optimal Contract? An Illustration with Respect to Tunisia's Weekly Markets," in *Contributions to Economic Analysis*, ed. Mustapha K. Nabli and Jeffrey B. Nugent, vol. 183, The New Institutional Economics and Development (Amsterdam: Elsevier, 1989), 178–99, https://doi.org/10.1016/B978-0-444-87487-0.50016-5.
5. Focus Group 6.
6. Focus Groups 1, 2.
7. While these goods are imported illegally, they are themselves licit goods—weapons or narcotics are not sold in the markets. The sale of gasoline will be discussed shortly.
8. Interview T84.
9. Interviews T15, T84.
10. Interview T39.
11. The breakdown of this agreement and its subsequent renegotiation will be discussed in chapter 8.
12. Interview T39.
13. Interview T35.
14. Interview T62.
15. Interview T32.
16. Interview T35.
17. Interview T62.
18. Interview T26.
19. Interview T26.
20. Michalak, "The Changing Weekly Markets of Tunisia."
21. Frances Cleaver, "Institutional Bricolage, Conflict and Cooperation in Usangu," *IDS Bulletin* 32, no. 4 (October 2001): 26–35.

4. REGULATING SMUGGLING IN THE BORDERLANDS

22. Hamza Meddeb, "Courir ou mourir: Course à el khobza et domination au quotidien dans la Tunisie de Ben Ali," PhD thesis, Institut d'études politiques, 2012.
23. Interview T41.
24. While this section focuses on Oujda, many of the observations made here also hold true for Nador, the second largest city of the Oriental region.
25. Interview M3.
26. Interview M53.
27. The Arabic title of the fee is الرسم المفروض على الباعة الجائلين المأذون لهم في بيع سلعهم على طرق العامة
28. Interview M17.
29. See Kristine Juul, "Decentralization, Local Taxation and Citizenship in Senegal," *Development and Change* 37, no. 4 (2006): 821–46, https://doi.org/10.1111/j.1467-7660.2006.00503.x. I will elaborate on this more extensively later.
30. The Arabic title of this fee is الرسم المفروض على شغل الاملاك الجماعية العامة مؤقتا لاغراض تجارية او صناعية او مهنية
31. Interview M17.
32. Interview M17.
33. Interview M60.
34. Interviews M48, M49.
35. Interview M36.
36. Interview M61.
37. Interview M34.
38. Interview M14.
39. Interview M70. The fixed locality contrasts to roadside vending.
40. Interview M59.
41. Interview M108.
42. Interview M63.
43. Interview T26.
44. One exception here is the role of the Spanish police in Melilla, which is somewhat more officially communicated. This relates to the fact that, as discussed in the previous chapter, smugglers at this crossing do not break any laws while they are still under the jurisdiction of the Spanish police.
45. See, for example, Maxim Bolt, "Navigating Formality in a Migrant Labour Force," in *The Political Economy of Life in Africa*, ed. W. Abdebanwi (Woodbridge, UK: James Currey, 2017).
46. Juul, "Decentralization, Local Taxation and Citizenship"; Hernando De Soto, *The Other Path* (New York: Basic Books, 1989).
47. Anuradha Joshi, Wilson Prichard, and Christopher Heady, "Taxing the Informal Economy: Challenges, Possibilities and Remaining Questions," *IDS Working Papers* 2013, no. 429 (2013): 1–37, https://doi.org/10.1111/j.2040-0209.2013.00429.x; Vanessa Van den Boogaard and Wilson Prichard, "What Have We Learned About Informal Taxation in Sub-Saharan Africa?" ICTD Summary Brief (Brighton, UK: International Centre for Tax and Development, 2016).
48. As later chapters will discuss, the informal importation of gasoline largely collapsed in Morocco in 2015 and has been significantly diminished in southeastern Tunisia since 2017. This section on distribution structures describes these

4. REGULATING SMUGGLING IN THE BORDERLANDS

structures as they were during their heyday. The same observations, however, apply to the smaller structures that continue to exist today, as the regulatory context within both countries has not changed significantly throughout this period.

49. One caveat applies here: the distribution structures described supply individual consumers of gasoline for cars, scooters, and motorcycles. It is likely that separate distribution channels exist for large-scale consumers, particularly in agriculture, that are built on direct supply by transporters, rather than through sales at roadside gas stations.
50. Lofti Ayadi et al., "Estimating Informal Trade Across Tunisia's Land Borders," Policy Research Working Paper, World Bank, December 1, 2013, https://documents.worldbank.org/en/publication/documents-reports/documentdetail/8562314 68173645854/estimating-informal-trade-across-tunisias-land-borders; Querine Hanlon and Matthew Herbert, *Border Security Challenges in the Grand Maghreb* (Washington, D.C.: United States Institute of Peace Press, 2015).
51. Interviews M7, M101.
52. Focus Group 7.
53. Interviews T94, T95.
54. Interview T94.
55. Interview T72.
56. *Nessma*, "Gabès: Saisie de 24 mille litres de carburant de contrebande," *Nessma Online*, February 9, 2017, https://www.nessma.tv/fr/regionale/actu/gabes-saisie-de -24-mille-litres-de-carburant-de-contrebande-5571/10026.
57. Interview M17.
58. Susanne Karstedt and Stephen Farrall, "The Moral Economy of Everyday Crime-Markets, Consumers and Citizens," *British Journal of Criminology* 46, no. 6 (November 1, 2006): 1011–36, https://doi.org/10.1093/bjc/azl082.
59. Tim Kelsall, "Going with the Grain in African Development?" *Development Policy Review* 29, no. s1 (2011): s223–51, https://doi.org/10.1111/j.1467-7679.2011.00527.x.
60. Kate Meagher, "Disempowerment from Below: Informal Enterprise Networks and the Limits of Political Voice in Nigeria," *Oxford Development Studies* 42, no. 3 (July 3, 2014): 419–38, https://doi.org/10.1080/13600818.2014.900005.
61. This particularly holds true for Libya. Hüsken, "The Practice and Culture of Smuggling"; Hüsken, *Tribal Politics in the Borderland*; Tuesday Reitano and Mark Shaw, "People's Perspectives of Organised Crime in West Africa and the Sahel," ISS Report (Dakar: Institute for Security Studies, April 2014); Kamel Laroussi, "Commerce informel et nomadisme moderne," Ecole des Hautes Études en Sciences Sociales, Paris, 2007; International Crisis Group, "Tunisia's Borders: Jihadism and Contraband," Middle East and North Africa Report, Geneva, 2013, http://www .crisisgroup.org/en/regions/middle-east-north-africa/north-africa/tunisia/148 -tunisia-s-borders-jihadism-and-contraband.aspx.
62. Scheele, *Smugglers and Saints of the Sahara*.
63. Interview T88.
64. Interviews T94, T95.
65. Interview M77.
66. Interview T110.
67. Interview T110.

68. Interview T70.
69. While there has been, among the people interviewed for this project, a notable diversity of these perspectives within informal trade networks, groups of local state employees, and social classes, it is possible that there are patterns along these lines. The data collected for this project, however, is insufficient to demonstrate this.
70. Interview T65.
71. Interview T68.
72. Interview T60.
73. Interview M36.
74. Interview T75.
75. Allan Christelow, "Property and Theft in Kano at the Dawn of the Groundnut Boom, 1912–1914," *International Journal of African Historical Studies* 20, no. 2 (1987): 225–43, https://doi.org/10.2307/219841.
76. Interview T110.
77. Interview T104.
78. Interview M39.
79. Memorandum of Understanding, signed in Zuwara on the first Sunday of January 2017.
80. Giorgio Agamben, *State of Exception* (Chicago: Chicago University Press, 2005).
81. Interview T96.
82. Interview T57.
83. To my knowledge, there have not been any official communications from the respective organs of the Tunisian state on the agreement. In an interview with the author, when asked about the issue, a local member of parliament who was not himself involved in the negotiation of the agreement criticized it harshly, highlighting that it was inappropriate for nonstate entities to conduct these kinds of negotiations (interview T101). The relevant minister (of trade and industry), when asked about the agreement, similarly highlighted that these types of agreements should not be negotiated outside of the institutions of the state, but also the difficulty of the political context in Libya and the importance of civil society initiative (interview T120).
84. Memorandum of Understanding, signed in Zuwara in January 2017. For full text, contact author.
85. Interview T97.
86. Interview T95.
87. Interview T98.
88. Interview T95.
89. Interview T66.
90. Purely functionally, one could argue that the traditional institution of the rotating market represents an exception to this. While it has a long local history and tradition and has been clearly hybridized with state institutional structures in the creation of the modern city markets, conversations with local traders did not exclude these markets from the wider unease about the smuggling economies they are embedded in or referenced them as a normatively embedded local institution.

5. SMUGGLING RENTS AND SOCIAL PEACE

1. Interview T42. For a more extensive discussion, see R. Prud'homme, "Informal Local Taxation in Developing Countries," *Environment and Planning C: Government and Policy* 10, no. 1 (March 1, 1992): 1–17, https://doi.org/10.1068/c100001.
2. It is worth noting that this story refers to the pre-2011 era. As the following chapter will discuss, the relationship between the police and the local population has become increasingly strained.
3. In Ben Guerdane, the police and the National Guard appear to have divided up the territory, where the police control the city center, while the National Guard controls the outskirts and space between the city and the zone south of the border crossing controlled by the military.
4. Interview M77.
5. Interview M106.
6. Interview T86.
7. Interview M40.
8. Interview M63.
9. Interviews T26, T84.
10. Interview T64.
11. Interview M7.
12. Interview M35.
13. Querine Hanlon and Matthew Herbert, *Border Security Challenges in the Grand Maghreb* (Washington, D.C.: United States Institute of Peace, 2015).
14. Interview T72.
15. Interviews T73, T97. A similar observation is made by Thomas Cantens and J. F. F. Raballand, "Cross-Border Trade, Insecurity and the Role of Customs: Some Lessons from Six Field Studies in (Post-)Conflict Regions," ICTD Working Paper (Brighton, UK: International Centre for Tax and Development, August 2017).
16. Interview M76.
17. Miguel Ángel Pérez Castro and Miguel Ángel Montero Alonso, "Estudios economicos sectorales de la Cuidad Autónoma de Melilla" (Melilla: Consejería de Economía y Hacienda de la Ciudad Autónoma de Melilla, December 2014).
18. Interviews M7, M101.
19. Interview M63.
20. Moncef Kartas, "On the Edge? Trafficking and Insecurity at the Tunisian-Libyan Border," Security Assessment in North Africa Working Paper (Geneva: Small Arms Survey, 2013).
21. Interviews T102, T22, T68.
22. Kate Meagher, "Taxing Times: Taxation, Divided Societies and the Informal Economy in Northern Nigeria," *Journal of Development Studies* 54, no. 1 (January 2, 2018): 1–17, https://doi.org/10.1080/00220388.2016.1262026; Erica Carroll, "Taxing Ghana's Informal Sector: The Experience of Women," Occasional Paper (Christian Aid, 2011); Anuradha Joshi, Wilson Prichard, and Christopher Heady, "Taxing the Informal Economy: Challenges, Possibilities and Remaining Questions," *IDS Working Papers* 2013, no. 429 (2013): 1–37, https://doi.org/10.1111/j.2040-0209.2013.00429.x.
23. The post-2011 phase will be discussed in chapter 6.

5. SMUGGLING RENTS AND SOCIAL PEACE

24. These numbers were attained through the municipality of Ben Guerdane in September 2014. The income from the stalls has been triangulated using the number of stalls and the individual stall fees, as reported by multiple sources.
25. Calculation by the author, based on budget data obtained from the municipality on Ben Guerdane.
26. Interview T84.
27. Interview T39.
28. Technically, Oujda has eleven "communes": three are urban and eight are rural. This section refers to the largest urban commune. Other important municipal markets play a smaller role, as the Souk Fellah is largely untaxed by the municipality, and the Souk Quds is now largely selling legally imported products. In the past few years an increasing amount of vendors are selling goods that are imported legally, but the driving force behind the markets for the past decades has been the smuggling economy (see chapter 7).
29. Calculation by the author based on data provided by the market association (interviews M48, M49) and triangulated with multiple vendors. Some additional income may be generated through a wider range of taxes and fees, but a precise calculation is difficult as the vast majority of vendors do not pay those.
30. Interview M17.
31. Strictly speaking, this has created another rent stream—vendors who were part of the original allotments were able to generate additional income by renting out their stalls at a higher rate. In both Ben Guerdane and Oujda, there are indications that personal and family connections have played a role in the original allotment, suggesting that there may be a small, elite-focused rent stream here. This issue will be discussed in subsequent chapters.
32. Interview M17.
33. Interview M61.
34. Interview M60.
35. Interview M47.
36. Lana Salman, "What We Talk About When We Talk About Decentralization? Insights from Post-Revolution Tunisia," *L'année Du Maghreb*, no. 16 (June 30, 2017): 91–108, https://doi.org/10.4000/anneemaghreb.2975; Anja Hoffmann, "Dezentralisierung in Marokko—Hohe Erwartungen," GIGA Focus (Hamburg: German Institute of Global and Area Studies, 2015), https://www.giga-hamburg.de/en/system/files/publications/gf_nahost_1508.pdf; Hoffmann, "Morocco Between Decentralization and Recentralization: Encountering the State in the 'Useless Morocco,'" in *Local Politics and Contemporary Transformations in the Arab World*, by Malika Bouziane, Cilja Harders, and Anja Hoffmann, Governance and Limited Statehood Series (Basingstoke, UK: Palgrave Macmillan, 2013).
37. Interviews T57, T68.
38. Interview T64.
39. Perhaps the most drastic illustration of this is that the Agence Oriental, an agency created by the Moroccan state to fund and coordinate development projects in the Oriental region, did not even have its headquarters located in the Oriental region for the first years of its existence. Between 2006 and 2014 it was located in Rabat, before moving to Oujda. See also Hoffmann "Morocco Between Decentralization and Recentralization."

40. Interview ML3.
41. John O. Igué and Bio G. Soule, *L'etat entrepot au Benin: Commerce informel ou solution a la crise* (Paris: Karthala, 1992).
42. Castro and Alonso, "Estudios economicos sectorales de la Cuidad Autónoma de Melilla."
43. Interview ML5.
44. Interview ML4.
45. While this section centers on the smuggling of licit goods, in keeping with the focus of this chapter, a serious of high-profile scandals in recent years have brought increasing attention to the cocaine trade in Algeria. See Matthew Herbert, "The Butcher's Bill—Cocaine Trafficking in North Africa" (Geneva: Global Initiative Against Transnational Organised Crime, September 21, 2018), https://global initiative.net/the-butchers-bill-cocaine-trafficking-in-north-africa/.
46. See Anouar Boukhars, "Barriers Versus Smugglers: Algeria and Morocco's Battle for Border Security" (Washington, D.C.: Carnegie Endowment for International Peace, March 19, 2019).
47. See, for example, Mark Micallef, "The Human Conveyor Belt: Trends in Human Trafficking and Smuggling in Post-Revolution Libya," Geneva: Global Initiative Against Transnational Organised Crime, March 2017; Thomas Hüsken, *Tribal Politics in the Borderland of Egypt and Libya* (New York: Palgrave Macmillan, 2018); Hamza Meddeb, *Peripheral Vision: How Europe Can Help Preserve Tunisia's Fragile Democracy*, ECFR Policy Brief, 2017, https://www.ecfr.eu/publications /summary/peripheral_vision_how_europe_can_preserve_tunisias_democracy _7215.
48. Hamza Meddeb, "Courir ou mourir: Course à el khobza et domination au quotidien dans la Tunisie de Ben Ali" (PhD thesis, Institut d'études politiques, 2012), 91–97.
49. International Crisis Group, "Tunisia's Borders: Jihadism and Contraband," Middle East and North Africa Report (Geneva: International Crisis Group, 2013), http://www.crisisgroup.org/en/regions/middle-east-north-africa/north-africa /tunisia/148-tunisia-s-borders-jihadism-and-contraband.aspx.
50. Prud'homme, "Informal Local Taxation in Developing Countries"; Peter Andreas, "Smuggling Wars: Law Enforcement and Law Evasion in a Changing World," in *Transnational Crime in the Americas*, by Tom Farer (New York: Routledge, 1999), 95.
51. Meddeb, "Courir ou mourir"; International Crisis Group, "Tunisia's Borders."
52. Interview T64. They naturally overlap with the groups' membership.
53. See chapter 6.
54. Caroline Freund, Antonio Nucifora, and Bob Rijkers, "All in the Family: State Capture in Tunisia," World Bank, March 1, 2014, http://documents.worldbank.org /curated/en/440461468173649062/All-in-the-family-state-capture-in-Tunisia."
55. Mariam Abdel Baky, "Peacebuilding in Tunisian Border Regions: A Missing Piece of the Transition Process," in *Accord Insight 4—Borderlands and Peacebuilding* (London: Conciliation Resources, 2018); Kartas, "On the Edge?" The role of the Trabselsi networks in Ben Guerdane changed over the years; see chapter 8.
56. Interviews M91, M102, M103.
57. Hanlon and Herbert, "Border Security Challenges."

5. SMUGGLING RENTS AND SOCIAL PEACE

58. Interviews M91, M67.
59. Interview M67.
60. Boukhars, "Barriers Versus Smugglers."
61. Adeel Malik, "Was the Middle East's Economic Descent a Legal or Political Failure? Debating the Islamic Law Matters Thesis," CSAE Working Paper Series (Centre for the Study of African Economies, University of Oxford, 2012), 30, https://ideas.repec.org/p/csa/wpaper/2012-08.html.
62. Interview T59.
63. Interview T42.
64. Interviews T94, T95.
65. This describes the situation before the effects of the conflict in Libya diminished supply in 2017. This will be addressed in chapter 6.
66. Interview T94.
67. Focus Group FG7.
68. Interview M35.
69. Interviews M41, M42.
70. Interviews T66, T68.
71. Interviews T96.
72. Interviews M24, M36, M55, M56.
73. Meddeb, "Courir ou mourir."
74. The discussion on access here contains one important simplification: it does not consider the lopsided gender balance within these access structures. While not directly relevant for the argument made here, this will be discussed in chapter 10.
75. Office de Développement du Sud, Ministère du Développement Régional et de la Planification, République Tunisienne, "Gouvernorat de Médenine en Chiffres 2012," ODS, 2012.
76. Interview T62; Mohamed Haddar, "Rapport sur les relations économiques entre la Tunisie et la Libye auprès du Plan Régional d'Environnement et de Développement Durable du Gouvernorat de Médenine (PREDD) et de la Table Ronde Économique (TRE) Médenine" (Tunis, 2013).
77. Interview T17.
78. Interview T61.
79. Ministry of Industry, Commerce, and Investment, Delegation of Commerce and Industry, Oujda.
80. Interview M80.
81. Interview M65.
82. Interview M76.
83. With Libya, the speaker here refers to the cross-border trade. Interview T112.
84. Interview T93.
85. Interview M54.
86. Interview M46.
87. Interview M108.
88. Interview T36, Focus Group FG6.
89. Interview T97.
90. Mushtaq Khan, "Political Settlements and the Governance of Growth-Enhancing Institutions," draft paper in Research Paper Series on Growth-Enhancing Governance, 2010; James Putzel and Jonathan Di John, "Political Settlements, Issues

Paper" (Governance and Social Development Resource Centre, University of Birmingham, 2009).
91. Khan, "Political Settlements and Governance," 53.
92. Here it is interesting to note that in Tunisia, where the military has commonly been considered relatively less powerful within the security apparatus, it also features less prominently in the distribution of rents. Zoltan Barany, "Comparing the Arab Revolts: The Role of the Military," *Journal of Democracy* 22, no. 4 (October 14, 2011): 24–35, https://doi.org/10.1353/jod.2011.0069; L. B. Ware, "The Role of the Tunisian Military in the Post-Bourgiba Era," *Middle East Journal* 39, no. 1 (1985): 27–47.
93. Steffen Hertog, "The Role of Cronyism in Arab Capitalism," in *Crony Capitalism in the Middle East: Business and Politics from Liberalizaton to the Arab Spring*, ed. Ishac Diwan, Adeel Malik, and Izak Atiyas (Oxford: Oxford University Press, 2019), 39–64; Jon Marks, "Nationalist Policy-Making and Crony Capitalism in the Maghreb: The Old Economics Hinders the New," *International Affairs* 85, no. 5 (September 1, 2009): 951–62, https://doi.org/10.1111/j.1468-2346.2009.00840.x; Mohammed Said Saadi, *Moroccan Cronyism: Facts, Mechanisms, and Impact* (Oxford: Oxford University Press, 2019), https://www.oxfordscholarship.com/view/10.1093/oso/9780198799870.001.0001/oso-9780198799870-chapter-6.
94. Herbert Kitschelt and Steven I. Wilkinson, "Citizen–Politician Linkages: An Introduction," in *Patrons, Clients, and Policies*, ed. Herbert Kitschelt and Steven I. Wilkinson (Cambridge: Cambridge University Press, 2007), 1–49, https://doi.org/10.1017/CBO9780511585869.001.
95. Ragui Assaad, "Making Sense of Arab Labor Markets: The Enduring Legacy of Dualism," *IZA Journal of Labor & Development* 3 (April 25, 2014): 2, https://doi.org/10.1186/2193-9020-3-6.
96. See also Steffen Hertog, "The Political Economy of Distribution in the Middle East: Is There Scope for a New Social Contract?" *International Development Policy | Revue internationale de politique de développement* 7, no. 7 (February 1, 2017), https://doi.org/10.4000/poldev.2270; Raymond Hinnebusch, "Authoritarian Persistence, Democratization Theory and the Middle East: An Overview and Critique," *Democratization* 13, no. 3 (June 1, 2006): 373–95, https://doi.org/10.1080/13510340600579243; Clement Moore Henry and Robert Springborg, *Globalization and the Politics of Development in the Middle East* (Cambridge: Cambridge University Press, 2010); Perry Cammack et al., *Arab Fractures: Citizens, States, and Social Contracts* (Washington, D.C.: Carnegie Endowment for International Peace, 2017).
97. On Tunisia, see Alexandra Blackman, "Ideological Responses to Settler Colonialism: Political Identities in Post-Independence Tunisia," working paper, February 2019.
98. Interviews T111, M106. While this dynamic is one of the most well-established and most discussed elements of the political and economic development of Tunisia and Morocco, it is not typically put in relation to the development of informal and illicit economies in these regions. Two notable exceptions include Meddeb, "Courir ou mourir"; and Béatrice Hibou, *The Force of Obedience* (Cambridge: Polity, 2011).
99. Timothy Raeymaekers, "Reshaping the State in Its Margins: The State, the Market and the Subaltern on a Central African Frontier," *Critique of Anthropology* 32, no. 3 (September 1, 2012): 334–50, https://doi.org/10.1177/0308275X12449248

100. Kristof Titeca, "Tycoons and Contraband: Informal Cross-Border Trade in West Nile, North-Western Uganda," *Journal of Eastern African Studies* 6, no. 1 (February 1, 2012): 47–63, https://doi.org/10.1080/17531055.2012.664703.
101. Khan, "Political Settlements and Governance," 7.

6. TUNISIA

1. Laryssa Chomiak, "The Making of a Revolution in Tunisia," *Middle East Law and Governance* 3 (2011): 68.
2. Margaret Williams and Youssef Mahmoud, "The New Tunisian Constitution: Triumphs and Potential Pitfalls," *IPI Global Observatory* (blog), February 27, 2014, https://theglobalobservatory.org/2014/02/the-new-tunisian-constitution-triumphs-and-potential-pitfalls/.
3. Michele Penner Angrist, "Understanding the Success of Mass Civic Protest in Tunisia," *Middle East Journal* 67, no. 4 (2013): 547–64.
4. International Crisis Group, "Tunisia: Confronting Social and Economic Challenges," (Geneva: International Crisis Group, June 6, 2012); Beátrice Hibou et al., *Tunisia After 14 January and Its Social an Political Economy: The Issues at Stake in a Reconfiguration of European Policy* (Copenhagen: Euro-Mediterranean Human Rights Network, 2011).
5. Ishac Diwan, Adeel Malik, and Izak Atiyas, eds., *Crony Capitalism in the Middle East: Business and Politics from Liberalization to the Arab Spring* (Oxford: Oxford University Press, 2019), chaps. 6 and 7.
6. Chomiak, "The Making of a Revolution in Tunisia."
7. Interview T39.
8. Querine Hanlon and Matthew Herbert, *Border Security Challenges in the Grand Maghreb* (Washington, D.C.: United States Institute of Peace, 2015), 14.
9. Wikileaks, "Corruption in Tunisia Part IV: The Family's Holdings," Wikileaks Public Library of U.S. Diplomacy (U.S. Embassy Tunis, July 5, 2006), https://wikileaks.org/plusd/cables/06TUNIS1672_a.html.
10. Hamza Meddeb, "Courir ou mourir: Course à el khobza et domination au quotidien dans la Tunisie de Ben Ali" (PhD thesis, Institut d'études politiques, 2012), 205.
11. Interview T49. It is unclear which policy Morjane is referring to here, but it appears likely that this could be the refusal of the Tunisian state to sell an oil distribution license to Libya (interview T8).
12. Interview T73.
13. Nawaat, Tunisie : Ben Guerdane est le théâtre d'événements sans précédent. La Population réclame 'Ras Jdir,'" *Nawaat*, August 15, 2010, https://nawaat.org/portail/2010/08/15/tunisie-ben-gardane-est-le-theatre-devenements-sans-precedent-la-population-reclame-ras-jdir/.
14. Interview T65.
15. Nawaat, "Tunisie: Ben Guerdane."
16. Christopher Barrie, "The Process of Revolutionary Protest: Development and Democracy in the Tunisian Revolution of 2010–2011," *SocArXiv*, August 10, 2018, https://doi.org/10.31235/osf.io/eu5b4.

17. Interview T12.
18. Interview T40.
19. Interview T76.
20. Interview T11.
21. Interview T40.
22. Interview T40.
23. Interview T40.
24. Interview T40. Both sides have confirmed to me the existence of this meeting.
25. Interview T45.
26. Interview T40.
27. Interview T40.
28. Kareem Fahim, "Slap to a Man's Pride Set off Tumult in Tunisia," *New York Times*, January 21, 2011, https://www.nytimes.com/2011/01/22/world/africa/22sidi.html.
29. Interview T64.
30. Interview T36.
31. Interview T84.
32. Interview T61. The name here is my translation.
33. Interview T56.
34. Interview T98.
35. Interview T41.
36. At the same time, the municipality had also engaged in a dialogue with the OTLB over payments at the Ras Jedir market, but these negotiations stalled almost immediately (interview T41).
37. Interview T64.
38. Ala Oueslati, "With Municipal Elections, Tunisia Moves Beyond 'Transition,'" *IPI Global Observatory* (blog), April 30, 2018, https://theglobalobservatory.org/2018/04/tunisia-municipal-elections-beyond-transition/.
39. "Tunisia Militants Jailed for 2015 Attacks," *BBC News*, February 9, 2019, https://www.bbc.com/news/world-africa-47183027.
40. "Tunisia Builds Anti-Terror Barrier," *BBC News*, February 7, 2016, https://www.bbc.com/news/world-africa-35515229.
41. Sarah Mersch, "Gegen Terroristen, Schmuggler Und Zivilisten—Wie Tunesien Seine Grenzen Aufrüstet," *Neue Zuricher Zeitung*, March 14, 2019, https://www.nzz.ch/international/tunesien-ruestet-die-grenzen-gegen-schmuggler-und-terroristen-auf-ld.1467111; Katherine Pollock and Frederic Wehrey, "The Tunisian-Libyan Border: Security Aspirations and Socioeconomic Realities" (Washington, D.C.: Carnegie Endowment for International Peace, August 21, 2018), https://carnegieendowment.org/2018/08/21/tunisian-libyan-border-security-aspirations-and-socioeconomic-realities-pub-77087.
42. Interview T68.
43. Heba Saleh, "Tunisia Border Attack by Suspected Isis Forces Kills 52," *Financial Times*, March 7, 2016, https://www.ft.com/content/e7a728be-e445-11e5-a09b-1f8b0d268c39.
44. Nate Rosenblatt, "All Jihad Is Local—What ISIS' Files Tell US About Its Fighters," New America International Security Program (New America, 2016); Sudarsan Raghavan, "Islamic State, Growing Stronger in Libya, Sets Its Sights on Fragile Neighbor Tunisia," *Washington Post*, May 13, 2016, https://www.washingtonpost

6. TUNISIA

.com/world/middle_east/islamic-state-threatens-fragile-tunisia-from-next-door-in-libya/2016/05/13/cd9bd634-f82e-11e5-958d-d038dac6e718_story.html.
45. Oussama Romdhani, "Ben Guerdane, a Year On," *Arab Weekly*, March 12, 2017, https://thearabweekly.com/ben-guerdane-year.
46. Thomas Cantens and Gael J. R. F. Raballand, "Cross-Border Trade, Insecurity and the Role of Customs: Some Lessons from Six Field Studies in (Post-)Conflict Regions," ICTD Working Paper (Brighton, UK: International Centre for Tax and Development, August 2017), 13, make a similar observation, though it is only briefly mentioned.
47. "Tunisie: Trois jihadistes tués à Ben Guerdane (officiel)," *L'Orient le jour*, March 10, 2016, https://www.lorientlejour.com/article/974761/tunisie-trois-jihadistes-tues-a-ben-guerdane-officiel.html.
48. "Tunisie: Cinq 'terroristes' tués au lendemain des attaques jihadistes de Ben Guerdane," *L'Obs.com*, March 8, 2016, https://www.nouvelobs.com/monde/20160308.AFP9231/tunisie-cinq-terroristes-tues-au-lendemain-des-attaques-jihadistes-de-ben-guerdane.html.
49. Interviews T68, T97, T94, T95.
50. Interview T69.
51. Interview T107.
52. From the author's field notes, February 14, 2017.
53. Interview T68.
54. Interview T97.
55. This has been triangulated through multiple interviews with different traders as well as informants involved in negotiating this agreement.
56. Interview T66, T68.
57. Frederic Wehrey, *The Burning Shores: Inside the Battle for the New Libya* (New York: Farrar, Straus and Giroux, 2018); Wolfram Lacher, "Fault Lines of the Revolution," SWP Research Paper (Berlin: Stiftung Wissenschaft und Politik, May 2013).
58. Tarek Megerisi, *Order from Chaos: Stabilising Libya the Local Way* (London: European Council on Foreign Relations, 2018), https://www.ecfr.eu/publications/summary/order_from_chaos_stabilising_libya_the_local_way.
59. Tim Eaton, *Libya's War Economy: Predation, Profiteering and State Weakness* (London: Chatham House, 2018), https://www.chathamhouse.org/sites/files/chathamhouse/publications/research/2018-04-12-libyas-war-economy-eaton-final.pdf.
60. Anouar Boukhars, "The Potential Jihadi Windfall from the Militarization of Tunisia's Border Region with Libya" (Washington, D.C.: Carnegie Endowment for International Peace, January 26, 2018), https://carnegieendowment.org/2018/01/26/potential-jihadi-windfall-from-militarization-of-tunisia-s-border-region-with-libya-pub-75365.
61. Michael J. Willis, "Berbers in an Arab Spring: The Politics of Amazigh Identity and the North African Uprisings," in *North African Politics: Change and Continuity*, ed. Yahia H. Zoubir and Gregory White (London: Routledge, 2015).
62. Mahmoud Bader et al., "Libyan Local Governance Case Studies" (Brussels: European Union Delegation to Libya, July 2017), 14–33.
63. Mark Micallef, "The Human Conveyor Belt: Trends in Human Trafficking and Smuggling in Post-Revolution Libya" (Geneva: Global Initiative Against

Transnational Organised Crime, March 2017), 11–12; Sami Zaptia, "Libyan Fuel Smuggling Is Part of an International Smuggling Network: Attorney General's Office," *Libya Herald*, March 15, 2018, https://www.libyaherald.com/2018/03/15/libyan-fuel-smuggling-is-part-of-an-international-smuggling-network-attorney-generals-office/.
64. Interviews T61, T68.
65. "Protests, Strike Shut Down Tunisian Town Over Libya's Halt of Border Trade," *Middle East Eye*, May 12, 2016, https://www.middleeasteye.net/news/protests-strike-shut-down-tunisian-town-over-libyas-halt-border-trade.
66. Réalités Online, "Ouverture du passage frontalier de Ras Jedir," *Toutes les dernières News en Tunisie et dans le monde* (blog), August 19, 2016, https://www.realites.com.tn/2016/08/ouverture-du-passage-frontalier-de-ras-jedir/; "Tunisie: Sit-in ouvert et actes de destruction à Ben Guerdane suite à la mort d'un contrebandier," *HuffPost Maghreb*, September 6, 2016, https://www.huffpostmaghreb.com/2016/09/06/ben-guerdane-contrebande_n_11871190.html.
67. "تواصل اعتصام بن قردان وغلق لحركة العبور نحو معبر رأس جدير," *Al-Wataniyya Tunis*, November 30, 2016, http://www.watania1.tn/%D8%AA%D9%88%D8%A7%D8%B5%D9%84-%D8%A7%D8%B9%D8%AA%D8%B5%D8%A7%D9%85-%D8%A8%D9%86-%D9%82%D8%B1%D8%AF%D8%A7%D9%86-%D9%88%D8%BA%D9%84%D9%82-%D9%84%D8%AD%D8%B1%D9%83%D8%A9-%D8%A7%D9%84%D8%B9%D8%A8%D8%A7%D8%B1 -%D9%86%D8%AD%D9%88 -%D9%85%D8%B9%D8%A8%D8%B1 -% D8% B1% D8% A3%D8%B3 -%D8%AC%D8%AF%D9%8A%D8%B1/%D9%85%D8%AD%D8%A A%D9%88%D9%89. Different interview partners have made conflicting reports as to whether the demands of the protesters also included calls for the removal of Ben Guerdane's police chief and the head of customs at Ras Jedir.
68. Interviews T101, T57.
69. Interview T61.
70. Interviews T57, T102; Memorandum of Understanding, signed in Zuwara in January 2017.
71. Interview T68.
72. Interviews T68, T102; Tunis Webdo, "A Ben Guerdane, les responsables libyens posent un lapin aux représentants du gouvernement tunisien," *Webdo* (blog), January 13, 2017, http://www.webdo.tn/2017/01/13/a-ben-guerdane-responsables-libyens-posent-lapin-aux-representants-gouvernement-tunisien/.
73. Interview T102.
74. Interviews T68, T57, T58.
75. Interviews T65, T101.
76. World Bank, "Impact of the Libya Crisis on the Tunisian Economy" (Washington, D.C.: World Bank, 2017), https://openknowledge.worldbank.org/handle/10986/26407.
77. Eaton, *Libya's War Economy*.
78. "Anti-Smuggling Protests as Zuwara Faces Fuel Crisis," *Libya Herald*, June 18, 2017, https://www.libyaherald.com/2017/06/18/anti-smuggling-protests-as-zuwara-faces-fuel-crisis/.
79. Interview T114.
80. Interview T102. The council's participation was confirmed via email by a member of the Zuwara Municipal Council, July 2017.

6. TUNISIA

81. Interview T106.
82. Interview T108.
83. Interview T106.
84. Youssef Cherif, "Tunisia's Risky War on Corruption," *Sada—Carnegie Endowment for International Piece*, July 18, 2017, https://carnegieendowment.org/sada/71569.
85. Tarek Kahlaoui, "Tunisia's 'War Against Corruption' Feels like a Fake," *Middle East Eye*, June 14, 2017, http://www.middleeasteye.net/columns/without-more-guarantees-tunisian-government-s-fight-against-corruption-feels-fake-862047549.
86. Kapitalis, "Arrestation de Wachwacha, Baron de La Contrebande a Ben Guerdane," *Kapitalis.com*, June 1, 2017, http://kapitalis.com/tunisie/2017/06/01/arrestation-de-wachwacha-baron-de-la-contrebande-a-ben-guerdane/.
87. Business News Tn, "Ben Guerdène: 3 millions de dinars saisis chez un réseau de financement de terroristes," *Business News Tn* (blog), June 28, 2017, http://www.businessnews.com.tn/ben-guerdene—demantelement-dun-reseau-de-financement-du-terrorisme-et-saisi-de-3-millions-de-dinars,520,73278,3.
88. DirectInfo, "Hédi Yahia, accusé de contrebande, vient d'être acquitté," *Directinfo.com* (blog), June 17, 2017, https://directinfo.webmanagercenter.com/2017/06/17/hedi-yahia-accuse-de-contrebande-vient-detre-acquitte/.
89. Lisa Anderson, *The State and Social Transformation in Tunisia and Libya, 1830–1980* (Princeton, N.J.: Princeton University Press, 1987), 66.
90. Interview T105.
91. Interview T119. The comment on the judiciary likely refers to the concern, referenced at another point in the interview, that the inefficiencies of the judicial system could slow down the process or make it impossible to bring forward charges at all.
92. Matthew Herbert and Max Gallien, "The Risks of Hardened Borders in North Africa" (Washington, D.C.: Carnegie Endowment for International Peace, August 16, 2018), https://carnegieendowment.org/sada/77053.
93. From the author's field notes, February 14, 2017.
94. This is based on interviews with smugglers, videos recorded by smugglers, and the visibility of tire marks along and across the fortifications on satellite images.
95. Harchaoui, Badi, and Gallien, project report for the Global Initiative Against Transnational Organized Crime (GITOC) forthcoming.
96. WIEGO, "Informal Workers in the COVID-19 Crisis: A Global Picture of Sudden Impact and Long-Term Risk," *Wiego.org*, July 2020, https://www.wiego.org/fr/node/8371; Max Gallien and Vanessa Van den Boogaard, "Informal Workers and the State: The Politics of Connection and Disconnection During a Global Pandemic" (Brighton, UK: Institute of Development Studies, 2021); Lucia Bird Ruiz-Benitez de Lugo, "Human Smuggling in the Time of COVID-19: Lessons from a Pandemic," in *The Routledge Handbook of Smuggling*, ed. Max Gallien and Florian Weigand (Abingdon, UK: Routledge, 2021).
97. Interview T90.
98. Interview T83.
99. Interview T90.
100. Author's field notes, March 2017.
101. The statue was finally inaugurated in March 2018.

7. MOROCCO

1. *Hajiira and the Issue of the Border Between Algeria and Morocco* (author's translation), Youtube video, 2013, https://www.youtube.com/watch?v=hDF-vMCBBu0&feature=youtu.be.
2. Mohammed Jaabouk, "Maroc/Algérie: L'armée Algérienne creuse des tranchées pour lutter contre le trafic des carburants," *Yabiladi.com* (blog), July 17, 2013, https://www.yabiladi.com/articles/details/18492/maroc-algerie-l-armee-algerienne-creuse.html.
3. Querine Hanlon and Matthew Herbert, "Border Security Challenges in the Grand Maghreb" (Washington, D.C.: United States Institute of Peace, 2015); Matthew Herbert, "At the Edge—Trends and Routes of North African Clandestine Migrants," ISS Paper (Pretoria, South Africa: Institute for Security Studies, November 2016).
4. Catherine Sweet, "Democratization Without Democracy: Political Openings and Closures in Modern Morocco," *Middle East Report*, no. 218 (2001): 22–25, https://doi.org/10.2307/1559306.
5. Katja Zvan Elliott, "Reforming the Moroccan Personal Status Code: A Revolution for Whom?" *Mediterranean Politics* 14, no. 2 (July 1, 2009): 213–27, https://doi.org/10.1080/13629390902987659; Human Rights Watch, "Morocco's Truth Commission—Honoring Past Victims during an Uncertain Present" (Human Rights Watch, November 2005), https://www.hrw.org/sites/default/files/reports/morocco1105wcover.pdf; Sweet, "Democratization Without Democracy."
6. Akbar Ahmed and Harrison Akins, "The Plight of the Rif: Morocco's Restive Northern Periphery," *Al Jazeera*, September 28, 2012.
7. HM King Mohammed VI, "Discours de S. M. Le Roi Mohammed VI à l'occasion de la visite officielle du Souverain dans la Région de l'Oriental" (speech, Oujda, Morocco, March 18, 2003), http://www.maroc.ma/fr/discours-royaux/discours-de-sm-le-roi-mohammed-vi-%C3%A0-loccasion-de-la-visite-officielle-du-souverain.
8. Timothee Boutry, "Le roi du Maroc réconforte les sinistrés," *Le Parisien*, February 29, 2004, http://www.leparisien.fr/faits-divers/le-roi-du-maroc-reconforte-les-sinistres-29-02-2004-2004792655.php.
9. James N. Sater, "Morocco's 'Arab Spring,'" Middle East Institute Policy Analysis (Washington, D.C.: Middle East Institute, October 1, 2011), https://www.mei.edu/publications/moroccos-arab-spring.
10. Sean L. Yom and F. Gregory Gause III, "Resilient Royals: How Arab Monarchies Hang on," *Journal of Democracy* 23, no. 4 (October 12, 2012): 74–88, https://doi.org/10.1353/jod.2012.0062.
11. Bruce Maddy-Weitzman, "Is Morocco Immune to Upheaval?" *Middle East Quarterly*, January 1, 2012, https://dev.meforum.org/3114/morocco-upheaval.
12. Interviews M80, M35.
13. Interview M60.
14. National Initiative for Human Development, "Activities Report 2005–2010" (INDH, 2010), http://www.indh.ma/sites/default/files/Publications-2017-10/rap3.pdf.
15. "INDH: Plus de 700 MDH pour 495 projets à Oujda-Angad entre 2005 et 2016," *Medias24*, January 26, 2017.

16. Driss Maghraoui, "Constitutional Reforms in Morocco: Between Consensus and Subaltern Politics," *Journal of North African Studies* 16, no. 4 (December 1, 2011): 679–99, https://doi.org/10.1080/13629387.2011.630879; Francesco Cavatorta, "Morocco: The Promise of Democracy and the Reality of Authoritarianism," *International Spectator* 51, no. 1 (January 2, 2016): 86–98, https://doi.org/10.1080/03932729.2016.1126155; Mohamad al-Akhssassi, "Reforms in Morocco: Monitoring the Orbit and Reading the Trajectory," *Contemporary Arab Affairs* 10, no. 4 (October 2, 2017): 482–509, https://doi.org/10.1080/17550912.2017.1343838.
17. Interview M108.
18. Interview M65. On the Technopole, see Agence Oriental, "Technopole d'Oujda," *Agence Oriental* (blog), accessed October 7, 2017, http://www.oriental.ma/fr/Page-16/les-grands-projets/grands-projets-structurants/technopole-doujda/86-1/.
19. Interview M67.
20. Interview M87.
21. Interview M108.
22. Interview M58.
23. Miguel Ángel Pérez Castro and Miguel Ángel Montero Alonso, "Estudios economicos sectorales de la Cuidad Autóonoma de Melilla" (Melilla: Consejería de Economía y Hacienda de la Ciudad Autónoma de Melilla, December 2014), 98.
24. Interviews M85, M77.
25. Interview M59.
26. Interview M106.
27. Interviews M76, M36.
28. Interview M46.
29. Interview M2.
30. Interview M14.
31. For the sake of illustration, this section focuses primarily on Oujda. The same dynamics described here—the associations, the markets, down to the fire leading to one of the markets' reconstruction—are largely mirrored in Nador, the other major city of the Oriental region.
32. Interview M16.
33. Interview M59.
34. Interview M14.
35. Interview M9; Mohammed Saddougui, "Les dysfonctionnements de l'impôt au Maroc: Cas des revenus professionnels" (PhD thesis, Faculté des scienes juridiques, économiques et sociales, université Mohamed premier Oujda Maroc, 2014), 264, https://tel.archives-ouvertes.fr/tel-01374198/document.
36. Interviews M34, M48.
37. Sylvia I. Bergh, "Traditional Village Councils, Modern Associations, and the Emergence of Hybrid Political Orders in Rural Morocco," *Peace Review* 21, no. 1 (March 1, 2009): 45–53, https://doi.org/10.1080/10402650802690060.
38. Interviews M94, M54.
39. Interview M14.
40. Interview M14.
41. Interviews M70, M91.
42. Interview M93.
43. Interview M58.

44. While the Souk Melilla contained two associations in 2017, conversations with the leadership of both associations as well as market vendors made clear that one of them had monopolized the intersection with local state structures, while the other was relatively small and largely reduced to voicing occasional frustration around the regulations for storefronts (interview M97).
45. Interview M14.
46. Interview M34.
47. Mohamed Zerhoudi, "Marjane Oujda ouvre ses portes," *L'Economiste*, December 11, 2007, no. 2670, https://www.leconomiste.com/article/marjane-oujda-ouvre-ses-portes.
48. Oujda Chamber of Commerce, "La grande distribution à Oujda & ses effets sur le commerce de proximité," unpublished report (Oujda, Morocco: Oujda Chamber of Commerce, 2009).
49. This is repeatedly evidenced through the ability of the Tunisian state to confiscate large cash deposits in the houses of traders, as in the raids mentioned in chapter 6.
50. Interview T93.
51. Interview M47.
52. Castro and Alonso, "Estudios economicos sectorales," 388. This contrast is notable given that Morocco has in recent years been lauded for its progress on money-laundering issues, contrary to Tunisia, which was even briefly added to the EU's money-laundry blacklist. Financial Action Task Force (FATF), "Improving Global AML/CFT Compliance: On-Going Process—23 February 2018" (Paris: FATF, February 23, 2018), http://www.fatf-gafi.org/countries/a-c/bosniaandherzegovina/documents/fatf-compliance-february-2018.html#Tunisia; FATF, "Improving Global AML/CFT Compliance: On-Going Process, 18 October 2013," http://www.fatf-gafi.org/countries/a-c/argentina/documents/fatf-compliance-oct-2013.html#Morocco; Hyun-Sung Khang, "MEPs Confirm Commission Blacklist of Countries at Risk of Money Laundering," press release, European Parliament, February 7, 2018, http://www.europarl.europa.eu/news/en/press-room/20180202IPR97031/meps-confirm-commission-blacklist-of-countries-at-risk-of-money-laundering.
53. Interview M33.
54. Interview M31.
55. Interviews M28, M29, M110, M62, M9.
56. Interviews M31, M65.
57. Interviews M66, M110, M111. This is not an untypical phenomenon in North Africa, as Luca Raineri has demonstrated in "Drug Trafficking in the Sahara Desert: Follow the Money and Find Land Grabbing," in *The Illicit and Illegal in Regional and Urban Governance and Development*, ed. Francesco Chiodelli, Tim Hall, and Ray Hudson (London: Routledge, 2017).
58. Interview M78.
59. Interview M33.
60. Interview M40.
61. United Nations Conference on Trade and Development, "An Investment Guide to the Oriental Region of Morocco—Opportunities and Conditions" (Geneva: UNCTAD, 2012), http://unctad.org/en/PublicationsLibrary/diaepcb2010d10_en.pdf.

62. Interview M108.
63. This is not to say that there are no protests along this border. Recent years have seen marches to the border to protest its closure as well as protests around a disagreement on the location of the border near Figuig (Max Gallien and Yasmine Zarhloule, "Moroccan Farmers' Protests Highlight the Human Toll of Border Dispute," *Middle East Eye*, April 5, 2021, https://www.middleeasteye.net/opinion/morocco-farmers-protests-highlight-human-toll-algeria-border-dispute). However, these were all comparatively small-scale and did not engage in the fundamental challenging of the regime that was visible in similar protests in Tunisia.
64. Jaabouk, "Maroc/Algérie"; Ziad Alami, "L'Algérie construit un 'mur de fer' à sa frontière terrestre avec le Maroc," *Le360* (blog), August 9, 2016, https://fr.le360.ma/politique/lalgerie-construit-un-mur-de-fer-a-sa-frontiere-terrestre-avec-le-maroc-82805.
65. Interview M100.
66. Idriss Houat, *Dhahirat At-Tahreeb* (The phenomenon of smuggling) (Oujda, Morocco: CCIS Oujda, 2004). There are severe methodological issues with this study, but its descriptive statistics are broadly illustrative of the large role that Algerian products played in the local informal trade structure before 2013.
67. Focus Group FG4.
68. Interview M29.
69. Interview M34.
70. Interview M95.
71. Interview M48.
72. Interview M83.
73. Interview M112.
74. Interview M102.
75. Interviews M54, M80, M100.
76. Interview M14.
77. Khalil Ibrahimi, "Développement: Un plan d'urgence pour L'Oriental," *Le360*, May 25, 2016, http://fr.le360.ma/economie/developpement-un-plan-durgence-pour-loriental-73699.
78. Interview M95.
79. Interview M4.
80. Interview M78.
81. Interview M108.
82. Interview M100.
83. Interview M71.
84. Interview M82.
85. Interview M82.
86. Interview M78.
87. Interview M89.
88. Interview M78.
89. Interview M80.
90. Interviews M96, M100, M101, M102.
91. Interview M101.

92. Interview M76.
93. Max Gallien and Matthew Herbert, "GITOC Report on Drugs in North Africa" (London: Global Initiative Against Transnational Organised Crime, 2019).
94. Interview M94.
95. Interview M22.
96. Interview M26.
97. Interview M94.

8. THE VALLEY AND THE MOUNTAIN

1. Name has been changed.
2. Interview M40.
3. Textile smuggling and gasoline smuggling in both locations are best conceptualized not as one network, but as a set of networks made up of different groups/families/businesses that broadly engage with the same formal and informal institutions and work with the same structures of access, supply, demand, marketing, and so on. As I am interested here in the effects of these institutions and structures, I am interested in them as sets of networks, as well as groups within them.
4. Interviews T105, T106.
5. Interview M102.
6. Interviews T106, T94, T95, T38.
7. Interviews T94, T95.
8. This is also evidenced by the selection of the communities in the borderlands that are prioritized in the emergency aid program by the Moroccan state after the border closure, as discussed in the concluding chapter.
9. Focus Group FG7.
10. Interview M54.
11. Interviews M111, M9, Focus Group FG4.
12. Interview M84.
13. Interview T105.
14. Interview T66.
15. Interview T94.
16. Interview M48.
17. Interview M83.
18. Interview M61.
19. Interview M51 and author's field notes, Oujda, June 5, 2017.
20. Tim Eaton, *Libya's War Economy: Predation, Profiteering and State Weakness* (London: Chatham House, 2018), https://www.chathamhouse.org/sites/files/chathamhouse/publications/research/2018-04-12-libyas-war-economy-eaton-final.pdf.
21. Interview T114. Smuggling of Libyan gasoline toward Malta and Italy was operated at a significantly larger scale and by actors who were seen as more influential and well-connected politically. On this, see Tim Eaton; "Libya—Rich in Oil, Leaking Fuel," Chatham House Shorthand Story (London: Chatham House, 2019).
22. Interview T102.

8. THE VALLEY AND THE MOUNTAIN

23. Max Gallien, "An Economic Malaise Lies at the Heart of Libya-Tunisia Border Standoff," *Middle East Eye*, July 31, 2018, https://www.middleeasteye.net/columns/economic-malaise-heart-libya-tunisia-border-standoff-883226567.
24. Rami Al-Talagh, "تتواصل .. أزمة المعابر الليبية التونسية," *Afrigate News*, August 27, 2018, https://www.afrigatenews.net/article/%D8%A3%D8%B2%D9%85%D8%A9-%D8%A7%D9%84%D9%85%D8%B9%D8%A7%D8%A8%D8%B1-%D8%A7%D9%84%D9%84%D9%8A%D8%A8%D9%8A%D8%A9-%D8%A7%D9%84%D8%AA%D9%88%D9%86%D8%B3%D9%8A%D8%A9-%D8%AA%D8%AA%D9%88%D8%A7%D8%B5%D9%84/; France24, "احتجاجات في جنوب تونس بعد إغلاق حكومة الوفاق الليبية معبر رأس جدير الحدودي," *France24* (blog), August 29, 2018, https://www.france24.com/ar/20180829-%D8%AA%D9%88%D9%86%D8%B3-%D9%84%D9%8A%D8%A8%D9%8A%D8%A7-%D9%85%D8%B9%D8%A8 D8%B1-%D8%AD%D8%AF%D9%88%D8% AF -%D8%A8%D9%86 -%D9%82%D8%B1%D8%AF%D8%A7%D9%86 -%D8%AA% D9%87%D8%B1%D9%8A%D8%A8-%D8%A7%D8%AD%D8%AA%D8%AC%D8% A7%D8%AC%D8%A7%D8%AA -%D8%B5%D8%AF%D8%A7%D9%85%D8%A7% D8%AA; Jawhara FM, "تتوتر الأوضاع في بنقردان بعد فتح معبر راس جدير," *Jawhara FM* (blog), September 9, 2018, https://www.jawharafm.net/ar/article/%D8%AA%D9%88% D8%AA%D9%91%D8%B1-%D8%A7%D9%84%D8%A3%D9%88%D8%B6%D8%A7 %D8%B9-%D9%81%D9%8A -%D8%A8%D9%86%D9%82%D8%B1%D8%AF%D8% A7%D9%86 -%D8%A8%D8%B9%D8%AF -%D9%81%D8% AA%D8%AD -%D9% 85%D8%B9%D8%A8%D8%B1 -%D8%B1%D8%A7%D8%B3 -% D8% AC%D8%AF% D9%8A%D8%B1-/105/121444.
25. There are important parallels in the argument presented here to the discussion of informal political voice and political alliances in the context of the informal organizations in Kate Meagher, "Disempowerment from Below: Informal Enterprise Networks and the Limits of Political Voice in Nigeria," *Oxford Development Studies* 42, no. 3 (July 3, 2014): 419–38, https://doi.org/10.1080/13600818.2014.900005.
26. Interview M35.
27. Interview M39.
28. Interviews M4, M12, M14, M110, M111, M102, M103.
29. Interview M80.
30. Interviews M54, M94, M96.
31. Interview M93.
32. Interview M94.
33. Interview M96.
34. Interview M108.
35. Interview M80.
36. Interview M98.
37. Interview M4.
38. Interview M102.
39. Interview M94.
40. Interviews M96, M22, M94, M63.
41. Interview M95.
42. From the author's field notes, Oujda, June 20, 2017.
43. Interview M100.
44. Interview M94.

45. Focus Group FG7.
46. Alcinda Honwana, "'Waithood': Youth Transitions and Social Change," *Development and Equity*, January 1, 2014, 28–40, https://doi.org/10.1163/9789004269729_004.
47. Interviews M63, M22, M94, M96.
48. Focus Group FG7.
49. Lesiteinfo, "Les chiffres chocs de la criminalité à Oujda," *Lesiteinfo* (blog), April 12, 2018, https://www.lesiteinfo.com/maroc/chiffres-chocs-de-criminalite-a-oujda/; Liberation Ma, "19.896 Arrestations à Oujda pour des actes criminels visant les biens et les personnes," *Liberation.Ma* (blog), August 5, 2016, https://www.libe.ma/19-896-arrestations-a-Oujda-pour-des-actes-criminels-visant-les-biens-et-les-personnes_a77421.html.
50. Jonathan Goodhand, "From War Economy to Peace Economy? Reconstruction and State Building in Afghanistan," *Journal of International Affairs* 1, no. 58 (2004).
51. Anuradha Joshi and Joseph Ayee, "Associational Taxation: A Pathway Into the Informal Sector?" in *Taxation and State-Building in Developing Countries*, ed. Deborah Brautigam, Odd-Helge Fjeldstad, and Mick Moore (Cambridge: Cambridge University Press, 2008), 183–211, https://doi.org/10.1017/CBO9780511490897.008.
52. Interview M85.
53. Interviews M76, M77, M83, M85.
54. Focus Group FG2.
55. The exceptions to this were vendors who were financially unable to move to the new, formalized markets. However, the number of vendors where this was an issue (such as at the Souk Melilla in Oujda) was generally low.
56. Interviews T61, T62.
57. Interview M46.
58. Interviews T61, T68, M81.
59. Interviews M34, M83.
60. Interview M70.
61. Interview M48.
62. Interview M60.
63. Interview M80.
64. Although this lies beyond the scope of the chapter, these observations also apply to the other larger Spanish enclave in Morocco, Ceuta.
65. Interviews M99, M55, M56.
66. Linda Pressly, "The 'Mule Women' of Melilla," *BBC News*, October 30, 2013, https://www.bbc.com/news/magazine-24706863.
67. Andries du Toit, "Forgotten by the Highway: Globalisation, Adverse Incorporation and Chronic Poverty in a Commercial Farming District of South Africa," SSRN Scholarly Paper (Rochester, N.Y.: Social Science Research Network, December 1, 2004), https://papers.ssrn.com/abstract=1753702.
68. Kate Meagher and Ilda Lindell, "Introduction," *African Studies Review* 56, no. 3 (December 3, 2013): 57–76.
69. T. Parks and W. Cole, "Political Settlements: Implications for International Development Policy and Practice" (San Francisco: Asia Foundation, 2010), 7, http://www.gsdrc.org/document-library/political-settlements-implications-for-international-development-policy-and-practice/.

70. Kate Meagher, "Informality, Religious Conflict, and Governance in Northern Nigeria: Economic Inclusion in Divided Societies," *African Studies Review* 56, no. 3 (December 2013): 231.

CONCLUSION

1. Marc Lynch, "The Arab Uprisings Never Ended: The Enduring Struggle to Remake the Middle East Essays," *Foreign Affairs* 100, no. 1 (2021): 111–22.
2. On the labor force numbers, see International Labour Organization, "Women and Men in the Informal Economy: A Statistical Picture," 3rd ed., ILO Report, April 30, 2018, http://www.ilo.org/global/publications/books/WCMS_626831.
3. On state-building and smuggling, see Peter Andreas, *Smuggler Nation: How Illicit Trade Made America* (Oxford: Oxford University Press, 2014); Jonathan Goodhand, "From War Economy to Peace Economy? Reconstruction and State Building in Afghanistan," *Journal of International Affairs* 1, no. 58 (2004); Kate Meagher, "Smuggling Ideologies: From Criminalization to Hybrid Governance in African Clandestine Economies," *African Affairs*, 2014. On African borderland studies, see Timothy Raeymaekers, "African Boundaries and the New Capitalist Frontier," in *Companion to Border Studies*, ed. Thomas M. Wilson and Hastings Donnan (Chichester, UK: Wiley, 2012); Kristof Titeca, "The Changing Cross-Border Trade Dynamics Between North-Western Uganda, North-Eastern Congo and Southern Sudan," Crisis States Research Centre Working Papers (London: London School of Economics and Political Science, 2009), 63; Kate Meagher, "The Strength of Weak States?: Non-State Security Forces and Hybrid Governance in Africa," *Development and Change* 43 (September 2012): 1073–1101.
4. James C. Scott, *The Art of Not Being Governed: An Anarchist History of Upland Southest Asia* (New Haven, Conn.: Yale University Press, 2009); R. I. Rotberg, *When States Fail: Causes and Consequences* (Princeton, N.J.: Princeton University Press, 2004).
5. Paul Nugent, *Smugglers, Secessionists and Loyal Citizens on the Ghana-Togo Frontier: The Life of the Borderlands Since 1914* (Oxford: James Currey, 2002); Raeymaekers, "African Boundaries."
6. Thomas Hüsken and Georg Klute, "Political Orders in the Making: Emerging Forms of Political Organization from Libya to Northern Mali," *African Security* 8, no. 4 (October 2, 2015): 320–37, https://doi.org/10.1080/19392206.2015.1100502."
7. Meagher, "Smuggling Ideologies"; Gregor Dobler, "The Green, the Grey and the Blue: A Typology of Cross-Border Trade in Africa," *Journal of Modern African Studies* 54, no. 1 (March 2016): 145–69, https://doi.org/10.1017/S0022278X15000993.
8. Douglass C. North, *Institutions, Institutional Change and Economic Performance* (Cambridge: Cambridge University Press, 1990); Mushtaq Khan, "Political Settlements and the Governance of Growth-Enhancing Institutions," draft paper, Research Paper Series on Growth-Enhancing Governance, 2010.
9. Kate Meagher, "Introduction: Special Issue on 'Informal Institutions and Development in Africa,'" *Africa Spectrum* 42, no. 3 (2007): 405–18; Ragui Assaad, "Formal and Informal Institutions in the Labor Market, with Applications to the

CONCLUSION

Construction Sector in Egypt," *World Development* 21, no. 6 (June 1, 1993): 925–39, https://doi.org/10.1016/0305-750X(93)90052-B.

10. Elinor Ostrom, *Understanding Institutional Diversity* (Princeton, N.J.: Princeton University Press, 2005).
11. Johannes Jütting et al., eds., *Informal Institutions: How Social Norms Help or Hinder Development*, Development Centre Studies (Paris: OECD Publishing, 2007); Ostrom, *Understanding Institutional Diversity*.
12. Gretchen Helmke and Stephen Levitsky, "Informal Institutions and Comparative Politics: A Research Agenda," *Perspectives on Politics* 2, no. 4 (2004): 725–40.
13. Frances Cleaver, *Development Through Bricolage: Rethinking Institutions for Natural Resource Management* (Abingdon, UK: Routledge, 2012).
14. This has previously been noted by Frances Cleaver, "In Pursuit of Arrangements That Work: Bricolage, Practical Norms and Everyday Water Governance," in *Real Governance and Practical Norms in Africa: The Game of the Rules*, ed. Tom De Herdt and Jean-Pierre Olivier de Sardan (London: Routledge, 2015), 209; and Kate Meagher, Kristof Titeca, and Tom de Herdt, "Unravelling Public Authority: Paths of Hybrid Governance in Africa," Justice and Security Research Programme Policy Brief (London School of Economics and Political Science, 2014).
15. David Booth, "Introduction: Working with the Grain? The Africa Power and Politics Programme," *IDS Bulletin* 42, no. 2 (March 1, 2011): 1–10, https://doi.org/10.1111/j.1759-5436.2011.00206.x; Brian Levy, *Working with the Grain: Integrating Governance and Growth in Development Strategies* (Oxford: Oxford University Press, 2014).
16. Martin Doornbos, "Researching African Statehood Dynamics: Negotiability and Its Limits," *Development and Change* 41, no. 4 (2010): 747–69, https://doi.org/10.1111/j.1467-7660.2010.01650.x; Meagher, "The Strength of Weak States?"
17. Abdul Raufu Mustapha, Kate Meagher, and Nicholas Awortwi, "Introduction and Overview," in *Political Settlements and Agricultural Transformation in Africa*, ed. Martin Atea and Abdul Raufu Mustapha (Abingdon, UK: Routledge, 2023), 3.
18. Jonathan Goodhand, "From War Economy to Peace Economy?"; Goodhand, "Frontiers and Wars: The Opium Economy in Afghanistan," *Journal of Agrarian Change* 5, no. 2 (April 1, 2005): 191–216, https://doi.org/10.1111/j.1471-0366.2005.00099.x.; Goodhand, "Corrupting or Consolidating the Peace? The Drugs Economy and Post-Conflict Peacebuilding in Afghanistan," *International Peacekeeping* 15, no. 3 (June 1, 2008): 405–23, https://doi.org/10.1080/13533310802058984; and Goodhand, "Bandits, Borderlands and Opium Wars in Afghanistan," in *A Companion to Border Studies*, ed. Thomas M. Wilson and Hastings Donnan, 332–53 (Chichester, UK: Wiley, 2012).
19. Mushtaq Khan, "Political Settlements"; Khan and Kwame Sundaram Jomo, *Rents, Rent-Seeking and Economic Development: Theory and Evidence in Asia* (Cambridge: Cambridge University Press, 2009); and Khan, "Rents, Efficiency and Growth," in Khan and Jomo, *Rents, Rent-Seeking and Economic Development*, 21–69, http://eprints.soas.ac.uk/9842/.
20. Jonathan Goodhand and Patrick Meehan, "Spatialising Political Settlements," in *Accord Insight 4: Borderlands and Peacebuilding*, ed. Sharri Polanski and Zahbia Yousuf (London: Conciliation Resources, 2018), 15.

APPENDIX 1

21. Andries du Toit, "Forgotten by the Highway: Globalisation, Adverse Incorporation and Chronic Poverty in a Commercial Farming District of South Africa," SSRN Scholarly Paper (Rochester, N.Y.: Social Science Research Network, December 1, 2004); du Toit, "Adverse Incorporation and Agrarian Policy in South Africa, or, How Not to Connect the Rural Poor to Growth" (Cape Town, South Africa: Institute for Poverty, Land and Agrarian Studies, 2009); Kate Meagher and Ilda Lindell, "Introduction," *African Studies Review* 56, no. 3 (December 3, 2013): 57–76.
22. Querine Hanlon and Matthew Herbert, *Border Security Challenges in the Grand Maghreb* (Washington, D.C.: United States Institute of Peace Press, 2015); Hannah Timmis, "Formalising Informal Trade in North Africa," K4D Helpdesk Report (Brighton, UK: Institute of Development Studies, 2017).
23. Alexander Babuta and Cathy Haenlein, "Commodity Smuggling in the Maghreb: A Silent Threat," Policy Brief (Rabat, Morocco: Policy Center for the New South, May 2018), https://www.africaportal.org/publications/commodity-smuggling-maghreb-silent-threat/; Hanlon and Herbert, "Border Security Challenges."
24. Max Gallien and Matthew Herbert, "GITOC Report on Drugs in North Africa" (London: Global Initiative Against Transnational Organised Crime, 2019).
25. For a full discussion of this argument, see Matthew Herbert and Max Gallien, "The Risks of Hardened Borders in North Africa" (Washington, D.C.: Carnegie Endowment for International Peace, August 16, 2018), https://carnegieendowment.org/sada/77053.
26. Babuta and Haenlein, "Commodity Smuggling"; Timmis, "Formalising Informal Trade in North Africa"; Economist Intelligence Unit, "The Global Illicit Trade Environment Index" (London: Economist Intelligence Unit, 2018), https://eiuperspectives.economist.com/sites/default/files/Illicit%20Trade%20WHITEPAPER%20(19%20June%202018).pdf.
27. Max Gallien and Florian Weigand, "Channeling Contraband: How States Shape International Smuggling Routes," *Security Studies* 0, no. 0 (March 12, 2021): 1–28, https://doi.org/10.1080/09636412.2021.1885728.

APPENDIX 1. STUDYING SMUGGLING IN NORTH AFRICA

1. Gregor Dobler, "Localising Smuggling," and Thomas Hüsken, "Research in Dangerous Fields: Ethics, Morals, and Practices in the Study of Smuggling," both in *The Routledge Handbook of Smuggling*, ed. Max Gallien and Florian Weigand (Abingdon, UK: Routledge, 2021).
2. For a comprehensive introduction to the quantitative methods used in studying smuggling, see Sami Bensassi and Jade Siu, "Quantifying Missing and Hidden Trade: An Economic Perspective," in Gallien and Weigand, *Routledge Handbook of Smuggling*.
3. Lofti Ayadi et al, "Estimating Informal Trade Across Tunisia's Land Borders," Policy Research Working Paper (World Bank, December 1, 2013), https://documents.worldbank.org/en/publication/documents-reports/documentdetail/856231468173645854/estimating-informal-trade-across-tunisias-land-borders; Sami Bensassi et al., "Commerce Algérie—Mali: la normalité de l'informalité" (World Bank,

APPENDIX 1

March 22, 2015), http://documents.worldbank.org/curated/en/202591468195569 460/Commerce-Alg%C3%A9rie-Mali-la-normalit%C3%A9-de-l-informalit %C3%A9; KPMG, "Illicit Cigarette Trade in the Maghreb Region," 2017.
4. Mohammed Reza Farzanegan, "Illegal Trade in the Iranian Economy: A MIMIC Approach" (ERF 14th Annual Conference, Cairo, 2007).
5. Friedrich Schneider and Dominik H. Enste, "Shadow Economies: Size, Causes, and Consequences," *Journal of Economic Literature* 38, no. 1 (March 2000): 77–114, https://doi.org/10.1257/jel.38.1.77.
6. For a more comprehensive introduction to qualitative methods in studying smuggling, see Stephen Ellis and Janet MacGaffey, "Research on Sub-Saharan Africa's Unrecorded International Trade: Some Methodological and Conceptual Problems," *African Studies Review* 39, no. 2 (September 1996): 19–41; Nikki Philline C. de la Rosa and Francisco J. Lara, "Lorries and Ledgers: Describing and Mapping Smuggling in the Field," in Gallien and Weigand, *Routledge Handbook of Smuggling*.
7. Ethnographic work includes Laia Soto Bermant, "A Tale of Two Cities: The Production of Difference in a Mediterranean Border Enclave," *Social Anthropology* 23, no. 4 (November 1, 2015): 450–64, https://doi.org/10.1111/1469-8676.12266; and Timothy Raeymaekers, *Violent Capitalism and Hybrid Identity in the Eastern Congo: Power to the Margins* (New York: Cambridge University Press, 2014). Market and social network analyses include Olivier J. Walther, "Trade Networks in West Africa: A Social Network Approach," *Journal of Modern African Studies* 52, no. 2 (June 2014): 179–203, https://doi.org/10.1017/S0022278X14000032; Kate Meagher, "The Hidden Economy: Informal and Parallel Trade in Northwestern Uganda," *Review of African Political Economy* 17, no. 47 (March 1990): 64–83, https://doi.org/10.1080/03056249008703848; and Kamel Laroussi, "Commerce informel et nomadisme moderne" (Ecole des Hautes Études en Sciences Sociales, Paris, 2007). Archival work includes Peter Andreas, *Smuggler Nation: How Illicit Trade Made America* (Oxford: Oxford University Press, 2014); Matthew H. Ellis, *Desert Borderland: The Making of Modern Egypt and Libya* (Stanford, Calif.: Stanford University Press, 2018); and Paul Nugent, *Smugglers, Secessionists and Loyal Citizens on the Ghana-Togo Frontier: The Life of the Borderlands Since 1914* (Oxford: James Currey, 2002). Legal scholarship is explored in Gabriella E. Sanchez, *Human Smuggling and Border Crossings* (Abingdon, UK: Routledge, 2015).
8. W. Prichard and V. van den Boogaard, "Norms, Power and the Socially Embedded Realities of Market Taxation in Northern Ghana," ICTD Working Paper (International Centre for Taxation and Development, 2015).
9. Ellis and MacGaffey, "Research on Sub-Saharan Africa's Unrecorded International Trade."
10. Mushtaq Khan and Kwame Sundaram Jomo, *Rents, Rent-Seeking and Economic Development: Theory and Evidence in Asia* (Cambridge: Cambridge University Press, 2009); Lindsay Whitfield et al., *The Politics of African Industrial Policy: A Comparative Perspective* (Cambridge: Cambridge University Press, 2015).
11. Jonathan Goodhand and Patrick Meehan, "Spatialising Political Settlements," in *Accord Insight 4: Borderlands and Peacebuilding*, ed. Sharri Polanski and Zahbia

APPENDIX 1

Yousuf (London: Conciliation Resources, 2018), 15. This similarly applies to the scarcity of scholarship on the role of marginalized communities within national political settlements and power held outside the formal political system, which Behuria et al. have noted, alongside calls for more fine-grained ethnographic work within the field. See Pritish Behuria, Lars Buur, and Hazel Gray, "Studying Political Settlements in Africa," *African Affairs* 116, no. 464 (July 1, 2017): 515–16, 525, https://doi.org/10.1093/afraf/adx019.

12. Ragui Assaad, "Formal and Informal Institutions in the Labor Market, with Applications to the Construction Sector in Egypt," *World Development* 21, no. 6 (June 1, 1993): 925–39, https://doi.org/10.1016/0305-750X(93)90052-B; Kate Meagher, *Identity Economics: Social Networks and the Informal Economy in Nigeria* (Woodbridge, UK: Boydell & Brewer, 2010); Frances Cleaver, "Reinventing Institutions: Bricolage and the Social Embeddedness of Natural Resource Management," *European Journal of Development Research* 14, no. 2 (December 1, 2002): 11–30, https://doi.org/10.1080/714000425; Kristof Titeca and Tom de Herdt, "Regulation, Cross-Border Trade and Practical Norms in West Nile, North-Western Uganda," *Africa* 80, no. 4 (November 2010): 573–94, https://doi.org/10.3366/afr.2010.0403. Additionally, Gretchen Helmke and Stephen Levitsky, "Informal Institutions and Comparative Politics: A Research Agenda," *Perspectives on Politics* 2, no. 4 (2004): 725–40, provide a prominent example of relatively rare comparative scholarship on informal institutions.

13. Judith Scheele, *Smugglers and Saints of the Sahara: Regional Connectivity in the Twentieth Century* (Cambridge: Cambridge University Press, 2012); Mareike Schomerus and Kristof Titeca, "Deals and Dealings: Inconclusive Peace and Treacherous Trade Along the South Sudan-Uganda Border," *Africa Spectrum* 47, no. 2–3 (November 23, 2012): 5–31.

14. Some quantitative work on the issue in the Maghreb in recent years that I have also been able to draw on includes Bensassi et al., "Commerce Algérie-Mali"; Ayadi et al., "Estimating Informal Trade"; Karim Trabelssi, "Current State of the Informal Economy in Tunisia as Seen Through Its Stakeholders: Facts and Alternatives" (UGTT union youth report, 2014); Idriss Houat, *Dhahirat At-Tahreeb* (The phenomenon of smuggling) (Oujda, Morocco: CCIS Oujda, 2004); Miguel Ángel Pérez Castro and Miguel Ángel Montero Alonso, Estudios conomicos sectorales de la Cuidad Autónoma de Melilla" (Melilla: Consejería de Economía y Hacienda de la Ciudad Autónoma de Melilla, December 2014).

15. Lisa Wedeen, "Reflections on Ethnographic Work in Political Science," *Annual Review of Political Science* 13, no. 1 (2010): 255–72, https://doi.org/10.1146/annurev.polisci.11.052706.123951; Edward Schatz, *Political Ethnography* (Chicago: University of Chicago Press, 2009); Erica S. Simmons and Nicholas Rush Smith, "Comparison with an Ethnographic Sensibility," *PS: Political Science & Politics* 50, no. 1 (January 2017): 126–30, https://doi.org/10.1017/S1049096516002286.

16. Lisa Wedeen, *Ambiguities of Domination: Politics, Rhetoric, and Symbols in Contemporary Syria*, 2nd ed. (Chicago: University of Chicago Press, 2015).

17. Edward Schatz, *Political Ethnography* (Chicago: University of Chicago Press, 2009), 11, 9.

18. Wedeen, *Ambiguities of Domination*, 1.

19. Schatz, *Political Ethnography*, 305–6.
20. Mark-Anthony Falzon, *Multi-Sited Ethnography: Theory, Praxis and Locality in Contemporary Research* (Abingdon, UK: Routledge, 2016).
21. Scheele, *Smugglers and Saints of the Sahara*, 19.
22. John Stuart Mill, *The Collected Works of John Stuart Mill*, vol. 8: *A System of Logic Ratiocinative and Inductive Part II*, 1843; Sidney Tarrow, "The Strategy of Paired Comparison: Toward a Theory of Practice," *Comparative Political Studies* 43, no. 2 (February 2010): 230–59.
23. A. George and A. Bennett, *Case Studies and Theory Development* (Cambridge, Mass.: MIT Press, 2005); A. Bennett, "Process Tracing: A Bayesian Perspective," in *The Oxford Handbook of Political Methodology*, ed. J. M. Box-Steffensmeier and D. Collier (New York: Oxford University Press, 2008), 702–21.
24. Sidney Tarrow, "The Strategy of Paired Comparison: Toward a Theory of Practice," *Comparative Political Studies* 43, no. 2 (February 2010): 245; R. D. Putnam, R. Leonardi, and R. Nanetti, *Making Democracy Work: Civil Traditions in Modern Italy* (Princeton, N.J: Princeton University Press, 1993); J. Linz and A. Valenzuela, eds., *The Failure of Presidential Democracy* (Balitmore: Johns Hopkins University Press, 1994).
25. R. M. Gisselquist, "Paired Comparison and Theory Development: Considerations for Case Selection," *PS: Political Science & Politics* 47, no. 2 (2014): 477–84; J. Moller and S. Skaaning, "Explanatory Typologies as a Nested Strategy of Inquiry: Combining Cross-Case and Within-Case Analyses," *Sociological Methods Research* (2015).
26. John Gerring, *Case Study Research—Principles and Practices* (Cambridge: Cambridge University Press, 2007); Jason Seawright and John Gerring, "Case Selection Techniques in Case Study Research: A Menu of Qualitative and Quantitative Options," *Political Research Quarterly* 61, no. 2 (June 1, 2008): 294–308, https://doi.org/10.1177/1065912907313077.
27. Tarrow, "The Strategy of Paired Comparison."
28. A. Bennett, "Process Tracing: A Bayesian Perspective," in *The Oxford Handbook of Political Methodology*, ed. J. M. Box-Steffensmeier and D. Collier (New York: Oxford University Press, 2008), 702–21; Tasha Fairfield and Andrew Charman, "Bayesian Probability: The Logic of (Political) Science Opportunities, Caveats, and Guidelines" (Annual Meeting of the American Political Science Association, San Francisco, 2015), https://www.researchgate.net/profile/Tasha_Fairfield/publication/281701239_Bayesian_Probability_The_Logic_of_Political_Science/links/55f4e74a08ae6a34f66096bb/Bayesian-Probability-The-Logic-of-Political-Science.pdf.
29. Patrick Biernacki and Dan Waldorf, "Snowball Sampling: Problems and Techniques of Chain Referral Sampling," *Sociological Methods & Research* 10, no. 2 (November 1, 1981): 141–63, https://doi.org/10.1177/004912418101000205.
30. In three cases I did pay money to people I had interviewed. However, this was not in connection with gaining access, but as a donation in the face of the interviewee's abject poverty. In all three cases, this was done at the end of our interaction, in one case weeks later, and had at no point been promised, anticipated, or suggested beforehand.

APPENDIX 1

31. Ellis and MacGaffey, "Research on Sub-Saharan Africa's Unrecorded International Trade"; Sanchez, *Human Smuggling and Border Crossings*.
32. H. Rubin and I. Rubin, *Qualitative Interviewing—The Art of Hearing Data* (Thousand Oaks, Calif.: Sage, 2005); Ellis and MacGaffey, "Research on Sub-Saharan Africa's Unrecorded International Trade"
33. Paul Atkinson and David Silverman, "Kundera's Immortality: The Interview Society and the Invention of the Self," *Qualitative Inquiry* 3, no. 3 (September 1, 1997): 322, https://doi.org/10.1177/107780049700300304; S. E. Baker, R. Edwards, and Mark Doidge, "How Many Qualitative Interviews Is Enough? Expert Voices and Early Career Reflections on Sampling and Cases in Qualitative Research," 2012.
34. Sanchez, *Human Smuggling and Border Crossings*, 13.
35. Fairfield and Charman, "Bayesian Probability."
36. M. Wolfgang, "Confidentiality in Criminological Research and Other Ethical Issues," *Journal of Criminal Law and Criminology* 72, no. 1 (1981); S. E Beckerleg and G. L. Hundt, "The Characteristics and Recent Growth of Heroin Injecting in a Kenyan Coastal Town," *Addiction Research & Theory* 12, no. 1 (2004): 41–53; M. Hammersley and A. Traianou, *Ethics in Qualitative Research—Controversies and Contexts* (Thousand Oaks, Calif.: Sage, 2012).

BIBLIOGRAPHY

Abaab, Ali, Mohamed Haddar, and Aida Tarhouni. "Plan Régional d'environnment et de Développement Durable (PREDD) Du Governorat de Médenine." Tunis: Deutsche Gesellschaft für Internationale Zusammenarbeit, 2014.

Abdel Baky, Mariam. "Peacebuilding in Tunisian Border Regions: A Missing Piece of the Transition Process." In *Accord Insight 4—Borderlands and Peacebuilding*. London: Conciliation Resources, 2018.

Acemoglu, Daron, and James A. Robinson. *Why Nations Fail: The Origins of Power, Prosperity and Poverty*. New York: Profile Books, 2012.

Advocats Sans Frontières. "The Kasserine 'Region as a Victim' Petition: A First in Transitional Justice in Tunisia." Tunis: Advocats Sans Frontières 2015. https://www.asf.be/wp-content/uploads/2015/11/20160615_DossierRegion_Victim_ENG.pdf.

Afsahi, Kenza, and Salem Darwich. "Hashish in Morocco and Lebanon: A Comparative Study." *International Journal on Drug Policy* 31 (2016): 190–98. https://doi.org/10.1016/j.drugpo.2016.02.024.

Agamben, Giorgio. *State of Exception*. Chicago: Chicago University Press, 2005.

Agence Oriental. "Technopole d'Oujda." *Agence Oriental* (blog). Accessed October 7, 2017. http://www.oriental.ma/fr/Page-16/les-grands-projets/grands-projets-structurants/technopole-doujda/86-1/.

Ahmad, Aisha. *Jihad & Co.: Black Markets and Islamist Power*. Oxford: Oxford University Press, 2017.

Ahmed, Akbar, and Harrison Akins. "The Plight of the Rif: Morocco's Restive Northern Periphery." *Al Jazeera*, September 28, 2012. https://www.aljazeera.com/indepth/opinion/2012/09/2012924103333182505.html.

Akhssassi, Mohamad al-. "Reforms in Morocco: Monitoring the Orbit and Reading the Trajectory." *Contemporary Arab Affairs* 10, no. 4 (October 2, 2017): 482–509. https://doi.org/10.1080/17550912.2017.1343838.

BIBLIOGRAPHY

Alami, Ziad. "L'Algérie construit un 'mur de fer' à sa frontière terrestre avec le Maroc." *Le360* (blog), August 9, 2016. https://fr.le360.ma/politique/lalgerie-construit-un-mur-de-fer-a-sa-frontiere-terrestre-avec-le-maroc-82805.

Al-Talagh, Rami. "تواصل ..أزمة المعابر الليبية التونسية." *Afrigate News*, August 27, 2018. https://www.afrigatenews.net/article/%D8%A3%D8%B2%D9%85%D8%A9-%D8%A7%D9%84%D9%85%D8%B9%D8%A7%D8%A8%D8%B1-%D8%A7%D9%84%D9%84%D9%8A%D8%A8%D9%8A%D8%A9-%D8%A7%D9%84%D8%AA%D9%88%D9%86%D8%B3%D9%8A%D8%A9-%D8%AA%D8%AA%D9%88%D8%A7%D8%B5%D9%84/.

Althai Consulting. "Leaving Libya—Rapid Assessment of Municipalities of Departures of Migrants in Libya," June 2017. http://www.altaiconsulting.com/wp-content/uploads/2017/08/2017_Altai-Consulting_Leaving-Libya-Rapid-Assessment-of-Municipalities-of-Departure-of-Migrants-in-Libya.pdf.

Al-Wataniyya Tunis. "تواصل اعتصام بن قردان وغلق لحركة العبور نحو معبر رأس جدير." November 30, 2016. http://www.watania1.tn/%D8%AA%D9%88%D8%A7%D8%B5%D9%84-%D8%A7%D8%B9%D8%AA%D8%B5%D8%A7%D9%85-%D8%A8%D9%86-%D9%82%D8%B1%D8%AF%D8%A7%D9%86-%D9%88%D8%BA%D9%84 D9%82-%D9%84 D8%AD% D8%B1%D9%83% D8%A9-%D8%A7%D9%84%D8%B9%D8%A8%D9%88%D8 %B1-%D9%86%D8%AD%D9%88-%D9%85%D8%B9%D8%A8%D8%B1-%D8%B1%D8%A3%D8%B3-%D8%AC%D8%AF%D9%8A%D8%B1/%D9%85%D8%AD%D8%A A%D9%88%D9%89.

Amin, Magdi, Ragui Assaad, Nazar al-Baharna, Kemal Dervis, Raj M. Desai, Navtej S. Dhillon, Ahmed Galal, Hafez Ghanem, Carol Graham, and Daniel Kaufmann. *After the Spring: Economic Transitions in the Arab World*. Oxford, New York: Oxford University Press, 2012.

Anderson, Lisa. *The State and Social Transformation in Tunisia and Libya, 1830–1980*. Princeton, N.J.: Princeton University Press, 1987.

Andersson, Ruben. *Illegality, Inc.* Berkeley: University of California Press, 2014.

Andreas, Peter. *Blue Helmets and Black Markets: The Business of Survival in the Siege of Sarajevo*. Ithaca, N.Y.: Cornell University Press, 2008.

———. *Border Games: Policing the U.S.-Mexico Divide*. Cornell Studies in Political Economy. Ithaca, N.Y.: Cornell University Press, 2009.

———. "Dirty Entanglements: Corruption, Crime, and Terrorism, by Louise I. Shelley." *Political Science Quarterly* 130, no. 2 (2015): 350–51. https://doi.org/10.1002/polq.12327.

———. "The Illicit Trade and Conflict Connection: Insight from US History." In Gallien and Weigand, *The Routledge Handbook of Smuggling*.

———. *Smuggler Nation: How Illicit Trade Made America*. Oxford: Oxford University Press, 2014.

———. "Smuggling Wars: Law Enforcement and Law Evasion in a Changing World." In *Transnational Crime in the Americas*, by Tom Farer, 87–100. New York: Routledge, 1999.

Andreas, Peter, and Ethan Nadelmann. *Policing the Globe: Criminalization and Crime Control in International Relations*. Oxford: Oxford University Press, 2008.

Andrews, Matt. *The Limits of Institutional Reform in Development: Changing Rules for Realistic Solutions*. Cambridge: Cambridge University Press, 2013.

Angrist, Michele Penner. "Understanding the Success of Mass Civic Protest in Tunisia." *Middle East Journal* 67, no. 4 (2013): 547–64.

BIBLIOGRAPHY

Assaad, Ragui. "Formal and Informal Institutions in the Labor Market, with Applications to the Construction Sector in Egypt." *World Development* 21, no. 6 (June 1, 1993): 925–39. https://doi.org/10.1016/0305-750X(93)90052-B.

———. "Making Sense of Arab Labor Markets: The Enduring Legacy of Dualism." *IZA Journal of Labor & Development* 3 (April 25, 2014). https://doi.org/10.1186/2193-9020-3-6.

Assaad, Ragui, and Mongi Boughzala, eds. *The Tunisian Labor Market in an Era of Transition.* Oxford: Oxford University Press, 2018.

Assaad, Ragui, and Caroline Krafft. "Labor Market Dynamics and Youth Unemployment in the Middle East and North Africa: Evidence from Egypt, Jordan and Tunisia." Economic Research Forum Working Paper. Cairo, April 2016.

Atkinson, Paul, and David Silverman. "Kundera's Immortality: The Interview Society and the Invention of the Self." *Qualitative Inquiry* 3, no. 3 (September 1, 1997): 304–25. https://doi.org/10.1177/107780049700300304.

Ayadi, Lotfi, et al. "Estimating Informal Trade Across Tunisia's Land Borders." World Bank Report. Policy Research Working Paper. World Bank, December 1, 2013. https://documents.worldbank.org/en/publication/documents-reports/documentdetail/856231468173645854/estimating-informal-trade-across-tunisias-land-borders.

Ayubi, Nazih N. *Over-Stating the Arab State: Politics and Society in the Middle East.* New ed. London: Tauris, 1996.

Azabou, Mongi, and Jeffrey B. Nugent. "Tax Farming: Anachronism or Optimal Contract? An Illustration with Respect to Tunisia's Weekly Markets." In *Contributions to Economic Analysis*, vol. 183, ed. Mustapha K. Nabli and Jeffrey B. Nugent, 178–99. Amsterdam: Elsevier, 1989. https://doi.org/10.1016/B978-0-444-87487-0.50016-5.

Babuta, Alexander, and Cathy Haenlein. "Commodity Smuggling in the Maghreb: A Silent Threat." Policy brief. Rabat, Morocco: Policy Center for the New South, May 2018. https://www.africaportal.org/publications/commodity-smuggling-maghreb-silent-threat/.

Bader, Mahmoud, Hanan Dakhil, Mohamed Eljarh, Mohamed Elmagbri, Faraj Garman, Jean-Louis Perroux, and Haitham Younes. "Libyan Local Governance Case Studies." Brussels: European Union Delegation to Libya, July 2017.

Baghdadi, Leila, Hassan Arouri, and Bob Rijkers. "How Do Dictators Get Rich? State Capture in Ben Ali's Tunisia." In *Crony Capitalism in the Middle East: Business and Politics from Liberalization to the Arab Spring*, ed. Ishac Diwan, Adeel Malik, and Izak Atiyas. Oxford: Oxford University Press, 2019.

Baker, S. E., R. Edwards, and Mark Doidge. "How Many Qualitative Interviews Is Enough? Expert Voices and Early Career Reflections on Sampling and Cases in Qualitative Research." 2012.

Barany, Zoltan. "Comparing the Arab Revolts: The Role of the Military." *Journal of Democracy* 22, no. 4 (October 14, 2011): 24–35. https://doi.org/10.1353/jod.2011.0069.

Barkey, Karen. *Bandits and Bureaucrats: Ottoman Route to State Centralization.* Ithaca, N.Y: Cornell University Press, 1994.

Barrie, Christopher. "The Process of Revolutionary Protest: Development and Democracy in the Tunisian Revolution of 2010–2011." *SocArXiv*, August 10, 2018. https://doi.org/10.31235/osf.io/eu5b4.

BIBLIOGRAPHY

Barzoukas, Georgios. "Drug Trafficking in the MENA—the Economics and the Politics." EISS Brief Issue. Paris: European Institute for Security Studies, 2017.

Bayart, Jean-Francois, Stephen Ellis, and Beatrice Hibou. *The Criminalization of the State in Africa*. Oxford: Boydell and Brewer, 1999.

Bayat, Asef. "Activism and Social Development in the Middle East." *International Journal of Middle East Studies* 34, no. 1 (2002): 1–28.

———. "Un-Civil Society: The Politics of the 'Informal People.'" *Third World Quarterly* 18, no. 1 (March 1, 1997): 53–72. https://doi.org/10.1080/01436599715055.

BBC. "Tunisia Builds Anti-Terror Barrier." *BBC News*, February 7, 2016. https://www.bbc.com/news/world-africa-35515229.

———. "Tunisia Militants Jailed for 2015 Attacks," *BBC News*, February 9, 2019. https://www.bbc.com/news/world-africa-47183027.

Beckerleg, S. E, and G. L. Hundt. "The Characteristics and Recent Growth of Heroin Injecting in a Kenyan Coastal Town." *Addiction Research & Theory* 12, no. 1 (2004): 41–53.

Behuria, Pritish, Lars Buur, and Hazel Gray. "Studying Political Settlements in Africa." *African Affairs* 116, no. 464 (July 1, 2017): 508–25. https://doi.org/10.1093/afraf/adx019.

Bellin, Eva. "Reconsidering the Robustness of Authoritarianism in the Middle East: Lessons from the Arab Spring." *Comparative Politics* 44, no. 2 (January 1, 2012): 127–49. https://doi.org/10.5129/001041512798838021.

Benda-Beckmann, Franz von. "Who's Afraid of Legal Pluralism?" *Journal of Legal Pluralism and Unofficial Law* 34, no. 47 (January 1, 2002): 37–82. https://doi.org/10.1080/07329113.2002.10756563.

Bennafla, Karine, and Montserrat Emperador Badimon. "Le 'Maroc inutile' redécouvert par l'action publique: Les cas de Sidi Ifni et Bouarfa." *Politique africaine* 120, no. 4 (2010): 67–86.

Bennett, A. "Process Tracing: A Bayesian Perspective." In *The Oxford Handbook of Political Methodology*, ed. J. M. Box-Steffensmeier and D. Collier, 702–21. New York: Oxford University Press, 2008.

Bensassi, Sami, Anne Brockmeyer, Gael J. R. F. Raballand, and Matthieu Pellerin. "Commerce Algérie-Mali: La normalité de l'informalité." World Bank, March 22, 2015. http://documents.worldbank.org/curated/en/202591468195569460/Commerce-Alg%C3%A9rie-Mali-la-normalit%C3%A9-de-l-informalit%C3%A9.

Bensassi, Sami, and Jade Siu. "Quantifying Missing and Hidden Trade: An Economic Perspective." In Gallien and Weigand, *The Routledge Handbook of Smuggling*.

Bergh, Sylvia I. "Traditional Village Councils, Modern Associations, and the Emergence of Hybrid Political Orders in Rural Morocco." *Peace Review* 21, no. 1 (March 1, 2009): 45–53. https://doi.org/10.1080/10402650802690060.

Berriane, Mohamed, and Andreas Kagermeier. *Remigration Nador I: Regionalanalyse der Provinz Nador*. Passau, Ger.: Passavia, 1996.

Biernacki, Patrick, and Dan Waldorf. "Snowball Sampling: Problems and Techniques of Chain Referral Sampling." *Sociological Methods & Research* 10, no. 2 (November 1, 1981): 141–63. https://doi.org/10.1177/004912418101000205.

Bierschenk, Thomas, and Jean-Pierre Olivier de Sardan. "ECRIS: Enquête Collective Rapide d'Identification des conflits et des groupes Stratégiques...." *Bulletin de l'APAD*, no. 7 (July 1, 1994). http://apad.revues.org/2173.

———, eds. *States at Work: Dynamics of African Bureaucracies*. Leiden: Brill, 2014.

BIBLIOGRAPHY

Blackman, Alexandra. "Ideological Responses to Settler Colonialism: Political Identities in Post-Independence Tunisia." Working paper, February 2019.
Blickman, Tom. "Morocco and Cannabis: Reduction, Containment or Acceptance." Drug Policy Briefing. Amsterdam: Transnational Institute, March 2017.
Boege, Volker, M. Anne Brown, Kevin P. Clements, and Anna Nolan. "On Hybrid Political Orders and Emerging States: What Is Failing—States in the Global South or Research and Politics in the West?" *Berghof Handbook for Conflict Transformation Dialogue Series*, no. 8 (April 9, 2009): 15–35.
Bolt, Maxim. "Navigating Formality in a Migrant Labour Force." In *The Political Economy of Life in Africa*, ed. W. Abdebanwi. Woodbridge, UK: James Currey, 2017.
Boone, Catherine. "Trade, Taxes, and Tribute: Market Liberalizations and the New Importers in West Africa." *World Development* 22, no. 3 (March 1994): 453–67.
Booth, David. "Introduction: Working with the Grain? The Africa Power and Politics Programme." *IDS Bulletin* 42, no. 2 (March 1, 2011): 1–10. https://doi.org/10.1111/j.1759-5436.2011.00206.x.
———. "Political Settlements and Developmental Regimes: Issues from Comparative Research." Addis Ababa: Ethiopian International Institute for Peace and Development, 2015.
Bouammali, Noureddine. "Emigration internationale de travail et mutations socio-spatiales d'une ville frontalière: Cas d'Oujda (Maroc)." PhD dissertation, Tours, Fr., 2006. http://www.theses.fr/2006TOUR1502.
Boukhars, Anouar. "Barriers Versus Smugglers: Algeria and Morocco's Battle for Border Security." Washington, D.C.: Carnegie Endowment for International Peace, March 19, 2019.
———. "The Potential Jihadi Windfall from the Militarization of Tunisia's Border Region with Libya." Washington, D.C.: Carnegie Endowment for International Peace, January 26, 2018. https://carnegieendowment.org/2018/01/26/potential-jihadi-windfall-from-militarization-of-tunisia-s-border-region-with-libya-pub-75365.
Boutry, Timothee. "Le roi du Maroc réconforte les sinistrés." *Le Parisien*, February 29, 2004. http://www.leparisien.fr/faits-divers/le-roi-du-maroc-reconforte-les-sinistres-29-02-2004-2004792655.php.
Bratton, Michael. "Formal Versus Informal Institutions in Africa." *Journal of Democracy* 18, no. 3 (July 31, 2007): 96–110. https://doi.org/10.1353/jod.2007.0041.
Brenner, David. "Rebels, Smugglers and (the Pitfalls of) Economic Pacification." In Gallien and Weigand, *The Routledge Handbook of Smuggling*.
Bromley, R. J., Richard Symanski, and Charles M. Good. "The Rationale of Periodic Markets." *Annals of the Association of American Geographers* 65, no. 4 (1975): 530–37.
Brown, Nathan. "Brigands and State Building: The Invention of Banditry in Modern Egypt." *Comparative Studies in Society and History* 32, no. 2 (April 1990): 258–81. https://doi.org/10.1017/S0010417500016480.
Business News Tn. "Ben Guerdène: 3 millions de dinars saisis chez un réseau de financement de terroristes." *Business News Tn* (blog), June 28, 2017. http://www.businessnews.com.tn/ben-guerdene—demantelement-dun-reseau-de-financement-du-terrorisme-et-saisi-de-3-millions-de-dinars,520,73278,3.
Cammack, Perry, Michele Dunne, Amr Hamzwy, Marc Lynch, Marwan Muasher, Yezid Sayigh, and Maha Yahya. *Arab Fractures: Citizens, States, and Social Contracts*. Washington, D.C.: Carnegie Endowment for International Peace, 2017.

BIBLIOGRAPHY

Cantens, Thomas, and Gael J. R. F. Raballand. "Cross-Border Trade, Insecurity and the Role of Customs: Some Lessons from Six Field Studies in (Post-)Conflict Regions." ICTD Working Paper. Brighton, UK: International Centre for Tax and Development, August 2017.

Carroll, Erica. "Taxing Ghana's Informal Sector: The Experience of Women." Occasional Paper. Christian Aid, 2011.

Cassarino, Jean-Pierre. "Approaching Borders and Frontiers in North Africa." *International Affairs* 93, no. 4 (July 1, 2017): 883–96. https://doi.org/10.1093/ia/iix124.

Castro, Miguel Ángel Pérez, and Miguel Ángel Montero Alonso. "Estudios economicos sectorales de la Cuidad Autónoma de Melilla." Melilla: Consejería de Economía y Hacienda de la Ciudad Autónoma de Melilla, December 2014.

Cavatorta, Francesco. "Morocco: The Promise of Democracy and the Reality of Authoritarianism." *International Spectator* 51, no. 1 (January 2, 2016): 86–98. https://doi.org/10.1080/03932729.2016.1126155.

Charrad, Mounira M. "Central and Local Patrimonialism: State-Building in Kin-Based Societies." *ANNALS of the American Academy of Political and Social Science* 636, no. 1 (July 1, 2011): 49–68. https://doi.org/10.1177/0002716211401825.

Cherif, Youssef. "Tunisia's Risky War on Corruption." *Sada—Carnegie Endowment for International Piece*, July 18, 2017. https://carnegieendowment.org/sada/71569.

Chomiak, Laryssa. "The Making of a Revolution in Tunisia." *Middle East Law and Governance* 3 (2011): 68.

Christelow, Allan. "Property and Theft in Kano at the Dawn of the Groundnut Boom, 1912–1914." *International Journal of African Historical Studies* 20, no. 2 (1987): 225–43. https://doi.org/10.2307/219841.

Cleaver, Frances. *Development Through Bricolage: Rethinking Institutions for Natural Resource Management*. Abingdon, UK: Routledge, 2012.

———. "In Pursuit of Arrangements That Work: Bricolage, Practical Norms and Everyday Water Governance." In *Real Governance and Practical Norms in Africa: The Game of the Rules*, ed. Tom de Herdt and Jean-Pierre Olivier de Sardan. London: Routledge, 2015.

———. "Institutional Bricolage, Conflict and Cooperation in Usangu." *IDS Bulletin* 32, no. 4 (October 2001): 26–35.

———. "Reinventing Institutions: Bricolage and the Social Embeddedness of Natural Resource Management." *European Journal of Development Research* 14, no. 2 (December 1, 2002): 11–30. https://doi.org/10.1080/714000425.

Collin, J., E. Legresley, R. MacKenzie, S. Lawrence, and K. Lee. "Complicity in Contraband: British American Tobacco and Cigarette Smuggling in Asia." *Tobacco Control* 13 Suppl 2 (December 2004): ii104–11. https://doi.org/10.1136/tc.2004.009357.

Coquery-Vidrovitch, Catherine. *Frontières, problèmes de frontières dans le tiers-monde*. Paris: Éditions L'Harmattan, 2000.

Daoudi, Fatiha. *Vécu frontalier algéro-marocain depuis 1994: Quotidien d'une population séparée*. Paris: Éditions L'Harmattan, 2015.

Devarajan, Shantayanan, and Lili Mottaghi. "Towards a New Social Contract." World Bank, April 1, 2015. http://documents.worldbank.org/curated/en/202171468299130698/Towards-a-new-social-contract.

BIBLIOGRAPHY

DirectInfo. "Hédi Yahia, Accusé de Contrebande, Vient d'être Acquitté." *Directinfo.com* (blog), June 17, 2017. https://directinfo.webmanagercenter.com/2017/06/17/hedi-yahia-accuse-de-contrebande-vient-detre-acquitte/.

Diwan, Ishac, Adeel Malik, and Izak Atiyas, eds. *Crony Capitalism in the Middle East: Business and Politics from Liberalization to the Arab Spring*. Oxford: Oxford University Press, 2019.

Dobler, Gregor. "The Green, the Grey and the Blue: A Typology of Cross-Border Trade in Africa." *Journal of Modern African Studies* 54, no. 1 (March 2016): 145–69. https://doi.org/10.1017/S0022278X15000993.

———. "Localising Smuggling." In Gallien and Weigand, *The Routledge Handbook of Smuggling*.

Doornbos, Martin. "Researching African Statehood Dynamics: Negotiability and Its Limits." *Development and Change* 41, no. 4 (2010): 747–69. https://doi.org/10.1111/j.1467-7660.2010.01650.x.

Eaton, Tim. "Libya—Rich in Oil, Leaking Fuel." Chatham House Shorthand Story. London: Chatham House, 2019. https://www.chathamhouse.org/2019/10/libya-rich-oil-leaking-fuel.

———. *Libya's War Economy: Predation, Profiteering and State Weakness*. London: Chatham House, 2018. https://www.chathamhouse.org/sites/files/chathamhouse/publications/research/2018-04-12-libyas-war-economy-eaton-final.pdf.

———. "Theft and Smuggling of Petroleum Products." In Gallien and Weigand, *The Routledge Handbook of Smuggling*.

Economist Intelligence Unit. "The Global Illicit Trade Environment Index." London: Economist Intelligence Unit, 2018. https://eiuperspectives.economist.com/sites/default/files/Illicit%20Trade%20WHITEPAPER%20(19%20June%202018).pdf.

Egg, Johny, and Javier Herrera. *Échanges transfrontaliers et intégration régionale en Afrique subsaharienne*. Paris: Éditions de l'Aube, 1998.

Eibl, Ferdinand, and Adeel Malik. "The Politics of Partial Liberalization: Cronyism and Non-Tariff Protection in Mubarak's Egypt." CSAE Working Paper Series. Centre for the Study of African Economies, Oxford University, 2016. https://ideas.repec.org/p/csa/wpaper/2016-27.html.

Eilat, Yair, and Clifford Zinnes. "The Shadow Economy in Transition Countries: Friend or Foe? A Policy Perspective." *World Development* 30, no. 7 (July 1, 2002): 1233–54. https://doi.org/10.1016/S0305-750X(02)00036-0.

El-Haddad, Amirah, and May Gadallah. "The Informalization of the Egyptian Economy (1998—2012): A Factor in Growing Wage Inequality?" Economic Research Forum Working Paper. Cairo, 2018.

El-Khawas, Mohamed A. "North Africa and the War on Terror." *Mediterranean Quarterly* 14, no. 4 (December 4, 2003): 176–91.

Elliott, Katja Zvan. "Reforming the Moroccan Personal Status Code: A Revolution for Whom?" *Mediterranean Politics* 14, no. 2 (July 1, 2009): 213–27. https://doi.org/10.1080/13629390902987659.

Ellis, Matthew H. *Desert Borderland: The Making of Modern Egypt and Libya*. Stanford, Calif.: Stanford University Press, 2018.

Ellis, Stephen, and Janet MacGaffey. "Research on Sub-Saharan Africa's Unrecorded International Trade: Some Methodological and Conceptual Problems." *African Studies Review* 39, no. 2 (September 1996): 19–41.

BIBLIOGRAPHY

Elloumi, M. *Développement rural, environnement et enjeux territoriaux: Regards croisés Oriental marocain et Sud-Est tunisien*, ed. P. Bonte, Henri Guillaume, and M. Mahdi. Tunis: Cérès, 2009. http://www.documentation.ird.fr/hor/fdi:0100 50190.

El-Said, Hamed, and Jane Harrigan. "Economic Reform, Social Welfare, and Instability: Jordan, Egypt, Morocco, and Tunisia, 1983–2004." *Middle East Journal* 68, no. 1 (2014): 99–121.

Fabiani, Riccardo. "The Multiple Types of Interaction between Jihadists, Criminals and Local Communities." In *Transnational Organized Crime and Political Actors in the Maghreb and Sahel*, by Jihane Ben Yahia, Riccardo Fabiani, Max Gallien, and Matthew Herbert. Mediterranean Dialogue Series 17. Berlin: Konrad Adenauer Foundation, 2019.

Fahim, Kareem. "Slap to a Man's Pride Set off Tumult in Tunisia." *New York Times*, January 21, 2011. https://www.nytimes.com/2011/01/22/world/africa/22sidi.html.

Fairfield, Tasha, and Andrew Charman. "The Bayesian Probability: The Logic of (Political) Science." American Political Science Association Conference, San Francisco, 2015. https://www.researchgate.net/profile/Tasha_Fairfield/publication/281701239 _Bayesian_Probability_The_Logic_of_Political_Science.

Falzon, Mark-Anthony. *Multi-Sited Ethnography: Theory, Praxis and Locality in Contemporary Research*. Abingdon, UK: Routledge, 2016.

Farzanegan, Mohammed Reza. "Illegal Trade in the Iranian Economy: A MIMIC Approach." Cairo, 2007.

FATF. "Improving Global AML/CFT Compliance: On-Going Process, 18 October 2013." Paris: FATF, October 18, 2013. http://www.fatf-gafi.org/countries/a-c/argentina /documents/fatf-compliance-oct-2013.html#Morocco.

———. "Improving Global AML/CFT Compliance: On-Going Process—23 February 2018." Paris: FATF, February 23, 2018. http://www.fatf-gafi.org/countries/a-c /bosniaandherzegovina/documents/fatf-compliance-february-2018.html#Tunisia.

Fawcett, Louise. "States and Sovereignty in the Middle East: Myths and Realities." *International Affairs* 93 (July 1, 2017): 789–807. https://doi.org/10.1093/ia/iix122.

Fearon, James D., and David D. Laitin. "Ethnicity, Insurgency, and Civil War." *American Political Science Review* 97, no. 1 (February 2003): 75–90. https://doi.org/10.1017 /S0003055403000534.

France24. "احتجاجات في جنوب تونس بعد إغلاق حكومة الوفاق الليبية معبر رأس جدير الحدودي." *France24* (blog), August 29, 2018. https://www.france24.com/ar/20180829-%D8%AA%D9% 88%D9%86%D8%B3 -%D 9%84 %D9 %8A %D8 %A8 %D9%8A %D8 %A7 -%D9% 85%D8%B9%D8%A8%D8%B1 -%D8%AD%D8%AF%D9%88%D8%AF -%D8 %A8% D9%86 -%D9%82%D8%B1%D8%AF%D8%A7%D9%86 -%D8%AA%D9 %87 %D8% B1%D9%8A%D8%A8 -%D8%A7%D8%AD%D8%AA%D8%AC%D8%A7%D8%AC% D8%A7%D8%AA-%D8%B5%D8%AF%D8%A7%D9%85%D8%A7%D8%AA.

Freund, Caroline, Antonio Nucifora, and Bob Rijkers. "All in the Family: State Capture in Tunisia." World Bank, March 1, 2014. http://documents.worldbank.org /curated/en/440461468173649062/All-in-the-family-state-capture-in-Tunisia.

Frey, Bruno S., and Hannelore Weck-Hanneman. "The Hidden Economy as an 'Unobserved' Variable." *European Economic Review* 26, no. 1–2 (1984): 33–53.

Gallien, Max. "Beyond Informality: The Political Economy of Illegal Trade in Southern Tunisia." MPhil thesis, University of Oxford, 2015.

BIBLIOGRAPHY

———. "Cigarette Smuggling: Trends, Taxes and Big Tobacco." In Gallien and Weigand, *The Routledge Handbook of Smuggling*.
———. "An Economic Malaise Lies at the Heart of Libya-Tunisia Border Standoff." *Middle East Eye*, July 31, 2018. https://www.middleeasteye.net/columns/economic-malaise-heart-libya-tunisia-border-standoff-883226567.
———. "Informal Institutions and the Regulation of Smuggling in North Africa." *Perspectives on Politics* 18, no. 2 (June 2020): 492–508. https://doi.org/10.1017/S1537592719001026.
Gallien, Max, and Matthew Herbert. "Divided They Fall: Frontiers, Borderlands and Stability in North Africa." North Africa Report. Pretoria, South Africa: Institute for Security Studies, March 3, 2021.
———. "GITOC Report on Drugs in North Africa." London: Global Initiative Against Transnational Organised Crime, 2019.
———. "Out of the Streets and Into the Boats: Tunisia's Irregular Migration Surge." Washington, D.C.: Atlantic Council, November 27, 2017. http://www.atlanticcouncil.org/blogs/menasource/out-of-the-streets-and-into-the-boats-tunisia-s-irregular-migration-surge.
Gallien, Max, and Vanessa van den Boogaard. "Formalization and Its Discontents: Conceptual Fallacies and Ways Forward." *Development and Change* 54, no. 3 (2023): 490–513. https://doi.org/10.1111/dech.12768.
———. "Informal Workers and the State: The Politics of Connection and Disconnection during a Global Pandemic." Brighton, UK: Institute of Development Studies, 2021.
Gallien, Max, and Florian Weigand. "Channeling Contraband: How States Shape International Smuggling Routes." *Security Studies* 30, no. 1 (March 12, 2021): 1–28. https://doi.org/10.1080/09636412.2021.1885728.
———, eds. Gallien, Max, and Florian Weigand. *The Routledge Handbook of Smuggling*. Abingdon, UK: Routledge, 2021
———. "Studying Smuggling." In Gallien and Weigand, *The Routledge Handbook of Smuggling*.
Gallien, Max, and Yasmine Zarhloule. "Moroccan Farmers' Protests Highlight the Human Toll of Border Dispute." *Middle East Eye*, April 5, 2021. https://www.middleeasteye.net/opinion/morocco-farmers-protests-highlight-human-toll-algeria-border-dispute.
Gambetta, Diego. *The Sicilian Mafia: The Business of Private Protection*. Cambridge, Mass.: Harvard University Press, 1996.
Gazzotti, Lorena. "The 'War on Smugglers' and the Expansion of the Border Apparatus." In Gallien and Weigand, *The Routledge Handbook of Smuggling*.
George, A., and A. Bennett. *Case Studies and Theory Development*. Cambridge, Mass.: MIT Press, 2005.
Gerring, John. *Case Study Research—Principles and Practices*. Cambridge: Cambridge University Press, 2007.
Ghorbal, Sami. "Tunisie: Aux origines de la chute de Chafik Jarraya, l'homme qui personnifiait l'impunité de la corruption." *JeuneAfrique.com* (blog), June 16, 2017. https://www.jeuneafrique.com/mag/444630/politique/tunisie-aux-origines-de-chute-de-chafik-jarraya-lhomme-personnifiait-limpunite-de-corruption/.
Gisselquist, R. M. "Paired Comparison and Theory Development: Considerations for Case Selection." *PS: Political Science & Politics* 47, no. 2 (2014): 477–84.

BIBLIOGRAPHY

Goodfellow, Tom. "Political Informality: Deals, Trust Networks, and the Negotiation of Value in the Urban Realm." *Journal of Development Studies* 56, no. 2 (March 4, 2019): 1–17. https://doi.org/10.1080/00220388.2019.1577385.

———. "Seeing Political Settlements Through the City: A Framework for Comparative Analysis of Urban Transformation." *Development and Change* 49, no. 1 (2018): 199–222. https://doi.org/10.1111/dech.12361.

Goodhand, Jonathan. "Bandits, Borderlands and Opium Wars in Afghanistan." In *A Companion to Border Studies*, ed. Thomas M. Wilson and Hastings Donnan, 332–53. Chichester, UK: Wiley, 2012. http://onlinelibrary.wiley.com/doi/10.1002/9781118255223.ch19/summary.

———. "Corrupting or Consolidating the Peace? The Drugs Economy and Post-Conflict Peacebuilding in Afghanistan." *International Peacekeeping* 15, no. 3 (June 1, 2008): 405–23. https://doi.org/10.1080/13533310802058984.

———. "Epilogue: The View from the Border." In *Violence on the Margins*, ed. Benedikt Korf and Timothy Raeymaekers, 247–64. Palgrave Series in African Borderlands Studies. New York: Palgrave Macmillan, 2013. https://doi.org/10.1057/9781137333995_10.

———. "From War Economy to Peace Economy? Reconstruction and State Building in Afghanistan." *Journal of International Affairs* 1, no. 58 (2004).

———. "Frontiers and Wars: The Opium Economy in Afghanistan." *Journal of Agrarian Change* 5, no. 2 (April 1, 2005): 191–216. https://doi.org/10.1111/j.1471-0366.2005.00099.x.

Goodhand, Jonathan, Jan Koehler, and Jasmine Bhatia. "Trading Spaces: Afghan Borderland Brokers and the Transformation of the Margins 1." In Gallien and Weigand, *The Routledge Handbook of Smuggling*.

Goodhand, Jonathan, and David Mansfield. "Drugs and (Dis)Order: A Study of the Opium Trade, Political Settlements and State-Making in Afghanistan." Working paper. London: Crisis States Research Centre, 2010.

Goodhand, Jonathan, and Patrick Meehan. "Spatialising Political Settlements." In *Accord Insight 4: Borderlands and Peacebuilding*, ed. Sharri Polanski and Zahbia Yousuf. London: Conciliation Resources, 2018.

Gray, Hazel. "Access Orders and the 'New' New Institutional Economics of Development." *Development and Change* 47, no. 1 (2016): 51–75. https://doi.org/10.1111/dech.12211.

———. *Turbulence and Order in Economic Development: Institutions and Economic Transformation in Tanzania and Vietnam*. Oxford: Oxford University Press, 2018.

———. "Understanding and Deploying the Political Settlement Framework in Africa." In *Oxford Research Encyclopedia of Politics*, ed. Hazel Gray. Oxford: Oxford University Press, 2019. https://doi.org/10.1093/acrefore/9780190228637.013.888.

Greif, Avner. *Institutions and the Path to the Modern Economy: Lessons from Medieval Trade*. Cambridge: Cambridge University Press, 2006.

Guillaume, Henri. *Entre désertification et éveloppement: La Jeffara tunisienne*. Tunis: Cérès Editions, 2006.

Haddar, Mohamed. "Rapport sur les relations économiques entre la Tunisie et la Libye auprès du Plan Régional d'Environnement et de Développement Durable Du Gouvernorat de Médenine (PREDD) et de la Table Ronde Économique (TRE) Médenine." Tunis, 2013.

BIBLIOGRAPHY

Hagmann, Tobias. *Stabilization, Extraversion and Political Settlements in Somalia*. London: Rift Valley Institute, 2016.
Hagmann, T., and D. Peclard. "Negotiating Statehood: Dynamics of Power and Domination in Africa." *Development and Change*, no. 41 (2010): 539–62.
Hajiira and the Issue of the Border Between Algeria and Morocco (author's translation). Youtube video, 2013. https://www.youtube.com/watch?v=hDF-vMCBBuo&feature=youtu.be.
Hale, Henry E. "Formal Constitutions in Informal Politics: Institutions and Democratization in Post-Soviet Eurasia." *World Politics* 63, no. 4 (October 2011): 581–617. https://doi.org/10.1017/S0043887111000189.
Hammersley, M., and A. Traianou. *Ethics in Qualitative Research—Controversies and Contexts*. Thousand Oaks, Calif.: Sage, 2012.
Hanlon, Querine, and Matthew Herbert. *Border Security Challenges in the Grand Maghreb*. Washington, D.C.: United States Institute of Peace Press, 2015.
Helmke, Gretchen, and Stephen Levitsky. "Informal Institutions and Comparative Politics: A Research Agenda." *Perspectives on Politics* 2, no. 4 (2004): 725–40.
Henry, Clement Moore, and Robert Springborg. *Globalization and the Politics of Development in the Middle East*. Cambridge: Cambridge University Press, 2010.
Herbert, Matthew. "At the Edge—Trends and Routes of North African Clandestine Migrants." ISS Paper. Pretoria, South Africa: Institute for Security Studies, November 2016.
———. "The Butcher's Bill—Cocaine Trafficking in North Africa." Geneva: Global Initiative Against Transnational Organised Crime, September 21, 2018. https://globalinitiative.net/the-butchers-bill-cocaine-trafficking-in-north-africa/.
———. "From Contraband to Conflict: Links Between Smuggling and Violence in the Borderlands of Meso-America and North Africa." PhD dissertation, Fletcher School of Law & Diplomacy, Tufts University, 2019.
———. "Rising Irregular Migration and Its Complicated Politics in the Maghreb." ISS Report. Institute for Security Studies, 2019.
Herbert, Matthew, and Max Gallien. "The Risks of Hardened Borders in North Africa." Washington, D.C.: Carnegie Endowment for International Peace, August 16, 2018. https://carnegieendowment.org/sada/77053.
Herdt, Tom de, and Jean-Pierre Olivier de Sardan, eds. *Real Governance and Practical Norms in Sub-Saharan Africa: The Game of the Rules*. London: Routledge, 2015.
Hertog, Steffen. "Is There an Arab Variety of Capitalism?" Working paper. Economic Research Forum, June 12, 2016. https://ideas.repec.org/p/erg/wpaper/1068.html.
———. "The Political Economy of Distribution in the Middle East: Is There Scope for a New Social Contract?" *International Development Policy | Revue internationale de politique de développement* 7, no. 7 (February 1, 2017). https://doi.org/10.4000/poldev.2270.
———. "The Role of Cronyism in Arab Capitalism." In *Crony Capitalism in the Middle East: Business and Politics from Liberalizaton to the Arab Spring*, ed. Ishac Diwan, Adeel Malik, and Izak Atiyas, 39–64. Oxford: Oxford University Press, 2019.
Heuser, Cristoph. "The Effect of Illicit Economies in the Margins of the State—the VRAEM." *Journal of Illicit Economies and Development* 1, no. 1 (January 14, 2019): 23–36. https://doi.org/10.31389/jied.7.
Hibou, Béatrice. *The Force of Obedience*. Cambridge: Polity, 2011.

———. "The 'Social Capital' of the State as an Agent of Deception: Or the Rules of Economic Intelligence." In *The Criminalization of the State in Africa*, ed. Jean-Francois Bayart, Stephen Ellis, and Beatrice Hibou. Oxford: Boydell and Brewer, 1999

Hibou, Beátrice, Hamza Meddeb, Mohamed Hamdi, and Euro-Middelhav Menneskerettigheds Netværket. *Tunisia after 14 January and Its Social and Political Economy: The Issues at Stake in a Reconfiguration of European Policy*. Copenhagen: Euro-Mediterranean Human Rights Network, 2011.

Hinnebusch, Raymond. "Authoritarian Persistence, Democratization Theory and the Middle East: An Overview and Critique." *Democratization* 13, no. 3 (June 1, 2006): 373–95. https://doi.org/10.1080/13510340600579243.

Hoffmann, Anja. "Dezentralisierung in Marokko—Hohe Erwartungen." GIGA Focus. Hamburg: German Institute of Global and Area Studies, 2015. https://www.giga-hamburg.de/en/system/files/publications/gf_nahost_1508.pdf.

———. "Morocco Between Decentralization and Recentralization: Encountering the State in the 'Useless Morocco.'" In *Local Politics and Contemporary Transformations in the Arab World*, by Malika Bouziane, Cilja Harders, and Anja Hoffmann. Governance and Limited Statehood Series. Basingstoke, UK: Palgrave Macmillan, 2013.

Holland, Alisha C. "The Distributive Politics of Enforcement." *American Journal of Political Science* 59, no. 2 (April 2015): 357–71.

———. "Forbearance." *American Political Science Review* 110, no. 2 (May 2016): 232–46. https://doi.org/10.1017/S0003055416000083.

Honwana, Alcinda. "'Waithood': Youth Transitions and Social Change." *Development and Equity*, January 1, 2014, 28–40. https://doi.org/10.1163/9789004269729_004.

Houat, Idriss. *Dhahirat At-Tahreeb* (The phenomenon of smuggling). Oujda, Morocco: CCIS Oujda, 2004.

HuffPost Maghreb. "Tunisie: Sit-in Ouvert et Actes de Destruction à Ben Guerdane Suite à La Mort d'un Contrebandier." *HuffPost Maghreb*, September 6, 2016. https://www.huffpostmaghreb.com/2016/09/06/ben-guerdane-contrebande_n_11871190.html.

Human Rights Watch. "Morocco's Truth Commission—Honoring Past Victims During an Uncertain Present." Human Rights Watch, November 2005. https://www.hrw.org/sites/default/files/reports/morocco1105wcover.pdf.

Hüsken, Thomas. "Die Neotribale Wettbewerbsordnung Im Grenzgebiet von Ägypten Und Libyen." *Sociologus* 59, no. 2 (April 1, 2009): 117–43. https://doi.org/10.3790/soc.59.2.117.

———. "The Practice and Culture of Smuggling in the Borderland of Egypt and Libya." *International Affairs* 93, no. 4 (July 1, 2017): 897–915. https://doi.org/10.1093/ia/iix121.

———. "Research in Dangerous Fields: Ethics, Morals, and Practices in the Study of Smuggling." In Gallien and Weigand, *The Routledge Handbook of Smuggling*.

———. *Tribal Politics in the Borderland of Egypt and Libya*. New York: Palgrave Macmillan, 2018.

Hüsken, Thomas, and Georg Klute. "Political Orders in the Making: Emerging Forms of Political Organization from Libya to Northern Mali." *African Security* 8, no. 4 (October 2, 2015): 320–37. https://doi.org/10.1080/19392206.2015.1100502.

BIBLIOGRAPHY

Ianchovichina, Elena. "Eruptions of Popular Anger: The Economics of the Arab Spring and Its Aftermath." MENA Development Report. Washington, D.C.: World Bank, 2018. https://openknowledge.worldbank.org/handle/10986/28961.
Ibrahimi, Khalil. "Développement: Un plan d'urgence pour L'Oriental." Le360 (blog), May 25, 2016. http://fr.le360.ma/economie/developpement-un-plan-durgence-pour-loriental-73699.
Igué, J. Le Commerce de contrebande et les problèmes monétaires en Afrique occidentale. Cotonou: CEFAP, Université Nationale du Benin, 1977.
Igué, John O., and Bio G. Soule. L'etat entrepot au Benin: Commerce informel ou solution a la crise. Paris: Karthala, 1992.
Inkyfada. "تونس-أمراء-الحدود-مسالك-تهريب-السلاح," December 8, 2017. https://inkyfada.com/ar/2017/12/08/%D8%AA%D9%88%D9%86%D8%B3-%D8%A3%D9%85%D8%B1%D8%A7%D8%A1-%D8%A7%D9%84%D8%AD%D8%AF%D9%88%D8%AF-%D9%85%D8%B3%D8%A7%D9%84%D9%83-%D8%AA%D9%87%D8%B1%D9%8A%D8%A8-%D8%A7%D9%84%D8%B3%D9%84%D8%A7%D8%AD/.
International Alert. "Marginalisation, Insecurity and Uncertainty on the Tunisian-Libyan Border." International Alert, 2016. http://www.international-alert.org/sites/default/files/TunisiaLibya_MarginalisationInsecurityUncertaintyBorder_EN_2016.pdf.
International Crisis Group. "How the Islamic State Rose, Fell and Could Rise Again in the Maghreb." Geneva: International Crisis Group, July 24, 2017.
———. "Tunisia: Confronting Social and Economic Challenges." Geneva: International Crisis Group, June 6, 2012.
———. "Tunisia's Borders: Jihadism and Contraband." Middle East and North Africa Report. Geneva: International Crisis Group, 2013. http://www.crisisgroup.org/en/regions/middle-east-north-africa/north-africa/tunisia/148-tunisia-s-borders-jihadism-and-contraband.aspx.
International Labour Organization. "Women and Men in the Informal Economy: A Statistical Picture." 3rd ed. ILO Report, April 30, 2018. http://www.ilo.org/global/publications/books/WCMS_626831.
Jaabouk, Mohammed. "Maroc/Algérie: L'armée Algérienne creuse des tranchées pour lutter contre le trafic des carburants." Yabiladi.com (blog), July 17, 2013. https://www.yabiladi.com/articles/details/18492/maroc-algerie-l-armee-algerienne-creuse.html.
Jamal, Amaney A., and Michael Robbins. "Social Justice and the Arab Uprisings." American University of Beirut Working Paper Series. Beirut, April 2015. https://scholarworks.aub.edu.lb/bitstream/handle/10938/21216/20150401_sjau.pdf.
Jawhara FM. "توتّر الأوضاع في بنقردان بعد فتح معبر راس جدير." Jawhara FM (blog), September 9, 2018. https://www.jawharafm.net/ar/article/%D8%AA%D9%88%D8%AA%D9%91%D8%B1-%D8%A7%D9%84%D8%A3%D9%88%D8%B6%D8%A7%D8%B9-%D9%81%D9%8A-%D8%A8%D9%86%D9%82%D8%B1%D8%AF%D8%A7%D9%86-%D8%A8%D8%B9%D8%AF-%D9%81%D8%AA%D8%AD-%D9%85%D8%B9-%D8%A8%D8%B1-%D8%B1%D8%A7%D8%B3-%D8%AC%D8%AF%D9%8A%D8%B1-/105/121444.
Jean Ganiagé. Les origines du protectorat francais en tunisie (1861–1881) jean ganiage, 1957. http://archive.org/details/OriginesProtectoratFrancaisEnTunisie.

Jenzen-Jones, N. R., and Ian McCollum. "Web Trafficking—Analysing the Online Trade of Small Arms and Light Weapons in Libya." Small Arms Survey Working Paper. Geneva: Small Arms Survey, 2017.

Joshi, Anuradha, and Joseph Ayee. "Associational Taxation: A Pathway Into the Informal Sector?" In *Taxation and State-Building in Developing Countries*, ed. Deborah Brautigam, Odd-Helge Fjeldstad, and Mick Moore, 183–211. Cambridge: Cambridge University Press, 2008. https://doi.org/10.1017/CBO9780511490897.008.

Joshi, Anuradha, Wilson Prichard, and Christopher Heady. "Taxing the Informal Economy: Challenges, Possibilities and Remaining Questions." *IDS Working Papers* 2013, no. 429 (2013): 1–37. https://doi.org/10.1111/j.2040-0209.2013.00429.x.

Jütting, Johannes, Drechsler Denis, Bartsch Sebastian, and de Soysa Indra. *Informal Institutions: How Social Norms Help or Hinder Development*. Development Centre Studies. Paris: OECD Publishing, 2007.

Juul, Kristine. "Decentralization, Local Taxation and Citizenship in Senegal." *Development and Change* 37, no. 4 (2006): 821–46. https://doi.org/10.1111/j.1467-7660.2006.00503.x.

Kahlaoui, Tarek. "Tunisia's 'War Against Corruption' Feels Like a Fake." *Middle East Eye*, June 14, 2017. http://www.middleeasteye.net/columns/without-more-guarantees-tunisian-government-s-fight-against-corruption-feels-fake-862047549.

Kapitalis. "Arrestation de Wachwacha, baron de la contrebande a Ben Guerdane." *Kapitalis.Com*, June 1, 2017. http://kapitalis.com/tunisie/2017/06/01/arrestation-de-wachwacha-baron-de-la-contrebande-a-ben-guerdane/.

Karstedt, Susanne, and Stephen Farrall. "The Moral Economy of Everyday Crime Markets, Consumers and Citizens." *British Journal of Criminology* 46, no. 6 (November 1, 2006): 1011–36. https://doi.org/10.1093/bjc/azl082.

Kartas, Moncef. "On the Edge? Trafficking and Insecurity at the Tunisian-Libyan Border." Security Assessment in North Africa Working Paper. Geneva: Small Arms Survey, 2013.

Katan, Yvette. *Oujda, une ville frontière du Maroc (1907–1956): Musulmans, juifs et chrétiens en milieu colonial*. Paris: Éditions L'Harmattan, 2000.

Kelsall, Tim. "Going with the Grain in African Development?" *Development Policy Review* 29, no. s1 (2011): s223–51. https://doi.org/10.1111/j.1467-7679.2011.00527.x.

———. "Thinking and Working with Political Settlements." ODI Briefing Papers. ODI, January 2016.

Khaldûn, Ibn. *The Muqaddimah—an Introduction to History*, 1377.

Khan, Mushtaq. "Political Settlements and the Governance of Growth-Enhancing Institutions." Draft paper, Research Paper Series on Growth-Enhancing Governance, 2010.

———. "Rents, Efficiency and Growth." In *Rents, Rent-Seeking and Economic Development: Theory and Evidence in Asia*, ed. Mushtaq Khan and Kwame Sundaram Jomo, 21–69. Cambridge: Cambridge University Press, 2000. http://eprints.soas.ac.uk/9842/.

Khan, Mushtaq, and Kwame Sundaram Jomo. *Rents, Rent-Seeking and Economic Development: Theory and Evidence in Asia*. Cambridge: Cambridge University Press, 2000.

Khang, Hyun-Sung. "MEPs Confirm Commission Blacklist of Countries at Risk of Money Laundering." Press release, European Parliament, February 7, 2018.

http://www.europarl.europa.eu/news/en/press-room/20180202IPR97031/meps-confirm-commission-blacklist-of-countries-at-risk-of-money-laundering.

Kireyev, Alexei, et al. "Economic Integration in the Maghreb: An Untapped Source of Growth." Washington, D.C.: IMF, 2019. https://www.imf.org/en/Publications/Departmental-Papers-Policy-Papers/Issues/2019/02/08/Economic-Integration-in-the-Maghreb-An-Untapped-Source-of-Growth-46273.

Kitschelt, Herbert, and Steven I. Wilkinson. "Citizen–Politician Linkages: An Introduction." In *Patrons, Clients, and Policies*, ed. Herbert Kitschelt and Steven I. Wilkinson, 1–49. Cambridge: Cambridge University Press, 2007. https://doi.org/10.1017/CBO9780511585869.001.

Kopytoff, Igor. *The African Frontier: The Reproduction of Traditional African Societies*. Bloomington: Indiana University Press, 1987.

KPMG. "Illicit Cigarette Trade in the Maghreb Region." 2017.

La Porta, Rafael, and Andrei Shleifer. "Informality and Development." Working paper. National Bureau of Economic Research, June 2014. http://www.nber.org/papers/w20205.

Lacher, Wolfram. "Fault Lines of the Revolution." SWP Research Paper. Berlin: Stiftung Wissenschaft und Politik, May 2013.

Laroussi, Kamel. "Commerce informel et nomadisme moderne." Paris: Ecole des Hautes Études en Sciences Sociales, 2007.

———. "Mutations de la Société Nomade et du commerce caravanier dans le Sud-Est Tunisien à la fin du XIXe siècle." Working paper. 2008. http://www.academia.edu/25965603/Mutations_de_la_soci%C3%A9t%C3%A9_nomade_et_du_commerce_caravanier_dans_le_Sud-Est_tunisien_%C3%A0_la_fin_du_XIXe_si%C3%A8cle.

Laws, Edward. "Political Settlements, Elite Pacts and Governments of National Unity: A Conceptual Study." DLP Background Paper, 2012.

Ledeneva, Alena V. *How Russia Really Works: The Informal Practices That Shaped Post-Soviet Politics and Business*. Ithaca, N.Y.: Cornell University Press, 2006.

Lesiteinfo. "Les chiffres chocs de la criminalité à Oujda." *Lesiteinfo* (blog), April 12, 2018. https://www.lesiteinfo.com/maroc/chiffres-chocs-de-criminalite-a-oujda/.

Levy, Brian. *Working with the Grain: Integrating Governance and Growth in Development Strategies*. Oxford: Oxford University Press, 2014.

Liberation Ma. "19.896 arrestations à Oujda pour des actes criminels visant les biens et les personnes." *Liberation.Ma* (blog), August 5, 2016. https://www.libe.ma/19-896-arrestations-a-Oujda-pour-des-actes-criminels-visant-les-biens-et-les-personnes_a77421.html.

Libya Herald. "Anti-Smuggling Protests as Zuwara Faces Fuel Crisis." June 18, 2017. https://www.libyaherald.com/2017/06/18/anti-smuggling-protests-as-zuwara-faces-fuel-crisis/.

Linz, J., and A. Valenzuela, eds. *The Failure of Presidential Democracy*. Baltimore: Johns Hopkins University Press, 1994.

L'Obs/AFP. "Tunisie: cinq 'terroristes' tués au lendemain des attaques jihadistes de Ben Guerdane." *L'Obs.com*, March 8, 2016. https://www.nouvelobs.com/monde/20160308.AFP9231/tunisie-cinq-terroristes-tues-au-lendemain-des-attaques-jihadistes-de-ben-guerdane.html.

Long, David E., and Bernard Reich, eds. *The Government and Politics of the Middle East and North Africa.* 3rd ed. Boulder, Colo.: Westview Press, 1995.

L'Orient le Jour. "Tunisie: trois jihadistes tués à Ben Guerdane (officiel)." *L'Orient le Jour,* March 10, 2016. https://www.lorientlejour.com/article/974761/tunisie-trois-jihadistes-tues-a-ben-guerdane-officiel.html.

Lugo, Lucia Bird Ruiz-Benitez de. "Human Smuggling in the Time of COVID-19: Lessons from a Pandemic." In Gallien and Weigand, *The Routledge Handbook of Smuggling.*

Lynch, Marc, ed. *The Arab Uprisings Explained: New Contentious Politics in the Middle East.* New York: Columbia University Press, 2014.

———. "The Arab Uprisings Never Ended: The Enduring Struggle to Remake the Middle East Essays." *Foreign Affairs* 100, no. 1 (2021): 111–22.

Maddy-Weitzman, Bruce. "Is Morocco Immune to Upheaval?" *Middle East Quarterly,* January 1, 2012. https://dev.meforum.org/3114/morocco-upheaval.

Maghraoui, Driss. "Constitutional Reforms in Morocco: Between Consensus and Subaltern Politics." *Journal of North African Studies* 16, no. 4 (December 1, 2011): 679–99. https://doi.org/10.1080/13629387.2011.630879.

Malik, Adeel. "Was the Middle East's Economic Descent a Legal or Political Failure? Debating the Islamic Law Matters Thesis." CSAE Working Paper Series. Centre for the Study of African Economies, University of Oxford, 2012. https://ideas.repec.org/p/csa/wpaper/2012-08.html.

Malik, Adeel, and Bassem Awadallah. "The Economics of the Arab Spring." *World Development* 45 (May 2013): 296–313. https://doi.org/10.1016/j.worlddev.2012.12.015.

Malik, Adeel, and Max Gallien. "Border Economies of the Middle East: Why Do They Matter for Political Economy?" *Review of International Political Economy* 27, no. 3 (May 3, 2020): 732–62. https://doi.org/10.1080/09692290.2019.1696869.

Manocchi, Francesca. "How Libya's Oil Smugglers Are Bleeding Country of Cash." *Middle East Eye,* January 29, 2019. https://www.middleeasteye.net/news/how-libyas-oil-smugglers-are-bleeding-country-cash.

Marks, Jon. "Nationalist Policy-Making and Crony Capitalism in the Maghreb: The Old Economics Hinders the New." *International Affairs* 85, no. 5 (September 1, 2009): 951–62. https://doi.org/10.1111/j.1468-2346.2009.00840.x.

Martin, Jean-François. *Histoire de la Tunisie contemporaine: de ferry à Bourguiba 1881–1956.* Paris: Éditions L'Harmattan, 2003.

Masbah, Mohammed. "Transnational Security Challenges in North Africa: Moroccan Foreign Fighters in Syria 2012–2016." *Middle Eastern Studies* 55, no. 2 (March 4, 2019): 182–99. https://doi.org/10.1080/00263206.2018.1538972.

Masri, Safwan M. *Tunisia: An Arab Anomaly.* New York: Columbia University Press, 2017.

McMurray, David A. *In and out of Morocco: Smuggling and Migration in a Frontier Boomtown.* Minneapolis: University of Minnesota Press, 2001.

Meagher, Kate. "A Back Door to Globalisation? Structural Adjustment, Globalisation & Transborder Trade in West Africa." *Review of African Political Economy* 30, no. 95 (2003): 57–75.

———. "Beyond the Shadows: Informal Institutions and Development in Africa—Introduction." *Afrika Spectrum* 43, no. 1 (2008). http://hup.sub.uni-hamburg.de/giga/afsp/index.

———. "Disempowerment from Below: Informal Enterprise Networks and the Limits of Political Voice in Nigeria." *Oxford Development Studies* 42, no. 3 (July 3, 2014): 419–38. https://doi.org/10.1080/13600818.2014.900005.

———. "The Hidden Economy: Informal and Parallel Trade in Northwestern Uganda." *Review of African Political Economy* 17, no. 47 (March 1990): 64–83. https://doi.org/10.1080/03056249008703848.

———. *Identity Economics: Social Networks and the Informal Economy in Nigeria*. Woodbridge, UK: Boydell and Brewer, 2010.

———. "Informal Integration or Economic Subversion? Parallel Trade in West Africa." In *Regional Integration and Cooperation in West Africa: A Multidimensional Perspective*, ed. Real Lavergne. Ottawa: IDRC, 1997.

———. "Informality, Religious Conflict, and Governance in Northern Nigeria: Economic Inclusion in Divided Societies." *African Studies Review* 56, no. 3 (December 2013): 209–34.

———. "Introduction: Special Issue on 'Informal Institutions and Development in Africa.'" *Africa Spectrum* 42, no. 3 (2007): 405–18.

———. "Smuggling Ideologies: From Criminalization to Hybrid Governance in African Clandestine Economies." *African Affairs*, 2014.

———. "The Strength of Weak States? Non-State Security Forces and Hybrid Governance in Africa." *Development and Change* 43 (September 2012): 1073–1101.

———. "Taxing Times: Taxation, Divided Societies and the Informal Economy in Northern Nigeria." *Journal of Development Studies* 54, no. 1 (January 2, 2018): 1–17. https://doi.org/10.1080/00220388.2016.1262026.

Meagher, Kate, and Ilda Lindell. "Introduction." *African Studies Review* 56, no. 3 (December 3, 2013): 57–76.

Meagher, Kate, Kristof Titeca, and Tom de Herdt. "Unravelling Public Authority: Paths of Hybrid Governance in Africa." Justice and Security Research Programme Policy Brief. London School of Economics and Political Science, 2014.

Medani, Khalid Mustafa. *Black Markets and Militants: Informal Networks in the Middle East and Africa*. New ed. Cambridge: Cambridge University Press, 2021.

Meddeb, Hamza. "Courir ou mourir: Course à el khobza et domination au quotidien dans la Tunisie de Ben Ali." PhD thesis, Institut d'études politiques, Paris, 2012.

———. *Peripheral Vision: How Europe Can Help Preserve Tunisia's Fragile Democracy*. ECFR Policy Brief, 2017. https://www.ecfr.eu/publications/summary/peripheral_vision_how_europe_can_preserve_tunisias_democracy_7215.

Medias24. "INDH: Plus de 700 MDH pour 495 projets à Oujda-Angad entre 2005 et 2016." *Medias24*, January 26, 2017.

Megerisi, Tarek. *Order from Chaos: Stabilising Libya the Local Way*. London: European Council on Foreign Relations, 2018. https://www.ecfr.eu/publications/summary/order_from_chaos_stabilising_libya_the_local_way.

Meier, Daniel. "Introduction to the Special Issue: Bordering the Middle East." *Geopolitics* 23, no. 3 (July 3, 2018): 495–504. https://doi.org/10.1080/14650045.2018.1497375.

Mersch, Sarah. "Gegen Terroristen, Schmuggler Und Zivilisten—Wie Tunesien Seine Grenzen Aufrüstet." *Neue Zuricher Zeitung*, March 14, 2019. https://www.nzz.ch/international/tunesien-ruestet-die-grenzen-gegen-schmuggler-und-terroristen-auf-ld.1467111.

Micallef, Mark. "The Human Conveyor Belt: Trends in Human Trafficking and Smuggling in Post-Revolution Libya." Geneva: Global Initiative Against Transnational Organised Crime, March 2017.

———. "Shifting Sands—Libya's Changing Drug Trafficking Dynamics on the Coastal and Desert Borders." Background paper commissioned by the EMCDDA for the EU Drug Markets Report 2019. European Monitoring Centre for Drugs and Addiction, 2019.

Michalak, Laurence. "The Changing Weekly Markets of Tunisia: A Regional Analysis." University of California, Berkeley, 1983.

Middle East Eye. "Protests, Strike Shut Down Tunisian Town Over Libya's Halt of Border Trade." *Middle East Eye*, May 12, 2016. https://www.middleeasteye.net/news/protests-strike-shut-down-tunisian-town-over-libyas-halt-border-trade.

Miles, William F. S. "Jihads and Borders—Social Networks and Spatial Patterns in Africa, Present, Past and Future." In *African Border Disorders*, ed. Olivier Walther and William F. S. Miles. London: Routledge, 2018.

Mill, John Stuart. *The Collected Works of John Stuart Mill*. Vol. 8: *A System of Logic Ratiocinative and Inductive Part II*. 1843.

Mirgani, Suzi, and Suzi Mirgani, eds. "An Overview of Informal Politics in the Middle East." In *Informal Politics in the Middle East*. Oxford, UK: Oxford University Press, 2021. https://doi.org/10.1093/oso/9780197604342.003.0001.

Mohammed VI, King. "Discours de S. M. le Roi Mohammed VI à l'occasion de la visite officielle du souverain dans la région de l'Oriental." Speech, Oujda, Morocco, March 18, 2003. http://www.maroc.ma/fr/discours-royaux/discours-de-sm-le-roi-mohammed-vi-%C3%A0-loccasion-de-la-visite-officielle-du-souverain.

Moller, J., and S. Skaaning. "Explanatory Typologies as a Nested Strategy of Inquiry: Combining Cross-Case and Within-Case Analyses." *Sociological Methods Research* (2015).

Mullin, Corinna, and Brahim Rouabah. "Decolonizing Tunisia's Border Violence: Moving Beyond Imperial Structures and Imaginaries." *Viewpoint Magazine* (blog), February 1, 2018. https://www.viewpointmag.com/2018/02/01/decolonizing-tunisias-border-violence-moving-beyond-imperial-structures-imaginaries/.

Mustapha, Abdul Raufu, Kate Meagher, and Nicholas Awortwi. "Introduction and Overview." In *Political Settlements and Agricultural Transformation in Africa*, ed. Martin Atela and Abdul Raufu Mustapha. Abingdon, UK: Routledge, 2023.

Naceur, Sofian Philip. "Decrypting ICMPD." Tunis: Forum Tunisien pour les Droits Economiques et Sociaux, 2011. https://ftdes.net/en/decrypting-icmpd.

National Initiative for Human Development. "Activities Report 2005—2010." INDH, 2010. http://www.indh.ma/sites/default/files/Publications-2017-10/rap3.pdf.

Nawaat. "Tunisie: Ben Guerdane est le théâtre d'événements sans précédent. La population réclame 'Ras Jdir.'" *Nawaat*, August 15, 2010. https://nawaat.org/portail/2010/08/15/tunisie-ben-gardane-est-le-theatre-devenements-sans-precedent-la-population-reclame-ras-jdir/.

Nessma Online. "Gabès: Saisie de 24 mille litres de carburant de contrebande." *Nessma Online*, February 9, 2017. https://www.nessma.tv/fr/regionale/actu/gabes-saisie-de-24-mille-litres-de-carburant-de-contrebande-5571/10026.

Nordstrom, Carolyn. *Global Outlaws: Crime, Money, and Power in the Contemporary World*. Berkeley: University of California Press, 2007.

BIBLIOGRAPHY

North, Douglass C. *Institutions, Institutional Change and Economic Performance.* Cambridge: Cambridge University Press, 1990.

Nugent, Paul. *Smugglers, Secessionists and Loyal Citizens on the Ghana-Togo Frontier: The Life of the Borderlands Since 1914.* Oxford: James Currey, 2002.

Office de Développement du Sud, Ministère du Développement Régional et de la Planification, République Tunisienne. "Gouvernorat de Médenine en Chiffres 2012." ODS, 2012.

Organisation for Co-operation and Development. *Interactions entre politiques publiques, migrations et développement au Maroc.* Paris: OECD Publishing, 2017.

Ostrom, Elinor. *Understanding Institutional Diversity.* Princeton, N.J.: Princeton University Press, 2005.

Oueslati, Ala. "With Municipal Elections, Tunisia Moves Beyond 'Transition.'" *IPI Global Observatory* (blog), April 30, 2018. https://theglobalobservatory.org/2018/04/tunisia-municipal-elections-beyond-transition/.

Oujda Chamber of Commerce. "La grande distribution à Oujda & ses effets sur le commerce de proximité." Oujda, Morocco, 2009.

Oviedo, Ana María, Mark Roland Thomas, and Kamer Karakurum-Özdemir. *Economic Informality: Causes, Costs, and Policies: A Literature Survey.* World Bank Publications, 2009.

Parks, T., and W. Cole. "Political Settlements: Implications for International Development Policy and Practice." San Francisco: Asia Foundation, 2010. http://www.gsdrc.org/document-library/political-settlements-implications-for-international-development-policy-and-practice/.

Pelham, Nicolas. "Gaza's Tunnel Phenomenon: The Unintended Dynamics of Israel's Siege." *Journal of Palestine Studies* 41, no. 4 (July 1, 2012): 6–31. https://doi.org/10.1525/jps.2012.XLI.4.6.

Perkins, Kenneth. *A History of Modern Tunisia.* 2nd ed. New York: Cambridge University Press, 2014.

Perry, Donna. "Rural Weekly Markets and the Dynamics of Time, Space and Community in Senegal." *Journal of Modern African Studies* 38, no. 3 (September 2000): 461–85.

Pham, J. Peter. "Foreign Influences and Shifting Horizons: The Ongoing Evolution of al Qaeda in the Islamic Maghreb." *Orbis* 55, no. 2 (January 1, 2011): 240–54. https://doi.org/10.1016/j.orbis.2011.01.005.

Pollock, Katherine, and Frederic Wehrey. "The Tunisian-Libyan Border: Security Aspirations and Socioeconomic Realities." Washington, D.C.: Carnegie Endowment for International Peace, August 21, 2018. https://carnegieendowment.org/2018/08/21/tunisian-libyan-border-security-aspirations-and-socioeconomic-realities-pub-77087.

Prentis, Jamie. "Zuwara Feels the Effect of Petrol Smuggling." *Libya Herald* (blog), February 13, 2018. https://www.libyaherald.com/2018/02/14/zuwara-feels-the-effect-of-petrol-smuggling/.

Pressly, Linda. "The 'Mule Women' of Melilla." *BBC News*, October 30, 2013. https://www.bbc.com/news/magazine-24706863.

Prichard, W., and V. van den Boogaard. "Norms, Power and the Socially Embedded Realities of Market Taxation in Northern Ghana." ICTD Working Paper. International Centre for Taxation and Development, 2015.

BIBLIOGRAPHY

Pritchett, Lant, Kunal Sen, and Eric Werker, eds. *Deals and Development: The Political Dynamics of Growth Episodes*. Oxford: Oxford University Press, 2017.

Prud'homme, R. "Informal Local Taxation in Developing Countries." *Environment and Planning C: Government and Policy* 10, no. 1 (March 1, 1992): 1–17. https://doi.org/10.1068/c100001.

Putnam, R. D., R. Leonardi, and R. Nanetti. *Making Democracy Work: Civil Traditions in Modern Italy*. Princeton, N.J: Princeton University Press, 1993.

Putzel, James, and Jonathan Di John. "Political Settlements, Issues Paper." Governance and Social Development Resource Centre, University of Birmingham, 2009.

Qorchi, Mohammed El, Samuel Munzele Maimbo, Samuel Munzele Autmainbo, John F. Wilson, and World Bank. *Informal Funds Transfer Systems: An Analysis of the Informal Hawala System*. Washington, D.C.: International Monetary Fund, 2003.

Raeymaekers, Timothy. "African Boundaries and the New Capitalist Frontier." In *Companion to Border Studies*, ed. Thomas M. Wilson and Hastings Donnan. Chichester, UK: Wiley, 2012.

———. "Reshaping the State in Its Margins: The State, the Market and the Subaltern on a Central African Frontier." *Critique of Anthropology* 32, no. 3 (September 1, 2012): 334–50. https://doi.org/10.1177/0308275X12449248.

———. *Violent Capitalism and Hybrid Identity in the Eastern Congo: Power to the Margins*. New York: Cambridge University Press, 2014.

Raghavan, Sudarsan. "Islamic State, Growing Stronger in Libya, Sets Its Sights on Fragile Neighbor Tunisia." *Washington Post*, May 13, 2016. https://www.washingtonpost.com/world/middle_east/islamic-state-threatens-fragile-tunisia-from-next-door-in-libya/2016/05/13/cd9bd634-f82e-11e5-958d-d038dac6e718_story.html.

Raineri, Luca. "Cross-Border Smuggling in North Niger: The Morality of the Informal and the Construction of a Hybrid Order." In *Governance Beyond the Law: The Immoral, the Illegal, the Criminal*, ed. Abel Polese, Alessandra Russo, and Francesco Strazzari, 227–45. International Political Economy Series. Cham, Switz.: Springer International, 2019. https://doi.org/10.1007/978-3-030-05039-9_12.

———. "Drug Trafficking in the Sahara Desert: Follow the Money and Find Land Grabbing." In *The Illicit and Illegal in Regional and Urban Governance and Development*, ed. Francesco Chiodelli, Tim Hall, and Ray Hudson. London: Routledge, 2017.

Raineri, Luca, and Francesco Strazzari. "Drug Smuggling and the Stability of Fragile States. The Diverging Trajectories of Mali and Niger." *Journal of Intervention and Statebuilding* 16, no. 2 (May 17, 2021): 1–18. https://doi.org/10.1080/17502977.2021.1896207.

Réalités Online. "Ouverture du passage frontalier de Ras Jedir." *Toutes les dernières news en Tunisie et dans le monde* (blog), August 19, 2016. https://www.realites.com.tn/2016/08/ouverture-du-passage-frontalier-de-ras-jedir/.

Reitano, Tuesday, and Mark Shaw. "People's Perspectives of Organised Crime in West Africa and the Sahel." ISS Report. Dakar: Institute for Security Studies, April 2014.

Renard, Thomas, ed. *Returnees in the Maghreb: Comparing Policies on Returning Foreign Terrorist Fighters in Egypt, Morocco and Tunisia*. Brussels: Egmont—Royal Institute for International Relations, 2019.

Reno, William. "Clandestine Economies, Violence and States in Africa." *Journal of International Affairs* 53, no. 2 (2000): 433–59.

———. *Warlord Politics and African States*. Boulder, Colo.: Lynne Rienner, 1998.
Reyntjens, Filip. "Legal Pluralism and Hybrid Governance: Bridging Two Research Lines." *Development and Change* 47, no. 2 (March 1, 2016): 346–66. https://doi.org/10.1111/dech.12221.
Romdhani, Oussama. "Ben Guerdane, a Year on." *Arab Weekly*, March 12, 2017. https://thearabweekly.com/ben-guerdane-year.
Rosa, Nikki Philline C. de la, and Francisco J. Lara. "Lorries and Ledgers: Describing and Mapping Smuggling in the Field." In Gallien and Weigand, *The Routledge Handbook of Smuggling*.
Rosenblatt, Nate. "All Jihad Is Local—What ISIS' Files Tell Us About Its Fighters." Washington, D.C.: New America, 2016.
Rotberg, R. I., ed. *When States Fail: Causes and Consequences*. Princeton, N.J.: Princeton University Press, 2010.
Rubin, H., and I. Rubin. *Qualitative Interviewing—The Art of Hearing Data*. Thousand Oaks, Calif.: Sage, 2005.
Saadi, Mohammed Said. *Moroccan Cronyism: Facts, Mechanisms, and Impact*. Oxford: Oxford University Press, 2019. https://www.oxfordscholarship.com/view/10.1093/oso/9780198799870.001.0001/oso-9780198799870-chapter-6.
Saddougui, Mohammed. "Les dysfonctionnements de l'impôt au Maroc: Cas des revenus professionnels." PhD thesis, Faculté des scienes juridiques, économiques et sociales, université Mohamed premier Oujda Maroc, 2014. https://tel.archives-ouvertes.fr/tel-01374198/document.
Saleh, Heba. "Tunisia Border Attack by Suspected ISIS Forces Kills 52." *Financial Times*, March 7, 2016. https://www.ft.com/content/e7a728be-e445-11e5-a09b-1f8b0d268c39.
Salihi, al-Saghir. *Al-Istiʿmār al-Dākhilī Wa-al-Tanmiyah Ghayr al-Mutakāfiʾah: Manẓūmat al-Tahmīsh Fī Tūnis Namūdhjan*. Al-Ṭabʿah al-Ūlá. Tunis: al-Ṣaghīr al-Ṣāliḥī, 2017.
Salman, Lana. "What We Talk About When We Talk About Decentralization? Insights from Post-Revolution Tunisia." *L'Année du Maghreb*, no. 16 (June 30, 2017): 91–108. https://doi.org/10.4000/anneemaghreb.2975.
Sanchez, Gabriella E. *Human Smuggling and Border Crossings*. Abingdon, UK: Routledge, 2015.
Sater, James N. "Morocco's 'Arab Spring.'" Middle East Institute Policy Analysis. Washington, D.C.: Middle East Institute, October 1, 2011. https://www.mei.edu/publications/moroccos-arab-spring.
Schatz, Edward. *Political Ethnography*. Chicago: University of Chicago Press, 2009.
Scheele, Judith. *Smugglers and Saints of the Sahara: Regional Connectivity in the Twentieth Century*. Cambridge: Cambridge University Press, 2012.
Scheele, Judith, and James McDougall, eds. *Saharan Frontiers: Space and Mobility in Northwest Africa*. Bloomington: Indiana University Press, 2012.
Schneckener, Ulrich. *States at Risk—Fragile Staaten Als Sicherheits- Und Entwicklungsproblem*. Berlin: Stiftung Wissenschaft und Politik, 2004.
Schneider, Friedrich. "The Size of the Shadow Economies of 145 Countries All Over the World: First Results Over the Period 1999 to 2003." IZA Discussion Paper. Institute for the Study of Labor (IZA), 2004. https://ideas.repec.org/p/iza/izadps/dp1431.html.

BIBLIOGRAPHY

Schneider, Friedrich, and Dominik H. Enste. "Shadow Economies: Size, Causes, and Consequences." *Journal of Economic Literature* 38, no. 1 (March 2000): 77–114. https://doi.org/10.1257/jel.38.1.77.

Schomerus, Mareike, and Kristof Titeca. "Deals and Dealings: Inconclusive Peace and Treacherous Trade Along the South Sudan–Uganda Border." *Africa Spectrum* 47, no. 2–3 (November 23, 2012): 5–31.

Schramm, Matthias, and Markus Taube. "Evolution and Institutional Foundation of the Hawala Financial System." Special issue: "Alternative Perspectives in Finance," *International Review of Financial Analysis* 12, no. 4 (January 1, 2003): 405–20. https://doi.org/10.1016/S1057-5219(03)00032-2.

Schuster, Caroline E. "Gender and Smuggling." In Gallien and Weigand, *The Routledge Handbook of Smuggling*.

Scott, James C. *The Art of Not Being Governed: An Anarchist History of Upland Southeast Asia*. New Haven, Conn.: Yale University Press, 2009.

Seawright, Jason, and John Gerring. "Case Selection Techniques in Case Study Research: A Menu of Qualitative and Quantitative Options." *Political Research Quarterly* 61, no. 2 (June 1, 2008): 294–308. https://doi.org/10.1177/1065912907313077.

Shelley, Louise I. *Dirty Entanglements*. New York: Cambridge University Press, 2014.

Sherwood, Harriet, and Hazem Balousha. "Palestinians in Gaza Feel the Egypt Effect as Smuggling Tunnels Close." *Guardian*, July 19, 2013. https://www.theguardian.com/world/2013/jul/19/palestinians-gaza-city-smuggling-tunnels.

Simmons, Erica S., and Nicholas Rush Smith. "Comparison with an Ethnographic Sensibility." *PS: Political Science & Politics* 50, no. 1 (January 2017): 126–30. https://doi.org/10.1017/S1049096516002286.

Snyder, Richard. "Does Lootable Wealth Breed Disorder? A Political Economy of Extraction Framework." *Comparative Political Studies* 39, no. 8 (October 1, 2006): 943–68. https://doi.org/10.1177/0010414006288724.

Snyder, Richard, and Angelica Duran-Martinez. "Does Illegality Breed Violence? Drug Trafficking and State-Sponsored Protection Rackets." *Crime, Law and Social Change* 52, no. 3 (September 1, 2009): 253–73. https://doi.org/10.1007/s10611-009-9195-z.

Soto Bermant, Laia. "Consuming Europe: The Moral Significance of Mobility and Exchange at the Spanish-Moroccan Border of Melilla." *Journal of North African Studies* 19, no. 1 (January 1, 2014): 110–29. https://doi.org/10.1080/13629387.2013.862776.

——. "The Myth of Resistance: Rethinking the 'Informal' Economy in a Mediterranean Border Enclave." *Journal of Borderlands Studies* 30, no. 2 (April 3, 2015): 263–78. https://doi.org/10.1080/08865655.2015.1046993.

——. "A Tale of Two Cities: The Production of Difference in a Mediterranean Border Enclave." *Social Anthropology* 23, no. 4 (November 1, 2015): 450–64. https://doi.org/10.1111/1469-8676.12266.

Soto, Hernando De. *The Mystery of Capital*. New ed. London: Black Swan, 2001.

——. *The Other Path*. New York: Basic Books, 1989.

Soufan Group. "Foreign Fighters—an Updated Assessment of the Flow of Foreign Fighters Into Syria and Iraq." Soufan Group, December 2015.

Sweet, Catherine. "Democratization Without Democracy: Political Openings and Closures in Modern Morocco." *Middle East Report*, no. 218 (2001): 22–25. https://doi.org/10.2307/1559306.

BIBLIOGRAPHY

Tabib, Rafaâ. "Effets de la frontière tuniso-libyenne sur les recompositions économiques et sociales des Werghemmas: de la possession à la réappropriation des territoires." PhD dissertation, Cités Territoires Environnement et Sociétés, Tours, Fr., 2011.
Tarrow, Sidney. "The Strategy of Paired Comparison: Toward a Theory of Practice." *Comparative Political Studies* 43, no. 2 (February 2010): 230–59.
Tendler, Judith. "Small Firms, the Informal Sector, and the Devil's Deal." *IDS Bulletin* 33, no. 3 (2002): 1–15. https://doi.org/10.1111/j.1759-5436.2002.tb00035.x.
Thakur, Shalaka. "Checkpost Chess: Exploring the Relationship Between Insurgents and Illicit Trade." In Gallien and Weigand, *The Routledge Handbook of Smuggling*.
Thompson, Edwina A. "An Introduction to the Concept and Origins of Hawala." *Journal of the History of International Law* 10 (2008): 83.
Tilly, Charles. *Coercion, Capital and European States, A.D.990–1990*. New ed. Cambridge, Mass.: Wiley-Blackwell, 1993.
———. *Trust and Rule*. Cambridge Studies in Comparative Politics. Cambridge: Cambridge Univ. Press, 2005.
Timmis, Hannah. "Formalising Informal Trade in North Africa." K4D Helpdesk Report. Brighton, UK: Institute of Development Studies, 2017.
Titeca, Kristof. "The Changing Cross-Border Trade Dynamics Between North-Western Uganda, North-Eastern Congo and Southern Sudan." Crisis States Research Centre Working Papers. London: London School of Economics and Political Science, 2009.
———. "Tycoons and Contraband: Informal Cross-Border Trade in West Nile, North-Western Uganda." *Journal of Eastern African Studies* 6, no. 1 (February 1, 2012): 47–63. https://doi.org/10.1080/17531055.2012.664703.
Titeca, Kristof, and Rachel Flynn. "'Hybrid Governance,' Legitimacy, and (Il)Legality in the Informal Cross-Border Trade in Panyimur, Northwest Uganda." *African Studies Review* 57, no. 1 (April 2014): 71–91. https://doi.org/10.1017/asr.2014.6.
Titeca, Kristof, and Tom de Herdt. "Regulation, Cross-Border Trade and Practical Norms in West Nile, North-Western Uganda." *Africa* 80, no. 4 (November 2010): 573–94. https://doi.org/10.3366/afr.2010.0403.
Toit, Andries du. "Adverse Incorporation and Agrarian Policy in South Africa, or, How Not to Connect the Rural Poor to Growth." Cape Town, South Africa: Institute for Poverty, Land and Agrarian Studies, 2009.
———. "Forgotten by the Highway: Globalisation, Adverse Incorporation and Chronic Poverty in a Commercial Farming District of South Africa." SSRN Scholarly Paper. Rochester, N.Y.: Social Science Research Network, December 1, 2004.
Trabelssi, Karim. "Current State of the Informal Economy in Tunisia as Seen Through Its Stakeholders: Facts and Alternatives." UGTT Union Youth Report, 2014.
Tsai, Kellee S. "Adaptive Informal Institutions and Endogenous Institutional Change in China." *World Politics* 59, no. 1 (October 2006): 116–41. https://doi.org/10.1353/wp.2007.0018.
Tsai, Lily L. "Solidary Groups, Informal Accountability, and Local Public Goods Provision in Rural China." *American Political Science Review* 101, no. 2 (May 2007): 355–72. https://doi.org/10.1017/S0003055407070153.
TunisWebdo. "A Ben Guerdane, les responsables libyens posent un lapin aux représentants du gouvernement tunisien." *Webdo* (blog), January 13, 2017. http://www.webdo

.tn/2017/01/13/a-ben-guerdane-responsables-libyens-posent-lapin-aux-repres entants-gouvernement-tunisien/.

United Nations Conference on Trade and Development. "An Investment Guide to the Oriental Region of Morocco—Opportunities and Conditions." Geneva: UNCTAD, 2012. http://unctad.org/en/PublicationsLibrary/diaepcb2010d10_en.pdf.

Van den Boogaard, Vanessa, and Wilson Prichard. "What Have We Learned About Informal Taxation in Sub-Saharan Africa?" ICTD Summary Brief. Brighton, UK: International Centre for Tax and Development, 2016.

Varese, Federico. *The Russian Mafia: Private Protection in a New Market Economy.* Oxford, UK: Oxford University Press, 2001.

Vishwanath, Tara, Umar Serajuddin, Irene Jillson, Matteo Morgandi, Maros Ivanic, and Gloria La Cava. "Promoting Youth Opportunities and Participation in Morocco," World Bank, June 1, 2012. http://documents.worldbank.org/curated/en/681321468276890567/Promoting-youth-opportunities-and-participation-in-Morocco.

Vorrath, Judith. "On the Margin of Statehood? State-Society Relations in African Borderlands." In *Understanding Life in the Borderlands: Boundaries in Depth and in Motion*, ed. I. William Zartman. Athens: University of Georgia Press, 2010.

Walther, Olivier J. "Trade Networks in West Africa: A Social Network Approach." *Journal of Modern African Studies* 52, no. 2 (June 2014): 179–203. https://doi.org/10.1017/S0022278X14000032.

Walton, Oliver, Sharri Plonski, Zahbia Yousef, Jonathan Goodhand, and Patrick Meehan. *Borderlands and Peacebuilding: A View from the Margins*. Bath, UK: Conciliation Resources, 2018. https://researchportal.bath.ac.uk/en/publications/borderlands-and-peacebuilding-a-view-from-the-margins.

Ware, L. B. "The Role of the Tunisian Military in the Post-Bourgiba Era." *Middle East Journal* 39, no. 1 (1985): 27–47.

Waterbury, John. *The Commander of the Faithful: The Moroccan Elite: A Study in Segmented Politics*. London: Weidenfeld and Nicolson, 1970.

Wedeen, Lisa. *Ambiguities of Domination: Politics, Rhetoric, and Symbols in Contemporary Syria*. 2nd ed. Chicago: University of Chicago Press, 2015.

———. "Reflections on Ethnographic Work in Political Science." *Annual Review of Political Science* 13, no. 1 (2010): 255–72. https://doi.org/10.1146/annurev.polisci.11.052706.123951.

Wehrey, Frederic. *The Burning Shores: Inside the Battle for the New Libya*. New York: Farrar, Straus and Giroux, 2018.

Werenfels, Isabelle, Anette Weber, and Anne Koch. "Profiteers of Migration? Authoritarian States in Africa and European Migration Management." SWP Research Paper. Berlin: Stiftung Wissenschaft und Politik, July 2018.

Whitfield, Lindsay, Ole Therkildsen, Lars Buur, and Anne Mette Kjær. *The Politics of African Industrial Policy: A Comparative Perspective*. Cambridge: Cambridge University Press, 2015.

WIEGO. "Informal Workers in the COVID-19 Crisis: A Global Picture of Sudden Impact and Long-Term Risk." WIEGO, July 2020. https://www.wiego.org/fr/node/8371.

Wikileaks. "Corruption in Tunisia Part IV: The Family's Holdings." Wikileaks Public Library of US Diplomacy. Tunis: U.S. Embassy, July 5, 2006. https://wikileaks.org/plusd/cables/06TUNIS1672_a.html.

Williams, Margaret, and Youssef Mahmoud. "The New Tunisian Constitution: Triumphs and Potential Pitfalls." *IPI Global Observatory* (blog), February 27, 2014. https://theglobalobservatory.org/2014/02/the-new-tunisian-constitution-triumphs-and-potential-pitfalls/.

Willis, Michael J. "Berbers in an Arab Spring: The Politics of Amazigh Identity and the North African Uprisings." In *North African Politics: Change and Continuity*, ed. Yahia H. Zoubir and Gregory White. London: Routledge, 2015.

———. *Politics and Power in the Maghreb: Algeria, Tunisia and Morocco from Independence to the Arab Spring*. London: Hurst, 2012.

Witte, Ann Dryden, Kelly Eakin, and Carl P. Simon. *Beating the System: The Underground Economy*. Boston: Praeger, 1982.

Wolfgang, M. "Confidentiality in Criminological Research and Other Ethical Issues." *Journal of Criminal Law and Criminology* 72, no. 1 (1981).

World Bank. "Impact of the Libya Crisis on the Tunisian Economy." Washington, D.C.: World Bank, 2017. https://openknowledge.worldbank.org/handle/10986/26407.

———. "Tunisia—Breaking the Barriers to Youth Inclusion." Washington, D.C.: World Bank, November 1, 2014. http://documents.worldbank.org/curated/en/753151468312307987/Tunisia-Breaking-the-barriers-to-youth-inclusion;jsessionid=d+bm9vJUVM9ziRbDmLDeJM39.

Yom, Sean L., and F. Gregory Gause III. "Resilient Royals: How Arab Monarchies Hang on." *Journal of Democracy* 23, no. 4 (October 12, 2012): 74–88. https://doi.org/10.1353/jod.2012.0062.

Zaptia, Sami. "Libyan Fuel Smuggling Is Part of an International Smuggling Network: Attorney General's Office." *Libya Herald*, March 15, 2018. https://www.libyaherald.com/2018/03/15/libyan-fuel-smuggling-is-part-of-an-international-smuggling-network-attorney-generals-office/.

Zartman, I. William. "States, Boundaries and Sovereignty in the Middle East: Unsteady but Unchanging." *International Affairs* 93, no. 4 (July 1, 2017): 937–48. https://doi.org/10.1093/ia/iix118.

Zerhoudi, Mohamed. "Marjane Oujda ouvre ses portes." *L'Economiste*, December 11, 2007, no. 2670. https://www.leconomiste.com/article/marjane-oujda-ouvre-ses-portes.

Zoubir, Yahia H., and Gregory White. *North African Politics: Change and Continuity*. London: Routledge, 2015.

INDEX

adverse incorporation, 201, 222, 224, 231, 237
Andreas, Peter, 21, 26
Arab Spring, 7, 40, 121, 145, 178
armed groups, 2, 48, 64, 66, 161–62
arms, 157, 163, 253; on smuggling, 6, 37, 40, 78, 81; on trade, 42, 46, 54
authoritarian, 5, 175, 185, 197, 207, 226–27; regime, 6, 10, 41, 51, 53, 130
authoritarian bargains, 8, 9, 16, 35, 113, 137, 141, 147, 227, 230. *See also* informal authoritarian bargain

barriers to entry, 127, 207, 214, 229, 240–41; types of, 131–33, 203, 216, 234
Barrio Chino, 3–4, 67, 71–74, 133, 286n24
Ben Ali, Zine El-Abidine: on clientelism, 39, 53–54, 118, 128–29; regime of, 7, 58, 145–50
Ben Guerdane, 2, 49–50, 128–29, 134–35, 186, 226, 250, 257, 293n24, 293n31; attack on, 16, 117, 144, 157–58, 160–62, 164–66, 255; geography of, 52–54, 61, 64, 66, 79, 88, 115; history of, 89–90, 92, 94–95; and municipalities, 119–22, 154–56; protests in, 145–52, 168–70, 172, 178, 219; resident accounts of, 105–107, 109, 112, 114, 116, 132, 136–37
border: effects of fortification, 17, 43, 176, 190, 195–96, 200, 237–38; porosity, 6, 189, 238; walls, 140, 238
bribe, 2–4, 150, 230; demand for, 76–77, 90, 114–15, 118, 191, 203–4; refusal to, 70, 73, 80, 83, 100, 111–12, 116, 123, 126, 135, 140, 234, 239; and religion, 104–05, 107; value of, 62, 66, 68–69, 101, 117, 285n5
Bouazizi, Mohamed, 7–9, 145, 154

cannabis, 6, 9, 46–47, 151; in Morocco, 57, 78, 104, 129, 141, 227
Chahed, Youssef, 136, 165, 169, 172
checkpoints, 66, 81, 101, 109, 115, 117, 119–20, 134, 159–61, 171, 255
citizen-state relationships, 6, 9, 113, 141, 227–28
cocaine, 6, 46–47, 78
colonialism, 18, 36–38, 40, 52–53, 55–56, 142; colonialization, 26
conflict, 25, 55, 66, 75, 161, 184, 226, 237; and borders, 166–67; and smuggling, 6, 23, 45–46, 56, 59, 272n3

INDEX

corruption, 1, 3–4, 22–23, 39, 59, 61, 63, 238–39; role of, 82–83, 114, 138, 140–41; war on, 164–65, 168, 172, 176–77, 228
Covid-19, 11, 146, 164, 224; and effects on smuggling networks, 167, 195–96, 207, 226, 237
cross-border trade, 2, 18, 22, 24–26, 35, 39, 82, 119, 239; geographies of, 48, 50, 52, 54, 57, 61, 66–68, 71; Morocco-Algeria; 75–76, 189; scholarship on, 104, 243–46, 250, 252–53; Tunisia-Libya, 88. *See* informal trade
customs, 150–51, 153–54, 162, 164, 285n5 ; agreement, 2, 62–63, 65–66; regulation, 67; role of officials, 3, 25, 54, 61, 68–70, 73–74, 79–80, 83, 90, 97, 100, 109, 114–18, 129, 234
currency, 49

democracy, 7–8, 157, 175, 185, 226, 245; democratic, 1, 7, 31, 51, 145–47, 150, 152, 154, 166, 230; democratization, 6–7, 31, 169

Egypt, 25, 27, 36, 40, 42 , 44–45, 180
Ellis, Mathew, 35–36
employment, 42, 50, 54, 98, 127, 135, 137, 190–91, 203, 240–41, 249; alternative, 118, 162, 177, 210, 234; formal, 8, 39, 41, 53, 106, 136, 227, 230; informal, 7, 10, 18, 41, 141
Europe, 1, 46, 160; migration, 10, 40, 48, 57, 141, 197; trade relations with, 39, 49, 57, 187
European Union, 44, 47, 57, 180

Fikri, Mohsen, 8, 10
formalization: of smuggling, 116, 182–83, 186, 218, 227, 231–32; of borderlands, 11, 17, 175, 190, 195; of employment 13, 250; of institutions, 31, 155, 219, 220–24, 237

gasoline, 6, 12, 61–63, 81, 87, 90, 116, 124–25, 160, 163; and comparisons with textile, 13, 17–18, 199–201, 214–22, 251, 306n3; features of, 202–3; inclusion of traders, 204–9, 211–14, 224, 229; and other goods, 39, 54, 57, 76, 104, 129, 159, 231, 248–49; roadside gasoline, 98–102, 112, 115, 132–34, 151; trade of, 44, 75, 77, 102, 163–64, 174, 188, 190–91, 207
Goodhand, Jonathan, 23–24, 33, 235, 244
governance, 23–24, 29–30, 35, 37, 49, 87, 123, 231–32, 235; on "good governance," 27, 82, on "real governance," 5, 9, 227. *See also* hybrid governance; nonstate governance

Hüsken, Thomas, 24, 25, 232
human trafficking, 42, 47, 80, 125, 159, 251
hybrid governance, 25–28, 30, 32, 86, 98, 103, 110. *See also* governance; nonstate governance
hybrid institutions, 16, 31, 60, 82, 97, 100, 103, 110–11, 142, 218, 235

illegal activities, 9, 14, 24, 83, 112, 168, 227–28, 243, 254, 257
illegality, 5, 8–9, 24, 154, 251
illicit goods, 81, 103, 104, 123, 128, 239; arms, 6, 46, 99; drugs, 6, 19, 46, 99, 238; trade of, 42, 50, 76–77, 129, 131, 188
INDH. *See* National Initiative for Human Development (INDH)
inequality, 7–8, 10, 146, 178, 227
informality, 9, 29, 31, 40, 93–94, 98, 103, 119, 201
informal authoritarian bargains, 5, 9, 11, 16, 113, 137, 141, 147, 222, 230. *See also* authoritarian bargains
informal incorporation, 17, 175, 237
informal institutions, 97, 100, 138; inclusion through, 201, 203, 207, 209, 214, 216, 220, 223, 229, 231; and legitimacy, 103, 110; political settlements, 232, 235–36; and regulation of smuggling, 15–16, 33–34, 60–61, 81–86, 111, 238, 244–47, 255, 306n3; role of, 27, 30–34, 64–65, 138, 235–36; and state-building, 232–36
informal trade, 6, 18, 54, 59, 61, 63, 66–67, 72, 76, 93, 106, 120, 140, 184, 186;

INDEX

networks, 57–58, 88–89, 180, 187, 247–48; on routes, 42, 45, 49–50, 54. *See also* cross-border trade
ISIS (Islamic State in Iraq and Syria), 10, 16, 48, 122, 137, 144, 146, 157, 172
Islam, 53, 103–4, 107, 110

jihadi movements, 40, 110, 157, 171

Khan, Mushtaq, 32, 235
Klute, Georg, 24, 232

law and order, 5, 227, 240–42
licit goods, 87, 123, 159, 187–88, 190, 249; smuggling of, 18, 78, 81, 114, 117, 119, 126, 128, 131, 137, 229, 231, 238–39, 248. *See also* illicit goods
lived political settlements, 33, 199, 201, 222. *See also* political settlements
livelihoods, 8–9, 11–12, 24–25, 35, 86, 106, 109, 161, 196, 205, 227- 28
legitimacy, 105–6, 108–9, 235; of borders, 37, 55; of smuggling, 18–19, 28, 35, 85, 87, 94, 103, 229
Levitsky, Stephen, 32
Lynch, Marc, 227

Maghreb, 15, 20, 38, 226, 228, 232, 237, 313n14
Mali, 6, 10, 22, 40, 45, 174
Meagher, Kate, 25–26, 103, 223, 233, 235
Medenine, 21, 50, 64, 97, 99, 101, 106, 150, 153, 157, 236, 249–50; history of, 52–56; markets at, 87–88, 91–92, 94, 215
Meehan, Patrick, 33, 236, 244
Melilla, 3–4, 12, 40, 44, 48, 55, 117–18, 180–81, 207–8, 238, 249, 255; administration of, 123–24, 190–91, 195–96; regulation of smuggling in, 57, 60, 67–68, 71–77, 80–82, 94, 118, 133–34, 175–76, 221–22, 233
methodologies, 12, 14, 18, 21, 243–45, 247, 250, 252; ethnographies, 13, 29, 244–47, 269n5, 313n11; fieldwork, 13, 18, 245–46, 248, 250–51, 255–57; interviews, 13–15, 18–19, 65, 121, 126, 130, 136, 179–80, 187, 193, 196, 204,

209, 244–46, 250–57; participant observation, 12–14, 246, 250–51, 255
migration, 6, 10–11, 20, 35, 40–41, 47, 67, 141, 168. *See also* trafficking
military, 6, 23, 36–37, 48, 52, 66, 76, 108, 114, 116, 138, 157–58, 161, 165–67, 251, 253
Mohamed VI (king), 7, 57, 176, 178, 188
Mohsen Fikri, 8–10
moral perceptions, 16, 86, 103, 109, 245
municipality, 2, 62, 89–92, 94–98, 119–22, 148, 152, 154–56, 169, 172, 182–83, 185, 216, 220, 226, 293n24, 293n28, 298n36
muqatila, 100–101, 110

narcotics: as illicit goods, 46, 99, 104, 188; smuggling of, 12, 19, 54, 62, 81, 129, 195–96, 213
National Initiative for Human Development (INDH), 8, 95–96, 178–79, 183, 185
Neo-Weberian, 27, 31, 33, 232
New Institutional Economics, 27, 30–32, 83, 138
nonstate actors, 8, 15, 23, 113, 126–27, 272–73
nonstate governance, 5, 28. *See also* governance and hybrid governance

Oriental (region in Morocco), 21, 50, 69, 87, 129, 137, 192, 195, 217, 236, 249; development of, 176–80, 186–88; fragility, 196–98; history of, 55–58; regional administration, 95, 97, 122, 179, 188, 192, 210, 293n39
Ottoman, 27, 36, 52, 130
Oujda, 50, 55, 57, 59, 76 –77, 92, 94, 96, 102, 106, 115, 119 –20

parliament, 2, 59, 64–65, 128, 146, 161–162, 178, 211, 226
police, 66, 69, 90, 130, 150–51, 154, 157–59, 162, 166, 213, 251, 255; and bribes, 101, 105, 114–17, 119–20, 123; cooperation, 2–3, 8, 65, 72–73, 80–81, 83, 89, 100, 221, 234; harassment of smugglers, 9, 95, 169–71, 177, 188, 197

INDEX

political economy, 10, 23, 27, 82–83; approach, 5, 15, 17, 20–21, 29–30, 41, 60–61, 65, 84, 111, 139–41, 232–36, 244, 269n5; and smuggling, 30, 111, 229–30, 247

political settlements, 5, 7, 51, 113, 123, 127, 137–40, 142–43, 200, 202–3, 230–33; framework, 30, 32–34, 83, 138–139, 155, 223, 235–37, 244, 248–49; in Morocco, 56, 58, 144, 175, 180, 189–90, 195, 197–98, 207–9, 212–14, 225; of textile traders, 217, 219–20; in Tunisia, 53, 145–48, 150–51, 155, 159, 160–61, 163, 166, 168, 205–7, 227, 241; and smuggling, 11–12, 16–17, 35. *See also* lived political settlements

popular diplomacy, 159–65, 168, 216

protests, 40, 227–28; in Morocco, 8, 10, 121, 137, 172, 175, 177–78, 184, 188, 190, 197, 219, 305n63; in Tunisia, 9, 54, 145–48, 150, 161, 167

Ras Jedir, 77, 81, 92, 115, 148, 170–71, 203–4, 207; and Covid-19, 167–68; crossing formalities at, 61, 66–67, 75, 108–9, 121, 131, 152–54, 174, 206, 233, 255; goods smuggled through, 78, 79, 106, 132–33; popular diplomacy in, 160–65; terrorist attack on, 157–59

rents generated by smuggling economies, 5, 15, 16, 32, 34, 96, 111–15, 117–20, 123, 126–28, 130, 134–35, 138–43, 148, 150, 160, 163, 173, 175, 180, 194–95, 208, 223, 230, 235–36; distribution of, 128, 140, 143, 197–98, 225; stall rents, 96

Rif Mountains, 36, 38, 56–57, 142, 227

Saied, Kais, 7, 146, 165, 226
Scheele, Judith, 22, 35, 45, 104, 246
social contract, 7–8, 10–11, 20, 40–41, 141, 227, 235
social peace, 112, 114–15, 121, 136
Souk Maghrebi, 89–90, 92–93, 95, 216; and employment, 134–35; and income, 119–21, 152, 226; and vendors, 148, 154–55, 172, 204, 217

Souk Melilla, 94–97, 107, 117, 120, 122, 179, 181–82, 205, 208, 215, 217–18, 220, 304n44

special economic zones, 44, 240

stability, 16, 32–33, 116–19, 121, 138, 177, 193; and the border, 6, 17, 114–15, 127, 140, 142, 190, 224, 237, 241; and fragility, 194–95, 198, 236; and smuggling economies, 1, 23, 126, 136, 140, 148–49, 158, 160, 163, 166, 200, 214, 231

state-building, 5, 30, 36–38, 54, 82, 140, 235, 249; and smuggling, 15–17, 20–22, 24, 26–27, 29, 31–34, 58, 111–12, 138, 228, 232, 247

state institutions, 25–26, 35, 141, 150, 251; formal, 32, 34, 139; and informal markets, 96–98, 111, 183, 200; and smuggling economies; 152, 201, 208–10, 213, 219, 228–30, 240

tariffs, 6, 39, 44, 57, 61, 65, 150, 180, 231; evasion of, 22, 44, 57, 63, 67, 102, 180; as state's income, 44, 62, 104, 117

taxes, 42, 92, 94–96, 98, 105, 119, 121, 148, 151–52, 155, 216, 230, 234, 241; right to tax, 88, 91, 106; and smuggled goods, 16, 85, 87, 94, 102, 119–20, 122–23, 220, 226

terrorism, 1, 2, 17, 35, 81, 153, 156–57, 162, 165–166, 170, 226; and smugglers, 22–23, 59, 153, 158, 229, 238; terrorist organizations, 23, 152, 165, 170

textiles, 191, 204, 206, 234; comparison with gasoline 13, 17, 102, 200–2, 214, 218–19, 229, 231, 251; and employment, 106, 136, 185, 210; networks for smuggling, 215–17

Titeca, Kristof, 25–28

trade agreements, 8, 11–12, 17, 176; free-trade agreements, 35, 180, 189, 218, 231, 240

trade networks, 25, 45, 58, 125, 160, 180, 187, 247, 248, 253–54

trafficking. *See* human trafficking; narcotics

women, 15, 68–69, 165, 171, 210–11, 221, 251–52

Printed and bound by CPI Group (UK) Ltd, Croydon, CR0 4YY
08/02/2024

08233904-0003